A DRINK WITH THE ANCESTORS

A DRINK WITH OUR ANCESTORS

A Pub Crawl Through History

The history of public houses past and present in Stocksbridge, Deepcar, Bolsterstone, Wigtwizzle, Hunshelf and Green Moor, from their early days until the eve of World War Two

By Claire Pearson

Copyright © 2020 Claire Pearson
All rights reserved.
ISBN: 9798691140174

I am grateful for all the help I have received from Sheffield Archives & Picture Sheffield, Barnsley Archives, the National Library of Scotland and OpenStreetMap. Thanks to Janet Sanderson and Dave Pickersgill for the proofreading, suggestions and corrections.

Most of the photographs are reproduced by kind permission of Sheffield Archives / Picture Sheffield, unless otherwise stated. The Ordnance Survey maps are reproduced under a Creative Commons Attribution-NonCommercial-ShareAlike 4.0 International licence with permission from the National Library of Scotland. The overlay map of Broomhead Reservoir is reproduced with permission of the National Library of Scotland and OpenStreetMap. OpenStreetMap® is open data, licensed under the Open Data Commons Open Database License (ODbL) by the OpenStreetMap Foundation (OSMF).

Remembering my mum Margaret, who, along with her mother Connie, gave me my love of history and writing. And thank you to my dad, Trevor Pearson, an electrician contracted to all the Tetley pubs in south Yorkshire, north Derbyshire and north Nottinghamshire. Thank you for the stories you couldn't make up, the tales of the characters you met every day, and for taking me in those basic back-street pubs in the steel working and mining areas, where I was too young to drink, but made very welcome, the men shouting, "*mind thy language, there's a lady present!*" Little did we know back then how much life was changing and how these pubs, busy with the working-class men who poured out of the steelworks and the mines to slake their thirst, would, within a few years, become nothing but a memory, like the mighty steelworks of Sheffield's east end and the coal mines and factories of further afield.

Contents

PREFACE ....
INTRODUCTION ....
THE CASTLE INN, BOLSTERSTONE 1
A PROPOSED NEW PUB FOR BOLSTERSTONE – 1876 15
THE COACH & HORSES INN, MANCHESTER ROAD, STOCKSBRIDGE... 17
THE BROOMHEAD MILL INN, WIGTWIZZLE, near BOLSTERSTONE 47
THE SPORTSMAN'S ARMS or INN, WIGTWIZZLE 57
THE ROYAL OAK, MANCHESTER ROAD, DEEPCAR 71
THE KING AND MILLER, MANCHESTER ROAD, DEEPCAR 99
THE MINERS ARMS, BRACKEN MOOR 137
SPORTSMAN'S ARMS, MANCHESTER ROAD, DEEPCAR 159
THE NEW INN, STOCKSBRIDGE 171
TRAVELLERS INN, VAUGHTON HILL, DEEPCAR 183
THE ROCK INN, GREEN MOOR ROAD, GREEN MOOR 203
THE BUTCHER'S ARMS, HUNSHELF 223
THE RISING SUN INN, HUNSHELF 227
THE FRIENDSHIP HOTEL, MANCHESTER ROAD, STOCKSBRIDGE 259
A MISCELLANY 307
A (VERY) BRIEF HISTORY OF LICENSING LAW 309
GLOSSARY 317
BIBLIOGRAPHY 325

PREFACE

I am an amateur historian and keen genealogist with over forty years' experience of researching the area in which I live and the people who went before me. Winter evenings in my childhood were spent sitting with my grandma in front of the coal fire, listening as she told me stories about her family; myth and legend woven into tales of hardship and strife. She instilled in me a love of history and the tales it had to tell about ordinary folks and how they lived their lives. Although I studied history to A level, it never really came alive for me until I ignored Kings and Queens and political intrigues and concentrated instead on the lives of the common people; those ancestors, farmers mainly, tied to the land on which generations of their family had lived and worked. All my early research was done in person, at record offices up and down the country, trawling through original documents and microfiche. Today it is so much easier, with huge amounts of material being digitised and put online; parish registers, newspapers, wills, out-of-print books; it's all there at the click of a mouse.

Researching local history inevitably throws up references to public houses, and over the years I have collected so many I thought I would collate them all, add to them, and make them more widely available by writing a book. I was not expecting it to take me so long, or to take up so much of my time, but I have enjoyed it all. Basing all the stories I have collected around the central theme of public houses seemed as good a way as any to share these stories with others.

I hope you enjoy reading them.

Claire Pearson

INTRODUCTION

Pubs in their various forms have been around for centuries, so it is not surprising that they have so many tales to tell. Inns, public houses, beerhouses, taverns, coaching inns, and hostelries have played a big part in all levels of society and they were not merely social hubs where people met to drink and talk. They played host to coroners' courts, manorial courts, Friendly Societies, political hustings, auctions of property and livestock, the payment of rents, the hiring of staff (especially in rural areas), and they were where people met to conduct business, whether honest or dishonest. Many provided horses for hire and stabling for travellers and stagecoaches. Their yards were used by carriers, blacksmiths, wheelwrights and travelling salesmen. They provided a convenient base for all kinds of itinerant traders, from dentists, quack doctors, and portrait painters to travelling shows, menageries, and waxworks. Many a soldier and sailor has been recruited in a public house, either through official means or by being press-ganged. Soldiers and mariners who were travelling, or who were sick or injured, could also get free food and accommodation at pubs thanks to legislation dating back to the time of Elizabeth I. The churchwardens and constables of a parish collected money from the inhabitants in order to meet this obligation. They were responsible for finding accommodation for soldiers in alehouses, inns, livery stables, victualling houses and so on. Anyone who refused to billet soldiers could be fined, as could anyone who took payment from them. In 1841 licensed victuallers in Sheffield complained to the magistrates that the unequal billeting of horse soldiers was unfair, placing a heavy burden on some innkeepers whilst others got away without having any soldiers and horses forced upon them.

The history of our public houses provides us with a mixture of comedy, tragedy, violence, happiness, and sadness. There are both banal and extraordinary stories about the day-to-day lives of our ancestors and their neighbours, be they working men, landowners, travellers, rogues, vagabonds, thieves, prostitutes, farmers, miners, steelworkers, fishermen, villagers, townspeople, stagecoach drivers, or their passengers. Not forgetting the odd travelling bear – as the saying goes, *"All Human Life is There."*[1]

Much has been written in both fact and fiction about the English public house, some writers praising or idealising the pub, others being critical in the extreme. *"To write of the English inn is almost to write of England itself [...] as familiar in the national consciousness as the oak and the ash and the village green and the church spire,"*[2] wrote Thomas Burke, in a rather romantic vein. On the other hand, Henry Zouch, a Yorkshire vicar, magistrate, and social reformer, wrote that public houses were, *"Licensed receptacles for rogues, vagabonds, night-poachers, and dangerous persons of all kinds. It is here that the scanty earnings of the manufacturer and labourer, which ought to be applied to the maintenance of their families at home, are improvidently squandered away. Nor doth anything contribute so much to increase the poor rates, as such places…"*[3] And even further back in time, Stubbs wrote, *"Every country, city, town, village, and other places hath abundance of alehouses, taverns, and inns, which are so fraught with malt-worms, night and day, that you would wonder to see them."*[4]

This is not a history of pubs in general – there are many good books on this subject already in print – but it is a book about the history of the pubs around Stocksbridge; a book of real-life stories, or what the locals got up to in their Locals.

One of the main sources of stories are old newspapers. These are a fascinating window into the lives of our ancestors and their neighbours, and a valuable resource, although what was reported could vary on who was reporting it and how they interpreted what was happening. Then, as now,

---

[1] This was the motto of The News of the World, taken from a quote by Henry James, "Cats and monkeys; monkeys and cats; all human life is there."
[2] Burke, Thomas. The English Inn. Herbert Jenkins: 1930
[3] Zouch, Henry. Hints Respecting the Public Police. London: John Stockdale: 1786
[4] Stubbs, Philip. The Anatomie of Abuses. 1583

one should not believe everything one reads in the papers! Two different newspapers might differ so much in their reporting of events that it is easy to wonder which version is the truth. Sometimes in their reporting of court cases, one questions if both reporters were even at the same trial. As far as possible, I have tried to find out the truth by using other sources to confirm or refute what was written in the papers. Just because it was printed did not make it true. That fact notwithstanding, the newspapers are the best source for unearthing some fascinating tales.

The criteria for inclusion in this book include:
The pubs that would have been within walking distance for our ancestors
Those with a fairly long history, with a cut-off point of 1939[5]
Public houses as opposed to Working Men's Clubs

Headlines in the text are taken from the newspapers; where quotes have been used, these are from the newspaper reports or Coroner's notebooks unless otherwise stated. Spellings are as in the original document.

It is not always possible to find out precise opening dates of pubs and also the exact dates when landlords came and went. There is a wealth of information out there but sometimes the facts are just not available. In which case I prefer to err on the side of caution and, rather than give exact dates, I will say "*about*" or "*approximately.*"

Thank you to all the people, experts in their field, who have contributed their knowledge, especially those who have explained legal terms to me. Any mistakes are purely mine.

The use of an apostrophe in pub names has been inconsistent over the years, with pub sign boards, reports in the press and in official records all at variance. For example, The Miner's Arms could also be the Miners' Arms and was often the Miners Arms. After taking conflicting advice from several experts about the use of an apostrophe I have decided to standardise the

---

[5] The reason for the cut-off is twofold. After this date records are not so easily available, and a lot of the later newspapers have not been digitised. I also want to avoid possible offence by talking about people who may still be alive.

spelling of Miners Arms, Travellers Rest and Travellers Inn to have no apostrophe, except where one occurs in a quote.

So here is a potted history of our local pubs, where generations of locals and a succession of travellers have spent their leisure hours. A few of these pubs are still with us, and some have gone, but their stories, recorded here, will live on. It is easy to get side-tracked when researching, and if the footnotes sometimes seem a bit random, that's because I have wandered off topic and found a story that I think is interesting enough to be included. Footnotes also contain extra information for anyone who might be researching their family history.

There is, on occasion, reason to refer to the laws that were passed regarding public houses. Licensing Laws are incredibly complex, and even local magistrates, who were responsible for putting the legislation into practice, admitted to not really understanding their complexity. I have tried to simplify them, and there is a brief history at the end of this book, but if anyone is interested, the details of several centuries-worth of licensing law, including the full texts of some of the Acts, are readily available online, should you require some soporific bedtime reading…

NOTE: To keep printing costs down, I have not been able to include as many photographs as I would have liked. In addition, many of the photographs I have are not of a high enough resolution and would not reproduce well. To compliment this book, I have built a website with a dedicated section devoted to all the local pubs (not just those in the book) containing all the photos I have collected over the years. I would like to thank all those who have contributed their photographs.

The website address is: stocksbridgetimespast.co.uk/pubs

"No, Sir; there is nothing which has yet been contrived by man, by which so much happiness is produced as by a good tavern or inn."

Samuel Johnson

"The candles were brought, the fire was stirred up, and a fresh log of wood thrown on. In ten minutes' time a waiter was laying the cloth for dinner, the curtains were drawn, the fire was blazing brightly, and every thing looked (as every thing always does in all decent English inns) as if the travellers had been expected and their comforts prepared, for days beforehand."

Pickwick, on the Saracen's Head in the old innkeeping town of Towcester
Charles Dickens, The Pickwick Papers

THE CASTLE INN, BOLSTERSTONE

The Castle Inn is situated on the edge of the moors in the small stone-built village of Bolsterstone and at one time had a brewhouse attached. This photograph was taken between 1905 and 1907 when John Jordan was the landlord. The cottage where the cart stands was later demolished to make way for an extension. The Castle is said to date back to 1840 but may have been opened in around 1833.

The first landlord of the Castle Inn was John Bramall. He was living at Bolsterstone and was described as an innkeeper in 1833, but the Castle Inn as we know it dates back to 1840; an old photograph shows this date carved on a stone above the door, although this is no longer there. There were also some initials above the date, but unfortunately these are not as clear. It is possible that the pub was built as a beerhouse, but it is also possible that an existing building was converted, the date stone being added then. In 2015 the pub celebrated its 175th anniversary.

The Castle was one of several beerhouses that opened locally in the 1830s. Legislation had been passed in 1830 which allowed householders to brew and sell beer (nothing stronger) without the need to obtain a licence from the magistrates. Many of these early beerhouses did not have a name, but a board would be hung outside the house bearing the name of the landlord. John Bramall was listed in a trade directory of 1833 under the heading "*Inns and Taverns*" at Bolsterstone, but the exact location was not given. The pub had not yet been given a name, and the entry reads "*Board, John Bramall.*" There was a brewhouse attached to the pub.

The Sheffield Independent of May 1833 reported on the opening of a new beershop at Bolsterstone, but it was not positive news; the paper was condemning a report of cruelty to a cockerel for "*entertainment*" purposes. No indication of the landlord's name was given, but it seems likely that the article was referring to John Bramall.

John and his family moved from Oughtibridge to Bolsterstone sometime between 1829 and 1833. When their daughter Emma was baptised at Bolsterstone church in April 1833 her father's occupation was given as "*Innkeeper*" and his home as "*Bolsterstone*".[6] Sadly, baby Emma died later that year, and her mother died the following year. John stayed at the Castle until 1848 when he transferred the licence to his son-in-law Samuel Knutton.

John Bramall had married Ann Grayson in 1817. Her family (The Graysons of Spink Hall) owned a lot of land in the area including the Castle and the land around it. Perhaps this would explain why John made the move from

---

[6] When their previous child had been baptised in 1829 the family were still living at Oughtibridge.

his home at Oughtibridge to Bolsterstone; he had also inherited some money (and a cow) from his mother in 1830. He was certainly no stranger to the pub trade because his mother Ann had been the licensee of the White Hart at Oughtibridge.

HORSE STEALING: 1833

One Saturday night in June 1833, two horses belonging to John Bramall were stolen from their field. John and a man called George Ronksley set off on horseback in pursuit of the thieves, following the prints that had been left and picking up information and a description of the two thieves as they went, as well as recruiting more men to join the chase. They got as far as Nottingham before John's horse got distressed and he had to return home to Bolsterstone. The others that had joined in the search carried on, eventually ending up at Nether Broughton, Leicestershire, near to where there was a horse fair taking place. At 5pm on Monday, they passed an inn called The Red Lion and saw the two thieves inside. The men made a run for it when they saw that they had been recognised, but they were soon captured. One of the men, Joshua Froggatt, offered his captor his purse containing £8 and the five horses they had with them if he would let him go. The other thief was called Thomas Richardson. The stolen horses were found tied up in the stable at the Red Lion.

The following morning, the local constable took the prisoners on a cart to Nottingham, followed by the men who had been pursuing them. More drama ensued, because the prisoners, who were not shackled, attacked the constable, and tried to get away. The men galloped after them, thrashed them when they caught them, chained them together, and took them onwards to Nottingham. On reaching Sheffield on Wednesday, the men were locked up in the town jail. They appeared before the magistrates, but because of the seriousness of the charge, they were committed to be tried at the Assizes, to be held at York Castle the following month. Both men were found guilty and were sentenced to be transported for life. It was noted in the newspaper that since the abolition of the death penalty for horse stealing, the number of such crimes had greatly increased. Both men were deported aboard the convict ship The Hive, which set sail on 15th January 1834 and arrived in New South Wales after a five-month journey on the 11th June 1834.

John Bramall's daughter Mary married Samuel Knutton in 1842, and John transferred the licence for the pub to him in 1848. John married again in 1843 and went to live at Spink House Farm, where he farmed 40 acres. He must have had this property from his late wife, whose family owned Spink House (among other properties and land). John held the freehold of this, which entitled him to vote. When his daughter married Samuel Knutton, John's occupation was entered on the marriage certificate as farmer, not innkeeper, which perhaps indicates that Samuel and his wife were already running the pub for him. Like John before him, Samuel was also a farmer as well as a pub landlord; many innkeepers had dual occupations at this time. Joseph Hunter[7] wrote back in 1819 about how common it was for men in this area (not just innkeepers) to have two occupations, it being common to combine farming with a craft, the better to eke out a living from the shallow clay soil. Many farmers also kept dogs for hunting.

When John Bramall was widowed for a second time, he moved next door to his other daughter Hannah, whose husband James Vaughton was the landlord of the Travellers Inn at Vaughton Hill, Deepcar.

In 1850 both Samuel Knutton and George Grayson (landlord of The King and Miller at Deepcar) had their licences suspended for two weeks because of complaints that had been made about their pubs – possibly drunkenness, noise, or disorderly conduct; they would have been unable to trade for those two weeks and would probably have had to remove the pub's sign for that fortnight. Samuel remained as landlord of the Castle for sixteen years until his death in 1864, running it with the help of his family and servants, his wife having died in 1856 when she was only 36 years old.

The licence stayed in the family when Samuel's daughter Ann [Knutton] and her husband John Bower took over, but John died just two years later in 1866 after a long illness. He was only 28 years old. A year later his widow married again, to Elijah Askew, and they went on to run the Coach and Horses and the Friendship Inn. The Bramall family did not own the pub or the land around it (this was still in the ownership of the Grayson family), but they did have the licence on and off for many years. After Ann Bower left, the licence

---

[7] Hunter, Joseph. The History and Topography of the Parish of Sheffield. London: 1819

passed out of the hands of the Bramalls for a short time, John Dronfield being the licensee between about 1866 and 1870.

The original landlady had been Ann Bramall nee Grayson. When her brother John Grayson of Spink Hall died in 1869, part of his estate included *"two freehold cottage houses and garden with the appurtenances situate at Bolsterstone now in the occupation of John Charlesworth and John Fish and of the public house known by the name of* "The Castle Inn" *situate at Bolsterstone with the brew house, barn, stabling, cow house, shed and appurtenances and the following Fields namely Calf Croft [...] Low Cross Ing, yard and buildings containing 30 acres and 2 roods [...] in the occupation of John Dronfield with a filemakers shop in the occupation of Thomas Bramall..."* all of which was left in trust for his wife Lydia to provide an income for her.

Opening after 11pm one Sunday night in January 1869 earned John Dronfield a ten shilling fine, which in turn placed him on the magistrates' *"blacklist."* When the time came to renew the licence at the annual Brewster Sessions, his application could have been refused it there had been any further trouble, but there hadn't been, so his name was removed from the blacklist and his licence granted. The following year the Castle was once again in the hands of the Bramall family, the new landlord being Thomas Bramall, son of the original landlord John.

Thomas Bramall ran the Castle with his wife Mary Ann Helliwell for thirteen years until his death in 1883. They also farmed about thirty acres of land. A couple of years after they moved into the Castle, one of their sons Thomas Henry fell about nine feet from a hayloft and was badly hurt, but luckily, he survived. In 1874 Mary Ann was visiting Sheffield and was crossing the road in Haymarket when she was knocked down by a horse and cart. Her injuries were attended to at the Sheffield Hospital and Dispensary.

"To be Sold, a Ginger-Beer Machine, with Bottles and Hampers. – Apply to Thos. Bramall, Bolsterstone; or Mr. Elijah Askew, Stocksbridge."[8]

---

[8] Sheffield Daily Telegraph 11th March 1871

SERIOUS ASSAULT AT THE CASTLE: 1873

A fight broke out one night between four men, one of whom was knocked unconscious. All the men worked as colliers, but the man who was attacked, John Dyson, also worked as a *"watcher"* over some land belonging to local landowner Mr. Rimington Wilson of Broomhead Hall.[9] Dyson had seen the men who assaulted him, along with some others, near this land. They had dogs and ferrets with them and were no doubt set on a spot of poaching. The three attackers were Joseph and John Walton, and George Staniforth.[10]

It was a Monday night at a quarter to eleven, and the men had all been drinking in the Castle. Afraid that Dyson would report them for poaching, they threatened to *"do for him"* if he did so. As he was leaving the pub, one of them grabbed him by the neck, held him down, and brutally kicked and punched him. The attack was so severe that he became unconscious and had to be carried home. John Walton had a large clasp knife in his hand, and he threatened to stab Dyson with it, as well as anyone else who might interfere in the fight.

The three men appeared in court and witnesses were called. Thomas Green confirmed Dyson's version of the assault. Mary Dyson (his sister-in-law) said that she heard Joseph Walton say that *"he was as pleased as if someone had given him £5 that he had done Dyson."* The Defence, however, argued that Dyson was a *"very quarrelsome man,"* and that it was he who had started the fight by striking the first blow. Each man was said to have had a *"fair fight"* with him, one after the other. Three witnesses backed up this alternative version of events. It was decided that the Walton brothers and George Staniforth had started the assault, and they were each fined ten shillings.

A request was made that the conduct of the landlord, Thomas Bramall, should be looked into because it was most important that village inns should be *"respectably conducted."*

---

[9] A Watcher was a man employed by a Lord of the Manor or landowner to watch his game preserves. He had the authority to apprehend night poachers.
[10] Joseph and John Walton were brothers, the sons of Christopher Walton. This family were originally from Hunshelf Bank. In 1871, Joseph was lodging at Bolsterstone with the Charlesworth family, and John was lodging at Ughill, Bradfield with the Smith family.

When George Staniforth was a child, his father (also called George) was killed during a fight at the Broomhead Mill Inn in 1855. When the census was taken in 1881, the enumerator wrote that George was of *"weak mind."* He never married, and ended his days at Grenoside Workhouse, dying there in 1913.

A HUNGRY THIEF: 1874

A man named Henry Charlesworth was employed by Thomas Bramall as a farm servant. He was living at the Castle when the 1871 census was taken. In 1874, whilst a butcher was delivering to the pub, Charlesworth stole a stew bone of beef from the cart that was parked outside. He was seen by the delivery man, who was standing in the doorway at the time, and was arrested. He was committed to be tried at the Sessions where was found guilty and sent to jail for six months, with hard labour.

Thomas Bramall seems to have kept an *"orderly house"* after his warning in 1872, with no further trouble being reported. He died in 1883, and the following year his son, the local auctioneer and valuer John Bramall, auctioned off his father's animals and farm machinery at Spink Hall Farm. The sale included ten beasts, one horse, two pigs, as well as farming equipment. The beasts were described as a red heifer (newly calved), a roan heifer (in calf), a red cow, a white heifer, two barren cows in milk, two stirks, and two Wye calves.

In his will, Thomas asked that his wife should be allowed to carry on the pub business if that is what she wished. Upon her death, any property could be sold if need be, and the proceeds divided up as legacies.

The pub was then run for a short time by Elijah Askew, one-time landlord of the Coach and Horses and The Friendship, who had been married to Thomas and Mary Ann's niece Ann Bower.[11] A newspaper report of 1884 said that Mr. Askew of the Castle Inn had provided *"an excellent dinner"* for the Bolsterstone and Wigtwizzle Ploughing Society. Mary Ann moved away at some point; when the next census was taken in April 1891, she was living

---

[11] Ann Knutton was the widow of John Bower, former landlord of the Castle. She was the daughter of Mary Bramall and Samuel Knutton, and the granddaughter of the original landlord John Bramall. She married Elijah Askew in 1867 and died in about 1882. Elijah married Lydia Grayson of Spink Hall in 1884 and retired from pub life.

with her son Thomas Henry at Townend Farm. She died the following month.

The next landlord was James Bulloss Nichols.

In September 1885, Elijah Askew (who, as a former publican himself, should have known better) was found inside the Castle drinking and gambling at 2am. Two policemen had entered the pub and found Askew, John Longford and James Kilner sitting around a table with drinks in front of them, a pack of cards, and £2 in silver. They said they were celebrating the landlord's birthday [Mr. Nichols] and had stayed after closing time as his guests. This did not impress the magistrates, who fined each man £1.

In 1888 Mr. Nichols sued the Stocksbridge Local Board for £45 in damages when his horse died after falling over a low wall on the roadside in Yew Trees Hill - presumably because the Board was responsible for the upkeep of roads and fences. They denied any liability, however, and he had to stand the loss himself. A few years later, in 1894, he stood for election to the Local Board but was unsuccessful. His pub venture came to an end in the Bankruptcy Court in 1898, with him owing debts of £444.

By 1901 the landlord was John Helliwell, who, like the former landlords, was also a farmer. Originally from Ridgeway in Derbyshire (where his father had been a publican), John had previously been the landlord of the Coach & Horses in Stocksbridge and the Newmarket Hotel in Sheffield. His wife Sarah Grace Woodcock was the daughter of Joseph Woodcock, late landlord of the King and Miller at Deepcar. John only had the Castle for a few years, until 1905, before he left the pub trade and moved to a farm at Howbrook.

The next landlord, John Jordan, was also only at the pub a short while, from 1905 until 1907. Jordan had been born in Clun, Shropshire, where he worked as a groom before coming north to live and work at Broomhead Hall as a coachman. He married Ruth Fox in 1886, the daughter of farmer and gamekeeper William Fox of Mortimer House at Smallfield, Bradfield. John and Ruth lived at Broomhead Hall before moving to Bolsterstone to run the Castle.

As mentioned above, when John Grayson died in 1869, he left his land and property, including the Castle and its land, to his widow Lydia Ann. When she died in 1905, the Castle and land should have passed to Thomas Bramall (John Grayson's nephew, and son of the original landlord John Bramall). However, he had died in 1883, so the property was inherited by his son Thomas Henry Bramall. A year after inheriting, in October 1906, Thomas Henry Bramall put the pub (with Jordan still its tenant), along with some cottages and fields, up for auction.

At this time, the pub was a lot smaller than it is now. There was a taproom, a front room, kitchen, larder, cellar, beer cellar, washhouse, coal house, and a storeroom. Upstairs were three bedrooms and a large club room. Included in the sale were outbuildings on the opposite side of the road which were being used as stables, a barn, and a turnip house, with a hay chamber above. All this was in the occupation of the current landlord John Jordan. The sale of the inn also included some adjoining cottages, both of which have now been demolished. The cottages on one side were occupied by John Charlesworth and Mrs. Oswald Dyson; these were demolished at some point and an extension to the pub built on their site. An old cottage on the other side was being used as a storeroom but had the potential to be converted into a farmhouse. This was eventually demolished, and a carpark now occupies the site. The tenants at this time were Mark Shaw and Herbert Hague; perhaps they were renting the cottages to use as stores.

According to the sale advert, *"The Castle Inn has a great reputation as an excellent licensed property, is situated in a capital and unique position, commands a very extensive and ever-increasing trade, and is worth the special attention of brewers and capitalists."* Possession would be given to the purchaser on the 25th March the following year.[12]

The landlords of the Castle had always farmed about thirty to forty acres of land belonging to it, and all this was now for sale as a separate lot, together with some stone-built farm buildings, a cow house large enough to hold

---

[12] 25th March, or Lady Day, was one of the *"Quarter Days"*, the others being 24th June (Midsummer Day), 29th September (Michaelmas Day) and 25th December (Christmas Day). It was on these days that rents were due to be paid and houses or lands entered into or quitted. The 25th March was the first day of the New Year according to the Old Style (Julian) calendar until 1752 when the New Year began on 1st January.

twelve head of cattle, a bull house, a stable for three large horses, a hay chamber, wagon and cart sheds, a workshop, a large yard, some piggeries, and sheds, etc.

The pub and its cottages, and the land, were bought for £3,750 and £975 respectively by Ann Bramall in January 1907. She was the widow of local auctioneer John Bramall of Leeke House, Old Haywoods, who had died in 1904. His father Thomas had once been the landlord (and his grandfather John before that). Ann was the daughter of Joseph Grayson, a coal merchant.

Ann Bramall's name is over the door, which dates this photograph post-1907. The cottages to the right have been demolished and a garage and car park now occupy the site. The cottages on the left were demolished to make way for an extension.

John Jordan was due to move out on the 25th March. On the 16th March he advertised for a *"Farm Man, good, all round, Wanted; to live in - Jordan, Castle Inn, Bolsterstone."*[13] He perhaps stayed on until April, when his name appeared in an advertisement for one of the regular livestock sales which

---

[13] Sheffield Daily Telegraph, 16th March 1907

took place there.[14] He then moved to Dronfield, where he continued in the pub trade. He died in 1932, after a short illness, at the Norton Hotel, Meadowhead, aged seventy-one.[15]

And so, the Castle Inn was once again in the hands of a Bramall. It is possible that, as the widow of John Bramall (one of the heirs of John Grayson), Ann inherited some money when John Grayson's widow Lydia Ann died in 1905, and that she used the money to buy the Castle which her late husband's brother Thomas Henry had put up for auction in 1906. When her husband's will was proved in 1908, his effects were £3,265 (which equates to around £439,357 today).

Ann stayed at the Castle until her death in 1931 at the age of 83; she was one of the oldest residents in the area and had been the licensee for about twenty years. She lived there with her sister Jemima Grayson, her daughter Mary Ann and her husband William Kay, and other family members.

In 1909 Ann applied for an eight-hour licence for drink and dancing for the annual Church School's ball. Police Superintendent Bielby objected to this, arguing that the licence, which would be from 9pm until 5am, was unreasonable and would mean that his men would have to be on duty until that time in the morning. The magistrates agreed, and the licence was granted with reduced hours, until 3am.

It was during Ann Bramall's time at the Castle that the building was significantly altered. Work on the construction of the two dams at More Hall and Broomhead had begun in 1913, resulting in an increased population of

---

[14] Sheffield Daily Telegraph, 13th April 1907: "*The Wigtwizzle Half-Yearly Sale of Cattle, Sheep, Pigs, Horses, Etc.*" was to be held at the Castle Inn, Bolsterstone, on Wednesday 24th April 1907. Entries were invited and could be made to Mr. J. Jordan, among others.

[15] The Derbyshire Times, Saturday 16th January 1932. "Mr. John Jordan [...] was one of the best-known sportsmen in Dronfield and district. Previous to becoming licensee at the Norton Hotel, when it was opened three years ago, Mr. Jordan was tenant of the Horse and Jockey Inn, Dronfield, for many years. He had also held licences at Bolsterstone, Stocksbridge and Sheffield." Mourners who attended the funeral from this area were Mr. & Mrs. W. Jordan, Stocksbridge and Mrs. H. Crosland, Bolsterstone.

drinkers - the navvies working on building the reservoirs. In November 1913 she applied for, and was granted, permission to enlarge and modernise the pub, and the work was put out to tender.

Ann did not have the monopoly however, because in 1914 the Sheffield Corporation were granted a licence for a canteen at Ewden. The canteen would form a necessary part of the model village for the workers, and the Corporation promised that it would be conducted *"in the best possible way"* under the supervision of the manager of the Water Department, Mr. Terry. The sale of liquors would be regulated in a way that the progress of work would not be interfered with. The man in charge would receive no interest on the sale of intoxicants but would have commission on the sale of non-alcoholic drinks, so that it would be to his benefit to push the sale of these. The canteen would be open for eight hours a day; an hour in the morning, two hours at noon and from 5pm until closing time. The beer supplied would be of a *"thoroughly wholesome kind."* Mr. Terry said that the canteen at the Langsett works sold to the workmen an average of half a pint of beer to each man per day, and that a large proportion of the men were teetotallers. This is rather at odds with reports from ten years previously, when there was an outcry about *"Shebeening"* at Langsett, with men selling alcohol illegally from their huts.[16]

In 1925, Ann put her former home Leeke House up for sale, as well as three adjoining cottages and three cottages at Leeke Bank, all of which were let to tenants. She was also selling a plot of land opposite the Castle Inn with farm buildings on it (there was enough good building material to erect *"six good cottages"*) and a plot of building land called Calf Croft, near to the Castle, fronting Stone Moor Road. Whether these sold was not reported, but both were put up for sale again in 1935 when the Castle was sold once more. The buildings were in a state of disrepair by then, but, again, the notice said that there was enough material to build six cottages.

AUCTION OF TEAROOM: 1928
On the 18th July 1928 a house, grocer's shop and tearoom, the property of the late John Kenworthy, went to auction at the Castle. The downstairs consisted of a shop, living room, scullery, and a spacious tearoom at the rear of the

---

[16] A Shebeen was an illicit bar or club where exciseable liquor was sold without a licence

house with an inside w.c. There were three bedrooms, an attic, and a bathroom with the luxury of hot and cold water, a lavatory, and a stock room. There was also a gas supply laid on. According to the sales advert, the property occupied the *"best position in the village"* and was a profitable concern.

In about 1927, Ann Bramall transferred the licence of the Castle to her son-in-law George Leonard Brook Sampson (husband of her daughter Ada Bramall). For many years Sampson was the manager for Thomas Brooke and Sons at their pipe works at Bracken Moor. He went on to start a business as a coal dealer and also set up as a charabanc proprietor under the name Sampson & Mann. The junior partner in the company was his nephew Frank Grayson Mann (1900-1931). Sampson continued to run the coaches after becoming the licensee of the Castle. His health, however, was failing, and he died only a month after Ann Bramall, on the 3rd April 1931 aged fifty years. Frank Grayson Mann died a few months after his uncle. Ada ran the pub for the next four years until it was put up for sale by the mortgagees [lenders] in July 1935.

Lot 1 consisted of the Castle (a fully licensed free house), and two cottages, the latter providing a rental income. The advert for the sale[17] noted that: *"The present very substantial trade is capable of being considerably increased by modernising the premises, and a good catering business for visitors to the beautiful Ewden Valley and the Old-World Village of Bolsterstone might be further developed."* A full description of the pub was also given: *"Entrance with enclosed service bar, smoke room, tap room with enclosed service bar and separate entrance, best room, private sitting room, large kitchen, pantry, very large rock-built beer cellar, wash kitchen, billiards or club room with separate entrance, 4 bedrooms, bathroom, W.C. and the usual outside conveniences."* Lot 2 was the building land opposite the pub (with outbuildings and enough material to erect six cottages) and Lot 3 was building land at Calf Croft. Ada Sampson was the occupier, but arrangements could be made for early possession.

The Castle and two freehold cottages sold for £5,000. Whoever bought it kept Ada on as landlady, for she remained there until her death in 1949 at the

---

[17] *Sheffield Independent* 29th June 1935

age of 72.[18] The freehold plot of land opposite the pub sold for £180 and the freehold plot of building land called Calf Croft, fronting Stone Moor Road, sold for £50.

Ada Sampson died at the Castle in 1949, and the following year her furniture and effects were up for sale by auction there. Her possessions included a pianola player with 60 music rolls.

The Castle Inn and St. Mary's church. The cottage on the left of the pub was demolished to make way for an extension. The name above the door is John Jordan, who was the landlord from 1905 until 1907. There is a date stone above the centre window which reads 1840.

---

[18] According to the website breweryhistory.com, The Castle became a William Stones house in September 1935.

A PROPOSED NEW PUB FOR BOLSTERSTONE – 1876

Spring View, Sunny Bank Lane, Bolsterstone in 1986.

At the West Riding Brewster Sessions, held at Sheffield in September 1876, William Shaw applied for a publican's licence for a house he had recently built at Spring View, Bolsterstone (on Sunny Bank Lane, just down the hill from the village). There were four rooms downstairs in addition to the kitchen, and upstairs there were five chambers and a club room. Outside there was stabling accommodation for 10 horses. In anticipation of having a licence granted, he had named it *"The Spring View Hotel."*

Unfortunately for Shaw, the application was objected to, on the grounds that another licensed house *"was not in the least required for the neighbourhood."* Superintendent Kershaw of the West Riding Constabulary told the Bench that the population of Bolsterstone would not in his opinion amount to more than a hundred people, and there was already a public house half a mile away, Thomas Bramall's Castle Inn. The magistrates were unanimous in refusing the application.

THE COACH & HORSES INN, MANCHESTER ROAD, STOCKSBRIDGE

Originally a small wayside inn surrounded by fields, this pub began life as a small beerhouse in the 1830s before gaining a full licence. It pre-dates the steelworks – indeed it is said that Samuel Fox called in at this pub when he was looking to acquire the cotton mill which stood nearby. Mr. Fox bought the mill and began his wire-drawing business, which grew over the years until it completely dominated the valley floor. The Coach and Horses gradually became surrounded by buildings as the steelworks expanded and more shops were built to serve the growing population. This photo was taken from Knowles's garden, and dates from 1916 when Tennant Brothers acquired the pub from A. H. Smith's brewery.

The Coach and Horses started out, as did many pubs, as simply a beer house – that is, it did not have a licence to sell stronger drink like spirits. Early records are patchy, but it seems likely that its first landlord was George Siddons, and that he took advantage of the new Beerhouse Act of 1830 which paved the way for any householder who met certain conditions to brew and sell beer from his own home. George was listed in trade directories as a *"retailer of beer"* rather than a licensed victualler in 1833 and 1834. In 1833 he gave notice that he intended to apply for a full licence for his pub; he called it the Travellers Inn, and it was *"at Stocks Bridge in Bradfield [...] on the Turnpike Road leading from Sheffield to Manchester."* He rented the premises from John Burkinshaw of Wortley.[19] Siddons signed a document to say that the house had not been used as an inn for the past three years (which was standard wording on the form), but that it was licensed for the sale of beer. The full licence was granted at some point, but he didn't stay long, because in August 1836 he transferred the licence to a John Siddons, who had been living in Manchester, and he in turn transferred it to Willie Jubb a few months later.

Local historian Joseph Kenworthy tells the story of when Samuel Fox - the *"founder"* of Stocksbridge - first came to this valley in the early 1840s, looking to take premises for a wire-drawing business in the Old Cotton Mill. He did not meet with much success and decided to go home. Passing a coal pit on the top of Dark Rocher at Wood Willows, he was startled when someone called out: *"Hello, Sam! What ar' tha dooin heear?"* Mr. Fox recognised a fellow workman whose name was Tom Jubb, this man having changed occupations from wire drawer to coke burner. Mr. Fox told him what he wanted, and how a tenant of the mill, Mr. Hemingway, had been most unwilling to entertain his application. Tom Jubb, who lived at Thurgoland, replied rather sternly: *"Tha's noan seen t'reight chap, tha mun see Jossie Newton,"* and he called a young lad named Tom Hawley, saying: *"Tak this chap to Willie Jubb's* [Coach and Horses], *and shew him Owd Jossie, he's sure to be theear."* He told Mr. Fox: *"Jossie's t'mester, an' yo mun settle wi' him. I'll follow thee when aw've putten another hillion[20] on."* And so Samuel Fox retraced his footsteps and was introduced to old Jossie,

---

[19] The Bradfield parish land tax records list a William Burkinshaw renting out a house [the pub] to George Siddons, and a house and shop to Edward Askew, who was a blacksmith. The pub tenancy was transferred to William Jubb in 1836.
[20] A cover; he meant to put more coal on top of the coke he was burning.

with whom he had a long talk, made known his wishes, and then after a pleasant chat over some refreshments, Mr. Fox sealed his bargain. He then left, no doubt feeling highly pleased that he had come across Tom Jubb so opportunely. Whether this is true or not, it makes for a fine tale![21]

INQUEST ON SARAH BATTY: 1837

An inquest was held at William Jubb's pub[22] on the 10th August 1837 upon the body of Sarah Batty. This tragic tale of a young servant girl who found herself pregnant made only a single short paragraph in the Sheffield Independent, with just a bare reporting of the facts. The Sheffield Iris provided more detail. Sarah had been in the service of Mr. Hague of Hoyle House for about ten weeks but had become unwell and was unable to do her work. Mrs. Hoyle noticed her pregnancy, which was quite advanced, and gave her a month's notice to quit. The girl worked her notice and then went to Penistone, where she called upon Mr. Booth, a surgeon who also kept a druggist's shop. She asked for half a pound of arsenic, which she said her master wanted to mix with some sheep salve he was preparing. Mr. Booth, knowing her master, gave her the arsenic, and told her to be careful with it, because it was poison, and she went away apparently in good spirits. That evening she was seen within three fields of her master's house, vomiting in a violent manner, and a boy who went up to her left her alone when she said she was going to her master's house. She never got there. The next morning she was found dead in the same field. About an ounce of arsenic was found in her basket; she had swallowed the rest.

The Jury, after the examination of a number of witnesses, returned a verdict of *"felo de se"* (suicide, literally *"felon of himself,"* because suicide was regarded as a crime). She was buried the same night in Penistone churchyard between the hours of nine and midnight, without the Christian rights of burial. There was no entry in the parish burial register. It wasn't until an Act of 1882 that suicides could be buried in a churchyard at any hour and with the usual religious rites. The tale was even sadder because about six months

---

[21] Kenworthy, J. The Early History of Stocksbridge & District Vol. 9. 1914
[22] Mistakenly reported in both the Sheffield Independent and Iris as the Waggon & Horses

previously her brother had been killed when he was run over by a wagon on the Bitholmes.[23]

Jubb was at the Coach and Horses until 1845. The 1841 census gives his occupation as a farmer, not an innkeeper. His wife Hannah would have helped with the running of the pub whilst he was working on the farm. In 1841 there were nine other people in the pub on census night, one servant and the rest presumably lodgers. All the lodgers were recorded as having been born in Scotland, Ireland or abroad. Two of them worked as cotton spinners and would have worked in the mill that Samuel Fox was to acquire for his wire-drawing business. Jubb appears to have bought the pub from Mr. Burkinshaw in about 1841. A blacksmith called Edward Askew was living in the adjoining house and renting the smithy too; he would one day become the pub's landlord, assisted by his wife.

Willie Jubb also owned a coal pit on Hunshelf Bank, and he was interviewed in 1842 as part of an investigation into the employment of children.[24] Here is what he said in defence of employing children in the mines:

"*Mr. William Jubb, owner of the coal pit at Henshelf Bank* [sic], *and publican about 40 years of age. Examined February 18th. He depones: - I think it would be impossible to heighten the gates in the pits so as to use ponies in them for hurrying because of the expense. It would not pay to have a pony even though the gates would admit it. We could not contrive to do without the children at all, that I can see of. I am not an advocate of having girls to hurry in the pits. There are people in this neighbourhood which can't do without their children working in the pits. If they go to the Union for relief, the Board says,* "you must get a job for your children at Mr. Jubb's or Mr. Webster's coal pits and let them work, girls as well as boys." *I don't think it hurts them to work in the pits. They run about after they have done their work and don't seem tired. There was a fever about here a few years since and those that worked in the pits did not have it. We don't consider it bad*

---

[23] Sarah was possibly the daughter of James Batty and Sarah Brown of Damstakes, Langsett, born 14th December 1819. The brother could have been Martin or William, but there is no record of an accident or burial to anyone of this name in this timescale.

[24] Children's Employment Commission 1842. Report by Jelinger C. Symons Esq., on the Employment of Children & Young Persons in the Mines and Collieries of the West Riding of Yorkshire, and on the State, Condition and Treatment of such Children & Young Persons.

work for children in this coal. I don't think it makes girls impudent. I had a servant girl live with me who was as well behaved as possible and she had worked in the pits. They don't get ill-treated. I pay the hurriers myself in my own pit. It would be an injury to the parents to prevent children from working, before they were 11 or 12 years old."

Jubb's wife Hannah died at the young age of 28. She was buried at Bolsterstone on the 4th May 1845 and ten days later Willie signed a declaration that he intended to transfer the licence to Thomas Hague at the next licensing sessions in June. Hague had recently been the licensee of a pub at Ingbirchworth, and before that, he had been at the King and Miller, Deepcar (until 1842). Jubb left the Coach and Horses and went to live with his mother Mary at Segg Hole farm, Hunshelf. He was working as a coke burner when the 1851 census was taken. He later moved to Stocksbridge and in 1861 and 1871 he was working as a butcher. He did not marry again and died in 1872 aged 67.

Thomas Hague died only a year after moving to the Coach & Horses. His widow Nellie took over, but she died not long afterwards. In 1847 her executor, Benjamin Coldwell of the Royal Oak at Deepcar, transferred the licence for the Coach and Horses to Edward Askew.[25]

Edward was a blacksmith and had been living next to the pub. The smithy was behind the Coach and Horses, and the road that runs down from the main road to Hunshelf Bank was always known as "*Smithy Hill*" because of this [this road has been re-named Fox Valley Way, and the corner house of this block, formerly Bamforth's shop, has been lost to road widening]. Edward carried on his trade of blacksmith as well as running the Coach and Horses; indeed, it seems to have been his main occupation. His wife Elizabeth, along with paid help and family, would have helped to run the pub. Whether the Coach received a lot of trade from being on the Sheffield to Manchester route isn't clear, but the main stopping-off point for the stagecoaches was The King and Miller at Deepcar, where the horses were changed. Askew bought the pub, the house, and the smithy from William Jubb in about 1851. It remained

---

[25] White's Directory of Sheffield, published in 1849, lists William Wagstaff as the victualler, Coach and Horses, and Edward Askew as a blacksmith. The directory would have been compiled the previous year, and it seems likely that he was only the landlord for a short time before moving to take a pub at Barnsley.

in the family until 1902 when it was sold to a brewery. Edward's daughter Ann married William Helliwell, and they opened a beerhouse called The Sportsman's Arms at Old Haywoods in about 1864.

INQUEST ON FANNY BROADHEAD: 1846
An inquest was held at the Coach and Horses on the body of Fanny Broadhead of Avice Royd, Hunshelf, aged five years, who drowned in the Porter Brook (the Little Don), the river that runs through the valley towards Sheffield. It appeared that the child had accompanied an elder sister, aged eleven years, to fetch a pair of boots home from the shoemaker. They had to pass over the Porter on a single plank, twelve or fourteen feet long. In returning, the elder girl first carried the boots over, and then returned for her sister. With the weight of the two girls together, the plank sprung considerably, and they were both thrown into the water. A man who was nearby saw one of the children in the water and ran to get her out. He did not see the sister, however; people only realised she was missing when the older girl recovered her senses and asked about her. Sadly, it was several hours before the body was found. The coroner passed a verdict of accidental death. A similar accident had occurred five years previously when another five-year-old girl died after falling from a plank spanning the River Don at Wharncliffe.

STOLEN PIGEONS: 1849
Like many pub landlords with a bit of land, Edward Askew organised pigeon shooting matches. In November 1849, his wife purchased a dozen pigeons for this purpose from a young man called Joshua Batty, paying him sixpence for each one. It turned out that he had stolen the pigeons the night before, taking ten from a pigeon cote belonging to John Redfearn at Gate, Oughtibridge, and two from Samuel Crawshaw of Coumes. Batty was arrested and, along with the pigeons, was taken to be locked up at Sheffield Town Hall. The pigeons were placed in a basket on a ledge over the cells, but when an officer went to feed them that night, Batty had somehow managed to open their basket and set them free. When he came up for trial, Batty swore that the pigeons belonged to his brother, and his defence rested on the fact that the liberated pigeons had not found their way home to Oughtibridge. The jury found him guilty, and he was sentenced to six months in jail, with hard labour.

Seven months later, Joshua and his brother Charles were arrested in possession of ten stolen ducks in Sheffield. One of the constables recognised Joshua from his previous conviction. The two lads (Joshua was 20 years old and Charles was 19) were arrested, and further investigations proved that the ducks had been stolen from Mr. B. Charlesworth of Hunshelf and George Jubb of Hayfolds [Haywoods?] near Hunshelf. In court, a note was produced from the boys' father, who lived at Midhopestones, saying that the ducks were his, and he had given them to the boys to sell at Sheffield. As a similar defence had been used previously, they were not believed, and the boys were committed to be tried at the Sessions. Charles was imprisoned for three months, but Joshua was sentenced to be transported (probably to Australia or Tasmania) for seven years, although this did not actually happen. Joshua was sent to Wakefield jail and then to Portland jail, Dorset, where his behaviour was reported to have been mostly *"exemplary."* After a few years he was recommended for discharge by licence in consequence of his *"very good character"* and the offer of employment by Mr. J. Helliwell of Damstakes, Midhope (which was where his father had farmed). He was discharged on licence on the 29th December 1853. Joshua and Charles were the brothers of Sarah Batty, who had committed suicide in 1837.

INQUEST ON CHARLES WEBSTER: 1852
Another inquest at the pub, this time on the body of Charles Webster, aged 49, a carter in the employ of Samuel Fox. Charles was returning from Sheffield and was riding in his cart without using the reins when the horse bolted, and he lost control. He jumped out of the cart to catch the horse, and in doing so he fell under the wheels, fracturing his jaw and injuring his head. He was taken home but died that night. The Coroner said the man was entirely to blame, for his *"reprehensible practice of riding without reins."*

INQUEST ON JOSEPH BURROWS: 1854
On the 3rd June 1854, the Sheffield Independent reported on a fatal accident that had occurred a month earlier. Joseph Burrows was 18 years old and worked for Samuel Fox at the wire mill. He and some fellow workers had assembled in the upper room of the mill to drink some ginger beer. Burrows sat down upon a *"swift"* (a plate fastened upon the top of a spindle). His weight broke the plate, and the sharp spindle ran into him a considerable depth. He was attended by Penistone surgeon Mr. Ward, but he did not survive. The coroner recorded a verdict of accidental death.

AUCTION OF PROPERTY: 1852
An auction of some property at Horner Houses belonging to William Helliwell was held at Mr. Edward Askew's Coach and Horses in November 1852. For sale in three lots, the property consisted of a homestead (consisting of two cottages, cow-houses, a barn, a stable, etc.) as well as fields and woods, all fronting the Turnpike (Manchester Road) and suitable for use as building land. The cottages were tenanted by Thomas Firth and Thomas Kay.

Edward Askew was in trouble with the licensing board in 1853, there having been complaints made about the manner in which he ran his house [pub]. He received a caution and was warned that if there was any further trouble during the following year, his licence would be taken from him at the next Brewster Sessions. It seems that there was no more trouble, for he continued as landlord there until his death in 1856. His widow then ran the pub until she died three years later in January 1859. Their son Elijah Askew took over, and like his father before him, he kept on with his main trade of blacksmith. He was also in partnership with a man called John Ramsden as grocers and provision dealers at Stocksbridge trading under the name of "*Ramsden and Co.*" In 1871 John and his wife Hannah were living at Bolsterstone, possibly in one of the cottages adjoining the Castle. His occupation was recorded as a butcher, and he was 26 years old. John Ramsden died in 1876, and the partnership was dissolved, the business then belonging solely to Elijah. He was described as a grocer in 1880 when he chaired a meeting of the creditors of a Stocksbridge surgeon Rowley Connolly in Sheffield.[26]

Elijah had married Mary Coldwell in 1858; her father Benjamin was the landlord of the Royal Oak at Deepcar. They had six children: James, Harriet Elizabeth (who married Elijah Batty of the Friendship), Ann, Clara, Emily, and Ada.[27]

ROBBERY BY A SERVANT GIRL: 1860
Elijah had hired a young live-in servant girl on the 28th November 1859 called Sarah McKay or Mackey. On Wednesday 11th January she was "*very pressing*" for permission to go home to Oughtibridge, but Elijah was

---
[26] Elijah had moved to the Friendship by 1880.
[27] James (1858-1858), Harriet Elizabeth (1860-1888), Ann (died young in 1861), Clara (1862-1932), Emily (1863-) who married George Cook, and Ada (1864-1888) who married Henry Sanderson.

suspicious and insisted on knowing what money and possessions she had upon her before she went. After some questioning and evasion, it was found that she had concealed quite a stash: 10s. 6d. in copper, about 5s. 6d. in silver, two ginger-beer bottles (one containing rum and the other gin), a few cigars, and two ounces of tobacco. She appeared before the Sheffield petty sessions that Friday and was committed to trial at the Sheffield Quarter Sessions. She pleaded guilty and was sent to prison for three months.

AUCTION AT THE COACH: 1866
Auctioneer Mr. James Taylor advertised an auction at the *"House of Mr. Elijah Askew"* [the pub] to sell a stock of groceries, black and green teas, soap, mustard, coffee, spices, washing crystals, and also some household furniture. These were the property of an unnamed person who was giving up the grocery trade.

Mary Askew died in 1866 at the age of 27, and a year later Elijah married again, to a widow called Ann Bower. Ann and her husband John Bower had been the licensees of the Castle Inn at Bolsterstone, as had Ann's parents and grandparents, so she was well-qualified to help her husband run his pub. The 1871 census recorded Elijah and Ann at the Coach and Horses, Elijah being both a publican and blacksmith. They had six children: Marion Ellen, Florence, Kate Annie, Elijah Edward, Tom, and Charles Ernest.[28] Tom didn't live with his parents but with Joseph Staniforth and his wife Esther Whittington, at their home in Bolsterstone village. In 1881 he was described as their *"nurse child,"* which implies that this was a temporary situation, but because his mother Ann died in about 1882, this became permanent and they adopted him.[29] They did not have any children of their own. Joseph Staniforth's father George had been killed in a fight at the Broomhead Mill Inn in 1855 when Joseph was only 12 years old. Tom's father Elijah died in 1892 and he made sure he provided for whoever had the care of his son by allocating them ten shillings a week for his maintenance, clothing, and living expenses. Joseph Staniforth died in 1897, leaving Esther to care for Tom

---

[28] Marion Ellen (1868-1943) married Samuel J. Moorhouse; Florence (1870-1870); Kate Annie (1871-1922) married Sydney Hague; Elijah Edward (1873-1898) married Lucy Cooke; Tom (1878-1902); Charles Ernest (1880-1882).
[29] There is no record of the death or burial of Elijah's second wife Ann Askew that fits the dates 1881 (when she was at the Coach and Horses) and 1884 when Elijah married for a third time to Lydia Ann Grayson nee Bramall of Spink Hall.

who, according to the 1901 census, had been *"feeble-minded from birth."* He died in 1902, and Esther died a few years later, in 1906.

Elijah was the landlord of the Coach and Horses for almost twenty years, before installing a tenant and moving up the road to run the Friendship Hotel in 1878.

Elijah Askew involved himself in many local events. In 1868 he provided a supper for the Paragon Cricket Club at the Old Church School to mark the conclusion of their first season. According to one newspaper report, over 400 people attended a pigeon shoot which was held in a field adjoining the pub in 1870. In 1873 he was treasurer of the Stocksbridge Feast (Second Annual Sports and Gala). This event offered *"valuable and useful"* prizes. Events included a sack race, egg and spoon race, high jump, races, and *"a great number of very Laughable Sports"* to take place at intervals, *"which will cause great amusement."* Stocksbridge Brass Band would be there playing some of the most fashionable dance music of the day, there would also be *"splendid Montgolfier balloon ascents"* and a fireworks display. The event was advertised in the Sheffield Daily Telegraph, but no mention was made of where the event was to take place - probably because all the locals would have known.[30] The prizes went on show at the pub before the event. In 1873, a new Stocksbridge Local Board [council] was founded to administer the new Sanitary District of Stocksbridge, and Elijah was one of those who were elected to the board, as was fellow publican Benjamin Couldwell of the Royal Oak. Samuel Fox was also elected, with the majority of the votes.

FATAL ACCIDENT AT STOCKSBRIDGE: 1873

The coroner held an inquest on the body of 30-year-old Peter Brady, who was killed at work in Mr. Helliwell's colliery. Mr. Wardle, one of Her Majesty's inspectors of mines, reported that the pit shaft was in a bad state, and he was duty-bound to report the case to the Secretary of State. The Jury returned a verdict of accidental death. A few days earlier, however, a different newspaper had said that Peter Brady and some other men were *"half- intoxicated"* and were *"amusing themselves"* at Helliwell's coal pit,

---

[30] The Sheffield Independent 14th August 1872 mentioned that the Stocksbridge Athletic Sports took place on *"Mr. Helliwell's large field, near the Coach and Horses."*

which was close to the Miners Arms. Brady, a labourer, bragged that he could descend the shaft (which was 35 yards deep), by climbing down the rope. He did so, and safely reached the corve (wagon) which hung at the end of the rope. The rope hung only about half-way down the shaft, but Brady thought the corve stood on the pit bottom. He stepped upon it, let go of the rope, and fell to the bottom of the shaft. He was brought back up to the surface but died soon after. The body was taken to the Coach and Horses in readiness for the inquest. Brady lodged in Chapel Row (near the Ebenezer Chapel) and was unmarried.

SLANDEROUS STATEMENTS AND A PUBLIC APOLOGY: 1875
"I, William Marsden, of Heywoods, Deepcar, APOLOGISE to Mr. JOSEPH HATTERSLEY, of Bolsterstone, Farmer, for the slanderous statements I made reflecting upon his character, on Saturday Evening, the 23rd. Inst., at the Coach and Horses Inn, Stocksbridge; and I hereby admit that the statements were untrue, and in order that my withdrawal of them may be as public as possible, I authorise the said Mr. HATTERSLEY to publish this Apology in the Sheffield and Rotherham Independent and the Sheffield Daily Telegraph."[31]

ALLEGED DEATH OF A CHILD BY POISON: 1875
The newspapers made much of the suspected death by poisoning of a 6-year-old girl called Ann Nichols of 52 Haywoods Park, Deepcar. The Coroner held the inquest at the Coach and Horses. The case heard from witnesses, and post-mortem results were presented. The girl had eaten breakfast and gone off to school as normal, but whilst at school she was taken ill and started to vomit and fit. Dr. Davison attended the girl at her home the next day and arranged to call again that evening, but sadly she had died by the time he returned. He initially refused to issue a death certificate because another child in the house seemed to be suffering from the same complaint. In the end, it was ascertained that there was no poison of any kind about the house, and the girl had not eaten anything out of the ordinary. She had always been a sickly child. The jury returned a verdict of death from natural causes. Today there might be a more definitive explanation of what caused her death – intestinal blockage seems a likely explanation.

---

[31] Printed in the Sheffield Daily Telegraph 30th January 1875

A SHOCKING FATAL SAW ACCIDENT AT STOCKSBRIDGE: 1877
The Coroner held an inquest at the Coach and Horses in 1877 on the body of a joiner called Mellin Wilkinson, who was killed at Stocksbridge Works when he fell on a circular saw whilst it was in motion. A man named Joseph Birkhead was operating the saw at the time, and he told the Coroner that Mellin had climbed onto a beam nine feet from the saw to reach some wood, walked along the metal frame to speak to him, but had slipped and fallen over the saw. It severed his left thigh and cut off his right foot. Fenton Wilkinson, his son, told the Coroner that his father, who was 61 years old, was subject to fits of dizziness, and often fell against the furniture at home. The jury returned a verdict of accidental death, and Birkhead was instructed that he must not allow anyone to walk on the frame of the saw. This is just one example of the many, many deaths that occurred in the steelworks before the modern notions of Health and Safety were implemented.

ALLEGED BRUTAL ATTACK UPON POLICEMAN: 1878
Trouble outside a pub is nothing new, as this report shows. One evening in June 1878, two police officers were on duty when they witnessed Stocksbridge man Walter Wood, a collier, drunk outside the Coach and Horses. He was using abusive language, and Sergeant Waight, who knew the man, cautioned him saying, "*Now, Walter, such language will not do.*" He was so drunk he started fighting his friends, who were trying to get him away. Scuffles ensued, which got violent. Constable Delve was struck on the ear, Sergeant Waight was bitten, and both policemen were violently kicked. Wood's friends also set a bull terrier on the policemen. Waight had been unfit for duty following the attack. Wood swore at Waight and said he didn't care if he got twenty years for his behaviour. Eventually, he was cuffed and taken to the Hillsborough lock-up by pony and trap. The defence maintained that Wood was normally a peaceful man, but he was attacked and "*throttled*" by the police. Several witnesses were called to back this up and swear that Wood was sober - his sister and his mother being two of them. He was bailed and committed for trial at the Quarter Sessions, which is where the more serious offences were tried. The three men accused of trying to help Wood escape from the police were Joseph Brooke, Vernon Booth and John Buckley, all colliers. Buckley, who was said to have set the dog on the constables, was fined £3, or two months in jail; Brooke and Booth were fined £2 each, or two months' imprisonment. When Wood appeared at the Sessions, he was acquitted, although no explanation was given as to why.

A few months later, in October 1878, The Coach and Horses was looking for a new tenant: *"To be Let, at once, that old Licensed House, the* "Coach and Horses," *at Stocksbridge, now in the occupation of Mr. Elijah Askew. For a business man this is an opportunity rarely to be met with. Apply Messrs. Richdale and Tomlinson, Britannia Brewery, Bramall Lane."* Elijah then moved a short way up the main road to the Friendship Inn.

The Friendship had been opened in the 1850s by George Batty, who had been married to Elijah Askew's sister Hannah. When George died, his second wife, Harriet, ran the pub, and after her death in 1874, George and Hannah's son Tom Batty ran it for a short while. After his young wife died only two years into their marriage, Tom left the pub and went to Penistone, where he ran the Bridge Inn. Elijah was Tom Batty's maternal uncle, and perhaps he wished to keep the pub in the family, which is why he advertised for a tenant for the Coach and moved to run the Friendship. The Friendship had been left to George Batty's youngest son, Elijah Batty, but despite being old enough to run the pub by 1878 – he was 21 years old – he did not take on the licence until about 1884.

The man who took the Coach after Elijah left was John Bramall. An auctioneer and valuer by trade, his father Thomas Bramall had been the landlord of the Castle Inn at Bolsterstone, and his grandfather before that, way back in 1833. Many years later, after John's death, his widow Ann would become the owner and licensee of the Castle Inn (in 1907).

John Bramall had been living at Wadsley before returning to Stocksbridge and moving to the Coach and Horses. His family had been involved in the pub trade for years, so perhaps that was his reason for the move. His stay, however, was brief, and after three years he went to live at Leeke House, Haywoods, and carried on in trade as an auctioneer and valuer.

DRUNK AND REFUSING TO QUIT: 1879
Two Stocksbridge miners, James Curley and Thomas Curley, were summoned before the magistrates for refusing to leave the Coach and Horses Inn when asked. They were drunk and were fighting in the taproom. John Bramall asked them to leave but they refused and were ejected by force. Thomas Curley was well known to the police - he had been in trouble twenty times previously. He was fined forty shillings (or two months in prison with

hard labour, should he default on payment). James Curley was also known to the police, and he was ordered to pay twenty shillings (or one month's hard labour). The two men were brothers; they lived at Bracken Moor and their parents were James Curley senior and Mary Ann, both from Ireland.

For whatever reason, John Bramall only stayed at the pub for three years. In 1881 he transferred the licence to John Helliwell, who ran the Coach with his wife Ann until his death in 1890. His son, John Thomas Helliwell then briefly took over. John Thomas married Sarah Grace Woodcock in 1891, the daughter of Joseph Woodcock of the King and Miller at Deepcar.

John Helliwell senior had only been in the pub for three months when he was assaulted by a customer. The assailant, a Stocksbridge man called Isaac Silverwood, was prosecuted for the attack and sent to jail for one month, with hard labour. The case was reported in the newspaper, who said that Silverwood, *"conducted himself in an improper manner in the complainant's house, and on being requested to desist, he struck him a blow on the face."*

Pubs served as the meeting places of choice for local clubs and organisations. The Stocksbridge Steel and Iron Works Cricket Club held their annual supper at the Coach and Horses in 1881, with over fifty people sitting down to an *"excellent repast,"* after which *"a very enjoyable evening was spent."* Also meeting at the Coach were members of the Good Intent Lodge of the Oddfellows. In July 1885 they met to celebrate their 22nd anniversary. After a procession through the village, they called at the Travellers at Deepcar for lunch before returning to their Lodge Room at the Coach where 120 people sat down to dinner. The Oddfellows were a Friendly Society, and workers who joined could protect themselves and their families against illness, injury, or death, like an insurance policy. Men paid into the Society and could claim if they fell on hard times. At the meeting after the meal, it was reported that they had paid out a total of £1,600 for sickness and death claims that year. The total amount of money held by all the Lodges was almost £3 million, *"the savings from the wages of working men."* Another Friendly Society that met in the pub's large club room was the Stocksbridge Pride Lodge, which was part of the Sheffield Equalised Independent Druids.

Auctions were regularly held in public houses. In 1881 John Bramall (the previous landlord, who had reverted to his trade of auctioneer and valuer) held an auction at the Coach and Horses to sell a stone-built house with garden and outbuildings at Common Piece, Stocksbridge, in the occupation of the Rev. David Waters. The house consisted of a dining and drawing room, a kitchen, four bedrooms, a pantry, and a good cellar. Water came from a pump on the premises. David Waters had been born in Scotland and was an Independent Minister.

A LOCAL DIGNITARY IN HIS CUPS: 1883
It was an offence to be drunk in public, and it was even an offence to be found to be drunk in the pub. It was also an offence for a landlord to permit drunkenness. Even more scandalous was for a fine, upstanding member of the community to be found drunk in public, or *"in his cups,"* as one newspaper reported it. James Grayson, of Old Haywoods, Deepcar, vice-chairman of the Stocksbridge Local Board [the Council], was summoned to the West Riding Court in June 1883 for having been drunk on licensed premises, the Coach and Horses.

Constable Morley saw Grayson drunk in the street at Stocksbridge one morning at 11.30am. An hour and a half later, the policeman went into the Coach and Horses and found Grayson sat in the bar with a glass of whisky in front of him. He was drunk, used bad language towards him, and had to be led home. In court, Sergeant Herry and Superintendent Gill swore that Grayson was drunk and disorderly in the police station at Stocksbridge before he went to the Coach. Grayson swore he was not drunk, but merely excited, and a man named Herbert Woodhouse stated that he had seen Grayson in the pub and did not think he was drunk. The magistrates did not agree and fined him ten shillings. The landlord Mr. Helliwell was summoned for permitting drunkenness on his premises, but the summons was dismissed upon him paying the costs of the case.

A DRAMATIC THUNDERSTORM: 26th June 1883
A little before 2pm a heavy thunderstorm passed over the neighbourhood. The lamp at the Coach and Horses was struck and broken, the spout being broken at the same time. Fox's premises for coal-washing were struck by lightning, with part of the roof being knocked off and some of the wall too. Pieces of brick were found sixty feet away. The electrical current followed

the *"endless chain"*[32] for about six hundred yards down the coal pit in the Holme. Severe and repeated shocks caused the men to refrain from touching the chain, as a flash was seen to issue from it. Stokers in other parts of the works had their pokers knocked out of their hands. The heavy rains severely damaged the roads.

FATAL ACCIDENT AT STOCKSBRIDGE WORKS: June 1888

At 5.30pm on the 27th June 1888, William Woodhead was killed in an accident in the Bessemer department at Fox's works. Several men were loading a tyre plate in the department when the chain gave way, and the plate, weighing about a ton and a half, fell on him, crushing the lower part of his body and killing him instantly. William's body was taken to his home at 60 New Haywoods to await the coroner's inquiry. Coroner Wightman held the inquest at the Coach and Horses with Mr. Edwin Bamforth as the foreman of the jury. A verdict of accidental death was returned. Woodhead was about 37 years old, and he left a wife, Harriet, and a large family, the youngest only six months old.

SAD SUICIDE AT BOLSTERSTONE.
A CASE OF RELIGIOUS MANIA: 1888

In 1888 an inquest was held at the Coach and Horses on 23-year-old Eli Hattersley of Holly Bush (Hollin Busk). Eli was the son of Joseph Hattersley (who had been the slandered by William Marsden back in 1875). Eli taught at the Sunday School at Bolsterstone, and one Sunday afternoon his behaviour became rather erratic, and, after shaking hands with the scholars, he told them he would not be seeing them again. He did his milk round as usual the following day, and then went out to rake a field, but by 3pm he had vanished, and he was not seen again. His body was found later that night at the bottom of a disused pit shaft.

At the inquest, his father said that Eli had been so uneasy on the Sunday night that he decided to sleep with him in order to keep an eye on him. Eli spent the night praying and asking his father if he had ever done anything wrong. He told his father, *"my soul has departed from me about a fortnight since. I am happy; the angels have taken it."* Mr. Hattersley's farm labourer John Walton went to search for Eli, eventually looking into the pit shaft, which

---

[32] A device for hauling coal

was about 36 yards deep. After tying a light to a piece of rope and lowering it into the shaft, he saw the body. Walton was fastened to a rope and lowered down into the shaft by his companions, and Eli was brought up. No one knew of any reason why Eli might have committed suicide, but Walton had been told by someone that it could be to do with a girl.

The Coroner stated that the pit shaft was very well protected and that no one could have fallen down it by accident. The Deputy Inspector of Mines had examined the shaft and was quite satisfied with the fences. The jury returned a verdict that Eli committed suicide by throwing himself down a pit shaft whilst in a state of temporary insanity.

SAD SUICIDE OF WIDOW
HER RELIEF HAD BEEN STOPPED: 1890
In November 1890, another inquest was held at the Coach, this time regarding the suicide of a 42-year-old widow called Clara Drinkhall. Her husband Joseph, a miner, had died two years previously, and she was struggling to make ends meet. She had two daughters, one of whom was at school, the other working in Fox's. Clara was in receipt of parish pay, which was a dole payment administered by the Guardians of the Poor. The Guardians could be very strict about the criteria for receiving this money, and one day Mrs. Drinkhall received a letter informing her that she would get no more money because she had "*wilfully deceived*" the Guardians when she told them that her daughter only earned four shillings a week. They ordered her and her children to be removed from their home and admitted to Bradfield Workhouse.

Workhouses were places where the poor, who had no job or home, were obliged to live. They were not nice places and people lived in fear of being admitted to them. Life there was intended to be harsh, to deter the able-bodied poor, and to ensure that only the truly destitute would apply. Inmates were provided with a roof over their head, clothes, and food, but they had to earn their keep by doing jobs - often back-breaking work such as breaking stones, crushing bones to make fertiliser, or picking oakum.[33] Also in the

---

[33] Oakum is tarred fibre used in shipbuilding and used to be recycled from old tarry ropes. Prisoners and workhouse inmates had to unravel and take this apart, which was tedious but at least it did not involve hard manual labour.

workhouses were orphaned children, the sick, the mentally ill, unmarried pregnant women, and unmarried mothers.

Mrs. Drinkhall could not bear the thought of being sent to the workhouse, and she was found in her attic by neighbours, having slit her own throat. A surgeon was called, but she died a few hours later. The Guardians, it seems, had been too hasty, because it was revealed that the daughter only occasionally made "*a trifle*" more than the four shillings which her mother had told them was her usual wage. A tragic outcome from an over-zealous decision by officials.

AUCTION: 1889
The property of the late Samuel Newton, who had died in 1886, was being auctioned off at the Coach and Horses. This included Hoyle House Farm at Stocksbridge, together with the farmhouse, stables, cowhouses, barns, and other outbuildings, and about sixty acres of land. Also for sale were some plots of building land adjoining the main road at Stocksbridge and on the road leading to Bolsterstone. The Hoyle House Estate was bought by John Grayson Lowood; he sold most of his land to Thomas Oxley in 1894, who used some of it to start his fruit farm at what is now Garden Village.

John Helliwell died at the Coach and Horses on the 30th January 1890 and was succeeded very briefly by his son, John Thomas Helliwell, who was one of the executors of his will (along with John's widow Ann and Charles Thickett of Hawthorn Brook). He left estate valued at just over £270.

JOHN HELLIWELL vs. JOHN GRAYSON LOWOOD: 1890
In March 1890, Coach landlord John Thomas Helliwell sued Messrs. J. Grayson Lowood & Company, Ganister Miners, for damages of £30. The previous November at about 5pm, Helliwell had picked up two friends, Mr. and Mrs. Lunn, from Deepcar railway station in his dogcart. He was going downhill when he met a man called Ridall coming the other way in his carriage. Ridall was a driver for Grayson Lowood. He had pulled out onto the wrong side of the road so that he could turn into the firm's gates. The shaft of his carriage entered the chest of Helliwell's horse, injuring it so badly that it died a few days afterwards. Ridall maintained that he never saw Helliwell coming. The court had to decide if he was negligent - the judge decided he was and allowed damages of £30 to be paid to Helliwell.

John Thomas Helliwell left the Coach and Horses not long after the death of his father in 1890. By the time the 1891 census was taken in April of that year, he had moved to the Newmarket Hotel in Sheffield (on the junction of Broad Street and Sheaf Street). He later returned to this area, becoming landlord of the Castle Inn at Bolsterstone from about 1898 to 1904.

The Coach and Horses then passed into the hands of Joseph Scott and his wife Mary Ann Mellor. Joseph had been born in Durham and was an engineer by trade, but his wife was from Oughtibridge and her family had been the licensees of the White Hart there. She was also the great niece of John Bramall who had first opened the Castle Inn at Bolsterstone. Joseph and Mary were at the Coach for about seven years before they moved to Scarborough where they ran a hotel at 34 & 36 Queen's Street. The 1901 census recorded them at the hotel along with Frances Mellor (Mary Ann's daughter), William Henry Scott (Joseph and Mary Ann's son), five female servants (two from Oughtibridge), nephew Harry Trickett from Oughtibridge, two "*Hotel Boots*" and one visitor. The "*Boots*" were male servants responsible for cleaning guests' boots as well as running errands, and probably carrying the cases too.

Elijah Edward Askew was the next landlord, moving to the Coach in about 1897. He had been born there in 1873 and was the son of Edward Askew and his second wife Ann Bower. When the 1891 census was taken, Elijah Edward had been living at Watson House, Deepcar, with his stepbrother Samuel Horace Bower, a farmer, and his wife Emily Maplebeck Kenworthy. He was working as a farm labourer.[34] When he married Lucy Cooke at Bolsterstone in August 1897, Elijah Edward gave his occupation as a grocer. The couple lived at Grimethorpe Road, Sheffield before moving into the Coach and Horses. They had only been there for about a year when Elijah died, in October 1898. He did not leave a will, and he was only 25 years old,

---

[34] Emily Maplebeck Kenworthy was the daughter of William Bramall Kenworthy, the son of Harriet Bramall of Oughtibridge and George Kenworthy. Harriet's sister Lydia Ann Bramall married John Grayson of Spink Hall; he died in a carriage accident only six months after their marriage. Lydia Ann later married Elijah Askew (Elijah Edward's father) of the Coach and Horses and the Friendship in 1884. Elijah then left the pub trade to live at Spink Hall and died there in 1892. These publican families certainly wove a tangled web!

so his death was probably unexpected. Lucy was granted *"Letters of Administration"* so that she could sort out his affairs.[35]

The next landlord was Samuel Joseph Moorhouse. He was married to Marion Helen Askew, Elijah's daughter. When the 1901 census was taken, they were living at the pub with three children, Joseph Alan, Sydney, and a month-old baby called Elijah. Also living with them were two domestic servants Ann Revitt (niece) and Angelina Brooks.

On the 1st November 1898, local man Joseph Moxon noted in his diary, *"My son Leonard is working at the "Coach" today* [he was a carpenter], *and while there the Stocksbridge Sergeant of Police comes in and gets several glasses of Beer. I wish I had seen him instead of my son then I would have laid a charge against him."*[36] Moxon was a member of the Temperance Society and was always trying to get people to sign The Pledge and agree to stop drinking. The police were not supposed to drink whilst they were on duty, and in 1894 a leaflet was circulating locally called *"How to form a public-house watch committee,"* which in effect was calling upon all those interested in sobriety to act as spies, watching and reporting on public houses and recording any breaches of the law, both by publicans and the police. The writer advised: *"write to the Police Inspector of the Division in which you are working, inform him of the fact that you intend to have every [public] house in the district watched; the police cannot then complain if they are caught."* The writer added that *"Drunkenness will then decline amazingly."*

In January 1899, an intriguing advertisement was placed in the Sheffield Evening Telegraph:

> *"Man Wanted, to travel with a 6½d. Bazaar; able to assist in shop; must be used to horses; references required. - Apply Coach and Horses, Stocksbridge."*

---

[35] Probate Index 1898: Elijah Edward Askew, Coach & Horses Inn, Stocksbridge, innkeeper, died 5th October 1898. Administration Wakefield 1st November to Lucy Askew, widow. Effects £1,230 5s. 11d.

[36] The Diary of Joseph Moxon, MS. Entry for Tuesday 1st November 1898. He was a *"Local Worthy,"* and was secretary and manager of the Stocksbridge Band of Hope Co-operative Society 1868-1906

Was this something organised by the landlord of the Coach, or was he was just the point of contact for the person who wanted an assistant? A *"sixpence ha'penny bazaar"* was so-called because everything it sold - mostly toys and fancy giftware - was that price, six and a half old pennies. Marks and Spencer was originally known as the *"Penny Bazaar"* because everything it sold cost one penny. The owner of the bazaar would have had a shop somewhere and employed men to go out and sell his goods. In 1901, a case came up in front of the Sheffield magistrates when a hawker called George Ernest Steel was accused of stealing goods worth over £4 belonging to James Edward Wild, who ran a sixpence ha'penny bazaar at 721 Attercliffe Road. Steel went out with his horse and dray carrying goods worth over £25, and when he returned, goods worth £4. 6s. 8d. were missing and could not be accounted for. The case was eventually dropped.

Almost every week in the yard at the back of the Coach and Horses a travelling *"Quack"* would arrive to sell his wares; apparently, these were coloured patent medicines and *"wondrous salves."* [37]

CLAIM FOR PERSONAL INJURIES
DAMAGES AGAINST A WAITER: 1900

Moorhouse had employed a man called Tom Revitt as a waiter for two years. Because of his *"unusual size and strength,"* he also used him as a *"chucker-out"* or bouncer, when the occasion arose. Or, as was alleged, he was kept as a *"public house bully."* Revitt also worked as a labourer. One day in March, a miner named John Dixon Haigh of Old Corn Mill, Stocksbridge, sued Tom Revitt for £10, alleging that he had assaulted him in the pub. Haigh had been drinking heavily all day (whisky and port mixed, and beer), both in the Coach and elsewhere. Moorhouse asked him to leave but he would not go, so he asked Revitt to evict him. Which he did, apparently knocking him down and kicking him in the mouth - he lost five teeth. In court, Haigh was asked if he had swallowed his teeth, but he said not, though he had gone looking for them the next morning! Revitt said that Haigh had taken a running kick at him, so he had defended himself with his fist. Haigh admitted he had once been fined for assault.

---

[37] This information came from local man Arnold Palmer

Judge Waddy told Revitt's solicitor, *"you have succeeded in indicating that [Haigh] was a drunken beast; but you have no right to strike even a drunken beast. This is another instance of a sink of iniquity."* When a witness called Thomas Burgin said he was outside the pub and saw Revitt make a kick at Haigh, the judge commented, *"you were not one of this* 'blessed army of martyrs' *who were drinking themselves blazing drunk?"* "No, sir," replied Burgin. Haigh's uncle, John William Haigh, swore that his nephew was not "*right drunk*," to which His Honour replied, "*no man ever is* 'right drunk,' *he is always wrong drunk.*" Passing further comment, Judge Waddy thought that, in his opinion, this was *"a drunken row amidst a lot of besotted blackguards. The sooner one faces it the better. It is a disgrace that such a thing is possible in a Christian country. It gives a melancholy view of the land to which we belong."*

The landlord, Samuel Joseph Moorhouse, said that Haigh had been to another public house before he visited the Coach and Horses, and that he had served him with three *"two pennyworths,"* and then gave him a soda to persuade him to go. The Judge remarked that *"this was about a disgraceful a thing as it was possible to conceive. That in the twentieth century and in a country supposed to be Christian, conduct like this was to be tolerated would seem incredible if they did not hear of it constantly."*

The Judge thought that a report should be made to the magistrates about the Coach and Horses, with a view to stopping the licence, and awarded Haigh the £10 damages he had asked for. At the end of the hearing the judge said that he'd been under the impression that it was Samuel Moorhouse, the landlord, who was on trial, and seeing as it was the waiter who was on trial he changed his mind and reduced the amount of damages awarded to £7.

When the time came for Moorhouse to renew the licence in August that year, he was summoned before the magistrates because this incident had put him on their *"blacklist."* Reference was made to Judge Waddy's remarks that "*it would be a public calamity if the magistrates did not institute an investigation into the matter, with a view of stopping the license of the house."* Superintendent Bielby reported that had made a thorough inquiry into the case, thinking to bring proceedings against Moorhouse for permitting drunkenness on his licensed premises. However, he said that the statements from witnesses told conflicting stories and nothing could be proved. He thought that there was no doubt that Hague [sic] was made drunk on Moorhouse's premises, and while he (the Superintendent) did not offer any objection to the renewal of the licence, he hoped the landlord would be more careful in the future. As the waiter was no longer in Moorhouse's employ, the licence was renewed.

AUCTION OF PROPERTY - 1901
A sale took place at the Coach and Horses of some freehold property at Bracken Moor near Stocksbridge, the property of the late Mrs. E. Smith. The auctioneers were selling three stone-built dwelling houses, which were in the occupations of Messrs. McKay, Bocking, and Shaw. The net yearly rental income from these was just over £34.

FOR SALE – THE COACH AND HORSES – 1902
In November 1902, auctioneer and former landlord John Bramall advertised a forthcoming auction re. Elijah Askew, deceased.[38] The property was offered in four lots. Lot 1 was the Coach and Horses and included stables, a carriage shed, outbuildings, and a large yard; the yard faced the main road (the Turnpike road, or Manchester Road as it is now known) and Oak Green.[39] The sales particulars said that this land allowed room for extending the pub - this was done between 1902 and 1916. The pub was being let to the Sheffield brewery Whitmarsh, Watson & Co. on a quarterly tenancy.[40] Samuel Moorhouse, the landlord, was an undertenant of the brewery. Lot 2 consisted of the two shops and houses adjoining the pub, on the corner of the Turnpike road and Hunshelf Road, together with a yard at the back. The tenants were Mr. Edwin Bamforth, Grocer, and Mrs. Blackburn, Draper. A storeroom adjoining the stable was being let to Mr. Bamforth. The remaining lots were plots of land in Orchard Road, Deepcar. The pub sold for £6,700, the shops and houses for £1,255, and the plots of land at Deepcar were withdrawn from sale.

---

[38] He had died in 1892 at Spink Hall.
[39] This was the piece of land adjoining the pub, Hawke Green. An extension to the pub was later built on some of this land and can be seen on later photographs.
[40] Brewers in Sheffield, Earl Street, South Street [later The Moor]. William Whitmarsh bought William Jepson's Free Trade Brewery in 1852 and built the South Street Brewery on the site. They were registered in October 1895 with a total of 140 houses, none of which included the Coach and Horses because they did not own it. They were acquired by Duncan Gilmour & Co. in 1906.

Moorhouse left the pub after it was sold and moved to Parkgate, Rotherham, to run the Sportsman's Arms. He died two years later in March 1904.[41]

The Coach and Horses was bought by A. H. Smith, whose Don Brewery was on Penistone Road. It was Smiths who undertook the enlargement of the premises, which would have been worthwhile with a growing population who were coming into the area to work at the rapidly expanding steelworks. The Don Brewery covered about one acre. There was a 224' deep artesian well on the site, and twenty stone Yorkshire Square fermenters. Smiths were taken over by Tennant Brothers in 1916.

For the next two years, the landlord was Peter William Ridings. He had previously run The Locomotive Inn on Carlisle Street, Brightside, with his second wife Sarah Allen. He hadn't been at the Coach and Horses long before he was summoned to the West Riding Police Court for permitting drunkenness on his licensed premises. Two policemen had gone into the Coach around 10pm on the 13th June and found a man asleep, drunk. Ridings told them that he had only just noticed the man's condition, and was on the point of turning him out, adding that he had only served him with one glass of beer. Superintendent Bielby said that he believed the landlord was doing his best, but unfortunately for him, the man had been drinking elsewhere, and that last glass in the Coach had *"finished him."* He did not wish to press the case, and it was agreed that payment of costs would settle it. The summons was withdrawn upon Riding paying the costs of six shillings.

MIDHOPE STONES SENSATION.
SUPPOSED PTOMAINE POISONING EPIDEMIC.
MANY PERSONS AFFECTED: July 1903
It appears from a report in the newspapers that Ridings was responsible for an outbreak of food poisoning. It was said to be a case of *"ptomaine poisoning,"* but this phrase is now obsolete. It was thought that ptomaines, which were found in food that was going off, had a serious and sometimes fatal effect on the body when ingested. We now know that food poisoning is due to the action of bacteria such as salmonella and e-coli. The report was

---

[41] He died at the Sportsman's on the 20th March 1904, Administration granted, London, [no will] to his widow Marion Ellen Moorhouse, effects £1,118 9s. 8d.

rather sensational and lurid, almost taking delight in describing the symptoms and the after-effects of the poisoning.

There had been a sports gala at Midhope, and a great many people, including the brass band, were taken ill after eating ham sandwiches. Even those who only had "*a preliminary nibble or two*" before deciding to eat no more because they noticed an odd taste, fell ill. Rumour and gossip, ably abetted by the newspapers, greatly magnified the results of the epidemic, adding in a few deaths for good measure, which was blatantly untrue.

Dr. Ross of Penistone noted that the weather was hot, muggy, and thundery, and he said he would not be surprised if meat cooked the day before the sports had been turned mouldy.

Ridings had been contracted to provide the refreshments for the gala, and he complained that the circumstances surrounding the poisoning had been greatly exaggerated. He said that he had bought the ham and some pressed beef from a Sheffield firm, ready cooked, and totally denied the rumour that the hams were boiled in a copper at his premises. Samples were sent for analysis, but there were no further reports in the newspapers about who was to blame for the food poisoning.

Ridings left the Coach and Horses in 1905 to run another pub, the Shakespeare in Sycamore Street. A few years later he moved to Langsett Road; his occupation in 1911 was given as the Managing Director of a Picture Palace.

The next landlord was Edgar Whittaker. Newspaper reports from about this time onwards consist mainly of reports about sports and shooting matches, including pigeon and starling shoots. Starlings were very numerous in the early years of the twentieth century; my grandma's uncle, George Crawshaw, said they used to call them sheps, and his brother Tom Crawshaw (born in 1886) used to sit in the kitchen doorway at their home at Horner Houses with his small-bore rifle shooting sparrows and sheps.

Whittaker had previously had the Black Bull at Thurlstone and the White Hart at Penistone. However, within two years of taking on the Coach and

Horses, he was bankrupt. In August 1907 he filed for bankruptcy, moved out of the pub, and went to lodge with a Mrs. Spooner on Manchester Road.

The cause of Whittaker's downfall was borrowing from money lenders at high rates of interest - or loan sharks as we would call them today. His debts amounted to over £1,300 and he estimated his assets to produce only £14 2s. Whittaker had left the White Hart for the Coach and Horses in 1905, receiving a valuation of £450, and he used £250 of this towards the ingoing valuation of the Coach (which was £450). The balance - and more - he raised by borrowing money. In January 1906 he sold his interest in the pub as well as all the fixtures, fittings, furniture, etc. to the Don Brewery Company for £509, and he used this money to pay several of his creditors. He had borrowed from money lenders and friends as well as having an overdraft with the bank. He also owed £175 to the brewery for beer and rent. He had been asked to provide a cash account for the last twelve months, but it was reported that *"his idea of a cash account, however, is distinctly original, for he wrote quite a long narrative of what had led to his bankruptcy. Naturally there was considerable laughter when the Official Receiver humorously asked, 'Does it balance?'"*

One newspaper report called him an *"imaginative debtor."* On making loan applications, he had stated that the pub's furniture was his own, and he also overstated how much it was worth. He applied for a loan whilst still owing over £1,300 but lied when he said that his debts did not exceed £150. He also said he had a main share in a butcher's shop, which was equally untrue, although he had been working as a butcher's salesman in 1901 at Thurlstone. *"Imaginative"* seems to have meant *"liar"* in this instance. By 1911 Edgar, his wife Emily, and their family moved to Carcroft near Doncaster where he worked as a self-employed butcher.

The next landlord was David Robert Dove, former landlord of the Wheatsheaf on Bridge Street, Sheffield. Dove was originally from Hindley, Wigan, and his father ran the Imperial Hotel, Market Street, there. Soon after he moved into the Coach, Dove instructed auctioneers to sell the furniture and effects that were there. These items included a 7-piece upholstered drawing room suite, an oak sideboard, a Jones sewing machine, iron bedsteads, a spring mattress, a walnut bedroom suite, various kitchen utensils, a harness, and other *"useful effects."*

Mr. Dove was at the Coach for a couple of years. In February 1908 he was granted a licence for music and dancing for one year. He occasionally placed advertisements for staff, like this one in September 1908:[42]

"General, age 19 to 23; wash, bake; another kept, references required. - Dove, Coach and Horses, Stocksbridge."

A DRUNKEN FREAK: 1908

Edith Greavett had been shopping in Stocksbridge and called in at the Coach to fetch her husband. When she left, she forgot her shopping bag, which contained a couple of rabbits, 1½ lbs of bacon, some suet, 1lb of steak, and a quantity of vegetables. This bag was taken by William Helliwell, a labourer from Bolsterstone. The next day (Sunday), Helliwell and four or five other men made a feast of the food in a hut in a garden at Bolsterstone. He came up before the magistrates charged with stealing the bag. He maintained that he *"remembered nought except having some cabbage."* He was fined £1 (or 14 days in prison) for what was said to be just a foolish trick (a drunken freak).

On the 26th May 1910 Mr. Dove left these shores for a new life in Australia. He made the journey alone, sailing from London to Sydney. His wife and daughter followed the next year and they settled in Burwood, New South Wales.

The next landlord was Tom Haigh from Skelmanthorpe. Tom and his wife Emma (nee Field) had three children living with them at the pub when the 1911 census was taken: Alice, Albert, and Rupert. Three servants were living there too, and the pub was recorded as having eleven rooms.

A PUBLIC HOUSE BRAWL: November 1910

Two Stocksbridge steel workers called Robert Aistrop and Harry Firth got into a fight in the taproom and refused to leave, so a policeman was summoned to eject them. Aistrop maintained that they were only having a friendly wrestling match and that the landlord had encouraged them, saying, *"Give 'em room: let 'em have a reight do."* Firth on the other hand said that there had been some trouble and that he had tried to calm it down, but he was

---

[42] Printed in the Sheffield Daily Telegraph, 15th September 1908

hit on the head by Aistrop, so he retaliated. Aistrop was fined £1 and Firth was fined 12s. 6d. The case was prosecuted on behalf of the Sheffield, Rotherham and District Licensed Victuallers' Association.

MOTORIST'S DEATH.
STOCKSBRIDGE LANDLORD'S FATAL MISJUDGEMENT: 1913

A Sunday afternoon outing ended in tragedy when Tom Haigh was killed in a motorbike accident in September 1913. He was riding his bike along the Ingbirchworth Road near Penistone, with his neighbour Ernest Jackson of Rimington Row in the sidecar, when he collided with another motorbike. A landau cab that was going in the opposite direction had prevented him from seeing the other motorbike and sidecar, which was standing on the left side of the road. He thought that he had room to pass between the two vehicles, but when he tried, he caught the footboard of the other bike, and the impact threw him and his passenger to the ground. After being seen by a doctor, Haigh was taken to Penistone workhouse hospital and later sent home. Initially, it was reported that he had suffered a concussion of the brain, among other injuries, and that Jackson had severe bruising. However, his condition deteriorated, and he was moved to Sister Tait's nursing home where he died. He was 43 years old.

Haigh's wife Emma ran the pub for a few months before transferring the licence in January 1914 to Joseph Batty (no relation to the Battys who had the Friendship). Joseph had been born in 1870 to Benjamin Batty (who had been born at Hepworth) and Mary Kay, from Fulstone. Benjamin and Mary lived at Crimbles on Hunshelf Bank. Joseph had married Edith Gabbitas in 1893 and lived at Hunshelf, working as a coal carter before moving to the Coach, which he kept for fifteen years until 1929. He died at the age of 67 in the Sheffield Royal Infirmary after a short illness in November 1937 and is buried at Bolsterstone with his parents and his wife.

TROUBLESOME CUSTOMERS: 1914

One Friday in September at about 7pm, a man named Robert Richard Archer, a labourer of no fixed abode, was already drunk when he entered the Coach. The landlord refused to serve him and asked him to leave. Archer refused, so Mr. Batty threatened to put him out himself; the drunken man picked up a customer's heavy glass mug, which was full of beer, and threw the liquid into the landlord's face, before hitting him on the head with the mug. Batty and his son managed to evict the man, and he was arrested. In court, Archer expressed great regret at his behaviour. He explained that he had served in the Militia for ten years, and he offered, if the Bench would give him a chance, to go with a policeman to the recruiting office and enlist with the colours. However, because he had been convicted once before for drunkenness and violence, and he was sent to prison for one month with hard labour.

On the 1st October 1929, the licence of the Coach and Horses was transferred from Joseph Batty to Samuel Archer at the Sheffield Transfer Sessions. Almost immediately, Samuel was in trouble for allowing betting to take place in his pub. It was illegal for anyone other than a licensed bookmaker at a racecourse to take bets, but a man named Wilfred Hamlin Paul Rodgers was caught by undercover police taking bets in the Coach. They found evidence of 39 bets on 29 horses running at Manchester that day. Archer was fined £20 despite, it was said, not being aware of the betting, and Rodgers, who pleaded guilty, was fined £25 for betting and £12 for acting as a bookmaker without a certificate. Archer was told that this would not affect the renewal of his premises licence, but that he would be dealt with *"very severely"* if any further betting was discovered. Archer was still the landlord in 1932 when he was granted a licence for *"music and singing"* by the magistrates.

In February 1934 there was a fatal accident outside the Coach and Horses involving two lorries. William Smith of Sleaford, Lincolnshire, was 29 years old, and a driver for vegetable merchants Cooper Brothers of Butterwick, near Boston. He was killed as a result of his lorry being involved in a head-on collision with another lorry being driven by W. H. Lilleker of Sheffield. It seems that neither vehicle was speeding – they were only doing about 20mph, but Lilleker said the other lorry was zigzagging all over the road and he could not avoid the collision. The jury returned an open verdict and said that they were dissatisfied with some of the evidence, which was conflicting. The accident only merited a short account in the Sheffield Independent, although a much more in-depth account was given in the Lincolnshire papers, along with a photograph of the wreck. Smith had been taking a load of potatoes and cabbages to Manchester.

In January 1937, Archer transferred the licence to John Edmundson, who had been living at Langsett Terrace, Horner Houses. The valuation of the pub was £605. The Magistrates' Clerk asked Mr. Edmundson if he was aware that Mr. Archer had been convicted twice for betting offences and asked him whether he was quite willing to take the pub *"with his eyes open."* Mr. Edmundson said that he was. Inspector Little said the police had no objection to the renewal of the licence to Mr. Edmundson. He took the pub with his wife Mary Jane and they were there until at least 1940. At fifty-nine years of age, John would have been too old to have been called up to fight.

The Coach and Horses is now closed.

This photo dates from between November 1902 (when Sheffield-based A. H. Smith & Company bought it and added the extension on the side) until 1916 (when they were taken over by Tennant Brothers).

THE BROOMHEAD MILL INN, WIGTWIZZLE, near BOLSTERSTONE

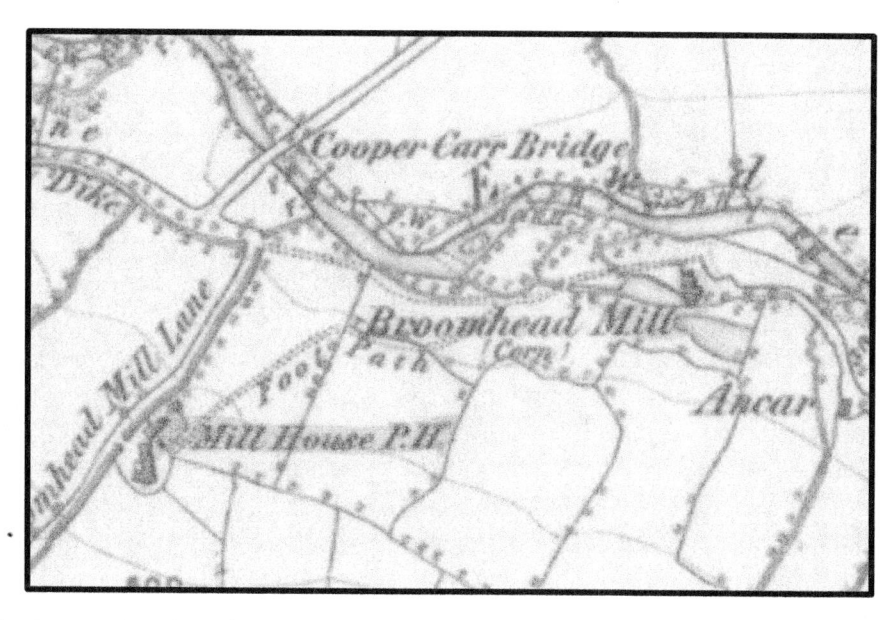

The Broomhead Mill Inn was a small wayside public house near the hamlet of Wigtwizzle, about a mile from Bolsterstone. It was a lonely building, standing in a deep valley on the edge of Broomhead Moors, and there was no other habitation within half a mile. A man was killed there in 1855, and the newspapers reported that the pub was remote and isolated, its interior accommodation very sparse, and that, over the years, the bleak weather that came in off the moors had almost obliterated the sign which denoted its name. It opened in about 1833 and closed in 1856 when its licence was rescinded. This map shows its location. There is no known photograph of the inn.

From at least 1833 Ellis Jackson, the miller at Broomhead mill, also ran a pub from the Mill House, a short distance away from the actual corn mill. A trade directory of 1833 lists him twice; once under the category of *"Corn Millers,"* and again under *"Inns and Taverns."* We can assume the pub was recently opened because it had not yet been given a name; the entry in the trade directory simply lists it as *"Board, Ellis Jackson, Broomhead mill."* Jackson ran the pub, a farm, and the corn mill until his death in August 1855 at the age of 77. He never married.

ROBBING A CLUB BOX: December 1835

Ellis Jackson's inn was the meeting place for one of the many societies or clubs that proliferated in the 19th century. A group of men would form a club, and each of them would contribute a few pence each week into a fund. The money collected would occasionally be used to enable each man in turn to own, for example, a watch, a clock, a piece of furniture, some clothing, and so on. In the 1780s, the Horns Inn at Bradfield hosted a *"Watch Club,"* whereby the men would meet up in the pub every week, contribute their fee, and each man would, in his turn, obtain a watch purchased from the funds. Clubs were immensely popular among workmen at this time and were usually based in a public house, as were the Friendly Societies which members paid into as a form of insurance to be paid out if they were too ill to work, or to cover their funeral expenses. Landlords didn't usually charge a fee for the use of the club room, but there was generally an agreement whereby a certain amount of each member's contribution should be spent in drink. Each member was expected to consume a pint or more of ale *"for the good of the house."* This was known as a *"Wet Rent."*

There was a club room at the pub, and at night it was used as a bedroom by a couple called George and Hannah Woodhead. The club box, which contained money that had been subscribed by the members, was kept in this room. One night in December 1835, George and his wife were asleep in the club room when Hannah was awoken by a noise. She saw a man's hand come through the door, holding a candle. She called out to her husband, and the light went out. By the light of the moon, she saw three men enter the room, one of them with a large stick in his hand. The men threatened to kill them if they didn't lie still and *"hold their noise."* The men took the club box, which contained over £30,[43] from the side of the couple's bed, before leaving and locking the door. Woodhead was forced to climb out of the window. He called up another man, William Helliwell, and they set off in pursuit of the robbers.

The thieves realised that they were being followed, and one of them shouted, *"They're coming, let's murder them,"* and the two pursuers, terrified, and having no shoes on, returned to the pub to fetch a gun. When they returned, there was no sign of the men; they had emptied the box of its contents and thrown it over a wall into a field.

The suspected thieves were Joseph Ibbotson and John Fox. Ibbotson was a member of the Club and would have known how much money was in the box. However, none of the witnesses could identify the men, nor could they agree on how many intruders there were, despite being able to see well in the moonlight. A woman called Mrs. Stanley of Oughtibridge stated that the two accused men were in company at her house just before the time of the robbery and could not have done it. And so, because none of the witnesses could identify the prisoners, they were dismissed without charge.

Ellis Jackson was a member of the Bradfield Association for the Prosecution of Felons. Back in the days when there wasn't the organised police force there is today, householders and others would want potential thieves to believe that if they were caught stealing, they would be prosecuted. But pressing a prosecution could be expensive, with legal fees, transportation costs and lodging expenses for the prosecutor and any witnesses. A successful prosecutor might be reimbursed for expenses by the court, but it was unlikely to cover all the expenses. If the criminal had to be located and apprehended before he was prosecuted there would be additional costs, possibly including the cost of advertising and paying a reward. Becoming a member of an Association for the Prosecution of Felons, which usually had between twenty and a hundred local members, was seen by many to be the answer. Each member contributed a fixed payment to a common pool of money, and this could be used to pay the cost of finding, apprehending, and prosecuting anyone who had committed a crime against a member. The list of members was published in the local newspaper (perhaps for the would-be

---

[43] The Bank of England's Inflation calculator puts this at over £3,800 in today's money

thieves to read and consider). Thousands of prosecution associations were established in England in the 18th and early 19th centuries. A document survives, written on the 4th December 1855, which reports on a meeting of the Bradfield Association. [44] They had discussed the best means to be adopted to apprehend several persons suspected of having committed a burglary at the house of Ellis Jackson at Broomhead Mill. It was ordered that the Clerk of the Association be instructed to employ Constable Crapper of Stannington, or any other person he thought fit, to find out the burglars and bring them to justice, and they authorised all reasonable expenses to be paid out of the Association's funds.

Ellis called on the Association again in 1849, and Constable George Elliott was paid five shillings expenses for one day's search for some property which had been stolen from him.[45]

A good description of the corn mill was given in the Sheffield Independent (1st May 1841). A boy called John Woolhouse was charged with stealing a *"chitty prat"* hen[46] and some eggs from Wigtwizzle farmer George Helliwell. He also stole from Ellis Jackson. Jackson appeared in court to say that he had gone to the mill one morning just before 5am and found two of the doors open, and a small hole in the roof, about the size for a lad to get through. He noticed some meal and flour were missing. He then described going into the drying kiln, where there was a fire, and found that someone had been making meal and flour into bread. One of Ellis's men, Thomas Shaw, was working in a field near his master's barn and saw John Woolhouse in the company of another boy coming down the lane from a barn carrying a bundle. He must have thought they looked suspicious because he ran after them, and he saw one of them throw eleven cakes (made of meal and flour) out of the bundle. In the barn he found the hen, now dead. John Woolhouse was arrested by constable John Grayson and remanded into custody whilst enquiries were made about his previous character and to find his companion. There was no further report on this case. This mill occasionally supplied Bradfield Workhouse.

---

[44] Bradfield Archives ref. 43000
[45] Bradfield Archives ref. 42956. Ellis was spelt as Elias in this document.
[46] Yorkshire dialect word for a black hen with white speckles.

Ellis Jackson, who had lived at Broomhead all his life (his father Richard had also been the miller), died there on the 15th August 1855 at the age of 77. He had been living at the mill house with his brother Samuel (also a miller), Samuel's daughter Grace and her husband Jonathan Hartley.[47] On the 4th September, the executors of his will signed a declaration that they intended to apply to transfer the licence from Ellis to Samuel at the next licensing sessions,[48] but a tragic event meant that this probably never happened. Signing the declaration of intent allowed Samuel to take over the pub before the official transfer date. Without this, he could have been prosecuted for selling intoxicating liquor without a licence. His daughter and her husband helped in the bar when Samuel was busy on the farm or at the mill.

FATAL AFFRAY NEAR BOLSTERSTONE: 1855

One Sunday evening, on the 23rd September 1855, a month after Ellis Jackson's death, five men were drinking in the bar when a fight broke out. They were Joseph Shaw of Poggs farm, aged 40; George Staniforth of Bolsterstone, a labourer and night game-watcher for Mr. Rimington Wilson of Broomhead Hall; Joseph Smith of The Green, near Bolsterstone, farmer/labourer; Alfred Shaw of Race House, mason; and Mark Helliwell of Load Field, labourer. These men knew each other well.

They drank for a few hours together until Staniforth left to attend his game preserves, returning a little after nine o'clock. The landlady, Grace, called time at ten o'clock, and they all got up to go home. At this point, Staniforth's dog, a bulldog, attacked Joseph Shaw's dog, a mongrel. Shaw did not want his dog to fight, and he parted them, only for it to happen again. Staniforth on the other hand was all for letting the dogs carry on, and he struck Shaw a violent blow across his forehead with a thick stick that he was carrying. Shaw fell back into a chair, stunned, before jumping up, grabbing the fire poker, and hitting Staniforth on the head and knocking him to the ground. He then kicked him a couple of times. Shaw was arrested by the parish

---

[47] Grace was the illegitimate daughter of Elizabeth Hattersley of Hollin Busk. It was standard procedure that only a father's name was recorded on a marriage certificate, and if a person was illegitimate, the space for the father's name was left blank. Unusually in this case, both of Grace's parents' names were given (although this information seems to have been added to the parish register entry afterwards, in a different ink)

[48] The annual Brewster Sessions had already been held in August, so they were to apply for the transfer at the next Special Sessions which would be held on the 20th November

constable, Jonathan Grayson of Storth House Farm. As was usual at that time, the coroner's inquest was held in a pub – in this case, the very pub in which the death had occurred.

The men who had been there that night were called to give evidence at the inquest. Joseph Smith swore that they were not drunk. He had helped the landlord Jonathan Hartley pick up Staniforth and put him on a sofa, where he breathed once or twice and then passed away. He then went to fetch Staniforth's wife. Alfred Shaw (no relation to Joseph Shaw) added that Staniforth's dog had originally been muzzled, but that when he returned to the inn after seeing to the game, the muzzle had been removed. He thought that Shaw was sober and Staniforth *"sharp fresh."* Mark Helliwell gave a more picturesque description, saying that the blow Staniforth struck Shaw *"maddled him,"* and he *"womalled"* into a chair.[49] He added that he saw Shaw punch Staniforth twice and say, *"I'll give the --- something to sigh for."*

Grace Hartley told the inquest that she ran to fetch her husband from his bed when the trouble started, and when she came back down the stairs, she saw Staniforth lying insensible on the floor.

Shaw did not have anyone for his defence, and when the coroner gave him a chance to cross-examine the witnesses, he refused to do so, saying that everything that had been said was true. He did say however that he was unaware of what he was doing because of the blow to his head; indeed, he was still suffering its effects.

A post-mortem had concluded that death was caused by the blow to the head. The jury unanimously agreed in returning a verdict of manslaughter, and because of the seriousness of the charge, Shaw was committed to Wakefield prison on the coroner's warrant, to be tried at the next York Assizes. One newspaper reported that *"this event has caused great excitement in the neighbourhood. The accused is a man moving in a respectable sphere of life,*

---

[49] Maddle: to cause distraction of thought, confusion of mind. Defined in Hunter, Rev. J. The Hallamshire Glossary. Wommal, also wamble: to stagger. Defined in Wright, Joseph. The English Dialect Dictionary

and his victim was a man well known and respected" [50] Staniforth left a wife and six children.[51]

Joseph Shaw appeared for trial at York three months later, in December 1855. This time he had a solicitor to defend his case, but the Judge said that he did not need to address the Jury, because, in his opinion, Shaw had not actually been guilty of an offence. He said, *"If a man received such a blow as the deceased first gave the prisoner, and the prisoner returned the blow with anything that might be in his way, and death ensued, it was, he would not say a justifiable, but an excusable act."* The Jury consequently found Shaw not guilty and he was discharged.

Four years before this incident, Joseph Shaw, who was a widower, had been living and farming at nearby Poggs. Living with him were a son and daughter, plus a housekeeper called Sarah Sanderson and her son. The census enumerator perhaps felt there was moral wrongdoing here because he listed the housekeeper's occupation as *"Concubine,"* and her child as *"Concubine's Son."* When the 1861 census was taken, Joseph's son John Shaw was recorded as head of household at Poggs farm (aged 26, occupation *"formerly farmer"*), as was William Sanderson, the *"concubine's son,"* now 11 years old and working for John. There is no record of Joseph marrying Sarah and it is not known what happened to her.

The Sheffield Independent of 3rd February 1855 printed the announcement of a marriage at Cromwell, Nottinghamshire between Mr. Joseph Shaw, farmer, of Poggs, to Mrs. Corbett of the King and Miller Inn, Deepcar, the widow of Nathaniel Corbett. This was seven months before the fight at the pub in which George Staniforth was killed. However, there is no record of this marriage. The couple actually married at St. George's Church, Sheffield, on the 28th October 1855, so Joseph must have been out on bail, although none of the reports mention bail being applied for.

---

50 Sheffield Daily Telegraph 26th September 1855
51 One of his sons, also called George, would later be in trouble (in 1873) for attacking a man named John Dyson in the Castle Inn, Bolsterstone. He and two other men were found guilty. When the census was taken in 1891, it was noted that George was of *"weak mind."* He ended his days at Grenoside Workhouse, dying there in 1913.

Jane Corbett was the daughter of William Spafford, and she had been born at East Stoke, Nottinghamshire, about nine miles away from Cromwell, so perhaps the couple had intended to marry in her home parish but for some reason they did not. Joseph Shaw was Jane's fourth husband. She wed her first husband in 1837 and was widowed two years later. She then married her second husband in 1840, only to be widowed again after three years. Her third husband was Nathaniel Corbett, who died five years after marriage. She also outlived Joseph Shaw and married for the fifth time in 1874.[52]

The inn closed in 1856. I have read that its licence was rescinded by Mr. James Rimington Wilson of Broomhead Hall, but I can find no proof of this. He had recently qualified as a magistrate for the West Riding (in 1854), and, as a magistrate, he could have been on the licensing bench, but the decision to take the licence away would not be his decision alone, even if he didn't want a public house on his own doorstep. It is possible that, as the landowner, he could stop his tenants from operating a public house from the premises they rented. When licenses were refused or taken away there was usually a report in the newspapers about it, but there is no report about the Broomhead Mill Inn.

In the absence of proof, it may simply be that Samuel, Grace, and Jonathan decided that innkeeping was not for them. In September 1856 Samuel, who was in his seventies, announced that he was retiring from farming, and there would be an auction at Broomhead Mill to sell two draught mares, cattle, a sow and her litter, fowls, bees, and even a "*cur dog*" (mongrel). Also being sold off were carriages, tools, corn, hay, potatoes, brewing vessels, dairy equipment, and furniture, including some of antique oak. Samuel, Jonathan, and Grace then moved away from the mill, and by 1861 they were all living at Low Bradfield.

In November 1856, the water corn mill and farm with 36 acres were advertised as being To Let, with immediate possession. The new tenant was a Mr. George Higham, but he only stayed there for four years. In September 1860 he announced that he was leaving, and instructed auctioneers to sell off

---

[52] For more information, see the chapter on the King and Miller, which the couple ran for a few years, the first time from 1858-1864 and a second time from around 1870; Joseph died there in 1871 and Jane ran the pub with her fifth husband Thomas Turton until around 1880/1.

his farm animals, some household furniture, dairy utensils, and farming equipment.

The Mill and Farm became available to rent the following month. The mill was described as being *"in capital working order,"* and there was also a brand new *"dwelling-house and homestead"* (pictured, left) as well as 36 acres of land.[53] The mill itself is to the left of the house.

There are no further mentions in documents or newspapers of Broomhead Mill House, only of Broomhead Mill. The mill house was demolished, and the new house or houses were built at the cornmill itself. The census returns from 1861 to 1901 refer only to *"Broomhead Mill,"* and there were usually two households listed, none of whose occupants gave their occupation as miller; there were no millers listed in the immediate vicinity either. It isn't until the 1911 census that a miller is recorded at the mill, one George Steel. This census also tells us that his house had seven rooms. The corn mill now lies submerged under the waters of Broomhead Reservoir. Work commenced on both Ewden and Broomhead Reservoirs in 1913 but was delayed by the First World War, the work not being completed until 1929.

But the days of the Broomhead Mill Inn were long gone by this point in time, and nothing remains to remind us of its existence except for a few stories. There is a new road which runs alongside the reservoir, and the mill house stood where there is now a junction at Mill Lane and New Road.

Photographs survive of the mill, and the new house which was built alongside it, but there are no known photographs of the old mill house and inn.

---

[53] The Collins English Dictionary defines a homestead as a farmhouse, together with the land around it.

Broomhead Mill in 1920. A mill has stood on this spot since the 13th century, and the mill in Ewden was known as New Mill as far back as 1275. It is not known when this mill at Broomhead was built.

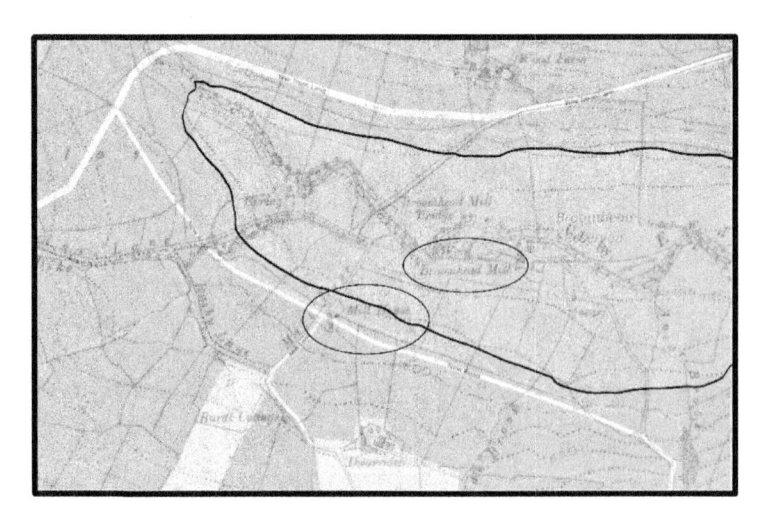

This overlay using the 1905 Ordnance Survey map and OpenStreetMap shows how the mill's location is now submerged under the waters of Broomhead Dam (outlined in black). The site of the public house, the Mill House, can also be seen.

THE SPORTSMAN'S ARMS or INN, WIGTWIZZLE

An isolated moorland country inn situated in a tiny hamlet, close to where Broomhead Hall once stood. The pub was opened as a beerhouse in the 1830s by Thomas Hollins, and the pub remained in the same family until it closed in 1904. The pub has been demolished but the barn still stands and has been converted into a private house. Sheffield City Council used this land as a wood yard before the current house was built.

For a time, there were two public houses in the sparsely populated moorland area around the (now demolished) Broomhead Hall - the Broomhead Mill Inn (which opened in around 1833 and closed after a murder occurred on its premises in 1856) and the Sportsman's Arms at Wigtwizzle hamlet, about a mile away. The Sportsman's Arms first opened as a beerhouse in the 1830s and gained a full wines and spirits licence in September 1841. Its first landlord was Thomas Hollins, and the pub remained in the Hollins family until it closed in 1904.

Born at Cawthorne near Barnsley in about 1772, Thomas Hollins married Mary Watson at Bolton-on-Dearne in 1795. They lived in Cawthorne for a while and had three children baptised in the church there: George (1796), Henry (1798), and Mary Ann (1801). Sometime after their daughter was born, they moved to a farm at Hoyle House, Stocksbridge. Five more children followed, all baptised at Bolsterstone[54] before they moved again to farm at Broomhead Hall, Wigtwizzle. Their youngest son James was baptised at Bradfield church in 1817. Broomhead Hall was owned by the Rimington family, who were the local landed gentry.[55] Perhaps Thomas Hollins worked for the family or leased one of the properties nearby.

From at least 1833, Thomas Hollins ran a beerhouse; its location isn't certain, but it was almost certainly at Wigtwizzle.[56] A beerhouse was not licensed to sell stronger drink such as wines and spirits, and Thomas was one of several people in the area who took advantage of the Beerhouse Act of 1830 which allowed a householder who met certain conditions to brew and sell beer from their own home upon a payment once a year direct to the Excise. In March 1836, Thomas applied for a licence for the Plough Inn at Low Bradfield, which was about four miles away. This pub had been open since at least January 1831 when its landlord was Benjamin Hobson. Hollins was only there just over a year before he transferred the license to his eldest son George, who had recently married Herodius Drury. She had been living at

---

[54] Thomas (1804), William (1807), John (1808), Frances (1811) and Samuel (1815)
[55] The family name changed to Rimington Wilson (no hyphen) in 1840 when James (a minor, son of the late James Rimington) took on the name Wilson following a direction contained in the will of his great uncle, Henry Wilson of Upper Tooting, Surrey.
[56] The 1833 directory does not give a location, and the 1834 directory merely says it was at "Bolsterstone", which could have meant Wigtwizzle. In March 1836, a document he signed stated that he had lived at Wigtwizzle for at least the previous six months.

Broomhead Hall, perhaps working there as a servant, and George was living at Wigtwizzle. George was the landlord at the Plough until 1851 when George Woodhead took over.

After leaving the Plough, Thomas returned to running a beerhouse at his farm in Wigtwizzle, and in 1839 he applied for a full license. Initially he was turned down, but he applied again, and his application was granted at the Sheffield Brewster Sessions in 1841. He was lucky – there were fifty new applications for licences, and thirty-seven were refused. He was about 69 years old at the time and carried on the two occupations of farmer and innkeeper side by side, renting the farm from Major Carlisle of Longstone, Derbyshire.

Thomas died two years later and was buried at Bolsterstone chapel on the 1st November 1843, aged 71. The running of the Sportsman now passed to his youngest son James Hollins.

In October 1844, the farm and 328 acres of land were put up for sale, but the Hollins family continued to live there as its tenants. The property was described as comprising *"a farm house, now occupied as a public house called the Sportsman's Arms, with outbuildings and offices, and over 328 acres of land, divided into suitable fields, in the possession of Widow Hollins. There is a Pew in Bradfield Chapel appurtenant to the Estate."* The advertisement said that it was in one of the best grouse districts, surrounded by moors, which were strictly preserved by the Bradfield Game Association, Mrs. Rimington [of Broomhead Hall], and others. *"Such an opportunity rarely occurs of becoming possessed of 300 Acres of capital Grouse Ground, combined with a Farm of most useful Land so near Home, and of such easy access to the Man of Business in Sheffield whose Transit to its locality may shortly be accelerated by the Manchester and Sheffield Railway, which passes near to it. Mr. James Hollins will shew the Estate."*

A FATAL SHOOTING: 1845

Sadly, James was not to be the landlord for long, because he was fatally wounded in a shooting accident in December 1845. He never regained consciousness and died the following January. He had invited eight friends to enjoy a day's grouse shooting on the moorland around his farm. At midday they broke off and went into a cabin for some refreshments. James went out to get some fuel for the fire and saw a covey of birds coming from the direction of Mrs. Rimington's moor. He called his friends from the cabin, and they came out with their guns, waiting until the birds got closer. James fired first, then his friend Swann, and thirdly James Helliwell of Reynold House. The instant that Helliwell fired, Hollins fell back, having received a severe wound to the back of his head. It seems that Hollins had crouched down to fire his gun and moved a short distance in front of Helliwell. The latter attempted to fire his gun, but it didn't go off; he was taking it from his shoulder when it fired, hitting Hollins. He was taken home and attended by Dr. Booth of Penistone, but he died on the 10th January. At the inquest (which was held at the Sportsman's Arms), no blame was attached to Helliwell, who knew how to handle a gun, was very careful, and a *"capital shot."* The Jury returned a verdict of accidental death, and James was buried at Bradfield on the 14th January aged 28 years.

James had an older brother called Henry, who had been living and farming at Swinton with his wife Martha Kemp and their family. After the death of his father and brother, Henry moved his family to Wigtwizzle to run the family farm and at the same time earn extra income as a publican. The 1851 census recorded that Henry was farming 72 acres, besides being a licensed victualler.

VIOLENT ASSAULT: 1856
On the evening of 11th August 1856 one of Mr. Rimington Wilson's gamekeepers, William Thornhill, was drinking in the pub when he was assaulted by two men from Bolsterstone, John Dyson and John Charlesworth. The men had a grievance against him because a few weeks previously the gamekeeper had given evidence in court against Dyson, and against Charlesworth's brother, because they had been poaching. His evidence convicted them, and they were out for revenge.

Thornhill had gone to the Sportsman's Arms to meet a man called Charles Spink, a fellow gamekeeper,[57] who had brought some dogs for Mr. Rimington Wilson, presumably gun dogs for the grouse shooting which was due to commence the following day, as the first day of the grouse shooting

---

[57] To a Mr. Aldam, possibly W. Aldam Esq. Of Frickley Hall, Doncaster, who was also a magistrate

season (known as the *"Glorious Twelfth"*). Outside the pub, Dyson challenged Thornhill to a fight. Having no wish to fight, Thornhill went inside, but Dyson followed him in, still wanting a fight and saying he would not rest till he had him by the throat, threatening that he *"would not leave life in him."* When Charlesworth entered, Dyson complained that the gamekeeper would not fight him, to which Charlesworth said, *"Can't you make him?"* and decided to move matters on by dragging the table away from Thornhill so that Dyson could throw a punch. The men took his stick and set upon him, dragging him across the floor towards the yard outside. The victim clung onto the doorpost, and the two men, now joined by another man, continued to kick and beat him. Eventually, some others intervened, and Thornhill crawled upstairs in great pain. He was battered and bruised and *"was obliged to have leeches on."* He dared not leave the inn until some of the other gamekeepers arrived. He was so badly injured that he was unable to fulfil his gamekeeping duties on the 12th.

When the case came to court, Dyson's defence was that Thornhill had offered to fight him for a gallon of ale, and that is how he got his injuries; he added that after they were separated (by Charlesworth and a man named Shaw), the gamekeeper wanted to carry on the fight in the yard.

Mrs. Hollins, the landlady, said that she saw the assault begin, and did not hear Thornhill say that he would fight for a gallon of ale. Rather, she heard him cry *"murder."* The other gamekeeper, Spink, confirmed all this.

The Defence called a young woman who was working in the pub that night, who immediately began to back up Dyson's version of events; the way it was reported implied she was rather too keen to defend him!

The verdict was that, even if the story were true that Thornhill agreed to fight, it was unacceptable to kick him as he sat in his chair, and for several men to hold him down and beat him. A very malicious and ferocious assault had been clearly proven, and the defendants were heavily fined; Dyson was fined £4 (or two months' imprisonment) and Charlesworth was fined £2 (or one month's imprisonment).

PAYING A NEIGHBOUR'S RATES WITHOUT AUTHORITY: 1858

As a householder/farmer, Henry was obliged to take his turn as a parish official. Before the modern system of government and poor relief, each parish was responsible for the relief of its own poor. The administration was carried out by the churchwardens and two or more overseers of the poor, who were chosen annually by the vestry,[58] and all this was overseen by Justices of the Peace. Provision was made for supplying work to the able-bodied, giving help to the deserving poor of the parish, and binding pauper children as apprentices. This whole system was financed by a rate levied on the occupiers of property. Henry Hollins served as Overseer in 1852, 1853 and 1854. It was an unpaid appointment, made on a yearly basis. A man could refuse to serve but would then have to pay a fine. An Overseer was originally required to be a *"substantial householder"* but this rather vague qualification was later changed (in 1819) to be *"any person assessed to the relief of the poor"* - to put it very simply, he had to be someone who was able to pay the poor rate and not one who received it.

The post was often seen as a burden, being troublesome and time-consuming. There were important decisions to make, including deciding who were the *"deserving poor"* as opposed to those who refused to work, the *"idle poor,"* and they had to decide when new levies on the poor rate had to be made. Overseers were thus under pressure from both the poor and the ratepayers. Any complaints made against them would be dealt with by the local Justice of the Peace. Henry Hollins experienced this to his cost.

In 1858 he sued Joseph Brook of Wigtwizzle for £2. 4d. During his years as Overseer, Hollins had been unable to get Brook to pay his highway rates. In the end, Hollins paid the money that Brook owed out of his own pocket, but Brook did not pay him back. Brook's defence was that there was no proof as to how the money was spent and that there were *"blurries"*[59] in the accounts. He added that the rate was illegally made without any vestry being called, which Hollins denied. He also wanted 20s. 9d. off-set for cutting snow and leading stones.[60]

---

[58] The vestry was a decision-making body which took its name from the room in the church in which it sat.
[59] Blurry is Yorkshire dialect for an error or a mistake
[60] Lead - a Yorkshire dialect word meaning to carry or convey something in a cart or other vehicle.

The overseer's accounts, certified by the magistrates, were produced, but Hollins was not able to swear that Brook had authorised him to pay the money. He alleged that if he had not paid it himself, he would, as collector and overseer, have had to *"stand to it"* [pay it] anyway. The Judge said that Hollins should not have paid the rate, but instead he should have sued Brook for it at the time. That way, if there had been any grounds for complaint as to the way in which business was conducted, it would have been adjudicated upon at the time…Hollins and his case were *"nonsuited"* [dismissed][61].

DISAGREEABLE RAILWAY PASSENGER PUNISHED: 1862

One November day, Henry Hollins, the son of the landlord [Henry senior] was travelling in a third-class carriage on the Manchester, Sheffield & Lincolnshire Railway. A young lady from Oughtibridge, Miss Swift, was also in the same carriage. Henry, it was alleged, kept putting his arm around her, asking if she was married, and *"indulging in other disagreeable familiarities."* He kept pestering her even when she moved to another carriage, and she complained to the railway authorities about him. Henry was charged with *"disorderly conduct in a railway carriage."* His defence was that he was drunk and did not know what he was doing. However, his behaviour earned him a fine of twenty shillings, plus another twenty shillings costs. He would have been about 28 years old. Henry went on to marry Ann Sorby of Sheffield in 1867.

Henry (senior) was the landlord of the Sportsman's Arms for about twenty years until his death in 1865 at the age of 66. As was common amongst publicans, his widow took over as the licensee after his death. Martha ran the pub and farmed the land for over twenty years, aided by her son Thomas. She died there in January 1891 aged 88 years.

In September 1882, Martha was called before the licensing magistrates, her name having appeared on their *"blacklist."* Back in April, she had been fined twenty shillings for keeping the pub open during prohibited hours. The licence was renewed, but she received a reprimand, which served as a caution; should there be any further trouble, she could lose her licence.

---

[61] A ruling of non-suit results in the dismissal of the case; a judgment given against a plaintiff [in this case, Hollins] who neglects to prosecute, or who fails to show a legal cause of action, or to bring sufficient evidence.

It was a few years before there was any more trouble reported. At the West Riding Brewster Sessions of 1887, Martha Hollins was fined for having "*unjust weights*" in her possession. Two others were fined for the same offence; a grocer from Penistone Road, Sheffield, and local man George Ronksley of Warrender Farm, Wigtwizzle.

After her death in 1891, Martha's son Thomas took over the pub. He had married Mary Ann Buckley from Snell House, Bradfield, in 1883 and they had a son, Bernard, in 1886. Thomas was widowed when Mary Ann died in 1889, and when the 1891 census was taken, his widowed sister Jane Wainwright was living with him, as was a servant called Arthur Buckley. Thomas married again in November 1891 to Mary Morris, who had been born in Denbigh, Wales.

BROOMHEAD AND WIGTWIZZLE C.C. ANNUAL DINNER: 1896
The Cricket Club's annual dinner was held at the Sportsman's Arms, and thirty members sat down to an "*excellent dinner*." Mr. J. B. Nicholls was voted to the chair; he was the landlord of the Castle Inn at Bolsterstone at the time.[62] The balance-sheet was read and passed and showed the club to be in a flourishing financial position, thanks to the untiring efforts of the Secretary, Mr. T. Swinburn. The past season was reported to have been a remarkably successful one, with seven out of sixteen matches having been won, eight drawn, and one lost. After votes of thanks had been passed to the various officers, the rest of the evening was spent with songs and recitations.

In 1899 Thomas Hollins was drinking in the Royal Oak pub at Deepcar. Also in the pub was John Bramall, a well-known Deepcar auctioneer and valuer. Hollins began to brag with another drinker about what they had got up to in their younger days (what they called their "*do's*") and mentioned a "*do*" at Wire Brigg[63], making an "*offensive allusion*" to Mrs. Bramall. Mr. Bramall said that his wife [Ann] would not have liked to have heard that, and "*there would have been some scratching.*" This careless pub talk resulted in Hollins being sued for slander by Mrs. Bramall. Thomas Hollins did not appear in

---

[62] He was landlord from 1888 until he was declared bankrupt in 1898.
[63] "*A do*" has a lot of meanings in the Yorkshire dialect. It can mean party or event, some trouble, merrymaking and entertainment, drunkenness, or a contest. The location of Wire Brigg remains a mystery as yet. Brigg is Yorkshire dialect for Bridge.

court (pleading ill health) and was found guilty in his absence. The jury then had to decide on the amount of damages to be awarded to Mrs. Bramall.

She admitted that she had known Hollins before her marriage but was adamant that there was no truth at all in his allegations. His defence said that there might have been some *"loose talk"* by Hollins when he was in *"a muddled condition"* [drunk], adding that, *"If they were all going to be held responsible for the tittle-tattle talked about women in public-houses, those rooms* [the court] *would be in constant use, and the Under-Sheriff would be there daily."* The Under-Sheriff did not agree, and stated that even in public houses men should not be allowed to make disgusting and disgraceful charges against respectable women, and added that *"if a man allowed his dirty tongue to run riot he must take the consequences."* He directed that Mrs. Bramall should be entitled to ask for a reasonable sum, and the jury awarded her damages of £20 - a huge sum of money, the equivalent to over £2,680 by today's reckoning.[64] Ann Bramall was, in later years, the landlady of the Castle Inn at Bolsterstone.

DRINKING OUT OF HOURS: April 1903

At 11.30am on Good Friday 1903, a policeman named Toase had found two men drinking in the pub during prohibited hours. The men, two Bolsterstone miners called Ben Crossland and Fred Curley, were charged with this offence, and the landlord Thomas Hollins was charged with keeping his public house open during prohibited hours. The two men were found in a shed adjoining the inn with some freshly-drawn beer in a jug. The jug and glass they were using belonged to Hollins. The defence tried to argue that the shed did not form part of the licensed premises, but the Bench ordered the trial to proceed.

The defence then argued that the jug and glass had been borrowed overnight by a neighbour, who had returned them when he had finished with them; this was apparently not unusual. The two men said they had simply found the beer, and that it was not fresh - Curley said that when he tasted the beer, he *"spitted it out"* because it was stale. Crossland said it tasted like cold tea. For his part, Hollins said he did not know the two men were in the shed, and

---

[64] According to The Bank of England's Inflation Calculator

that he had not supplied them with the beer. He added that his grandfather started the inn over eighty years ago and that he and his mother had kept it for fifty-eight years. None of them were believed, and Hollins was fined thirty shillings, whilst Crossland and Curley were fined 13s. 6d. each.

THEIR NOISE BETRAYED THEM: June 1903

Two months later Thomas Hollins was in trouble with the courts again. This time he was charged with being drunk on his own licensed premises, and also for permitting several men to get drunk there on the 2nd June. The men were a miller called George Steel (he lived at Broomhead Corn Mill), labourer Albert Clark, and groom John Thomas Marsh, all of Bradfield. The case had been adjourned for a fortnight because Hollins was ill. The charges against the others were proceeded with, but Steel did not appear. Again, P.C. Toase was called to give evidence, along with police sergeant Bellis. They told the court that when they went into the pub, they found Steel, Clark and Marsh in the taproom, very drunk. Clark admitted that if he got up to get a light he would fall into the fireplace. The sergeant stated that the landlord, who was in another room, was not in a fit condition to manage his house. Clark and Marsh were fined ten shillings each (or seven days' imprisonment), and Steel was fined fifteen shillings (or ten days' imprisonment).

When Thomas Hollins later appeared in court, evidence was given that, between nine and ten o'clock at night, three men were found drunk in the taproom of his pub. Hollins was lying on a sofa in another room, very drunk. His sister was in charge that day and had asked the men to leave, but they refused. Hollins denied that he was drunk, insisting that he had not had a drink all day, but that he was ill, and had been for some time. The Bench accepted his plea of illness and dropped the charge. However, he was fined forty shillings for permitting drunkenness.

DRUNK ON HIS LICENSED PREMISES: July 1903

One month later, Hollins was yet again in trouble - for being drunk on his own licensed premises (again), on the 28th July. P.C. Toase stated that Thomas was drunk, but two witnesses who were in the pub at the time said that he was only "*a little fresh.*" He did not claim illness this time and was fined ten shillings.

Such a run of trouble could not go unchallenged, and in February the following year the police objected to the renewal of the pub's license. In addition to the trouble Hollins had been in (being open during prohibited hours, permitting drunkenness and being drunk himself), the police also argued that the inn was "*not necessary*" for the needs of the neighbourhood and that it was so remote that adequate police supervision was almost impossible. Wigtwizzle consisted of very few dwellings - the pub itself, one farmhouse, two cottages, and Broomhead Hall. There were only fourteen houses within a mile of the inn, and there was a population of only fifty-eight. Hollins did not have legal representation and had nothing to say about the case. The application for the renewal of the licence was refused, and Hollins apparently did not seem too bothered by this.

Thomas Hollins died suddenly not long after losing his licence, on the 7th April 1904. He had complained of feeling unwell the previous evening and retired to bed at about 8pm. His son and a farm servant were sleeping in the same room. He was found dead by his sister, who had been keeping house whilst his wife was in the Sheffield Royal Hospital. The newspaper reported that, by strange coincidence, the inn would have been closed for the sale of drink that day, which probably meant that it was the day after the un-renewed licence had expired.

There were now no more public houses in this remote area. The contents of the pub were auctioned off, and the farm and its outbuildings were advertised as being available to rent with just over 75 acres, mostly grass, and well supplied with water. According to G.H.B. Ward, twelve fields and about fifty acres of the farm had been taken into Broomhead Park in about 1893. The farm itself was vacated in 1938.[65] For a while this site served as a wood yard for Sheffield City Council.

The old barn has been converted into a private house, but the pub building was demolished, and a garage to the house now stands on the site. I am told that at the base of a large tree was a large stone slab with hollows chiselled out, which was used as a skittle alley. People have unearthed beer bottles on the site, and an old midwifery book was found hidden in one of the walls when the pub was demolished.

---

[65] Ward, G.H.B. Across the Derbyshire Moors, Sheffield Telegraph & Star: 1946

Here is a list of the contents of the pub and house, which gives us a good insight as to how the family would have lived.[66] The advert added that the usual half-yearly sale of cattle, sheep, etc. would be held on the same date.

The following are Oak, and in a very good state: - Massive Chest of Drawers, 5ft 6in. high, with brass handles, in two parts; Chest of Drawers, large Oatmeal Chest, Linen Chest, panelled front; Langsettle[67], 6ft; Dresser, with 5 drawers and 2 cupboards; Delft 3Case, with 5 drawers; Corner Cupboard, Grandfather's Clock, 3 Tables, and 6 Chairs.

PARLOUR: - Square Table, with leaf and drawers; Card Table, Loose Cupboard, Hair-seated Couch, Armchair, 6 Small Chairs, Weather Glass, Case of Birds, Case Squirrel, Knife Box, Fender and Fireirons, Hearthrug, Cocoanut Matting, Linoleum, 2 Lamps, Flower Pots, etc.

LIVING ROOM: - Table with drawers; 2 Round Tables, Langsettle, Windsor Chair, 6 Wood Chairs, Small Cupboard, Bread Reel[68], Hastener[69], Salt Box, Lamp, Fender, and Fire-irons. Kitchen Table, Wringer, Looking-glass, Paraffin Tank, with brass tap, 10 gallons; Paraffin Can, 2 gallons.

STOREROOM: - Desk, 18 Chairs, 9 Stools, Round Table, 3 Tables and Trestles[70], 6 Forms, Oak Form, Cupboard, Bread Tub, Flour Chest, 2 Gantries[71], End-over-end Churn, new; Old Churn, Bacon Rack, Cross-cut Saw, Clothes Horse, Peggy and Pot.

BEDROOMS: - Four Wood Bedsteads, 2 Dressing Tables with drawers; Wardrobe, Night Chair[72], Folding Chair, 4 Small Chairs, 2 Mirrors, 2 Tables, Bird in case, Timepiece, Chamber Services[73], Hearthrugs, Carpeting, Mats,

---

[66] From a notice of auction placed in the Sheffield Daily Telegraph 23rd April 1904
[67] A long bench with arms and a high back
[68] A wooden frame, with wooden rails or ropes, suspended from the ceiling, on which oatcakes were dried and stored. Could be wound up and down – "*reeled*" - from the ceiling
[69] A semi-circular tin screen placed behind meat in roasting before the fire, to keep the cold air off and hasten the cooking by reflective heat
[70] A table, the support for a table or a form [bench without a back]
[71] In a bar, a structure containing inverted bottles and fitted with optics for serving measures
[72] Commode
[73] Could this mean dressing table items; "*service*" as in chinaware

etc.; Linen, 7 Pairs Blankets, 2 Rugs, 6 Quilts, Pillow and Bolster Slips, 5 Tablecloths, and 12 Teacloths.

PANTRY: - Six Saucepans, 2 Kettles, Dutch Oven, Bread Tins, Pudding Tins, 12 Meat Dishes, 40 Plates, 17 Small Plates, Pancheons[74], Stew Pots, Meat Covers, 35 jugs, Tea Service, 40 pieces; 5 Glass Dishes, 114 various Glasses, Lot of Sundry Crockery too numerous to mention. Five Hams, Flitch of Bacon.

There was a bread reel at the Rose and Crown Inn at Midhope (which closed in 1878). This pub was a staging point on the Wadsley to Langsett turnpike road, used by some of the stagecoach companies to change horses, and where their passengers could get some refreshment. In his book "*Tour of the Don,*" written in 1837, John Holland writes a very evocative account of calling at this hostelry:

"When a person enters the inn, at which the coaches stop at Midhope Stones, the first thing that strikes his eye, especially if he is hungry, is a sort of rack suspended on the joists of the ceiling of the kitchen, and overlaid with some scores of thin oat-cakes, or, as the batch is called, reed bread; having been placed on the rails of the rack in its flaccid state, the manner in which each cake is warped, first by hanging over the edges, and secondly by drying, gives it a curious appearance to a stranger. When eaten, it is found to be just so tenderly crisp, and withal so sweet, added to its undoubted wholesomeness, that many persons are extremely fond of it." [75]

---

[74] Wide shallow bowls for making bread or separating cream
[75] Holland, J. Tour of the Don, Volume 1. Sheffield: 1837

And finally ... The tiny hamlet of Wigtwizzle made the national newspapers in 1904 in an article about *"The Spanish Swindle,"* a con which had been doing the rounds in various places for a while. *"Right up in the wilds of the Bradfield Moors,"* the article said, *"some nine miles from the outskirts of Sheffield, and seven miles from the nearest railway station, there is a little hamlet called Wigtwizzle, pronounced* 'Weetwizzle' *by the moorsfolk."*

"One wild December morning about Christmas time one of the farmers at Wigtwizzle - there are only two farms in the place, which has about 25 inhabitants - received the Spanish swindle letter, telling him that there was £15,000 hidden in Wigtwizzle. Further, that part of this was to be his if only he would send a comparatively small sum to a poor languishing prisoner in the castle fort of Valencia."

The letter made its way to the police who were aware of similar letters. Indeed, New Scotland Yard was aware of it.

The newspaper thought that it was amazing that the fraudsters would single out a farmer in such an out-of-the-way spot, and said that Wigtwizzle did not appear in print from one year to the next, and didn't appear in any directory and was hard to spell. Plenty of people had fallen for the swindle, and the newspaper concluded that *"whilst there are fools in the world there will be rogues to cheat them of their money."*

THE ROYAL OAK, MANCHESTER ROAD, DEEPCAR

The Royal Oak (with the sign outside) in 1860. There used to be a grocer's shop adjoining (on the left), but today this forms part of the pub. The building standing at an angle was a shop, later demolished to make room for a car park. Behind the pub there was stabling for seven horses. The building on the left was the old toll bar, which was in operation until the end of 1875. The Royal Oak is supposedly haunted by a man who can be seen coming out of the taproom and heading through the bar towards the back, where the stables were.

Like many pubs, the Royal Oak started out as a beerhouse. It was built and owned by Benjamin Couldwell[76] who was a joiner and cabinet maker by trade. He also owned the adjoining shop and a house.

Benjamin had been born at Deepcar in 1807 and was the son of Benjamin, a cordwainer (shoemaker) and Mary. The exact date that he decided to turn his house into a beerhouse is not known, but by the time he applied for a full licence in 1836, he was already running a beerhouse alongside his main trade. There was a brewhouse on the premises, so either he or his wife would have brewed and sold their own beer.

People who wanted to turn their houses into licensed premises had to make their intentions known, and Bradfield Archives have two documents signed by Benjamin, dated 1836 and 1838,[77] which state that he owned the house at Deepcar, which was on the Turnpike Road between Sheffield and Manchester, and that it had not for at least three years past been used as an *"Inn, Alehouse, or Victualling House"* but that it was currently *"licensed and used for the sale of Beer by retail."*[78] He seems to have been unsuccessful both times, although he was eventually granted a full wines and spirits licence.

When the 1841 census was taken, Benjamin's occupation was recorded as both innkeeper and cabinet maker. With him in the house were his wife Harriet, their children James, Benjamin, Edmund, Mary, and Harriet, as well as an apprentice, two female servants, and two men who could have been visitors or lodgers. Benjamin had married Harriet Woodcock at Sheffield in 1830. They had seven children: James (a cabinet maker), John (a butcher), Benjamin (later the landlord of the Royal Oak), Edmund (also briefly a publican), Mary (married Elijah Askew of the Coach and Horses), Harriet, Mark (died young) and Ellen.

---

[76] The early spelling varies between Couldwell and Coldwell
[77] Reference numbers 42590 and 42600
[78] The wording is misleading. Beerhouses were not licensed by the magistrates, but beerhouse owners like Benjamin would have bought a certificate to sell beer direct from the Excise. He would not have been allowed to sell anything stronger.

RIDING WITHOUT REINS: 1836
Benjamin was fined twenty shillings in August 1836 for not using the reins whilst riding in his cart at Shalesmoor, Sheffield. In 1852, a man called Charles Webster, a carter working for Samuel Fox, was killed when he lost control of his cart whilst doing the same thing. The Coroner said Webster was entirely to blame for his own death, and he criticised the *"reprehensible practice of riding without reins."*

HIGHWAY ROBBERY ON THE WORTLEY ROAD: 1838
In 1838, Benjamin had to journey into Sheffield to give evidence in court regarding a robbery. George Guelder, a woodman who lived at Wellhouse, Wortley, was robbed whilst on his way home from Wadsley Bridge to Wortley. He had moved there from Worsbrough a year or two previously. His attackers, who all lived near Wadsley, were William Wilson, John Ibbotson, and William Charlesworth.

Guelder had been to Sheffield, where he received some money from a man named Youle. He was given £7, which consisted of a £5 note from the Retford bank[79], and two sovereigns. On his way home he called at the Gate pub and also at the New Inn at Wadsley Bridge. To use the newspapers' favourite phrase for drunk, he got *"very fresh."* George Woodhead, the landlord of the New Inn, gave evidence. He said that Wilson and Charlesworth had gone to his pub around midnight, followed shortly afterwards by Ibbotson. Guelder entered the pub with a Mr. Brown, who was the toll collector at the Parsons Cross toll bar, and they went into the back room, where Guelder *"treated"* Brown with spirits.[80] Guelder left with Wilson, but after a short distance, the other two men came upon them and they threw Guelder to the floor, two of them holding him whilst the other rifled his pockets. They took his money and stole his hat, which was one that had been specially made for him. Guelder went back to the toll bar and told the keeper he had been robbed, before setting off once more for Wortley. He slept the rest of the night in Luke Ogden's public house at Grenoside.

---

[79] At this point in history there were hundreds of private, provincial banks the length and breadth of England
[80] This simply means to buy another person a drink

Benjamin Coldwell, who was described as being a Deepcar beerhouse keeper, said that the three men had gone to the Royal Oak on the morning after the robbery. Ibbotson had asked him to change a £5 note – a Retford note. They went back that evening and asked for a bed for the night, but the constables must have known where to look for them, for they arrived soon afterwards and arrested them.

The Jury found Ibbotson guilty, and Wilson and Charlesworth not guilty. There seemed to be a lack of evidence, and there was a lot of discussion about the hat, which Ibbotson had been wearing when he was arrested. The Chairman said that this was one of the most serious charges that could come before the court – and if Ibbotson had been tried and convicted of this offence at the York Assizes instead, he would most likely have been sentenced to be transported for life, most likely to Australia or Van Diemen's Land (now Tasmania). He got off relatively lightly, being sentenced to eighteen months' imprisonment with hard labour. The judge must have thought them guilty, even if it could not be proved, because when Wilson cheekily asked for his money back (which had been taken from him when he was arrested), he said that he had "*no doubt*" that the money belonged to Guelder and should be given back to him, not to Wilson!

CHILD DROWNED: 1841
An inquest was held at the Royal Oak on the body of 5-year-old Sarah Brook of Deepcar, who was the daughter of a collier named John Brook. The inquest heard that she had been walking on a plank across the river Don at Wharncliffe when she fell in and was drowned. The verdict was Accidental Death. Five years later, another 5-year-old girl, Fanny Broadhead, died when she fell from a plank spanning the Little Don at Stocksbridge.

FATAL ACCIDENT IN WHARNCLIFFE WOODS: 1846
A 29-year-old Deepcar man named Richard Allen was working with some of his family in Wharncliffe Woods, peeling bark off trees. Whilst perched high up in a tree, the bough on which he was sitting gave way, plunging him sixteen feet to the ground. He suffered severe injuries to his back and his head and was taken home by his father and brother. A surgeon was called, but he died the following day. Richard was buried in his home village of Royston, Barnsley. The Coroner passed a verdict of accidental death, and

the vicar entered into the parish register that he was *"killed by falling from a tree in Wharncliffe Woods."*

AUCTIONS

Auctions were a common feature of pub life, and a lot of these took place at the Royal Oak. One of the regular sales was of trees which had been felled in Bitholmes Wood by John Haigh of Bolsterstone. Property was frequently auctioned, as were the household effects of those who had died, or whose possessions had been seized because of bankruptcy or non-payment of rent. In 1843, a farmhouse, barn, stable, cow house, and outbuildings at Bitholmes were advertised as being up for auction, with a tenant called George Housley. In addition, also available to buy were forty acres of arable and pastureland, and fourteen acres of woods and plantations, near the house.

THE REPEAL OF THE CORN LAWS: 1849

The Corn Laws were tariffs and trade restrictions placed on imported food and grain, which were in force from 1815. They were introduced to keep grain prices high so as to favour UK producers by making it too expensive to import grain from abroad, even when supplies here were short. There was a great deal of opposition to these laws, which were seen as profiting the landowners at the expense of the ordinary people. Food prices rose, and other economic sectors such as manufacturing suffered. Prime Minister Peel decreed that the Corn Laws would be abolished on 1st February 1849. This repeal was celebrated by a social meeting at the Royal Oak, with a Mr. J. Siddons in the chair. After tea there were speeches, and three cheers were given for the Queen.

Masbrough-born man Ebenezer Elliot became known as the Corn Law Rhymer for the poems he wrote to draw attention to the issue. He was a factory owner, but had known great hardship in his life, and knew how the poor struggled on a daily basis. His single-minded devotion to the welfare of the working classes, who were experiencing hardship and starvation, won him long-lasting fame, long after his Corn Law Rhymes and other works ceased to be read. He died on the 1st December 1849, the year the laws were repealed. There is a statue of him in Weston Park, Sheffield.

Ye coop us up, and tax our bread,
And wonder why we pine;
But ye are fat, and round, and red,
And fill'd with tax-bought wine.
Thus twelve rats starve while three rats thrive
(Like you on mine and me,)
When fifteen rats are caged alive,
With food for nine and three.[81]

When the 1851 census was taken, Benjamin's occupation was recorded as an innkeeper, cabinet maker, and farmer of sixteen acres of land. Another daughter, Ellen, had arrived, and there were two house servants, one agricultural labourer and two visitors at the pub on census night. In 1861 he was recorded as being a publican and grocer; the shop was attached to the pub and was to the left of its front door. For many years, this shop was run by the Dimmock family. It has now been incorporated into the pub.

CLUBS AND SOCIETIES

Pubs were very handy meeting places for clubs and societies, and the Royal Oak played host to several. One of these societies was The Rose of Britain's Isle Lodge. This was a lodge of the Loyal Order of Ancient Shepherds, one of the many Friendly Societies that existed at the time; in fact, it was one of the oldest mutual insurers in the world. It was a sickness and benefits society, whose objects were "*to relieve the sick, bury the dead, and assist each other in all cases of unavoidable distress, so far as in our power lies, and for the promotion of peace and goodwill towards the human race.*" An advert placed in the Stocksbridge Almanac of 1908 said that the Deepcar Shepherds' Friendly Society had been established in 1839 and met at the Royal Oak monthly; the secretary was Mr. Alfred R. Jackson of Common Piece and the treasurer was Mr. William Pearson of Derbyshire Row. In 1855, members of the lodge held their anniversary dinner at the pub. The officers and members assembled and marched to the Independent Chapel at Stocksbridge, the procession being headed by Mr. Westerman's band. A sermon was preached, and a collection was taken in aid of the Sunday School before everyone returned to the Oak and sat down to dinner. It was reported that there were 110 members, and that, although they had paid out rather a lot of

---

[81] A verse from Caged Rats, one of Elliot's anti-Corn Law Rhymes

money that year, they were still in a flourishing position. In 1863 there were 150 members, and £101 had been paid out in sick money during the previous year. The 1874 meeting was held on Whit Tuesday, and it was reported that there were 200 members. Mr. Couldwell provided "*a substantial repast.*"

In 1891 a man called Charles Fish took the society to court to recover some money that he thought was due to him. A member named Frederick Guest had fallen ill several times, and the society had paid him out some money whilst he was on the sick list. This lasted until he was admitted to the Workhouse one day. The Guardians of the Poor, who administered such things, put in a claim to the society for the sick pay, as was their legal right. Mr. Guest, however, died before any money could be paid out. He had nominated Charles Fish of Cliffe View, Deepcar, a shoemaker, as his beneficiary, and Mr. Fish was paid the £3 which was payable at death. Mr. Fish also thought he was entitled to the sick pay which had not been paid whilst Mr. Guest was alive, and to this end, he sued Thomas Hague of Bolsterstone, who was the secretary of the Royal Oak Lodge of Shepherds, for £3 16s. 6d. sick pay. The judge decreed that Fish was not entitled to the money, adding that the society would not "*pocket the money*" either, so presumably it would be paid to the Guardians.

Benjamin was involved in a serious accident in October 1842 when he was driving home from Midhopestones in his cart "*at a brisk rate,*" according to reports. As he was passing the sharp turn at "*Hunchcliff Bridge*" [Hunshelf], he was thrown out of the cart, breaking his collarbone and his arm. He was much bruised about the head, and the newspapers reported that he was "*lying in a very dangerous state,*" though luckily, he survived.

A MAN FOUND DROWNED NEAR DEEPCAR: 1864
Abraham Cooke, a Sheffield publican, was found drowned in the river Don one day, just below Deepcar. The inquest at the Royal Oak was told that he had been in a low state of mind for some time, and the verdict was that he drowned himself while in a state of temporary insanity.

THE DEATH OF BENJAMIN COULDWELL: 1865
Benjamin Couldwell died on the 17th July 1865 at the age of 57. His furniture, two carts and a horse, along with other effects, were auctioned off at the Royal Oak in October. His eldest son James, who, like his father, was

also a joiner and cabinet maker, succeeded to his father's business. Another son, Benjamin, moved back to the house and took over the running of the pub together with his wife Harriet Ridal.

POLITICS AND PUBS
Public houses were often used by political campaigners, and the Royal Oak was no exception. In November 1868, the Sheffield Daily Telegraph reported that the committees for promoting the return of Conservatives Messrs. Stanhope and Starkey sat daily at a number of pubs, the Royal Oak being one of them. Other local pubs used by campaigners were the Castle Inn at Bolsterstone, the Coach and Horses Hotel at Stocksbridge, and the Barrel Inn [later the Club Inn] at Midhope. The two men were well received by a large crowd when they spoke at a meeting held at Stocksbridge on Wednesday 15th November that year. They went on to address meetings at Ecclesfield and Handsworth Woodhouse on the same day.

Mrs. Mary Jagger, writing in her book The History of Honley, recalled how election candidates would arrive in Honley village (about fifteen miles away) on their electioneering trail. *"The coming of the Candidates in a carriage drawn by four spanking grey horses with mounted postilions, and accompanied by a cavalcade of horsemen was an enlivening sight,"* she wrote, adding that she could *"vividly recall such an arrival, when Messrs. Stanhope and Starkey, the Conservative Candidates for the Southern Division of the West Riding of Yorkshire in 1874, came to Honley. In an old-time election perhaps there was much bribery, treating and undue influence, but the retinues of men, horses and carriages passing to and fro were more animating to look upon than the present prosaic ballot-box."* She concluded that perhaps *"free-fights, broken heads, cheers, counter cheers, abundant supply of coloured liquids, and the general hurly-burly taking place around the hustings held more attraction for an old-time voter than the present lifeless proceedings."*[82]

ANTI TOLL BAR MEETING AT DEEPCAR: 1869
There was a toll bar at Deepcar, next to the Royal Oak. It had been installed to collect fees (tolls) when the Sheffield and Langsett turnpike road had been built in 1805, and the money collected was used to help maintain the road.

---
[82] Jagger, M. The History of Honley. Alfred Judd & Sons: 1914

These were obviously unpopular. In October 1869, a meeting was held at the Oak by a committee who were campaigning for the abolition of the toll bars on the road. It was reported that in all the districts which were *"injuriously affected by the tolls,"* the general feeling of opposition to the renewal of the Turnpike Trust[83] was deepening, and people were urged not to cease in their efforts until all the tolls on the road were abolished.

There were also disputes arising from the fees. In 1874 Samuel Barton, the keeper of the Deepcar toll bar, took Michael Mason, a road contractor, to court because he refused to pay a toll on a cart that passed through the bar. Mason had two horses drawing two carts, but one of the horses had suffered an accident, so he fastened the two carts together to be drawn by one horse. Barton wanted payment for two carts, but Mason argued that the toll was levied on the horse and not on the cart, therefore only one toll was due. The court agreed and the charge was dismissed, Mason being awarded a guinea in costs.

Samuel Fox was one of those leading the opposition. The fees must have had a big impact on his profits, as all his Works transport which passed through the toll bar would have had to pay. The matter went as high as the Home Secretary, and in 1872 a Select Committee of the House of Commons decided that the Turnpike Trust should be discontinued after the 31st December 1875. It was noted that *"parties using the road will not be sorry to learn that at the end of 1875 all the toll bars on the road will be done away with."* And so in 1875 the Trust was dissolved; in any case, the parishes through which the road ran had been paying towards its maintenance for some time anyway.

Before the Trust expired (at the end of 1875), the Stocksbridge Local Board served a notice on the Turnpike Trustees, requiring them to *"throw into the road"* the site occupied by the Deepcar toll bar and the garden attached to it, in order to widen the road. The Trustees appealed, and the issue was debated at length. Eventually, the magistrates ordered that the road be widened to thirty-six feet along the whole frontage, with each party paying their own costs.

---

[83] A Turnpike Trust was set up in 1805 to get an Act passed through Parliament to allow the road to be built; the committee wanted to prevent any further renewal of the Act.

The site needed to be cleared prior to it being auctioned off, and at the beginning of January 1876 this task was put out to tender. The site had to be cleared of all the building materials from the toll bar house and the site taken down to the level of the road. The auction of this plot of land took place at the Royal Oak on the 31st January 1876.

Deepcar Bar
To Be Sold By Auction
The Plot of Land forming the site of the Deepcar Toll Bar, Garden and Premises (except a portion thereof adjoining the Wadsley and Langsett road, which is required to be thrown out to make such road along its frontage thereto of the width of 36 feet).
The Plot of Land (exclusive of the above portion to be thrown out) contains 221 superficial square yards or thereabouts, and forms a very eligible situation for building purposes, being bounded on all sides by public roads.[84]
The Plot of Land will be conveyed to the purchaser free of cost.
The Buildings and Toll Gate will be included but the purchaser will have forthwith to remove such parts thereof as extend upon the said width of 36 feet.[85]

This wasn't the end of the matter, however, for in November 1877 the Barnsley Chronicle reported that complaints had been made to the Stocksbridge Local Board [council] about the dangerous state of the site of the Deepcar toll bar. The Clerk was instructed to request Mr. Fox to carry out the magistrate's order and make the road its proper width.[86]

SPORT
The Royal Oak does not seem to have been involved in sport as much as some other pubs, perhaps for lack of a suitable field. The land that adjoined the pub was used for getting stone and coal, and for farming. There are no reports of any shooting matches until a new landlord called Cornelius Tingle became the landlord in about 1888. The first mention of a pigeon ledger at the Oak appeared in the Sheffield Daily Telegraph in 1890. Pigeon shooting was a common activity at the pubs in this area.

---

[84] The toll bar was in a triangle of land at the top of Vaughton Hill.
[85] Advertisement placed in the Sheffield Independent 2nd January 1876
[86] Samuel Fox was the chairman of the Local Board.

A TROTTING MATCH: 1870

In 1870 a *"Trotting Match Against Time for £10"* took place. Priam Hudson of Yew Trees Farm, Bolsterstone, was to trot his pony 8½ miles in 35 minutes from Fiddler's Green (Saltersbrook) to Deepcar, with a gig carrying two men. The *"spirited little animal"* (accompanied by the referee on horseback, and a few interested spectators riding in a spring cart) trotted the distance in 33½ minutes with ease. Its owner and friends, along with Mr. John Charlesworth, the loser, supped at Benjamin Couldwell's Royal Oak.

THE PUB GOES TO AUCTION: 1870

Auctioneer Robert Lowe placed notices in the newspapers that he was instructed by the owner of the Royal Oak (James Couldwell, who was the late Benjamin's eldest son) to put up for auction various properties, including the Royal Oak. The sale was to take place on the 15th June 1870. Lot 1 included the Royal Oak, with stabling for seven horses, a hayloft, brewhouse, piggeries, etc. The advert said that the premises had been built by the late Mr. Benjamin Couldwell, who *"occupied and conducted an excellent business upon them until his death."* The tenant was Benjamin Couldwell junior, who was a yearly tenant. Also included in this sale was an adjacent provision shop, also occupied by Benjamin, and a house and garden occupied by the West Riding Constabulary. The total rental of all this stone-built property brought in £65 per year. Lot 2 consisted of about five acres of land, which was being dug for stone and coal. Lot 3 was a field of approximately two acres adjoining Lot 2, both of which fronted the Bolsterstone road [Carr Road]. According to the 1861 census returns, the occupations of both Benjamin and his younger brother Edmund were *"farmer & colliery 21 acres land,"*[87] although Edmund had briefly been the landlord of the King and Miller (from 1864-1868).

Edmund filed for liquidation in 1872, and his house on Carr Road, his business goods, and some furniture were auctioned off. He moved away from Deepcar to live in Sheffield.

Benjamin was still the publican when the 1871 census was taken. He was living there with his wife Harriet, six children, and two servants. P.C. John

---

[87] There is no mention of who, if anyone, bought the pub, but by 1898 it was in the hands of Whitmarsh, Watson & Co. Ltd., of the South Street (Moor) Brewery

Tomlinson was a neighbour. Records from the year 1881 tell us that as well as being a publican, he was also a farmer, shop keeper, and coke burner.

James Couldwell was in financial trouble by 1875. At a meeting of creditors, it was said that his liabilities were over £203 and his assets just over £78, not including book debts. It was agreed that the estate should be liquidated by arrangement. Like his brother Edmund, James also moved away from Deepcar to live in Sheffield.

ASSAULT ON A RAILWAY PORTER AT DEEPCAR: 1873

In January 1873 James Couldwell and his son Edmund (who would have been about 16 years of age) were summoned for assaulting William Hartley, a railway porter at Deepcar station. The court heard that on the afternoon of the 26th December 1872 the porter was walking from Deepcar to Stocksbridge, it being Boxing Day and a half-holiday. Some boys were playing in a field by the road and started to throw stones at him. One of them hit him in the middle of his back. He ran after the boys, following them over several fields into a lane, where he saw young Edmund Couldwell. Thinking that he was one of the group, he caught hold of him and asked him why he had been throwing stones at him. Edmund had a dog with him, threatened to "*set it*" at him if he didn't leave him alone; he then struck Hartley a violent blow in the face which knocked him over. James Couldwell arrived at this point and started kicking Hartley, and as a result of this, he was confined to his bed for four days and was not able to work for several days after he got up. Several witnesses confirmed this, including his doctor. The defence argued that Hartley was drunk and had attacked Edmund and that James had only attacked Hartley because he saw him beating his son. A summons had thus been taken out against Hartley for assaulting Edmund, but the magistrates thought there was "*an excuse*" for the assaults and dismissed both of them. However, they said that the case against James Couldwell was very different. He had assaulted Hartley in "*a violent and cowardly manner,*" and they fined him over £5, including costs.[88] James had been in trouble for attacking a man five years before this, in 1868. He was fined for assaulting Thomas Siddons at the King and Miller (the landlord of the Miller at the time was his brother Edmund).

---

[88] The newspaper reported that James was a publican, living at Deepcar, so he perhaps assisted his brother Benjamin in the running of the Royal Oak.

A HUGE STORM: July 1872
The Sheffield newspapers were full of reports about the damage caused by a huge storm in the district when at least four people in Sheffield were drowned. Work had to be suspended at Fox's rail mill, which stood several feet deep in water; the cellars of the melting furnaces were likewise flooded. The Independent wrote:

"Near the Coach and Horses [Stocksbridge] the turnpike was a pond several inches deep, and the shop and cellars of Mr. Williams, and the cellars of Mr. Brownhill, were flooded. At Deepcar, a swift river rolled down the lane called the Car, and washed holes in the lane and the turnpike 30 inches deep. Scores of tons of stones and gravel were brought down. The cellars of the King and Miller, the Royal Oak, and the Traveller's Rest were all flooded. Mrs. Hemsworth, a widow, in Couldwell's houses, was away, and the neighbours looking through the window of her house saw the furniture floating about. The river was fully three feet higher than is usual in floods, and a cow, some geese, and many poles and uprooted trees were brought down."[89]

SKELETON OF A WOMAN FOUND AT DEEPCAR: 1877
A gruesome discovery was made one day when the skeleton, hair, and clothing of a female were found in an old drift pit at Deepcar, belonging to James Grayson. It was supposed that the remains were of a young married woman called Keziah Beal, the daughter of James Ridal. She had been an inmate of the Wadsley Asylum and had escaped through a window one cold snowy night about six months earlier. She had escaped several times before, only to be taken back again. The pit was in the Clough (which we now know as Fox Glen), and when a man and boy went in to help put down a new shaft, they found the remains about 90 yards from the mouth. Her remains were taken to the Royal Oak to await a coroner's inquiry.

---

[89] Sheffield Independent 15th July 1872. Couldwell's Houses were better known as Mangle Row. This row of houses was listed on the 1871 census as James Couldwell Row and was also known as Wharncliffe View. Mrs. Sarah Ann Hemsworth and her husband Edward, a packing case maker, were living at Jas. Couldwell Row in 1871; he died about six weeks before this flood, and was buried at Wortley church in June 1872, aged 40. In 1911 three of these houses were sold at auction (their tenants being Oliver Shaw, Charles Emerson, and John Schofield).

The Coroner held the inquest a few days later. Keziah had been admitted to the Asylum around the beginning of 1876, suffering from *"melancholia."* She escaped four times during the year, and on the 4th January 1877, she escaped again. Nothing further was heard of her until her remains were found. Identification was only possible from her clothes, being those worn by patients in the Asylum, and a *"number of other circumstances."*

Deepcar farmer James Ridal said that his daughter was 29 years old, and was the widow of Luke Beal, a labourer.[90] He could not identify the body but did not doubt that it was his daughter. He blamed the Asylum for allowing her to escape so often. The head nurse of the female ward, Elizabeth Helliwell, said that Keziah had been admitted to the sick ward, but was removed to the refractory ward [for patients deemed unmanageable], which was above the sick ward. She thought this was done to prevent her from escaping; however, she was taken back down again after threatening to throw herself out of the window.

After she had gone missing, a nurse was sent to her mother's house to fetch back her asylum clothing (but not the girl herself, who they said was discharged). Dr. Mitchell, the medical superintendent at Wadsley, said that Keziah was not *"refractory,"* rather she was a *"pauper lunatic."* He said that she was *"full of cunning, in fact, in that respect, she was of sound mind."* He had an order for her discharge; she should have been discharged before her escape, except that she had suffered a *"slight attack"* in the meantime.

A lot of evidence was heard, and the Coroner informed the jury that he was satisfied with the conduct of the Asylum. The jury returned a verdict that Keziah Beal was found dead on the 13th June, having escaped from the South Yorkshire Lunatic Asylum on the 4th January, and having probably died from cold and exposure, being at the time a person of unsound mind. And whilst blaming no one, they thought Dr. Mitchell should have communicated with her friends and family respecting her escape sooner than he did.

---

[90] Luke and Keziah had married at Bolsterstone in 1875; he was 35 years old, and a furnaceman. She was 26 years old. The only burial that seems to fit is: Ecclesfield 5th March 1877, Luke Beal of the Workhouse, aged 36.

THE FATAL FALL AT DEEPCAR: 1883
An inquest was held at the Royal Oak on the body of John Pickford, aged 55, a labourer who lived at Royd. One Friday night, after receiving his wages, he called in at the Royal Oak to spend them, leaving there somewhat the worse for drink. He was on his way home, but he never arrived, having strayed from the path and fallen into a deep ditch near Lane End. When he did not return home the next day, a search was made and his body was eventually found face down in a ditch, in some water. There were bruises on his face caused by the fall. The Coroner gave the cause of death as asphyxia.

AUCTIONS
Many auctions were held at the Royal Oak by local auctioneer and valuer John Bramall, of Old Haywoods. Some of those held during the tenure of Benjamin Couldwell junior included:
- 1878: sale of five freehold cottages at Bolsterstone, in the occupation of Mary Staniforth and others
- 1880: sale of freehold land at Deepcar (pursuant to an order of the High Court of Justice, Chancery Division, made in an action of Hallam *v*. Grayson). This included a field of about an acre at Deepcar called Hagg Field in the occupation of Benjamin Couldwell as a yearly tenant. This was bought by Mr. Macro Wilson for £190.
- 1881: John Bramall put his own house and garden at Haywoods up for sale, and also five cottages and some vacant land. His own house was supplied with water from a pump on the premises, and the other houses were supplied with water from the Water Works of the Stocksbridge Local Board.
- 1883: Freehold properties Townend House and two cottages (the former being in the occupation of Benjamin Webster as a yearly tenant), and "*a small but comfortable homestead*" called Pen Nook.
- 1883: freehold building sites, cottages and land, and a valuable coke business and plant. The advertisement noted that building land was much sought after to provide houses for the ever-increasing workforce at Fox's. There were nine building plots fronting the main road; one adjoining the west of the Wesleyan Chapel at Deepcar; three cottages on the opposite side of the road (in the occupation of James Woodcock, Ernest Faulkner & Samuel Evans); four cottages nearby and also a parcel of land (with tenants George Parkin, John Spivey, Albert Crawshaw & John Grayson).

- 1890: for sale by auction were the sole rights to sell refreshments at the 14th annual athletic sports day; Lot 1 was the right to sell beer, wines, spirits, mineral waters, and cigars. Lot 2 was the right to sell luncheon, tea, coffee, and confectionary. Similar auctions were held at the King and Miller.
- 1898: an auction of the animals and farming implements belonging to Mr. George Fieldsend, who had given up farming. There were two horses, four beasts, two sows with litters of eleven and ten piglets, and all the farming equipment.

In January 1885 Benjamin Couldwell announced that he was giving up the coke business and the farm, and he instructed John Bramall to auction his horses, cattle, farm equipment, farm produce, etc. There were seven horses (one of which was said to be suitable for funeral work), nine cows, a great many farm implements, some hay and some straw. In 1891 Benjamin was living at Carr Road; he was 57 years old, and his occupation was *"retired publican."* He died in 1896 at the age of 62 and his widow Harriet died the following year aged sixty-one.

A man named John Kilner left the Bridge Inn at Penistone in January 1887 and took over at the Royal Oak. He took on both the shop and the pub, but he didn't last long in either venture. He had been at the Bridge Inn for almost four years, and he had also dealt in cattle. Just over a year after moving to Deepcar he gave up the butchers and grocery business to concentrate on the pub. He auctioned off his horse, dogcart (with lamps and cushions), delivery cart, dray, and other items such as harnesses, a barrel, and a churn. He placed several advertisements in the Sheffield Daily Telegraph looking for both staff and musicians; he was looking to hire a young male pianist and vocalist, and a lady pianist and vocalist (the latter to be in her twenties). He also advertised football matches.

However, in July 1888, after only 18 months in the Royal Oak, his business failed, and he filed for bankruptcy. He made an offer to his creditors to pay them five shillings in the pound, but upon examination it turned out that he could afford much more (18s. 6d. in the pound). He upped his offer to six shillings, but this was not accepted. He did have some property, but the solicitors thought there would not be much money left after the mortgages were paid off. Kilner accounted for his deficiency by bad debts, losses in cattle and pigs, and the business not having paid expenses.

On leaving his previous pub in Penistone, Kilner had received a valuation of just short of £400. He had to pay a valuation of £500 when he entered the Royal Oak, and in order to pay the £100 shortfall, he borrowed from the bank. However, he does not seem to have been very good at book-keeping. The Official Receiver said that Kilner's creditors had complained that he had been frequenting race meetings, spending large sums of money, getting drunk, and *"doing worse things,"* but what these things were was not disclosed. The Official Receiver wanted to know where Kilner's money had gone, commenting that it could not have simply *"vanished into thin air."* Kilner's solicitor remarked that he did not think his client was *"sharp enough to have made a nest egg or kept anything back."* This was eventually resolved in August 1888, and the examination was concluded [case closed].

The next landlord of the Royal Oak was Cornelius Robert Tingle. He had been born in West Bromwich, Staffordshire, in about 1857, although his parents moved to Brightside in Sheffield when he was young. His father William worked as a steel roller. Cornelius married Maria Snowden, and in 1881 they were recorded on the census as having a beerhouse at Savile Street, Brightside. This was the Victoria Arches, and it was surrounded by the steelworks and heavy industries of Sheffield's east end. By 1891 Cornelius had moved his family out of the city and into the more rural surroundings of Deepcar. Cornelius and his family were at the Royal Oak when the census was taken, together with two domestic servants and an ostler to look after the horses. In 1895 one of their daughters Florence Gertrude married Benjamin Couldwell, the grandson of the original landlord. The 1901 census records them at Carr Road, Benjamin's occupation being a self-employed cab driver. By the time the 1901 census was taken, Cornelius had moved back to Brightside.

WALKING MATCH AT DEEPCAR: 1887
A Deepcar man named Frank Ibbotson backed himself to walk or run fifty miles in twelve hours. A crowd turned out to see whether he made it – the course was from the Royal Oak to the top of the Bitholmes. Speculation was slightly in Ibbotson's favour in the morning, but he failed after covering

forty-two miles, two hours before the expiration of his time, though he had been *"training all the week."*

SAD SUICIDE AT DEEPCAR: 1892

Mark Couldwell, the eldest son of Benjamin and Harriet, and a grandson of the original landlord, committed suicide on the 23rd November 1892 in a building belonging to John Brearley.[91] He was 32 years old, unmarried, and lived with his parents at Rock View, Carr Road (which is behind the pub). When the census was taken the previous year, no occupation was recorded for him, and at the inquest his father said that his son did not have an occupation and enjoyed fairly good health. However, he had been drinking heavily for some time. His father was awoken about 6am that day, and shouted out, *"Who's there?"* His son replied, *"It's me, and you'll not see me [alive] any more."* He then went out, locking the door behind him. His father was worried, and he roused the rest of the family. Their search was hampered because they could not get out of the locked door, and it was still dark outside. Benjamin tragically found his son in an outbuilding belonging to his married daughter, who lived next door. He was dead, with his throat cut from ear to ear, his open razor lying on the floor beside him. The police were called, and the body removed to the Oak to await the inquest, which took place two days later. His father reported the circumstances and said that he knew of nothing which would have led Mark to commit suicide. He had left two notes, which were almost unintelligible, but which said things like, *"Dear Mother, - I gone for ever,"* *"I do not bear it"* and *"with love to all. I am not sane. But oblige."* The jury all knew Mark and were aware of the fact that lately he had given way to drink. They returned a verdict of *"Committed suicide while in a state of temporary insanity,"* and expressed sympathy with the father in his bereavement.

In July 1895, an advert was placed in the Sheffield Independent announcing that the freehold Royal Oak, with its yard, stables, piggeries, and other outbuildings was to go up for auction, along with two freehold shops and houses adjoining, one currently occupied by a Mr. Worthy as a Boot and Shoe and Milliner's Shop, and the other by Mr. Dimmock as a Provision and

---

[91] The body was reported to have been found in a closet belonging to Mark's married sister who lived next door; this was Mary Ellen, who had married John Tattersall in 1882; they had a draper's shop. This must have been owned by Mr. Brearley.

Grocer's Shop. Full particulars were to follow, but none appeared, so perhaps the sale was cancelled. In September, the same newspaper carried an advertisement for a shop to let (drapers and milliners) at Stocksbridge – interested parties to apply to Benjamin Couldwell and George Sampson of Deepcar.

In 1896 Cornelius Tingle was fined for failing to report the existence of swine fever on his premises. When the police visited, they found four pigs, two of which were suffering from swine fever.

In 1896, James Frederick Hewertson published in the newspaper – as was required – his intention to apply for an off-licence for his premises at Carr Road and the junction of New Street (now St. John's Road). Publishing intent was to give interested parties a chance to object – other beer retailers, the police, and so on. On this occasion, there were objections from Cornelius Tingle and the police. Hewertson had been the tenant of the premises, a shop, since 1893. He paid rent and rates of just over £20 a year, meaning the premises met the minimum rateable value required for it to be licensed. Almost all the houses surrounding his premises were new, and more building was planned.

His solicitor argued that the application was made *"in the interests of temperance and the well-being of the people."* This line of reasoning was that, in order to get a drink, a man had to go into a public house, but he should not have to enter a pub every time he wanted his *"supper beer"* because once he was in there *"temptations were held out to him which a man should avoid."* Furthermore, if a man could not fetch the beer himself, he would send his wife, child, or servant, and it was not good for them to mix with *"persons usually found in public houses."* There were three nearby *"on"* licences (The King and Miller, the Travellers Inn, and the Royal Oak). There were also two off-licences nearby (Moorhouse's, which was 700 yards away, and Helliwell's, 400 yards away), which negated the argument about there being nowhere other than public houses for a man to get a drink.

Superintendent Bielby objected to the application being granted because he argued that the rateable value of the house was much lower than stated; he seemed to think Hewertson was lying about the amount of rent and rates he paid, even though a book was produced. The application was refused.

DEEPCAR MINERS IN TROUBLE: 1896
George Shaw and Frederick Charlesworth, two Deepcar miners, were summoned before the West Riding Justices in April, charged with being drunk on the licensed premises of the Royal Oak. They were both intoxicated and were creating a disturbance and had to be ejected. Charlesworth was fined ten shillings and Shaw £1.

DEATH OF BENJAMIN COULDWELL: 1896
Benjamin died on the 12th November at Rock View, Deepcar. He was buried at Bolsterstone, and a large number of mourners attended, a sign that he was highly respected by all who knew him. He had been for a long time a member of the Stocksbridge Local Board [the council], and up to his death was one of the trustees of the United Shepherds' Club at Deepcar, which met at the Royal Oak. The mourners included Mr. William Beasley and family of Belmont; Mrs. Askew of Spink Hall; Messrs. Joseph Marsden (clerk to the Stocksbridge Local Board), George Sampson, John Dyson, John Bramall; Messrs. Joshua Kenworthy and Edward Thickett (his co-trustees of the Shepherds' Club).

The following year, his property was auctioned off at the pub he used to run. Lot 1 comprised his house, Rock View, which was off Carr Road (behind the pub), and also a stable and carriage house. The house had a large kitchen, dining and drawing rooms, four bedrooms, a bathroom, and lavatory, with hot and cold water, and w.c. A lot of houses at this time did not have an indoor bathroom and toilet. There was also a large garden at the back and an outhouse. Lot 2 consisted of three stone houses on Carr Road, with tenants. One was occupied by Dr. Maclaren and was quite substantial – there were four rooms on the ground floor, four bedrooms, two attics, a toilet, and cellars. This is probably the end terrace that still stands at the bottom of Carr Road. The other two houses were smaller, with two living rooms, two bedrooms, an attic, and a cellar. These were rented out to Mrs. Walton and Mr. G. Slater. In 1901 there was still a doctor in the larger house and widow Ann Walton was still in the adjoining house. Benjamin Couldwell's son (also called Benjamin) was in the third one – he was working as a cab proprietor. Lot 3 consisted of three freehold houses in Orchard Street, off Carr Road; these were being rented out to Mr. Tattersall, Mr. Newton, and Mr. Ridal.

Cornelius Tingle stayed at the Royal Oak for about ten years, from 1888 to 1898, before moving to Sheffield. It was possibly in 1898 that the pub was acquired by Whitmarsh, Watson & Co. Ltd.[92] This company was acquired by Duncan Gilmour & Co. Ltd. in 1906, who were in turn taken over by Leeds-based Joshua Tetley in 1954.

After Cornelius, the new landlord was George William Elliott, who had previously been the landlord of the Travellers Inn at Vaughton Hill, just across the road from the Oak; he was there from about 1893 until 1898.

George had been born into pub life in 1866. His parents were William and Ann Elliott, and they had the Strines Inn, out on the wild moors towards Derbyshire. William's parents had also had the Strines, as well as being farmers. When George married Adelaide Herbert at Bolsterstone in 1891, his occupation was given as a coke merchant. They had a daughter, Edith Phadorah, who was born at Haywoods in 1892, and a son called George Herbert, who was born at the Travellers in 1895.

DEEPCAR INNKEEPER FINED: February 1900
George William Elliott was summoned to court for permitting drunkenness, and Peter Bramwell, shoemaker, of Stocksbridge, was summoned for being drunk on licensed premises. Solicitor Mr. A. Muir Wilson appeared for the brewery. Around 3pm one day, P.C. Goldthorpe was in the process of locking up a man for being drunk and disorderly when he passed the Royal Oak and saw Bramwell outside, very drunk. Two hours later he and Sergeant Carter called at the Oak, and found Bramwell inside, still drunk. The landlord admitted that Bramwell was "*fresh*," and that he had been in the pub for about four hours, but he had not ordered him to leave because he wasn't causing any trouble. When he did order him to leave, Bramwell apparently declared himself too drunk to walk. The landlord added that Bramwell had been in the pub that morning and had gone back in the afternoon. He was then apparently sober, but the landlord refused to serve him "*on strap*"

---

[92] This according to Breweryhistory.com, but these records are sometimes patchy. There is no record of the pub being sold in this year, so perhaps it had been acquired back in 1870 (when James Couldwell put it up for sale), by John Watson or William Whitmarsh before they merged. A notice that the pub was going to be put up for auction appeared in the newspapers in 1895, with further particulars to follow, but none were ever printed, so the sale might not have happened.

[credit]. Bramwell himself denied that he was drunk, and said he fell down because the footpath was slippery. Two men called George Underhill and James Devine said that Bramwell was sober when he entered the pub. In the end, Bramwell was fined ten shillings and Elliott £1, including costs, but the licence was not to be endorsed.

RUNAWAY HORSE AND TRAP: 1907

A runaway horse caused some excitement when it bolted from outside the Royal Oak. A lady and gentlemen had just got into a horse and trap and were waiting while the groom put the bluffs (blinkers) on the horse. But before the bit was in its mouth, the horse bolted. The gentleman was thrown out when the trap hit a lamp post. The horse continued its panicked journey, and no control could be got with the reins. It was eventually stopped by Sergeant Vardy and Benjamin Couldwell. Beyond suffering from *"fright"* the lady escaped uninjured.

DEEPCAR COTTAGE GARDENERS' SOCIETY: founded 1882

In September 1905, the Sheffield Daily Telegraph reported on the 23rd annual show of the Deepcar Royal Oak Cottage Gardeners' Society. This being its 23rd year, it would have begun in 1882, though there is no previous record of such an event in the earlier newspapers. The 24th show, in 1906, was reported to have been an *"excellent"* exhibition of flowers, vegetables, and hothouse plants. There had been almost 100 entries, which were judged by Mr. George Stevenson, who worked as head gardener to Mrs. Macro Wilson of Waldershaigh. The 25th annual show had 109 entries. The club room of the Oak had been decorated with palms, foliage, flowering plants and cut blooms, and a collection of plants had been lent by Mr. C. E. Hayward. The judge was Mr. George Stevenson again, and he awarded prizes to the following: T. Dimelow, S. Revitt, J. Naylor, W. Race, William Booth, J. Mann, H. Haigh, S. Marshall, H. Burgin, C. Bullock, J. Naylor, G. H. Milnes, G. Smith, E. Harper, R. Wilson, George Tattersall, J. Naylor, G. Nance, C. Crawshaw, H. Ward. In later years, the Deepcar Allotment Society had their headquarters at the Travellers Inn on Vaughton Hill. Mr. J. Cairns of Wortley Hall Gardens judged their shows.[93]

---

[93] Their second annual show was on the 1st September 1919.

FOOTBALL - DEEPCAR'S OFFENCE: 1909

The Royal Oak had its own football team. In September 1909, the Sheffield Competition Committee met to decide whether a complaint brought by Midland Athletic against Deepcar Royal Oak should be upheld. Midland alleged that, in their Junior Challenge Cup-tie with Deepcar Royal Oak, the latter club played an ineligible player in J. Wade. Deepcar strenuously denied this and said that they had played a man called Saxby in the position Midland Athletic alleged that Wade had played. On the evidence submitted, and also information received by private inquiries, the committee was unanimous in agreeing that J. Wade did indeed play on that particular day. Therefore, Midland Athletic's complaint was allowed, and Deepcar was thrown out of the competition. They were also fined over £1 towards the expenses incurred by the committee. Houldsworth, the secretary, and Walton, the assistant secretary, were suspended *"sine die"* [indefinitely; with no fixed date of being allowed to play again]. Whittaker (the captain) and Saxby were suspended until the end of the season, and J. Wade was suspended until he appeared before the committee.

RIFLE CLUB: 1910

The Bolsterstone, Stocksbridge, and Deepcar Rifle Club held their annual dinner at the Royal Oak in 1910. Around sixty members turned up for the meeting and the dinner. Various toasts were drunk, including that of the president, Mr. Rimington Wilson of Broomhead Hall. Mr. Adams of Sheffield presented the prizes to the winners of various competitions, and winners included J. Brearley, G. Moorhouse, and J. Helliwell.[94]

The next landlord (c1904 to 1913) was John Arthur Addy. He had been born in Stocksbridge next to the New Inn beerhouse in 1880. His parents were Joseph Addy, a miner, and Ruth Gill. When John Arthur was born, his maternal grandmother Eliza Gill was the landlady of the New Inn. His parents had taken it over by the time the 1891 census was taken and were still there in 1901, as was John Arthur's future wife Elizabeth Ellen Moorwood. John Arthur himself was with his brother John William at Otley Road, Walkley; both were managers at a pawnbroker's shop. John Arthur married

---

[94] The *"Bolsterstone Rifle Club"* had met at the King and Miller in 1908; it is not clear whether they were two separate clubs.

Elizabeth Ellen at Woodhouse in 1903 and their first child was born in Sheffield later that year.

John Arthur and his wife were recorded at the Royal Oak when the census was taken in 1911. With them were their son John Arthur junior (born in Sheffield in 1904), an ostler [95] called Jabez Abbott from Huntingdonshire, and two female servants. The pub had ten rooms.

There is a reference in the Sheffield Daily Telegraph of January 1912 to a Mr. F. Jeffries of the Royal Oak at Deepcar, but I have found no record of this man anywhere else.[96] He wrote a letter to the newspaper expressing his willingness to match Bill Bennett to box Tom Mitchell of Chesterfield.[97] Later that month he wrote to say he was suffering from an attack of pneumonia and would be unable to meet Mr. Bone, the backer of Tom Mitchell, but as soon as he felt better, he would be prepared to carry out the challenge issued on Bill Bennett's behalf.

After leaving the pub in 1913, the Addys went to live at Old Haywoods and later Townend before moving to Skelton Villas / Skelton Grove (Pot House Lane) where they opened a shop. The row of houses where they had the shop was known locally as Addy Row.

From 1913 until 1925, Samuel Ernest Moorhouse ran the Royal Oak with his wife Emily. Emily was the daughter of Joseph Newton of the Rising Sun on Hunshelf Bank. Samuel had been born in Derbyshire but was brought up in Florence Buildings. His father George was a coal miner, and his mother Sarah was a grocer (unusually, the 1881 census recorded George's wife's occupation). After she was widowed, Sarah moved the family to Old Haywoods, and in 1891 she was recorded as a draper. Sam and Emily married in 1905 and lived at Old Haywoods with the widowed Sarah, Sam being employed as a banksman in the clay mine at a brick works. Joseph Newton died in 1911, and Emily inherited some money – perhaps they used

---

[95] An ostler looked after the horses
[96] Alternate spellings checked.
[97] 15 or 20 three-minute rounds, for £25 (open to £50) a-side, at 9 stone, weigh-in at two o'clock on the day of boxing. The challenge is also open to any 9 stone man in the North or Midlands. Joe Starmer, of Kettering, preferred.

this to set up at the Royal Oak. After leaving the Oak, they went to live at Prospect Cottages, next to the Rising Sun.[98]

In May 1914, Sheffield magistrates granted permission for structural alterations to be made at the Royal Oak, although what these consisted of was not mentioned. The Licensing Act of 1902 had given the magistrates power over structural alterations, and permission had to be sought from them before anything was changed. This allowed them to keep control over such matters as multiple and side entrances to pubs, and compartments and snugs within them. All these things made police supervision more difficult, and they were seen as encouraging excessive or secretive drinking, particularly by women.

MORE AUCTIONS
- 1915: valuable freehold property at Deepcar which included the row of shops opposite the King and Miller which were being used as a grocer's shop, blacksmith's shop (being used as a store-room), wheelwright's shop, stables, sheds, and conveniences, as well as some vacant land adjoining the site which fronted the main road and Carr Lane [Road]. There were being rented out to Messrs. Bramwell, Elson, Rushton, and others. There was room for the erection of additional shops or houses.
- 1915: Two stone-built houses in Ash Lane, Deepcar, tenanted by Mr. Tingle and Mr. Firth.
- 1920: Three stone-built houses known as Woodland View, Manchester Road, Deepcar, belonging to the late David Brearley. The tenants were Jane Hartley, Frederick Walton, and Benjamin Hoyle.

MINE DEPUTY ASSAULTED: 1923
Henry Ibbotson, a Deepcar miner, was fined forty shillings for assaulting a mine deputy called Thomas Dickinson one Saturday night. Dickinson was

---

[98] The Electoral Registers for 1919 through to 1925 list Samuel Ernest and "*Lydia*" Moorhouse. The only record of a Lydia Moorhouse living locally was born at Holmfirth and was married to Walter Edwin, born Hepworth; this was probably an initial error in compiling the register that was perpetuated. In 1926, a new entry was required when they moved, and this time his wife's name was correctly recorded as Emily.

drinking in the Royal Oak when some trouble arose, and he was knocked off his stool by Ibbotson. The men had *"had a few words"* down the mine the previous Tuesday; the next morning Ibbotson's lamp was stopped [taken away],[99] and he had told Dickinson, *"We will settle this job at the week-end."* And indeed he did – gaining a fine in the process.

Moorhouse left the pub in 1925 and the licence was transferred to Thomas (Tommy) Hughes, who had the large grocer's shop on the corner of Carr Road and Manchester Road. The Hughes family later lived at the house called Imbros, on the Bitholmes. Tommy Hughes had the pub for about five years before John (Jack) Schofield came across the road from the Travellers Inn at the top of Vaughton Hill when it closed its doors in January 1932.

Jack had been born in 1884, the son of Friend Schofield, who was a *"timber leader"* (carter) by trade. Jack followed his father into the business, which he worked at until becoming a pub landlord. He was at the Travellers from about 1926 until 1932 when he took on the Royal Oak. He had married Josephine Bodsworth in 1907 and they lived at Mangle Row. Josephine was the daughter of Harry Bodsworth, a local carrier. Jack Branston tells the story that Harry had a shop and used to go to Sheffield with his pony and dray to fetch his greengrocery from the wholesale market. As public houses back then were open from 5.30am, Harry was often drunk before most people were up in the morning. This happened so often that his pony seemed to sense he was asleep and used to make its own way back to Stocksbridge with its sleeping passenger, right up to the shop door.[100]

---

[99] Stopping a miner's lamp was a serious matter; it meant he could not work, and therefore he could not earn. Miners hired their Davey safety lamps from the company, and collected them at the beginning of their shift, hanging a *"lamp check"* in its place on the hook. This was a small round brass token with the colliery name and a miner's number on. It was a method of knowing who was underground. If the lamp was withheld, he could not work, because no other sort of illumination would be safe. In *"The Road to Wigan Pier,"* published in 1937, George Orwell describes a typical miner's payslip, where one of the deductions was *"hire of lamp."*

[100] Branston, J. The History of Stocksbridge p. 136. It was probably only the town pubs near the markets which opened at this hour, though I have heard that some of the local pubs were open early for the steelworkers coming off the night shift.

The Royal Oak still had entertainment; in 1934 they advertised for a lady pianist to play on Saturday evenings. Prospective pianists were to write, stating their terms.

CAR HITS POLE. ESCAPE FOR DEEPCAR PARTY: 1935
Jack Schofield, his daughter Doris, her husband Frank Hough, and Doris's 4-year-old daughter Dorothy Day, were involved in a car accident at Wiseton, near Gringley-on-the-Hill, Lincolnshire, whilst they were en route to Cleethorpes. They were following a coach when suddenly, on a bend, the coach swerved to the right to avoid a stationary vehicle. This caused Mr. Schofield's car to also swerve, and it hit a telegraph pole. His daughter was hit on the head, which caused some severe bruising, but apart from suffering from shock, everyone was uninjured.

John and Josephine were still at the Royal Oak when the 1939 Register was taken; his occupation was given as *"Hotel Proprietor,"* but he was also a special constable, probably for the duration of the war.

And here we leave the Royal Oak. It is still a pub today, somewhat larger than it was, the adjoining shop having been knocked through to create a bigger interior. The shop on the other side is long gone, but Benjamin Couldwell's house, Rock View, still stands behind the pub, and the three terraced houses that he owned at the bottom of Carr Road are also still there. Mangle Row has been demolished.

THE KING AND MILLER, MANCHESTER ROAD, DEEPCAR

The King and Miller, Deepcar c1910 when George Allen was the landlord. The sign is advertising Don Ales from the Don Brewery near Kelham Island, Sheffield (taken over by Tennant Brothers in 1916). This pub was one of the stopping-off points for the stagecoaches on their way from Sheffield to Manchester after the turnpike road (now Manchester Road) was opened in 1806. The old cottage to the left of the pub was said to have been used as a stable for a bear, which was taken around the district for entertainment purposes. There are rumours that, on occasion, prisoners who were being taken to York or Leeds were kept locked overnight in one of the cellars beneath this pub.

The King & Miller at Deepcar is an old inn dating back to at least 1802, way before a road was constructed along the valley floor between Deepcar and Langsett. When Lord Melbourne's Manor of Bolsterstone was put up for sale by auction in that year, the list of tenants included a miller called Thomas Grayson, who, in addition to the corn mill at Deepcar, also had, *"a dwelling house, used as a public house with brew-house and stable disjoined"* [not attached to the house][101] The stables were opposite the pub, on some waste or common ground, as was a blacksmith's smithy. The corn mill was situated behind the King and Miller, on the banks of the Little Don or Porter River.

TRAVELLING BEARS

Bear-baiting for *"entertainment"* purposes had been a popular pastime in England for hundreds of years, along with bull-baiting, dog-fights, and cock-fights. According to local historian Joseph Kenworthy, bears were baited at Deepcar in a field at Carr Head, and in a field opposite Blacking Mill Row. It is not known when this barbaric practice ended locally, but the Penistone Church Wardens' accounts for 1815 recorded that 4s. 10d. was spent in preventing bear-baiting at Thurlstone. Jack Branston, in his book the History of Stocksbridge, said the bull- and bear-baiting also took place at Bolsterstone in a disused quarry, where the National School was built (now the village hall)

According to an article in the Barnsley Chronicle[102], Barnsley was the last town in England to keep a living bear to bait; however the following week a letter was published which said that this was not true; the folk of Barnsley did not keep a bear, at public expense; rather the bears were brought into the town by their owners, who travelled with them. Bulls however were kept by men of the town for baiting. There was a *"bull stoop"* at May Day Green in Barnsley consisting of the root and a few feet of a tree, with a hole in the upper part through which the end of a rope was knotted. The other end, which was about 15' long, was tied around the neck of the animal. Men would converge on the ground with dogs and set them on the bull or the bear.

---

[101] Kenworthy, Joseph. The Early History of Stocksbridge and District, Handbook 15: Bolsterstone. Published by the author in 1915
[102] 20th March 1875

In 1783, a group of Barnsley men signed their names to a document in which they set out their objections against the practice in which, "*Inn-Keepers & private persons in the Township of Barnsley ... hire and bate Bulls and Bears.*" They decried the cruelty and declared that they would report and proceed to prosecute anyone found to be leading, tying up, or exposing any animal to baiting, including bears or bulls.[103] The practice continued however, and in 1858 Rowland Jackson noted that baiting had carried on for many years after these objections. He reported that bull- and bear-baitings had taken place on May Day Green, Barnsley, within living memory, and that no one dared to attempt to put a stop to them until one day a man called James Cocker went into the midst of the crowd that had gathered to see the baiting and inquired as to who owned the bear. When no one answered, he took out a pistol and threatened to shoot the animal (a small black bear), whereupon the bear's owner stepped forward, begged him not to shoot, and said that he would take it away and never use him in Barnsley again. Apparently, there were no more baitings on May Day Green.[104]

A man named William Cooper of High Green kept a bear called Boath, and one day it escaped, with tragic consequences. In December 1790 this bear, which was kept *"for the amusement of the country people at their wakes,"* got loose and entered the house of Francis Rodger, attacking his wife, who was sitting with her two children. Hearing the screams, her husband and Cooper ran to help. Cooper hit the bear with a hammer, but it broke, and the bear then turned on him. He ran for his life until one of the neighbours shot the animal. The poor woman died two days later. The Sheffield Register gave its opinion that *"we hope and trust this dreadful and unparalleled accident will finally abolish, in these parts, that unchristian, barbarous species of diversion – bear-baiting!"*[105]

The Sheffield bearward [bear warden] at one time was a man called James Lansley (alias James Runcorn). He bought one of his bears from a man called Hardisty. John Widdop, writing in the Barnsley Chronicle, recalled that he once saw old Hardisty walking up the Sheffield road with a bear walking

---

[103] Cites in the Barnsley Chronicle 20th March 1875
[104] Jackson, R. The History of the Town and Township of Barnsley. London: 1858. p.126
[105] Information from The Sheffield Register, 17th December 1790; Lister, Septimus. An Old Ecclesfield Diary. J.W. Northend: 1921 and the Ecclesfield parish register. The surname is given variously as Rogers, Rodgers and Rodger, and the woman's name as Sarah or Mary.

behind him on its hind legs, with each forepaw resting on its master's shoulders.

Runcorn and his bear would travel around the countryside visiting feasts and fairs ("*wakes*"). Runcorn would sometimes get drunk and fall asleep on the road, and the bear would then take himself off to his previous owner's house in Barnsley. He would arrive in the middle of the night and make his presence known, and Hardisty would hear him and let him in until Runcorn arrived the next day to collect him. "*Many times have the stage wagonners been startled on their night journey on meeting* 'Ned,' *as he was called, trudging on the road, but he always passed them quietly,*" said Widdop. He added that Runcorn and his bear were far better known in Barnsley than the inside of St. Mary's church! The inevitable happened one day in May 1824; Runcorn went to fetch Ned from his field at Sheffield Park, and the bear, who was not muzzled, suddenly attacked him, and wounded him so severely that he died a few days later.

It seems highly likely that this man and his bear visited Deepcar as well as Penistone and Barnsley, spending the odd night bedded down in the King and Miller. A travelling bear was also lodged on occasion in outbuildings behind the Sportsman's Arms at Old Haywards.

RAISING THE DEVIL
A man who went by the name of "*Finney Shay*" was in the King and Miller one night and he offer to raise the "*Evil One*" [the devil]. The landlady at the time was Mally Grayson. Shay then began chanting weird incantations, and a black, unearthly face was seen to be slowly lifting up the grate of a large fireplace in response. The whole of the large company who were there jumped up and "*fled in wild disorder*" ... all except the wizard, who, along with one James Ridal and the village chimney sweep, their partner in crime, remained behind to drink the ale that had survived the general overthrow of chairs and crocks![106]

---

[106] As told by Jack Branston in The History of Stocksbridge. He said her name was Molly, buy it seems to have been Mally. Both are pet names for Mary. In his book The History of Penistone, published in 1906, John Dransfield refers to Mally Grayson of the King and Miller keeping a hunting hound called Jinker at the beginning of the previous century [1800s]. Joseph Kenworthy also mentions a Mally Grayson.

A NEW ROAD ALONG THE VALLEY BOTTOM

Deepcar – or Deep Carr [meaning Deep Swamp] was an ancient settlement, and the remains of a Mesolithic settlement have been found close by. The town of Stocksbridge did not exist as even a village until the arrival of Samuel Fox in the 1840s, who founded a wire drawing business there; it was just a scattering of farms and homesteads. There was no direct route along the valley floor from Deepcar to Stocksbridge and beyond until one was built following the passing of the Turnpike Act in 1805. Travellers would have had to go over Hunshelf Bank. What we now know as Manchester Road opened to traffic in 1806, joining up with an existing road to Manchester at the Flouch. Turnpike roads usually followed existing trackways, but this road was unusual in that it was built where there was no previous route. The King and Miller became a coaching inn to service the coaches that used this new road.

The new road was mentioned by Joseph Hunter in his History of Hallamshire.[107] He wrote that *"A new road from Sheffield to Manchester which follows the course of the Don for many miles in this chapelry is singularly picturesque and romantic. It penetrates into Lancashire by the pass at Woodhead."*

Fees were collected along the route at toll bars; there was one at the crossroads at the top of Vaughton Hill and one at Unsliven Bridge. These were chain bars; those at Midhope, Middlewood and Oughtibridge were gates. Joseph Kenworthy wrote that the toll bar was spoken of as the chain bar. The tolls helped to pay for the upkeep of the road, often using labour obtained from able-bodied men who were claiming poor relief or dole from the parish they lived in. There is still a toll bar cottage at Deepcar, where the toll bar keeper lived. He would keep a chain across the road, which barred access to horses, carts, and cattle until a fee was paid. These tolls included 3d. for a horse-drawn carriage, 1d. for a horse, ½d. for a bull or cow, ¼d. for a pig or sheep, and so on, although some loads were exempt. These particular toll bars were let by auction every year to the highest bidder. The successful bidder would make a fixed payment to the Turnpike Trustees for the lease,

---

[107] Hunter, Joseph. The History and Topography of the Parish of Sheffield. London: 1819. p268

then organise the daily collection of tolls, hopefully leaving themselves with a profit over the year.

Amusingly, it was noted that milk delivery boys could be a nuisance: *"Quantities of milk are conveyed to Sheffield and elsewhere in barrels or tin cans upon horses, mules and asses generally conducted by boys; who after delivering the milk, indulge in races and make a great noise rattling the cans and barrels which annoys passengers along the roads. Accidents have already happened near Sheffield. For the easy detection of such nuisances, milk carriers must have the names of the owners fixed to the pack saddle or other conspicuous part in large legible letters – penalty for omission not to exceed 40/-. The same penalty for those who indulge in racing and committing a noise nuisance."*[108]

The King and Miller would have seen a big increase in traffic once the road was opened because this new route from Sheffield to Manchester passed right outside its door. In fact, this pub became one of the Stages, or stops, on the coach route to and from Manchester. Both people and horses needed regular stopping places, and coaching inns provided food, drink and lodging, as well as stables where staff would care for the horses - not only feeding and watering them but also changing a tired team for a fresh one. These were busy places and were used by private carriages, public stagecoaches (which ran to a timetable and ferried paying customers), and mail coaches.

Coaches drove to Manchester from Sheffield via Wadsley, Deepcar, Midhope, Langsett, Boardhill, Woodhead, Mottram, Stalybridge, and Ashton-under-Lyne. The Snake Pass route opened in 1821. In 1834 a new coach called *"The Regulator"* ran from Sheffield via Ashopton (the village which was demolished to make way for the Ladybower reservoir), Glossop, Stalybridge, and Ashton. In 1828 the Royal Mail coach ran from the Tontine Inn at Sheffield to Manchester *"on the new line of road"* through Deepcar every day at *"a quarter before two"* to the Royal and the Swan hotels.[109] When the King and Miller was put up for auction in 1836, the advertisement noted that *"The Mail [coach] and several other Coaches pass through Deep*

---

[108] This clause was included in the Sheffield-Halifax Road Act 23rd May 1817
[109] Blackwell's Sheffield Directory and Guide, published in 1828

Carr to Sheffield and Manchester every day." Some of the coaches changed horses at the Rose and Crown Inn at Midhope (now closed).

In 1831 the Sheffield Independent ran an advertisement for a *"New Coach to Manchester"* via Deepcar called *"The Railway."*[110] It left Sheffield from the Angel, Commercial, and Tontine Inns at 7am every day except Sunday and left Manchester every afternoon at 3pm - it took five hours - arriving back in Sheffield at 8pm. The Tontine Inn was one of the three main departure places in Sheffield for coaches that ran all over England. It was built in 1785 and was a very large concern, with stabling for sixty horses as well as its own brewery and accommodation for the footmen. It was demolished in 1851. Other departure points were the Angel at Snig Hill, the King's Head at Change Alley, the Commercial Inn at Haymarket, and the George Inn at Market Place.

The largest of the coaching inns on the major routes kept teams of horses in their stables, and both the stagecoaches and the mail coaches would stop at inns along the way to replace their tired horses with fresh ones. Each coaching inn was responsible for providing the horses over an agreed stage, which usually covered an area of ten to fifteen miles in each direction. This meant that the inns were quite regularly spaced, depending on the terrain.

One of the early landlords of the King and Miller was James Green. He was possibly married to Ann Grayson, and also worked as a miller.

TORMENTING STRANGERS: 1828
John Roebuck, William Roebuck, Samuel Firth, James Hague, and James Broadbent, who the Sheffield Independent newspaper described as *"five stout-working country men,"* were charged by Mr. Green with riotous conduct, and with breaking pots and glasses. The men were regulars in the King and Miller, where they felt confident in their united strength. They *"ruled the roost in great style, and had a voice in all things* 'double as the landlord's,' *and* 'more potential' *than his wife's."* Should a traveller, or a man from the next village or town sit down in their company, they would always bother and harass them. The newspaper reported on their conversation as being something like this:

---

[110] Sheffield Independent, 6th August 1831

"I say Bill, dost know un?"
"Non, dost thee Sam?"
"Nay, not I!"
"Well then," says Bill, *" --- un let's have some sturrings."*

The unfortunate man's hat would be tossed onto the fire, his tobacco-pipe broken, his beer drank off, and, if he was really unlucky, he might receive a punch as well. The men were ordered to pay the landlord eighteen shillings to replace the broken items or be committed to the Sessions, where the more serious charges were heard.

In 1829 Green transferred the licence to Thomas Hague or Haigh, a farmer from Roughbirchworth. The document which Green signed on the 16th July 1829 signalling his intention to transfer the licence is the first evidence I have found for the pub being called the King and Miller. For some reason, in about 1835 Hague transferred the licence to Charles Stones for a few years, before returning in 1837, staying until 1842.

The Graysons had been tenants of the Lord of the Manor, Lord Melbourne. When he put his Bolsterstone estates (which included Deepcar) up for sale in 1802, Thomas Grayson was renting a house (the one used as a public house) with a brew-house and stable, a water-powered corn mill with grinding stones, an oat kiln (for drying), outbuildings and land, all of which covered just over eighteen acres. The whole of Lord Melbourne's estate was bought by John Rimington Esquire, of Hillsborough and Sheffield, an attorney and banker, for £35,000. According to Joseph Kenworthy (citing *"an old tradition"*), Mr. Rimington found it necessary to re-sell some portion of the estate to enable him to complete the purchase. To do this, he expressed his willingness to meet any tenant who would like to buy his or her holding and talk the matter over with them, with the result that many of Lord Melbourne's tenants became their own landlord. This seems to be when the Graysons acquired the mill and the King and Miller.[111]

---

[111] Cited in Kenworthy, Joseph. The Early History of Stocksbridge and District, Handbook 15, Bolsterstone. published by the author in 1915. In Handbook 4, Kenworthy mentions that an Abraham Grayson recorded that he bought some land from Mr. Rimington in 1803, who had purchased them from Lord Melbourne a few months before. Page 17

In October 1836, the King and Miller was put up for sale. It formed part of the estate of the late Ellis Grayson.[112] Lot 1 included the corn mill, which was being tenanted by William Scholey, and a wire mill, occupied by William Beet, as well as the mill dam, goit, and some land. The King and Miller public house, stable, outbuildings, and garden were for sale as Lot 2, tenanted by the landlord Charles Stones. This lot also included two cottages adjoining the pub, occupied by Charles Stones and Thomas Bramall, and came with just over five acres of land. Lot 3 was "*excellent garden ground*" at Cinder Hill, which was being rented out to James Vaughton. In addition, there were four more lots of land available (all occupied by Thomas Bramall). These were Hay Woods or Ewes Wood (formerly one large field but now divided by the turnpike road), Hood Royd Green and Clough (containing a bed of coal), Clough (or Triangle), and Clough and Plantation (which included a coal pit).

Some, if not all of this, seems to have been bought by Windle and Surtees.[113]

Hague was back as the licensee by September 1837, and John Stones moved away to run a public house at Silkstone. When the 1841 census was taken, Thomas and his wife Ellen were in residence, along with a servant girl and two men who could have been lodgers (a wire drawer called John Beet and a saddler called Thomas Sutliffe). There was also a couple called Kerton - Edmund Kerton's occupation was recorded as "*traveller*" (which could mean a travelling salesman, or that they were en route somewhere else). Hague left in 1842 and took a pub at Ingbirchworth before taking over from Willie Jubb at the Coach and Horses, Stocksbridge in 1845. He died in June 1846.

In April 1842, the new landlord of the King and Miller was John Dixon of Sheffield, who was the driver of the Manchester stagecoach. Passing through Deepcar twice a day, he must have seen an opportunity to make good money

---

[112] This could have been Elias, born 1777, the eldest son of former landlord Thomas Grayson.
[113] Bradfield Archives have land tax records which mention these two men (Abraham Windle and Richard Surtees) as Proprietors, with tenants. For example, in 1841 the census records Thomas Hague as the pub landlord, and the land tax records for this year list him as one of the tenants of Windle and Surtees, for a house and land. The partnership was dissolved in 1847.

by taking on the tenancy of the (presumably busy) King and Miller, which was a scheduled stop on the route.

Dixon had been born in Bawtry at the turn of the century, and when he married Sarah Pybourne in 1825, he was making a living as a horse dealer. At some point he moved to Sheffield, where he entered into a partnership with a Mr. Bradley as joint owner of a coach called the *"Tantivy,"* which he also drove, and each of them supplied the horses for part of the route. Dixon left the partnership in about 1839, and an advert for a new coach called the *"Champion"* in May of that year said that it was driven by *"John Dixon, late Coachman of the Tantivy, with which Coach he has now no connection."* Mr. Bradley ceased to be concerned with the coach in 1841.

The fare at this time was ten shillings to sit inside, and six shillings to sit outside; it would have been cold and uncomfortable going over the bleak high moors at certain times of the year, especially as the journey took five hours. In 1812 there was a report in the newspapers that when the Bath coach reached Chippenham one bitterly cold morning in March, two of its outside passengers were found frozen to death, and a third was near death.

"Some of the coaches changed horses at the "Rose and Crown" Inn, at Midhope, and several people were living until quite recently, who vividly remembered the discomforts endured in travelling over the high moors during the storms of winter. Old Phoebe Winterbottom, of Midhope, could well remember how interested young and old were in watching the coaches come and go. To see the passengers alight to partake of refreshments whilst the horses were changed, and hear the cracking of whips and the merry sounds of tooting horns and prancing hoofs, was a picture of the good times, not soon forgotten."[114]

Phoebe Winterbottom (nee Grayson) had lived at the Pot Houses on Mortimer Road at Midhopestones, just across the road from the Rose and Crown. She died in 1902 aged 80. John Holling, who was born in 1901, wrote that he recalled stagecoaches coming through the village, but he could only remember two occasions, and both times the post horns were sounded.

---

[114] Joseph Kenworthy, writing in the Stocksbridge Almanac 1908.

The people inside threw copper coins to the lads running after them in the road.[115]

Going way back to around 1807, the Sheffield Weekly Independent of 1887 was printing various stories about the Sheffield of eighty years ago, drawing on interviews made with a Mr. James Bussey.

"There are lights [...] in the dark archway of the Tontine, and an occasional ring of harness is heard. The ostlers are there with a fresh relay of horses waiting for the arrival of the midnight mail from the north. At length a horn is sounded in the distance, at which Constable Flathers hurries down to hear the news from his friend the coachman, and in another minute, with a rumble of wheels, a crash of harness, and a clatter of horses feet, the coach drives up. Five minutes of busy confusion follow, during which the fresh horses are put in and the passengers crowd round the blazing fire in the bar of the Tontine, and then the voice of the guard is heard calling out, "all on," and with a great cracking of whips and a blast of the horn, which causes uneasy sleepers to turn over in their beds, with an anathema on the coach and all its belongings, they are off again round the low side of the Market, up past the King's Head, round into High street, and away in the direction of Pinstone street. There are still lights in the Tontine yard, where the ostlers are wiping down and stabling the horses which have done the last stage, and Constable Flathers has gone into the bar with a passenger who has arrived by the coach, but the market square is deserted, and the silence of the late bustle and excitement is oppressive."

---

[115] The Memoires of John Holling (MSS, Stocksbridge & District History Society) written in 1959/60. John was born in 1901 at Deepcar.

Drawing of the Tontine Inn, Haymarket, by W. F. Northend dated 1941. Image reproduced by kind permission of Sheffield Local Studies Library www.picturesheffield.com

In 1842 Dixon was again driving the Tantivy, which he and a new partner, a Mr. Barraclough, had taken over from Bradley. An advert in February of this year said that it was the *"only Direct Coach from Sheffield to Manchester."* It wasn't long after this, in March, that Dixon was fined twenty five shillings for overloading the coach; a man named Tinker alleged that, at Deepcar, the coach had more people on the outside than it was licensed to carry. Most of the passengers were a contingent of butchers from Manchester. Running a coaching company incurred a lot of expense, what with the registration fee, toll bar fees, taxes, the cost of feeding and caring for the horses, as well as the wages of those employed at the inn and the stables. It was quite common for the coachman to take on board more passengers than was allowed, to try and increase revenue, and newspapers often carried stories about overloaded coaches being involved in accidents where people were seriously injured or killed.

As mentioned previously, the King and Miller at Deepcar was one of the stopping points or "*Stages*" for the Sheffield to Manchester coaches. The distance covered was forty miles, and the journey was divided into six stages. At each stage, the coach would stop so that the horses could be changed for fresh ones. Dixon and his partner Barraclough each had three stages for which they supplied the horses. Interestingly, the eight-mile stage between Deepcar and Sheffield was regarded as actually being nine miles, on account of it being "*a bad road.*"

In June 1842 Barraclough added another partner to this enterprise, John Wing, selling him one of his "*stages,*" the final one from Ashton to Manchester, and four horses. Wing was the landlord of a pub in Ashton-under-Lyne. Every month the three partners sent all their receipts and costs to a fourth man named Fletcher, who then made up the accounts and sent a statement to the others letting them know the amounts they were either to receive or pay, the profits being divided among them according to the number of miles they horsed. This relationship soon soured though because in 1843 Dixon took Wing to court for a large amount of money owing to him, about £30.[116] The court found in favour of Dixon, and Wing had to pay him the money.

Three years later, Dixon was declared bankrupt. The opening of the Manchester, Sheffield and Lincolnshire railway in 1845 had quickly made coach travel unattractive, and there would have been a fall in coach trade as people opted to use the quicker and more comfortable railway instead, although coach travel was by no means at an end.[117] Dixon transferred the pub licence to a farmer and miller called Thomas Peace, but he and his wife Sarah continued to live at the King and Miller during the bankruptcy proceedings, Sarah being employed there at seven shillings a week.

An advertisement was placed in the newspaper that Dixon's possessions were to be auctioned off at the King and Miller on Wednesday 27th August 1845.

---

[116] The Law Times Vol. 1 (1843) p. 648, reports this amount as £45 (£30 is worth approximately £3,840 today, and £45 is worth about £5,760 according to the Bank of England's Inflation Calculator).

[117] As an example, in 1829, the year before the Liverpool and Manchester Railway opened, the Warrington and Lower Irlam Trust had receipts of £1,680 but by 1834 this had fallen to £332, a huge drop.

Items for sale included brewing vessels (which indicates that the landlords probably still brewed their own beer), household furniture, a horse, hay and manure, wood, and some crops in the field including corn, grass, and clover. However, when the bailiffs were sent in to seize Dixon's goods, they were ejected from the premises by two of Mr. Peace's men, Charles Wimpenny and John Hutchinson.

The case came to court, and Peace testified that he was now the tenant of the inn, not Dixon, and that everything in it was now his; he had taken the King and Miller on the 5th January 1845 and bought all the stock from Dixon, paying him £260. He produced the licence transfer document, dated February, and a receipt for six months' rent to prove his case. The prosecution tried to prove that Dixon and his wife were carrying on running the pub just as they always had done, and they wanted to lay a charge of common assault for the eviction of the bailiffs. Peace said that Dixon had no property at the premises and no authority. Peace did not live on the premises himself, but had put a man called William Fletcher in charge, and he visited the pub in person three to five times a week. In the end, the magistrates dismissed the case.

The bankruptcy process dragged on for over a year, with disputes about balance sheets, requests for adjournments, and excuses. Dixon had income from his coach earnings and expenses for the horses, but he could neither explain how he had earned the money nor provide receipts for his expenses. The Commissioner said that he had, *"scarce ever met with a man more obstinate in this respect"* than Dixon, and he was finally threatened with being sent to the jail at York Castle. As there is no further mention of this case in the newspapers, he must have finally submitted satisfactory accounts and escaped being sent to jail. Dixon stayed on at the King and Miller for a year or so, before moving away to Derbyshire, where he carried on driving coaches.

Jack Branston[118] wrote that Dixon lived at Midhope, next to the Post Office, though I have found no evidence of this. He also noted that he used to carry

---

[118] Jack Branston, The History of Stocksbridge

a shotgun by his side whilst driving.[119] It was certainly common for mail coach drivers to carry pistols and blunderbusses, but according to David Mountfield,[120] the mail coach guards used their firearms more often against rabbits or pheasants, or even stray chickens, than against highwaymen! After Dixon had moved away, there was a piece of local poetry that went:

> *"John Dixon the coachman,*
> *No more will be seen,*
> *Travelling from Sheffield,*
> *To Fiddler's Green"*[121]

Instead, John Dixon could be found living in a place called Stone Bench in Fairfield, Derbyshire, and driving coaches between Buxton and Sheffield. In 1841 he drove a new coach called the Defiance, which set off from the Commercial Inn, Old Haymarket, Sheffield twice a day, morning and afternoon (except Sundays), setting off after the arrival of various trains in Sheffield, including the Penistone train. In 1851 this coach was running reduced fares to Buxton of 2s. 6d. outside, or 5s. inside. He later drove a coach called the Enterprise. He died on the 30th October 1857 aged 58 – not a great age, but he was affectionately known to many as *"Old John."* The Buxton Advertiser printed an obituary, noting that he *"kept possession of the "ribbons" [reins] so long as he could, longer, in fact, than he ought."* Under a rough exterior, *"Old John"* apparently carried a tender heart, and the newspaper printed a story about him from a year or two previously. It was a sleety, drizzling, snowy day when John overtook a poor woman and several children tramping across Sheffield Moor. He pulled up and found out that they were headed for Bakewell. Having no *"insides,"* [inside passengers] he dismounted, lifted the children into the coach, then helped their mother into the coach as well, *"as tenderly as he would a lady,"* carrying them all to

---

[119] Branston wrote that John Dixon was the grandfather of William Dixon, who had, at the time of writing, in the 1980s, just retired from the Traffic Department at Fox's. Extensive research has not proved this link, unless Branston was writing about a totally unrelated John Dixon. John Dixon the coach driver / landlord of the King and Miller had been living at Castle Folds, Sheffield, in 1841, and was working as a coachman. He was the landlord of the King and Miller from 1842-1845, and he carried on living there for a year or so after being made bankrupt, but he had moved to Derbyshire by 1851. His family all stayed in Sheffield.

[120] Mountfield, David. Stage and Mail Coaches. Shire Publications: 2003

[121] Fiddler's Green is at Salter's Brook. There was a pub here.

Bakewell, where they were deposited, warm, dry, and overflowing with thanks. *"Poor things! poor things!"* said Old John, *"they'd ha'been starved t'deeth! and I shall be none the poorer."*[122]

A STOLEN WATCH: 1845

One Monday evening in 1845, a 23-year-old navvy called Henry Slater (nicknamed *"Bilper"*) was arrested in the King and Miller for attempting to sell a stolen silver pocket watch belonging to Jonathan Crabtree of Thurgoland. After leaving the Rock Inn at Green Moor one night, Crabtree fell asleep in a wood, and when he woke up, he found that his watch had gone, as well as thirty shillings. Several witnesses were called to give evidence that they had seen Slater trying to sell the watch, which he still had in his possession when he was arrested. He was charged with *"highway robbery"* and committed to be tried at the Sessions, where he was found guilty and sent to jail for three months.

After two years, Peace decided to leave, and in June 1847 he signed a document to say he intended to transfer the licence to John Surtees, who was the nephew of the joint owner of the pub, Richard Surtees, at the next Special Sessions in August;[123] Surtees and Windle advertised the pub as being available to let in July that year.

The King & Miller Public-House, Deepcar, near Wortley.
To be Let, the above well-accustomed public house, with about 10 Acres of excellent land. It is exceedingly low Rented, and the Rates and Taxes are very moderate. The Furniture to be taken to at a fair Valuation. It has extensive accommodation, and in a good district for business.
Apply to Mr. Nicholson, Auctioneer and Valuer, Sheffield; or Messrs. Surtees and Windle, Deepcar Mills; or on the Premises.[124]

John Surtees had been born at Wortley. In 1841 he was staying in a pub in Hull run by Isaac Sedgewick. His occupation was recorded as *"Ag"* [agricultural labourer], though he was a woodsman by trade. Amongst the household staff was a servant called Sarah Smith. In 1842, John married

---

[122] Starved to death is Yorkshire dialect for frozen.
[123] The Special Sessions were held in order to allow transfers to take place outside of the General Licensing Sessions.
[124] Sheffield Independent: 10th July 1847

Sarah, whose father was an innkeeper. It was a short-lived marriage however because in August 1847, during a visit to her uncle who lived near Barnsley, Sarah suddenly died; she was only 23 years old. The day after her death, John instructed an auctioneer to sell all his furniture, brewing gear, and farming tools. An advertisement in the newspaper said the sale would take place on the 16th August at the house [public house] of Mr. John Surtees *"who is leaving the premises."*

When the Special Sessions were held in August 1847, Thomas Peace transferred the licence not to John Surtees, as originally intended, but to George Grayson, a coke merchant. Grayson took on the pub and also farmed nineteen acres of land. He had his licence suspended for two weeks in 1850 because of a complaint made against him, but there was no report as to what the complaint was.

George died at the King and Miller in 1852 when he was only 45 years old, leaving a widow Ann and several children. Six months later, in August that year, a document was supposedly signed by George, signalling his intention to transfer the licence to Nathaniel Corbett of Wortley in September! The probable explanation was that he had signed it, leaving it undated - as was common practice - and when he died the document was used anyway.

Nathaniel was married to Jane Marsden. Jane was an interesting woman. Born in Nottinghamshire in about 1813, she was the daughter of William Spafford, a farmer. She had already been widowed twice by the time she married Nathaniel, who was ten years her junior. She had married her first husband Joseph Eaton in 1837, and he died in 1839 aged 30. The following year she married Jonathan Marsden, who was a butcher before they took on a pub at Finkle Street, Wortley. He died aged 32 in 1843. She married Nathaniel Corbett in 1848, and he died in 1853 aged just 28, a year after moving into the King and Miller. Jane took over the licence for two years after his death until a new tenant was sought in August 1855. Jane married for a fourth time in October that year. She later married a fifth husband.

Now with slightly less land, just over five acres, the pub was available to let with immediate possession. Jane instructed auctioneers to sell her some of her furniture, as well as some animals and farming implements, so we can see that farming was still being carried on at the King and Miller alongside innkeeping. She was selling:

"Eight Mahogany Hair-seated Chairs and one Armed Chair, Mahogany Sofa, Mahogany Spring Table, two Oak Dining Tables, old Piano, Bagatelle Table, three Windsor Chairs, five Elm Chairs, two Round Tables, Pictures, Brass Fender, Fire Irons, 30-hours' Clock, in Oak Case; two Four-post Bedsteads, Camp, short Post and Press Bedsteads, Feather and Flock Beds, Mattresses, Pillows, Quilts, Sheets, Blankets, Oak Desk, Book Case and Drawers, Painted Drawers, Carpeting, Night Chair, Dressing Tables and Glasses, Chimney Ornaments, ten Forms, three Langsettles[125], two Club Room Tables, Fenders and Fire Irons, twelve sundry Chairs, six Square Tables, Kitchen Dresser, Langsettle, two Cupboards, three Clothes Boxes, Spittoons, seven Pairs of Quoits, Candlesticks, Knives and Forks, Kettles, Saucepans, Earthenware, Glasses, Pitchers, Plated Pints, &c.
Two Beasts, namely, Red Milch Cow, barren; Roan Yearling Heifer, Straw Cutter, Rakes and Forks, &c. Also, two Closes of Mowing Grass, standing."

Jane married her fourth husband, Joseph Shaw of Poggs Farm, Wigtwizzle, at St. George's Church, Sheffield, in October 1855.[126] Shaw was on bail awaiting trial for killing George Staniforth during a fight at the Broomhead Mill Inn at Wigtwizzle the previous month. The men had dogs with them which were fighting, and this caused a disagreement. Staniforth had hit Shaw first, and Shaw retaliated, landing Staniforth a blow to the head which killed him. Shaw appeared for trial at York in December 1855, two months after his marriage to Jane. The Judge said that, in his opinion, Shaw had not actually been guilty of an offence; *"If a man received such a blow as the deceased first gave the prisoner, and the prisoner returned the blow with anything that might be in his way, and death ensued, it was, he would not say a justifiable, but an excusable act."* The Jury consequently found Shaw not

---

[125] A long bench, usually with a high back and arms at each end
[126] The Sheffield Independent, Saturday 3rd February 1855, printed a notice of a marriage at Cromwell, Nottinghamshire, on Wednesday, between Mr. Joseph Shaw, farmer, Poggs, to Mrs. Corbett, of the King and Miller Inn, Deepcar, widow of the late Mr. Nathaniel Corbett. Cromwell was about 9 miles from where Jane was born (Stoke, Nottingham). The couple must have intended to marry at that time but did not.

guilty and he was discharged.[127] Jane would return to the King and Miller a few years later, along with her husband Joseph.

Following Jane's departure, the next tenant was Thomas Dukes, a wheelwright and carpenter, but he only stayed for three years. He had been born in Shireoaks, Nottinghamshire in about 1810 and was married to Ann. They had moved to Deepcar in the 1830s.

A ROBBERY: 1856
In October 1856 Thomas Dukes and his wife were robbed by three Sheffield men who had lodged overnight. The men – brothers Samuel and William Knight, and Thomas Brown – had asked for lodgings for the night, saying that they had come from Sheffield to see their father-in-law at Deepcar, and were too late for the train that night. They had all slept in one room, along with four other men, and in the morning one of the Knights paid Mrs. Dukes 9d. for the lodging, and they left without eating breakfast. Mrs. Dukes then went upstairs and noticed that her bedroom door and a desk had been forced open, and quite a lot of money - £25 - was missing, including a five-pound note and some sovereigns. The other four men had left at 5am, so they could not have been the thieves, because Mrs. Dukes was still in her room at that time. She sent for her husband, who was on the farm, and he, along with the local blacksmith Aaron Sanderson, set off in pursuit of the men, armed with pitchforks. They caught up with the Knights near Worral, about five miles away, and took them to the house of the Oughtibridge constable, George Stephenson. Brown had split from them, choosing to avoid the turnpike road, and he made his way back to Sheffield by a different route. He was later apprehended in Sheffield on a separate charge of stealing from his employer. The missing money was never found. The Knights were "*remanded at large*"[128] and Brown was committed to the Sessions for the robbery against his employer; he was later sentenced to 4 months' imprisonment.

In January 1858 Thomas Dukes sold his household furniture and items from the pub, along with about 6 tons of hay, and went to live at Grove Row, Old

---

[127] For full details, see the chapter on the Broomhead Mill Inn
[128] Basically, they were free to go. Remanded at large is the opposite of remanded in custody. The police could look for more evidence, but if they didn't, or time ran out, then no further action would be taken against the accused. Should new evidence come up, then the case could be re-opened.

Haywoods, Deepcar, working in his original trade of carpentry. The licence was then transferred to C. Ramsden[129] but in less than six months Nathaniel Corbett's widow Jane was back, along with her husband Joseph Shaw.

ANOTHER ROBBERY: 1858

In September 1858 George Firth, a labourer living on Hunshelf Bank, was charged with stealing some cigars and an ivory bagatelle ball from the King and Miller. Jane Shaw gave evidence that she and her husband were in the cellar kitchen when they heard footsteps in the bar upstairs. As they had left no one there, she hurried upstairs and found Firth in the bar. He had opened a drawer and had his hand in a cigar box. He saw her and left, heading along the passage towards the street. She got hold of him and challenged him, but as he was struggling to escape, she called her husband, who came and escorted Firth into the kitchen; he was holding a handful of cigars and the bagatelle ball. Because they knew Firth, they let him go, on condition that he pay for the cigars, which he had crushed and damaged. However, when he went back to the pub the next night, he refused to pay for the cigars, and the police were called. In court, the Shaws were told they should not have let the man go free after they had caught him but should have called the police; Firth was remanded at large.

When the 1861 census was taken, Joseph Shaw was at the pub along with Jane's son Frederick Marsden, a visitor, two servants, and four lodgers. His wife was visiting her Spafford relations in Lincolnshire. At the end of January 1864, Joseph Shaw announced he was leaving the pub and instructed a firm of auctioneers to sell off a lot of his possessions. Up for sale were the following household goods and farming implements:

"Mahogany Hair-seated Sofa, six Mahogany Hair-seated Chairs, Brussels Carpet, Piano-forte, Eight-days' Spring Timepiece, Mahogany Sofa, in Black Merino; six Rush-seated Elm Chairs, Mahogany Stand, Eight-days' Clock, in Oak Case; Brass-mounted Fender, Fire Irons, Weather Glass, Oak Spring Table, Oak Chest of Drawers, four Sets of Camp and Four-post Bedsteads, Mattress, Hangings, Feather and Flock Beds, Pillows, and Bolsters; Wash

---

[129] C. Ramsden seems to have only been landlord for a few months, from February 1858 to September at the latest. He was possibly Charles Ramsden, a wheelwright and joiner who lived at Smithy Moor.

and Dressing Tables, Bedroom Carpets, Towel Rails, Cane-seated Chairs, Painted Cupboard and Drawers, two Kitchen Tables, with Drawers; two Round Tables, seven Elm Chairs, Flour Tub, large Oak Meal Ark, Wood Gantry, two Oak Chests, Musical Instrument called a Trombone; Fender, sundry Tin Ware, Churn, Milk Panshons [pancheons], and various Kitchen Utensils. Also a Stack of well-got Hay, about Five Tons; straw Cutter, Corn Chests, Side Saddle, Stone Trough, Wooden Pig Trough, six Ash Poles, &c."

The Shaws would return to the King and Miller in 1871. The next landlord was Edmund Couldwell, whose father Benjamin had been the landlord of the Royal Oak across the road for many years. Edmund had been born in 1835, the son of Benjamin Coldwell and Harriet Woodcock, and he was the landlord of the King and Miller for about three years.

ALLEGED ROBBERY AT DEEPCAR: 1865
In December 1855, one of Edmund's brothers, John Couldwell, who was 31 years old and who worked as a butcher, was accused of stealing a purse containing seven shillings and sixpence, a counterfeit crown piece,[130] and a pocket-knife, from John Firth, who was fast asleep, drunk, in the King and Miller at the time. Firth was a stone cutter and lived at Hunshelf Bank. When he woke up and found the items were missing, he suspected Couldwell, who was searched. The missing items were found; the coins were in one of his clogs. The defence argued that the whole thing was just a practical joke, and the jury agreed. Couldwell was acquitted but was given a warning as to his behaviour in the future.[131]

SAVAGE ASSAULT: 1868
Three years later, in March 1868, another of Edmund's brothers, James, was in court on a much more serious charge of assault. James, a master cabinet maker, was charged with assaulting 60-year-old Thomas Siddons, a labourer living at Deepcar. Siddons was drinking in the King and Miller when his son came in with James Couldwell; they had been quarrelling, and young Siddons' face was covered with blood. The argument continued, and

---
[130] Worth 5 shillings; Firth had perhaps taken it in change and not noticed at the time that it was a fake
[131] John Couldwell was born in about 1834, the son of Benjamin Couldwell landlord of the Royal Oak at Deepcar. One of the newspaper reports wrongly called him James, but that was his older brother, who was a cabinet maker.

Couldwell hit his companion, and so Thomas Siddons intervened, hitting Couldwell in the face with his stick. Couldwell grabbed the stick and hit the older man on the back of the head with it, knocking him senseless. He continued to assault the man, kicking and punching him whilst he was on the ground until his brother Edmund Couldwell, the landlord, took him away. This didn't stop him though, and he returned to the bar to carry on the attack until two men removed him again. Siddons was unconscious and had to be taken home in a spring-cart. He remained on a sofa for a few days until he could be moved upstairs, and he was unable to work. Witnesses said that the blow Siddons dealt Couldwell was not that heavy and that Siddons was "*most grossly abused*." The defence tried to argue that some of the older man's injuries were caused when he fell against some furniture and that none of this would have happened if he had not intervened in the argument. The landlord swore that he did not see his brother James attacking the man. After some consultation, the Bench said that they realised that Siddons had started the fight, but also that he was defending his son, and that the blows dealt by Couldwell were far more violent than was acceptable; therefore they fined Couldwell the maximum amount of £5.

Additionally, a warrant was taken out against Couldwell by Siddons' son for the assault committed upon him, but this case was not gone into, and it was remanded. There was no further report in the newspapers about this.[132]
Thomas Siddons had been attacked once before, in February 1863. He was on his way home from the Travellers Inn at Vaughton Hill when he was set upon by John Bland and George Dronfield of Wadsley.[133]

Five years later, James Couldwell was in trouble with the law again, this time for an assault on a railway porter called William Hartley. Also accused was his son, Edmund, who would have been about 16 years old. The newspaper said that James Couldwell was a publican, living at Deepcar, though it didn't say which pub. His brother Benjamin was the landlord of the Royal Oak, so he could have been helping him as well as carrying on his joinery business.

---

[132] Thomas Siddons' son could have been Joseph. In 1871 both men were farm labourers living at Town End, Deepcar; Thomas was a widower aged 62 and his son Joseph was born c1845. James Couldwell lived at Deepcar with his wife Mary and family. He was born in 1830 the son of Benjamin, landlord of the Royal Oak.
[133] See the chapter on the Travellers at Deepcar

Edmund's case was dismissed, but James's *"violent and cowardly"* attack got him a fine totalling more than £5 including costs.[134]

A COW CHOKED WITH A TURNIP: 1866

In January 1866, Edmund made the newspapers nationwide with a rather gruesome report about one of his cows, which met with a painful death when it choked on a turnip. The creature was in a yard adjoining the house eating from a pile of turnips when it choked on one. The services of a butcher had to be called upon to put the poor thing out of its misery, its body swelling rapidly. The butcher, unable to save it, pronounced the cow guilty of having *"brussen itsen."*[135]

Edmund left the King and Miller early in 1868 and went back to his old trade of farming and coal/coke dealing. His fortunes, however, took a downturn, and in January 1872, he instigated liquidation proceedings. Owlerton auctioneer and valuer Robert Lowe was appointed Trustee, and he auctioned off all of Edmund's assets. These included his house, some of his furniture, and his business goods. His stone-built freehold house faced the Bolsterstone road (Carr Road); it had two rooms on the ground floor, three bedrooms, two cellars, closets, and a garden and was supplied with gas and water. His business goods included the following: colliery plant, two draught horses, three carts, a cow in milk, ox and seed harrows, a wooden plough, a metal roller, a straw cutter, a bean-splitter, a three-hole corn bin, four old wheels, a cart body and shafts, a step ladder, 340 pairs of iron tram rails weighing about five tons, two corves, baskets, and so on. Edmund then moved away from Deepcar to live in Sheffield. The 1881 census recorded him and his family living at 21 Bamforth Street [between Langsett Road and Penistone Road], and he was working as a farm labourer. Two years after Edmund's liquidation proceedings, his elder brother James was in financial trouble. At a meeting of his creditors in January 1874, it was found that his liabilities were over £203, and his assets only £78. By now James had moved to Grove Cottage, Pye Bank, Pitsmoor. It was unanimously resolved by the meeting, which all the largest creditors attended, that the estate should be liquidated by arrangement.

---

[134] See the chapter on the Royal Oak
[135] A Yorkshire dialect word for stuffed full to bursting ... very apt in this case.

The next landlord was William Helliwell. He organised a lot of shooting events in a field adjacent to the pub, as well as Knur and Spell matches. One day in March 1869 over 500 spectators gathered to watch a match for £10 a side at Knur and Spell between C. Morton of Damflask and W. Sherdon of Stocksbridge. Helliwell was only at the King and Miller for a couple of years; it was advertised as to let, with stabling and about twelve acres of grass land, in August 1869, although Helliwell was still there in February 1870.[136]

VIOLENT ASSAULT IN A PUBLIC-HOUSE AT DEEPCAR: 1870
Samuel Gregg, a blacksmith living at Thurgoland, was accused of assaulting William Dyson, a collier living at Deepcar. Dyson was at the King and Miller when Gregg came in with several other young men and started to kick both him and some others that were in the pub. Dyson was kicked several times on the chest. Gregg was fined twenty shillings plus costs. Gregg then tried to bribe the Sheffield Independent's reporter not to report the case – an offer which was, of course, *"indignantly rejected,"* Gregg's actions being given full publicity![137]

The next landlord was Benjamin Horsfield, but he seems to have been there for less than a year. The only reference to his existence is in the Sheffield Independent of 18th January 1871 when it was reported that Benjamin Horsfield, landlord of the King and Miller Inn, Deepcar, was fined ten shillings and costs for allowing card playing in his pub.

At some point, Joseph and Jane Shaw moved back in, but Joseph died there not long after, on the 10th February 1871. He was 58 years old. When the 1871 census was taken in April, Jane was recorded as the publican.

---

[136] In September 1869, interested parties were to apply to Mr. Brear of Deepcar Mills. In December 1869/January 1870, the contact was the Don Brewery, Sheffield (or enquire on the premises). Another William Helliwell ran the Sportsman's Inn at Deepcar at this time.
[137] The Sheffield Daily Telegraph reported that Gregg was from Bolsterstone and that Dyson lived at Thurgoland, but this was wrong, whereas the Barnsley Chronicle had it the opposite way round. Gregg lived at Thurgoland; the 1871 census recorded Samuel G. Gregg living in Thurgoland at the house of William Mudd, a blacksmith. Gregg was 21 years old, unmarried, and a journeyman blacksmith.

QUARREL AMONGST WORKMEN: 1877

In 1877 a gang of workmen from the East Riding of Yorkshire were employed to build St. John's Church at Deepcar. Their foreman was a stonemason called William Fortescue. The fact that the men were not local was a source of resentment, and there was ill-feeling towards them and disputes about the number of hours worked. These incomers were often called "*black-legs.*" Matters came to a head when Henry Beever, a quarryman living at Deepcar, assaulted Fortescue in the King and Miller one day. There were about twenty locals and twenty incomers in the pub, and there was an unpleasant atmosphere. Beever entered and challenged a man called Chester to a fight; he refused, but Beever hit him anyway, knocking him down into the fireplace, where he was scalded by a kettle of boiling water. Beever was fined £2 and costs, or two months' imprisonment should he refuse to pay.

In around 1879 a man called Thomas Turton took over. He had run a grocery shop and beer off-licence very close to the King and Miller for many years and had applied for a licence to sell wine back in 1869, but this was refused because the rateable value of his premises was deemed too low. He was married to one of the Grayson family, Martha. Martha died in 1866 and Thomas carried on running the shop before marrying again in 1874 to Joseph Shaw's widow Jane – he was her fifth husband. The couple married over the Pennines, in Chorlton-upon-Medlock (now part of Manchester). Her niece lived here, so she had a connection to the area. The couple gave their wrong ages, and Thomas's occupation was recorded as "*painter,*" but the rest of the details tie in with what is already known about the couple. Thomas died at the King and Miller in 1880 aged 74. Jane continued to run it for about a year after his death, before handing the reins over to Joseph Woodcock. She died in 1889 aged 75, and she left just over £212 – worth around £27,447 today.[138]

Joseph Woodcock was the landlord for about fifteen years, until 1896. He and his wife Mary were there when the 1881 census was taken, along with their daughters Alice, Mary Elizabeth, Hannah, and Sarah Grace. Sarah Grace married John Thomas Helliwell in 1891, and they ran The Castle at Bolsterstone from around 1898 to 1905. Previous to taking the King and

---

[138] According to the Bank of England's inflation calculator.

Miller, Woodcock had lived at Pilley Hills, Tankersley, where he had been head gamekeeper.

INQUEST ON A MAN FOUND DEAD AT DEEPCAR: 1882
One night in November 1882, a 62-year-old man called William Sampson, of Old Haywoods, was found dead near to Blacking Mill Row, Deepcar. He had been to Sheffield with his son-in-law John Pears, returning by the last train which left Sheffield at 9pm. They called and had a drink at the Travellers Inn on Vaughton Hill, before going on to the King and Miller, drinking until almost 11 o'clock. When they were ready to leave, they realised that Sampson had left his basket in the previous pub, so Pears went back for it. When he got home, his father in law had not arrived, so he went back out to look for him, finding him lying dead in the road, just 200 yards away.[139]

QUARRELSOME IN HIS CUPS: 1883
In October 1883 William Newton, a Deepcar butcher, appeared in court for being drunk and disorderly in the King and Miller. He was drunk when he went into the pub and he started a fight with a man who was already in there. The landlord Joseph Woodcock evicted him, but he came back, and P.C. Goodlad had to be sent for. Newton was fined ten shillings.

INQUEST ON A SHEFFIELD PLATELAYER: 1884
The coroner held an inquest at the King and Miller on the body of a 44-year-old platelayer called Samuel Nadin of Fox Street, Pitsmoor. His wife gave evidence and said that her husband was *"out of work but not ailing."* He had come to Deepcar one Sunday morning to visit a friend and witnesses said they had seen him on Sunday night at 9pm. He was found drowned on Monday morning, in the weir at Messrs. T. Taylor's. A verdict of *"Found Drowned"* was returned.

ILLEGAL GAMING: 1888
Two labourers, Edward Curley of Bracken Moor and Lewis Fearn of Stocksbridge, were summoned for playing a kind of tossing game called

---

[139] The Sheffield Independent said he died at 11.30pm and was 65 years old. The Sheffield Daily Telegraph said he died at 7.30pm and was 56. According to the GRO death indexes, he was 62. There was no report of the inquest, but it was said he suffered from cramp.

"*marrying*"[140] on the licensed premises of the King and Miller. The landlord, Woodcock, said that he had warned the men, but they had carried on the game regardless. He was praised for upholding the law, whilst the men were fined; Curley was fined ten shillings plus costs, and Fearn, who had previous convictions, was fined £1 and costs. Curley was the son of James and Mary, who came from Ireland. His brother Thomas had been in trouble many times for fighting. Tossing was a gambling game, and became a real problem in Sheffield in the 1920s during what became known as the "*Sheffield Gang Wars.*"[141] Tossing could mean "*pitch and toss,*" which involved betting on the toss of three half-pennies, or it could refer to a bet being placed on the toss of two coins.

ACCIDENT AT DEEPCAR: 1892
A butcher by the name of Horton called at the King and Miller whilst returning home in his trap one night, and fell heavily; he was so stunned he had to be carried into the pub and was unable to resume his journey home.[142]

AUCTIONS
Auctions were sometimes held in the pub to raise money for local events, such as the flower show and sports days. Interested parties would bid for the sole right to sell refreshments, food, and tobacco at these events.

A MINER IN TROUBLE AT DEEPCAR: 1893
A Deepcar miner by the name of Joseph Dalton was summoned for being disorderly and refusing to quit the King and Miller, Deepcar. He was drinking in the pub and started to use abusive language to the other customers. Woodcock, who was still the landlord, asked him to leave, but he refused. P.C. Headland was sent for, and when he arrived, Dalton left. He did not appear in court and was fined £1 in his absence.

---

[140] One newspaper calls it *tossing* and another calls it *marrying*. The Sheffield Independent of 1896 reports a game of marrowing, which is probably the correct word, from the definition of marrow: a match, one of a pair. See the chapter on the Miners Arms for further explanation.
[141] See Bean, J. P. The Sheffield Gang Wars. Sheffield: 1981
[142] Possibly William Horton of Hunshelf Bank, butcher and draper.

Woodcock retired from the pub after fifteen years as its landlord, and in 1896 it became available to rent from the Don Brewery. He died at Deepcar in 1898 aged 66.

At some point – perhaps in 1882[143], the King and Miller had been acquired by the Don Brewery of Sheffield, A. H. Smith & Co. The brewery was on Penistone Road, opposite the Globe Works at Kelham Island. The brewery also had the Sportsman's Arms at Old Haywoods and the Coach and Horses at Stocksbridge. Smiths was acquired by Tennant Brothers Ltd. in 1916.

The next landlord was Francis Shaw, who, with his wife Martha, ran the pub for about five years until about 1900. Martha was the daughter of Henry and Ann Bradley, who ran the Rose and Crown inn at Penistone.

LANDLADY ASSAULTED AT DEEPCAR: 1897
Martha was assaulted one night by one of her customers, a man called Alfred Nixon, a collier who lived at Potter's Hill, High Green. He had been drinking in the pub for about six hours when he became violent; he went into the club room and *"being in a pugnacious mood invited the customers out to fight."* Martha Shaw asked him to leave, but he would not, and he hit her in the face, giving her two black eyes. She threatened to fetch the police, and he said that she could fetch as many as she liked, because he *"did not care for them."* Two policemen were called for, and they forcibly ejected him from the premises. He was fined twenty shillings for the offence of refusing to quit, and thirty-one shillings for the assault. If he did not pay the fines, he would be sent to prison for a month.

The Shaws had left the King and Miller by 1901 and were living with Martha's widowed mother at the Rose and Crown. Francis had taken a job as a railway clerk on the goods trains, a job which would have involved a lot of paperwork but presumably less fighting.

Edward Hawley was at the King and Miller when the 1901 census was taken, along with his wife Vashti and their daughters Florence and Kitty. Edward had been born in Midhope and was the son of John Hawley, a highway surveyor and collector of taxes who lived in what was known as the *"King's*

---

[143] Breweryhistory.com

House" at Midhope. Edward had served his apprenticeship with George Steel of Bolsterstone, a blacksmith, before moving around for work, living in Attercliffe, Sheffield and Thrybergh, Rotherham. He came back to Deepcar to run the King and Miller, but it must not have worked out because he only stayed a couple of years before moving away again, this time to Doncaster.

Dronfield-born man George Allen and his wife Mary Ann Goodwin were the next to take the pub. They had two children, Hilda Frances Goodwin (1879-1897) and Mabel Alice – known as May - (1884). George had worked as a rail finisher before moving to Sheffield and a change of career – when Mabel was born, he was working as a curator at the School of Art on Arundel Street. He ran the Shakespeare Hotel on Sycamore Street, Attercliffe for a while before he moved to the King and Miller. Mabel Alice married a silversmith called Arthur Robertson Buttery in 1906, and they had the Sportsman's Arms at Old Haywoods for a few years, from about 1906 to 1911.

George was an accomplished musician. He was a well-known operatic tenor, and he made his debut with Arthur Rousbey's Opera Company as a principal tenor, from which he transferred subsequently to various other companies. Ill-health forced his retirement from the stage. When he moved to Deepcar, he was elected as a local councillor.

SUDDEN DEATH AT DEEPCAR: November 1906
A barman at the King and Miller fell ill and died at work one morning. Arthur Firth was 33 years old, and suddenly staggered and fell, dying before medical help could be sought. The cause of death was thought to be heart failure.

AUCTION: 14th August 1907
The posting stables, where the stagecoach horses had once been housed, stood on some waste ground opposite the King and Miller. Customers' horses would also have been looked after there. Later, three stone-built houses were erected on this site, which are still there today. Many years ago, these three buildings were used as a blacksmith's shop, a wheelwright and joiner's shop, and a grocer's shop. There were also some outbuildings on the site. These three shops, along with stables, sheds, conveniences, and some vacant land, came up for sale in 1907, the auction taking place in the King and Miller. These buildings were rented out to Messrs. Charlesworth

(blacksmith), Gabbitas (wheelwright), Dalton, and others. The whole site fronted Manchester Road and Carr Road, and the vacant land was said to be suitable for building additional shops or houses. These were bought by Walter Tingle of Ash Lane, but he died the following year, and all these properties, plus two houses in Ash Lane, went back to auction on the 4th November 1908. The grocer's shop was being used as a storeroom, Harry Gabbitas still had the wheelwright's shop and Mr. Charlesworth had the blacksmiths. Two houses in Ash Lane in the occupations of Harry Gabbitas and William Tingle (junior) were also for sale.

BOLSTERSTONE RIFLE CLUB: 1908
The Bolsterstone Rifle Club held their annual dinner at the King and Miller in 1908, when around fifty or sixty members and visitors were present. The Chair was occupied by the Rev. W. C. Edgington, who gave a speech on how every man should be able to defend his country - this was before the First World War - and that, in his opinion, it was impossible to get a good army until the soldiers were paid a living wage, adding that there were over 4,000 men who had fought for the country currently living in workhouses. He believed that Rifle Clubs such as this one could form an army for policing the home shores and become a vital addition to the regular army, who fought abroad when and where necessary. Prizes were awarded and there were toasts to *"The King,"* and *"The Army"* as well as other patriotic toasts. Mr. W. H. Robinson sang *"The True British Soldier,"* a banjo solo was given by Mr. F. Bramley, and Mr. R. Thickett sang a song called *"I Heard a Song."*

THE STOCKSBRIDGE AND DISTRICT TRADESMEN'S ASSOCIATION: 1908
The local tradesmen's association held their annual dinner at the King and Miller in March 1908, with between thirty and forty attendees being present. The hon. Secretary in this year was Mr. Alfred Hague, who reported that there were funds of over £32, out of which it was decided to send £5. 5s. to the Royal Infirmary Extension Fund. During the evening Mr. T. Hitchin, a Yorkshire elocutionist, gave several *"humorous recitals,"* and several men played or sang.

In 1908, the government proposed a new Licensing Act. The origins of this Bill are complex and involve the breweries, the pub trade, the Temperance Movement, and bitter party politics, but to put it briefly, the pub trade was put under threat by this proposed new legislation, and there were nationwide protests against the new Bill. In February 1908, the Chancellor of the Exchequer, Herbert Asquith, had argued for an acceleration in the suppression of licences, with the aim of closing a third of all public houses in England and Wales. He also mentioned other measures such as a reduction in Sunday opening hours and a ban on the employment of women in pubs. Not surprisingly the trade was horrified by these proposals, and they immediately began a series of actions designed to defeat the Bill. This period of time coincided with the dominance of the tied-house system, and the big breweries feared for their investments. There were many Temperance campaigners on the licensing boards who could press for a pub's closure on tenuous evidence. Brewers who were also J.P.s were not allowed to attend licensing sessions, so tempers were running high.

Joseph Kenworthy[144] reported on two meetings locally; these were not reported in the Sheffield newspapers, although a great many reports of meetings in other parts of the district were published. On the 19th March 1908, meetings were held at the Friendship and the King and Miller to protest against this new Bill, whilst on the 19th May the same year, a meeting in favour of it was held in the British School, presided over by Dr. Robertshaw. The opponents of the Bill thought it went too far and threatened not just the breweries but the livelihoods of all those involved and employed in the pub industry, not to mention depriving the hard-working man of his beer. Those who supported the proposed new legislation thought it did not go far enough. One letter, published in the Sheffield Independent on the 16th March 1908 said: *"public houses are a curse and a danger to the nation [...] Through the many temptations there are thousands today victims of intemperance, brought down into the depths of poverty and degradation, and then when old-age comes many of them become a burden to the rate-payer. In the public interest it is time this great evil was grappled with."* Strong words indeed! In the end, the Bill was defeated in November.

George Allen left the pub in about 1911 and went on to have the Spring Vale Hotel at Walkley, Sheffield. He died in 1919 leaving a widow and one daughter, Mabel Alice.

---

[144] Writing in the Stocksbridge Almanac

William Smith was the next landlord of the King and Miller, remaining there until he retired in 1926.

William and his wife Martha had a son called Arthur, who was killed in action in the Great War. He was 23 years old when he was shot and wounded in 1915, having enlisted less than a year before. He was carried out of the trenches by the stretcher-bearers, and it is reported that he asked them to share his cigarettes among the men in his section. A bullet had lodged in his abdomen; initially, it was not thought that he was badly wounded, and he was reported to have been quite cheerful, but he passed away on the 28th June 1915. In a letter to Arthur's mother, Lieutenant Chamier said, "*I cannot tell you how sorry I am to have lost such a good man.*" He was William and Martha's only son and was buried in La Brique Military Cemetery no.2 in Ypres, Belgium. Local newspapers stated that he was the fourth local soldier to be killed.[145]

William Smith retired in 1926 and an auction was held at the King and Miller to sell off his surplus household furniture. Among the items for sale were a player organ with a hundred rolls, a grand piano, a 4-wheeled caravan, and a "*portable dwelling*" adapted from an old railway carriage, which contained a kitchen and three sleeping compartments.

George Henry Moorhouse took over from William Smith. He had been born in Dodworth, the son of Joseph Moorhouse, a farmer and one-time landlord of the Rising Sun Inn on the High Street there. After the death of his father, his mother Mary married again to George Depledge, and they came to Stocksbridge to live at Horner Houses. Charles married Annie Castle, whose father Henry Castle was the landlord of the Smiths Arms, which was also on the High Street at Dodworth. George farmed at Hoyle House before moving to run a grocer's shop on Manchester Road, Stocksbridge; he was also a beer retailer. He moved into the King and Miller when William Smith retired in 1926, but only stayed for about four years before retiring to a house on Halifax Road, Grenoside.

George and Lucy Eyre took over after Charles Henry's departure. When the 1939 Register was taken, George Eyre's occupation was recorded as a

---

[145] See the end of this chapter for more information about Arthur Smith.

process clerk in the steelworks, and his wife was recorded as the landlady of the pub.

The King and Miller is still a public house, having been serving beer for over 200 years. Its current owner is the Bradfield Brewery, a local independent brewery based on a working farm at High Bradfield.

Detail from a window panel in the King and Miller from the time it was a Tennant Brothers pub.
Photo credit: Dave Pickersgill

PRIVATE ARTHUR SMITH 3/8789
1st Battalion, West Yorkshire (Prince of Wales Own) Regiment
Enlisted in August 1914
Killed in Action June 1915

In February 1915, both the Sheffield Independent and the Penistone Express published extracts from a letter that Arthur had written to his family:

"I've had no chance to write since I came out here until now, so you will guess what we've been doing. The Germans hoisted the white flag, and then two companies went over to fetch them, and when within range they turned their guns onto us. This is our sixth day in the trenches, but we are getting relieved tonight all being well. The enemy's artillery fire is terrible. They fire a shell we call "coal boxes", owing to the dense cloud of black smoke. It makes a hole large enough to bury between 20 to 30 horses and when they start dropping around it puts the fear of God into your hearts. But I never mind, I'm glad to be doing my bit for the old country. I've just seen a paper that's been sent into the trench saying that the German Army on the Franco-Belgian battlefield is suffering awfully. Well we are back in the trenches, but the weather out here has changed from wet to hard frost. We suffer most in our feet. You can hardly tell you have any on at times. When we were coming into the trenches we came along a road just behind the firing line at the same time as the Germans made an attack. They don't half kick up a row, shouting and singing. A football match isn't in it I can tell you. They advance in thousands shouting "*Hock the Kaiser*" or something to that effect. You would think they couldn't help walking over you, and the stream of bullets just sounds like a flock of bees on a fine summer's day. But you soon get used to it.

I go for rations now. A distance like from Deepcar to Stocksbridge, and do not bother to look round, for if I did I would be doing cake walk in record time, trying to dodge Black Maria. I left the firing line the other day to fetch water at considerable risk from snipers. Looking for a pan in an old house which was deserted, I fell across a Shropshire Light Infantry man, dead. Of course it gave me a shock for a minute, but I am used to all that now. In our last trenches we had 12 piles of Germ-huns (*sic*) in front of us. They swept our "abode of love" the other day, killed one and wounded five on the right of me, so you needn't trouble much about me, as I think I am one of the lucky ones, or I would have been hit before now. Coming out of their trenches the other night, a bullet whizzed by my elbow, making a hole in my coat, and I've five or six in my top coat lapels so if they keep there it will be alright. Well the next time I write I'll give you my first experience on the battlefield. It was across an open ploughed field. I'll now conclude as a rifle butt doesn't make a good desk.

Well, much has happened since last week. I'm going to tell you about it, as it's the worst since we came out here. In the first place we've been soaking wet for six days and nights with no possible chance of getting dry, and stood knee deep in water all the time. So they thought they would give us a four days rest in a billet which was a flax mill, and on the last night the enemy started shelling the town just after we had got down to sleep. The shells (Jack Johnson's) were bursting four at a time over the mills. Of course they had got to know we were in (210 of us and waiting expecting to be blown to pieces any minute). Well, a shell burst on the mill, and we had orders to fall in. Out came matches and candle. I was rolling my blanket up when someone yelled the mill's on fire, and before anyone could say Jack Robinson the flames were licking the roof. We all made a dash for the door; some poor chaps lost all they possessed: I lost my rifle rucksack, containing my scarf and all the comforts you sent me; some lost everything. They marched us about 600 yards into a field. We were given a grand display by the German artillery. The sky was lit up for miles, it making a proper target for their gunners, and they kept it up all night. The French people had come back to their homes, and it was awful to hear the women and kiddies crying, but we shall pay the Germans back with interest shortly. I think we are going to do a big advance, and then there will be some fun.

I often think that if all those "royal standbacks"[146] at home could only know half of what's going on they would enlist to a man; that's if they are Englishmen, because to see the old folk and kiddies without home or habitation makes us eager to get at the foe. You mention reading about German brutality, I'll tell you what happened close to where we are. They set a house on fire. A party of our men went to see what they could do in the

---

[146] Military slang: a regiment imagined by others not to have known particular keenness about going into action. "First to the canteen - last to the front"

matter, and they found three young women locked up in a cupboard left to be burned to death, but thank God they were not much hurt. Nice chaps aren't they? Well I promised to tell you about my first lesson, but I'll leave it until I come back as I'm not likely to forget the smallest detail of it. Well my listing pal was shot dead yesterday. We were stood talking about what we were going to do and what tuck we were going to have when we got back home and in a few minutes a bullet came clean through his head. Now if you are sending me anything then let it be something to eat, as I've two pals who like tasty bits, and you cannot imagine what it's like having bully beef so long. Never mind we are getting to Berlin, if it's only step by step, it's sure. Tell my pals to get out here, as there's extra game to bag."

His last letter home was published in the Penistone Express on the 17th July 1915. They received it a few days before his death, which occurred on the 28th June.

"Dear Parents – I write just to let you know that I am quite well, so far as health is concerned, but I shall never be able to stamp out of my mind the terrible nights of the last few days. You will read about this battle we've been in, but no pen can describe the slaughter. It was victory for us – but at what a cost. You see in the paper British assault at ---- and the capture of two enemy trenches – but [unintelligible print] I only hope that I am not called upon to go through it again. We just landed in from the scene. We had been in the trenches for 14 days and under shell fire all the time. It was just like a place of music playing mezzo forte before crescendoing into double forte. Talk about hell let loose! The bombardment at Neuve Chappelle lasted 35 minutes, but this lasted 18 hours. Fancy [unintelligible print] guns belching out fire for 18 hours as fast as possible, and fancy me crouched against the trench side with a splitting headache expecting to be blown to atoms any minute; it started at 3 o'clock in the morning. The whiz and bursting of shells just over my head sounded like a huge wave, and the feeling was like being in an express train going through a tunnel, and then the Germans started. I don't know how many guns they had but it was a lot, and they caused great havoc.

The bravery of our lads is something wonderful. The third lines of enemy trenches fell to us in under an hour, and we took 400 prisoners, but they were too eager, instead of taking the trenches one by one, so as to allow the artillery to batter the other trenches – they flew on into the first, straight onto the second and then the third - of course [unintelligible print]. A Scots regiment took the fourth line, and were taking the fifth, but had to retire back to the second under machine fire. Some of our chaps started in with the boot and fist, and you should have seen some of the German prisoners, who hadn't received a wound at all except with the boot and fist or rifle butt. I think our Fred was behind us, as we were working with their division, and their infantry were in the charge supported by us. We are now in a wood, still in sound and range of guns, and some shells came over us this morning, but it seems peaceful after that hell-hole. Don't wait to see if I'm alive or not when you want to send a parcel, because if I'm not my mate would get it, and we really need things tasty to make life at all worth living."

Arthur's mother received the following letter from Lieut. Chamier, who was in charge of Arthur's company:

"Dear Mrs. Smith, I am very sorry to have to inform you of the death of your son Private A. Smith, which occurred yesterday (Monday) afternoon. He was standing in the trench early yesterday morning, about half past 2 o'clock with another man when a bullet, after wounding the other man, slightly through the back of the shoulder, went into his stomach on the right-hand side. The stretcher bearers at once bound him up, and carried him to the dressing station, where he died during the afternoon. Although the bullet had lodged inside him, we did not think him badly wounded, and he was very cheerful when they carried him away. Before they took him away he asked his section commander to distribute his cigs amongst the other men in his section. I cannot tell you how sorry I am to have lost such a good man. My platoon wish me to tell you how much they feel his death, as he was very well liked amongst them. His things will be sent to you by our Battalion H.Q. He was buried here, last night by the Chaplain."

Spelling and punctuation as in the original documents

THE MINERS ARMS, BRACKEN MOOR

The Miners Arms began life as a beerhouse in about 1860 and was run by John Helliwell. The pub has always (certainly within living memory) been known locally by its nickname The Wragg or Rag. The field opposite is known as the Wragg Field. Opinions are divided as to how the pub acquired this name.

Photo credit: Jon Allcard

John Helliwell was born in about 1822, and he opened the Miners Arms as a beerhouse in around 1860. The house had been built sometime between 1851 and 1860 - there was no building marked on the 1854 Ordnance Survey map (which was surveyed in 1850/1). The first reference to him selling beer occurs in a trade directory for 1860, when he was listed as a beer retailer and coke burner. Helliwell seemed to have entertained the idea of getting a full wines and spirits licence, and lodged an application with the magistrates in 1862, but for some reason he withdrew it, and the Miners carried on as a beerhouse for many years.

When the 1851 census was taken, John was living at nearby Common Piece and was working as a coal miner. He had a housekeeper living with him, Ann Williamson, and her two daughters, Mary Ann and Elizabeth. Ann was recorded as *"unmarried,"* but she was in fact married to John Williamson, whom she had wed in March 1844 at Sheffield parish church. Ann was the daughter of Patrick Maguire, a gardener. The Maguires came from Ireland. A daughter, Mary Ann, was born in December and was baptised at St. Marie's Catholic Church (now the Cathedral) in May 1846. The previous month, Jonathan had appeared in court charged with assaulting his wife and *"putting her in fear of her life."* He was bound over to keep the peace for twelve months or go to prison, as this was not the first time this had happened.[147]

John and Ann appear to have married sometime between 1851 and 1861. There was no marriage registered in the whole of the country for a John Helliwell marrying an Ann Williamson, so I did think it possible that they were never married.[148] When the 1861 census was taken, John Helliwell was recorded as living at the *"Beer House,"* Bracken Moor, his occupation being recorded as a coal merchant. More daughters had been born to the Helliwells since the 1851 census, but they don't appear to have had any sons.

---

[147] There were only two Jonathan Williamsons listed on the 1841 census for Sheffield: Ann's husband and her father-in-law. The man in court could have been Jonathan's father, but as Jonathan junior went on to have a violent, criminal lifestyle, it does seem highly likely that this was him and that his wife moved out to Stocksbridge to escape from him.

[148] A marriage took place at the Sheffield parish church in 1858 between a John Helliwell and a Mary Ann Williamson, where some of the facts seem to fit, but others do not.

ALLEGED BIBLE BURNING BY A CATHOLIC PRIEST: 1860

Ann Williamson / Helliwell was a Catholic, and her daughter Mary Ann had been baptised into the Catholic Church in 1846 when she was 2 years old. She and her sisters attended the Protestant schools at Bolsterstone because there was no Catholic school locally. When the new Catholic schools opened at Deepcar, her sisters went there instead, but Mary Ann, who was fifteen, wanted to stay where she was.[149] Father McKenna, who was attached to St. Vincent's church in Sheffield, visited her one day whilst her father was out and asked to see her school books. Mary Ann brought a catechism, a prayer book, and a Bible to show him. He apparently ordered the books to be burnt, for they would *"send her soul to hell."* He told Mary Ann's younger sister Sarah Jane (aged eight) to put them on the fire, which she did. Mary Ann said that she tried to save the books, but was held back by the priest, and she cried bitterly. Her mother did not intervene. Her father's banksman,[150] Stephen Hudson, reported seeing them in the fire, and when Helliwell returned, he was *"much annoyed"* at the proceedings. In his defence, Father McKenna denied that he wanted the girl to burn the Holy Bible. He said that she had told him she wanted to become a practising Catholic, so he promised to provide her with a Catholic prayer book, saying that she might destroy the previous one. The newspaper reported that *"considerable indignation has been excited in the neighbourhood"* by these reports.

Ann lived with John Helliwell as his housekeeper, having a daughter Elizabeth to him in 1850. They went on to have another eight daughters.[151] Elizabeth and her siblings were all baptised in 1862 at St. Vincent's Roman

---

[149] This must mean Sunday School, because a girl of fifteen years of age would not have still been attending school at this point in history. Sunday schools would have been held in the new Catholic church, St. Ann's, which had been built at Deepcar the previous year. It was formally opened and blessed on 14th October 1859.

[150] A banksman works at the mouth of a mine shaft or pit and supervises the loading of coal and the lowering and raising of the cage.

[151] Elizabeth was born in 1850, and her birth was registered as Helliwell, mother's maiden name Williamson. The census enumerator recorded her as *"housekeeper's daughter,"* presumably because Ann was not married to John. All the remaining children were registered with the mother's maiden name as Williamson, except their final daughter, Ellen, when the mother's maiden name was entered as McGuire. There is no record at all of a John Helliwell marrying an Ann Maguire/McGuire, and only one of a John Helliwell marrying a *Mary* Ann Williamson.

Catholic church in Sheffield with the exception of Emma (born 1854) who died young, and Ellen, who was born and baptised in 1866.

Ann's husband Jonathan Williamson was in and out of court over the years, and his charge sheet listed fighting, assault, malicious wounding, robbery, fighting in a brothel at Scargil Croft, and burglary. He had a couple of short spells in prison, then in 1869 he was sent to prison for seven years for an assault on a Sheffield veterinary surgeon. The vet, Mr. John William Moorwood, was returning home early one morning, rather drunk. He walked down West Street and turned into Rockingham Lane where he was attacked by three men and a woman. They seized him by the throat, knocked him to the floor, then began kicking him, before stealing £2. Moorwood managed to hang onto one of the men, Williamson, until a policeman arrived. The vet had to spend some time in hospital as a result. Williamson was living nearby at the time, on Orange Street, just off West Street. He was committed for trial at the Leeds Assizes.[152] The judge said that he thought Williamson was *"one of those pests to society who hang about public highways in gangs, making them impassable to respectable people,"* adding that anyone who was drunk was an easy target for them.

Because of his previous convictions, Williamson was sentenced to seven years in jail. The 1871 census recorded him in the male convict prison at Chatham, Kent. He eventually moved back to Sheffield and lived on Leadmill Road, dying there in 1886 at the age of 61. He had been out drinking and had arrived home at around 3pm. Neighbours reported hearing a crash, and he was found lying unconscious at the bottom of some steps with a fractured skull; he died shortly afterwards. The inquest returned a verdict of accidental death.

MAN FOUND DEAD AT STOCKSBRIDGE: 1865

Miles Durken was drinking in the Miners Arms one Saturday night in February and was too drunk to get home, so he went into an outhouse attached to the pub to sleep. He died during the night from the cold, and also from suffocation. He was 58 years old.

---

[152] The Assizes were where the more serious offences were tried. Williamson had previous convictions for serious offences, and this is another reason why he was tried by this higher court.

A MAN SHOT WHILE *"LARKING"* AT STOCKSBRIDGE: 1868
Around 11pm one Saturday night in October, a group of men left the Miners Arms after an evening's drinking. The group included Matthew Hinchcliffe, James Helliwell (a carter), and Helliwell's brother, who was not named in the newspaper reports. They were arguing, and Hinchcliffe went home. He lived close to the beerhouse and he (or his wife) kept a sweet shop, but his main occupation was stonemason. Helliwell and his brother began throwing stones at Hinchcliffe's windows and shouting to his wife to open up and serve them with *"spice"* [sweets]. The more he remonstrated with them, the worse they became. Hinchcliffe then armed himself with a single-barrelled gun loaded with a full charge of number 7 shot and threatened to shoot them. The men hid behind a wall, but Hinchcliffe fired upon them anyway, hitting James Helliwell on his face and shoulders. Some of the wounds bled profusely, and he was taken home and a doctor was called, who feared that he would lose the sight in his right eye. Hinchcliffe was arrested on a charge of *"Maliciously Wounding"* Helliwell and was committed for trial at the Doncaster Quarter Sessions, where the jury found him guilty. He was sentenced to twelve months' imprisonment with hard labour at the House of Correction in Wakefield. He was back home at Bracken Moor when the 1871 census was taken, living with his wife Harriett and five children. His wife had been born in Darnall, Sheffield, and Matthew came from Penistone. They lived in Darnall before moving to Stocksbridge.

In 1869 new legislation was brought in which returned all beerhouses back under the control of the licensing magistrates. Previously, a beerhouse keeper could obtain a certificate to sell beer by paying two guineas direct to the Excise.[153] Helliwell applied for, and was granted, a licence for the Miners Arms, which remained as a beerhouse for years to come.

REFUSING TO QUIT: 1871
In June 1871, a labourer called Thomas Curley of Bracken Moor was summoned to the West Riding Court by P.C. Tomlinson for refusing to quit the Miners Arms when asked. The case was proved, and the magistrates ordered him to pay a fine of ten shillings plus costs.

---

[153] The Wine and Beerhouse Act took effect on 15th July 1869; a justices' certificate was now required for both on- and off-sales of beer. The law was in place in time for the annual Brewster sessions and gave licensing benches the opportunity to get rid of any pubs that had been the subject of complaints.

It was reported at the West Riding Brewster Sessions of 1873 that several beerhouses in this area had all been classed as *"underrated"* at the previous Sessions. Only premises of a certain rateable value were allowed to be licensed as public houses or beerhouses, and this rating qualification had recently been altered. Consequently, the rateable value of these premises was now not considered to be high enough for them to operate as licensed houses. The beerhouses in question were the Miners Arms, the New Inn at Stocksbridge, the Sportsman's Arms at Deepcar, and the Reservoir Inn [Haychatter] at Bradfield. The magistrates had decided to grant the licences on condition that the tenants would, during the year, enlarge their premises so that their rateable value would be increased. A few days before the Sessions were held in August 1873, a valuer had been sent to inspect the pubs in question, and he reported that they were now of the rateable value required by the Act of Parliament.[154]

FATAL ACCIDENT AT STOCKSBRIDGE: 1873

On a Saturday afternoon in June, several men, who were fairly drunk, were amusing themselves at Helliwell's coal pit close to the Miners Arms.[155] Peter Brady, a labourer, was bragging to the others that he could descend the shaft, which was 35 yards deep, by climbing down the rope. He proceeded to do so, his companions holding the winding wheel still, and he reached the corve or wagon which hung at the end of the rope. He thought this rested on the pit bottom, but in fact the rope only went about halfway down the shaft. He stood on it, let go of the rope, and fell to the bottom. His companions managed to bring him back up, but he died fifteen minutes later. His body was removed to the Coach and Horses to await the inquest. Brady lived in Chapel Row,[156] was 30 years old, and not married. The inquest said that he was killed whilst at work, though the original newspaper report seems to hint that the men were not working and had been drinking. Mr. Wardle, who was

---

[154] The 1872 Act stated that no premises with an annual rateable value of less than £20 could be granted a beerhouse licence (this was £30 for fully licensed public houses). The previous rateable value had been based on how a householder was assessed for paying the Poor Rate, which was a tax on property that was used to provide help for those who had fallen on hard times. This new criterion was based on the annual rateable value of the house, and, of course, was a cause of much discussion and disagreement. A great many pubs and beerhouses were forced to close because of this.

[155] It is not known if the landlord of the Miners Arms owned the coal pit as well.

[156] This was near the now demolished Ebenezer Chapel / British Hall.

a mines inspector, gave evidence. He had been to inspect the shaft, and asked Mr. Helliwell, the owner, if the pit was in the same state as it had been before the accident. Mr. Helliwell replied that it was and had been for the last twenty years. The inspector said it was in a *"very disgraceful state,"* and he should report the case to the Secretary of State. The jury agreed. The coroner gave a verdict of accidental death.

SPORT, OR "SPORT"
Over the years, all the landlords at the Miners Arms played host to various sporting events. Regular advertisements were placed in the Sheffield newspapers promoting these and reporting the results. Knur and Spell was one such sport and was played at the Miners Arms from the 1870s until at least 1916. There were also pigeon shooting matches, with live pigeons as the target. Shooting was a popular pastime at pubs who had some land nearby. Pigeons were popular, but sparrows were also a target.

"There was a numerous attendance at the grounds of the Miners' Arms, Stocksbridge, on Saturday, on the occasion of a knur and spell match for £10 between S. Revitt and A. Staniforth, both well-known players, of Stocksbridge, the match to be played on level terms, with ½ oz. common pot knurs, and be decided by the longest knock. A good game was witnessed, Staniforth being the winner; his longest knock, scored from his third rise, being 9 score 8 yds., Revitt's best being 8 score 18 yds. The referee was F. Rodgers, of Stocksbridge."[157]

Knur & Spell was a game requiring great skill and technique and many years of practice. Old men would say that younger men could not play it properly. Two of my distant relations, Herbert Crawshaw and his son Ernest (known as Jim, born in 1891) were experts at it.[158]

"Herbert Crawshaw…was a great player and it is said that he could drive a knur (potty) from Green Moor Top (Pennine) into Station road at Deepcar. Jim's career was lived in a different era to his father, Jim's record knock was

---
[157] Sheffield Daily Telegraph 25th March 1907
[158] http://northernlifemagazine.co.uk/knur-and-spell/ has information about the game of knur and spell, as well as photographs and a film from 1972. There is a British Pathe film on www.youtube.com from 1933 featuring Jim Crawshaw playing this game; search for knur and spell.

262.5 yards. Then came the "Knur and Spell" challenge to the world from Stocksbridge, "Yorkshire Sport" staked £200 for anyone who could beat Jim, but there were no challengers so Jim Crawshaw became the World Champion. Our new world champion was filmed by the Pathe Gazette at Green Moor before a large crowd on 1st April 1929, drinks flowed freely. Yes! It was the 1st April but Jim was no fool." [159]

The 1871 census recorded John Helliwell's occupation as a coal merchant; it was usual at this time for publicans to have two occupations, and it was probably his wife who ran the bar in his absence. He was possibly widowed in December 1875[160] was the landlord of the Miners Arms until about 1876. By August 1876 the tenancy had passed to John Helliwell's son in law, George Mather Douthwaite. John still lived at Brackenmoor and carried on his old trade of coke merchant until his death on the 18th July 1884.[161] He made his will three days before he died, naming Isaac Waterhouse of Bush Flat [Hollin Busk] as his executor. Isaac was also the trustee, responsible for making investments on behalf of John's daughters, including managing income from rental properties and also from any sales of property to pay off mortgages or free up money (none of the properties were named but it seems likely that they included the Miners Arms and its attached cottages). Isaac was a carpenter, but he was briefly the landlord of the Club Inn at Midhope (he was there when the 1901 census was taken) before moving back to Holly Bush [Hollin Busk], dying there at the age of 80 in 1915.

In his will, John mentioned his daughters and their husbands; Elizabeth wife of William Thomas Hemsley, Sarah Jane wife of Thomas Bowman, Alice wife of William Patchett, Olive wife of Charles Barlow, and Louisa wife of Asey [Adin Asaph] Staniforth There were three unmarried daughters: Eva Helliwell (married John Crapper in 1884), Rebecca Helliwell and Ellen Helliwell.

---

[159] Jack Branston, writing in The History of Stocksbridge
[160] Death registered Wortley Registration District in the December Quarter 1875 of Mary Ann Helliwell aged 44. Mary Ann was the name given when John married a Mary Ann Williamson in 1858. A Mary Helewell was buried 31 December 1875 aged 44 in St. Michael's Roman Catholic cemetery in Sheffield, probably the same person.
[161] His effects were just over £82, which according to the Bank of England's Inflation calculator, is over £10,600 today.

George Douthwaite had married Mary Ann, John's stepdaughter, at Sheffield in 1863. She was living at Moorfields, Shalesmoor, and George was living in Sheffield. He was a wheelwright, and his father was George Douthwaite, a painter and decorator. George had been apprenticed to another John Helliwell, a wheelwright and farmer living at Bracken Moor, and he lived with this family during his apprenticeship. This other John Helliwell was born in 1824 and was married to Mary Ellison.

George does not appear to have worked as a wheelwright though. The 1871 census recorded him as a painter and paperhanger, which had been his father's occupation. He was living at the wonderfully named Hobson's Choice, which was off Walkley Lane in Sheffield. In 1876 George filed a liquidation petition in which he stated that he had been living at Langsett Road and working as a painter and paperhanger but was now living at the Miners Arms and was a beerhouse keeper. His creditors met later that year, and a statement showed that he had liabilities of just over £201 and assets of about £73.[162] A year or two later, he left the Miners Arms and moved back to Sheffield. He died in 1894.

Three of George Douthwaite's sons followed him into the family trade of wallpaper hanging, including a son called George. George junior (born in 1872) went on to be a publican; he had the Newmarket Inn at 11-13 Exchange Street, Sheffield before taking the Bazaar Hotel on South Street, Moor, in 1913. He had it through the First World War, and in 1915 was one of many Sheffield landlords who were fined for allowing too much light to show during the blackout. His wife Annie had the licence in 1918, transferring it back to him in 1919 so perhaps he had been called up or forced to take another occupation, perhaps in the steelworks. He had this pub for many years. His son George Herman died at the Bazaar in February 1927 aged 27. In October the same year, George was found suffering from a wound in this throat. He was taken to the Royal Hospital in the Fire Brigade ambulance.

---

[162] Liquidation is different from bankruptcy; with the latter, the bankrupt can avoid settling debts by showing that there is insufficient value in his business or assets to cover the debts. An undischarged bankrupt would then have trouble setting up another business. However, a voluntary liquidation means that the owner of the business does actually have assets which can be sold and agrees with the people to whom money is owed that he will realise (sell) the assets to pay them at least some of the money owed. In this way, the debts can be paid (at least in part) and the person can then go on to start another business.

Despite being in a serious condition he survived. At some point, he went back to his original trade of painter and decorator, and he died in 1955 aged 82.

After George, the next landlord at the Miners Arms was Alfred Shaw, who took over in late 1876 or early 1877. He was a mason by trade and came from Bradfield.[163] He had married his wife Mary Ann (nee Shaw) in 1856.

THE CURLEY FAMILY

The Curley brothers were in trouble not long after Alfred had become the landlord. They lived at Bracken Moor, and regularly featured in the court reports. Their parents James and Mary Ann (nee Connolly) came from Ireland and lived in Sheffield before moving to Stocksbridge. They had nine children. The eldest, John, died in 1863 when he was only 17. He worked in the rolling mill and was employed in the rolling of crinoline steel. His job was to catch the steel with a pair of tongs as it came through the rollers, but one day he missed, and the steel went through his thigh to a length of thirteen feet. The steel was withdrawn *"as soon as possible,"* something which would not be attempted these days, because it can cause even more damage. Curley was taken home, but he died a few hours later before the doctor could attend to him.

The Curleys' sons Thomas, James, Edward, and Patrick were often in trouble with the law, though it seems to be Thomas who was the biggest rogue. He was first reported in the newspapers in 1871 for refusing to quit the Miners Arms. He was summoned for the same offence in 1877, and on the same day he appeared in court with his brother Patrick charged with vandalism. In July 1878 he made his 18th appearance in court (again, for being drunk and refusing to quit the Miners Arms; this time he was reported to have been violent) and he was fined forty shillings, or if he didn't pay, two months' imprisonment with hard labour. He does not seem to have learned his lesson, because the following year he and his brother James were fined for refusing to quit the Coach and Horses at Stocksbridge. The papers reported that this was Thomas's 20th offence and that his brother *"was not unknown to the*

---

[163] He was born in 1831 and his parents John and Hannah lived at Canyards, Bradfield (1841 census). When the 1851 census was taken Alfred was living with a John Helliwell and his wife Mary at Raynor House, assisting John on the farm.

police." 1877 saw James being fined for trespass whilst out looking for rabbits, and in 1888 Edward was fined for gambling in the King and Miller at Deepcar.

In 1880 and 1881 Mrs. Curley, their mother, was fined for breaching or infringing the Education Act, probably for not sending her child to school. This would have been her daughter Elizabeth, born in 1871, who would have been 9 years old in 1880.[164] All the older children were in work by this date. Mary Ann had been widowed in 1878 when her husband had died at the age of 47. He was buried at St. Vincent's R.C. church in Sheffield. The tale has a sad ending, for Mrs. Curley committed suicide in 1899 after having got drunk and taken some laudanum. She had told some women that she had been suspected of theft. She was 75 years old.

In 1879 Alfred Shaw applied for a licence that would allow him to have a billiard table in his pub. This would not have been necessary had the pub been fully licensed, but because it was a beerhouse, he needed to apply for permission to have the table; he would also have had to display a notice that said he was *"Licensed for Billiards."* This was because the Gaming Act of 1845 had stated that billiard licences were to be granted like wine and spirit licences, at the licensing sessions. Anyone opening a billiard house who was not a licensed victualler could be fined if they did not have a billiard licence. Hours for playing were restricted and playing was not allowed on Sundays and other holidays such as Christmas Day and Good Friday. Even Licensed Victuallers would be fined if they allowed play outside of opening hours.

Alfred had the beerhouse for about fifteen years. When the 1881 census was taken, he was recorded as a beerhouse keeper and was living at the Miners with his wife Mary Ann and a 15-year-old domestic servant called Mary Alice Walton. Pigeon shooting matches were still a regular occurrence there. The 1891 census simply gave his address as Bracken Moor and his occupation as mason. He and his wife had an 11-year-old girl called Margaret Sullivan working for them as a general servant. Newspaper adverts continue to mention Knur and Spell matches at *"Mr. Shaw's"*

---

[164] The 1880 Act made it mandatory for local boards [councils] to impose byelaws on school attendance.

Alfred left the Miners Arms in about 1892. The new landlord was Joseph Smith Hemsley, whose brother William Thomas was married to former landlord John Helliwell's eldest daughter Elizabeth. Joseph worked as a tyre-dresser, and when the 1891 census was taken he had been living at Haywoods Park with his wife Priscilla (nee Platts) and their adopted daughter, 4-year-old Ethel.[165] Sadly, he was not in residence long; in 1895 Priscilla placed a notice the newspaper informing people of his death at the Miners Arms on Christmas Eve at the age of 43.

BOXING MATCHES
In 1894 the Miners Arms was the brief home of a boxer called Jack Brierly of Liverpool. Brierly was due to fight Sheffield man Pat Kelly, and both men went into strict training. Brierly took up quarters at the Miners Arms, under the care of his brother W. Brierley and another man called Chappy Moran. Kelly based himself in the hands of Sam Hayden at Eckington. The prize money was £100 – about £13,000 in today's money.[166] They were to fight the best of twenty rounds, but Brierley lost in the sixth round to the Sheffielder. Later that month there was another fight between Michael (Chappy) Moran of Coventry (but of Irish parentage), champion of America, and Tom Fitzpatrick of Birkenhead. Moran trained at the Miners Arms under his old trainer Will Glen, and Fitzpatrick trained at the Black Horse, West Kirby, under the charge of his brother Charles. This fight went the full twenty rounds, and the verdict was given to Moran.

After Joseph Hemsley's death at Christmas 1895, his widow Priscilla took over the licence. She carried on holding the pigeon shoots.

The following February, the Miners Arms, a *"freehold beerhouse"* was put up for sale, together with ten freehold cottages and some adjoining land. This sale was probably brought about by John Helliwell's executor, Isaac Waterhouse, who had the power to choose when to sell property left by John Helliwell in order to realise money. The new owner was George Lane

---

[165] Ethel was recorded on the 1891 census as a 4-year-old adopted daughter of Joseph Hemsley, born in Sheffield c1887. Her second name looks like Judge or Fudge, but there is no birth or baptism that fits. In 1901 she was recorded with the surname Hemsley, stepdaughter to Priscilla's second husband James Batty. When Ethel married Jonas Goodison in 1906, she gave her father's name as Joseph Hemsley (deceased), publican.
[166] According to the Bank of England's Inflation Calendar.

Hooson, who owned the Park Brewery in Sheffield. Priscilla was kept on as the landlady.

GAMING AT BRACKENMOOR: 1896

In March 1896, four young men *"of respectable appearance"* named Richard Dyson, Reginald Dyson, Fred Shaw, and Benjamin Firth, were charged with gaming [gambling] near Brackenmoor, at 11.20pm. P.C. Sagar testified that he saw the defendants in a field playing a game called *"marrowing."* This was a game played with coins, also called *"marrying,"* both words meaning to match or to equal.[167] After watching the men for half an hour, the policeman caught two of them. He went with the men to the Miners Arms, where there was *"a bother,"* but he did not charge them that night. The day after, Firth [or Frith as it was spelt the second time], who had escaped, admitted the offence. They were fined ten shillings.

A DISORDERLY MINER AT STOCKSBRIDGE: 1896

On the 31st October 1896 two miners named William Woodhead and William Young were in trouble for being been drunk and disorderly, and with having refused to quit the Miners Arms. They appeared in court on these charges, and also with having committed wilful damage. The men had been quarrelling and fighting, and Mrs. Hemsley had asked them to leave. They refused and were eventually thrown out by James Batty, a local farmer. The door was locked, but the men then threw stones, breaking a window and doing damage to the amount of 2s. 6d. Young appeared in court and pleaded guilty to the disorderly conduct but denied wilful damage. He was fined ten shillings for refusing to quit, and 7s. 6d for the damage. Woodhead did not appear, and a warrant was issued for his apprehension.

DOMESTIC SERVANT'S FOLLY: 1898

In June 1898 Priscilla Batty married again, to James Batty, presumably the man who had evicted Young and Woodhead two years earlier. The marriage

---

[167] Defined by Joseph Wright in The English Dialect Dictionary. In Yorkshire dialect he gives the example of tossing coins for money: *"Will thou marrow me, or shall I marrow thee?"* and says it means, *"Shall I put a coin down covered by my hand, and will you put down another?"* Paul Jennings writes that some men, *"At the alehouse […] would play at dominoes,* "shuvving the penny," "marrowing each other's coins," *or* "odd man-ing," *and at puff and dart; or, if during the day, they might play at brass, quoits, and skittles – all for ale."* Jennings, P. The Public House in Bradford 1779-1970.

certificate said he was a farmer and lived at Bracken Moor. Three days after she married, Priscilla engaged a young girl called Charlotte Ulyett as a domestic servant. A month later Priscilla left the house for a few days, leaving her nephew and the girl to look after things. On her return she found that £3 in gold and £2 in silver was missing. She accused the servant of taking it and she admitted that she had taken nine shillings, offering to pay it back. Mrs. Batty refused, and P.C. Carter was summoned; when he examined the girl's room, he found £2. 14s. 9d. in a purse. Charlotte was taken to Hillsborough Police Station and confessed to buying some clothes with the money. When she appeared before the magistrates, she sobbed and pleaded guilty. She was bound over under the First Offenders' Act to come up for judgement when called upon.

Later that year, in September, Mrs. Batty's licence came up for its annual renewal, but it was opposed by Superintendent Bielby ... or rather, it was her new husband that he was objecting to. No reasons were given for this objection; Bielby merely stated that the applicant had married a man named Batty, and he did not consider him to be suitable to hold a licence, so he was opposing it.[168] It was reported that the pub's owners had found a new tenant, who would be installed as soon as possible. On the understanding that this would indeed happen, and there being no conviction against the house [pub], the renewal application was granted.

Priscilla Batty moved away from the Miners Arms and away from Stocksbridge. She took the Birmingham Arms on Lambert Street, just off West Bar, in June 1899. However, when she attended court to get the licence transferred, the magistrates refused to renew it because of previous breaches of the law there. Even though these offences had occurred before Priscilla took over, the magistrates allowed themselves to be swayed by the objections raised. These previous breaches of the licence included illicit drinking, selling beer out of hours and it being a disorderly house. The police complained that it was almost impossible for them to supervise; one officer said that it took him six weeks to find a place of concealment from which he could observe what went on in there. There was also an accusation that the

---

[168] There are no reports in the newspapers of any wrongdoings by James Batty, at least not at this period in time. He was in trouble later, in 1905, for being drunk and disorderly, refusing to quit and assault. Perhaps he just had a reputation locally with the police.

pub sold beer to a lodging house adjacent to it, and that beer was passed through the back windows, presumably out of hours. The pub was also deemed to be *"unnecessary"* because, within 200 yards there were 26 other licensed premises. Despite Priscilla having a good reputation and a character reference from the vicar of Bolsterstone, the magistrates refused to transfer the licence to her, and she took the Falcon Inn on Leicester Street, Netherthorpe, instead.

Five months later, in February 1900, Priscilla sued the Britannia Brewery of Bramall Lane,[169] claiming £50 damages for misrepresentation by the brewery upon the letting of the Birmingham Arms. Priscilla argued that she had paid over £52 for the fixtures and fittings (also known as the valuation). She alleged that during a meeting with the brewery manager, she was not made aware of the previous black marks against the pub, and consequently had no idea that its licence was in danger. The brewery completely denied this and said that she had been made aware of all the facts. The judge did not agree, and the verdict went in Priscilla's favour, although she was only awarded £27, not the £50 she was asking for.

On the 1901 and 1911 census returns, James is recorded as the landlord, although the licence was always in his wife's name. The couple were at the Falcon in 1901 with Ethel Hemsley, Priscilla's adopted daughter, and also *"two children, lost from Leeds,"* girls aged fifteen and nine (no names were given). By 1905 they had moved to the Victoria beerhouse on Thomas Street, Broomhall. James Batty was in trouble in this year for having been drunk and refusing to quit the Royal Hotel, Stoney Middleton, in Derbyshire. He was also charged with assaulting the landlord, Robert Gerrard. He denied being drunk, but witnesses confirmed it, and he was fined £1 for being drunk and refusing to quit, and £2 for the assault on the landlord. James and Priscilla stayed on at The Victoria until it closed in 1915.

The next landlord of the Miners Arms was Charles Herbert Moorhouse, who became the landlord in 1899. He had married Priscilla's niece Hannah Platts in 1896. The couple adopted a daughter, Lucy, who had been born in 1904

---

[169] The brewery had leased the pub, but when the lease expired, the pub passed into the hands of the executors of the late James Mudford, who did not want the house coming under the control of a brewery again.

to Hannah's sister Azalea Podoski; when Azalea died in 1905, Lucy was adopted by the Moorhouses. Lucy's grandfather Leon Constantine Podoski had been born in Poland in 1829.

Charles carried on with the tradition of holding pigeon shoots and Knur & Spell matches at the pub, which was still classed as a beerhouse. He had been born at Hepworth in 1867, the son of George and Jane Moorhouse. He was the landlord until his death in 1914, after which his widow took over.

UNSUSTAINED CHARGE AGAINST A PUBLICAN
POLICE & PUBLICANS: 1900
Moorhouse was in trouble with the police within his first year when he was summoned for allowing beer to be drunk during prohibited hours. One of his customers also had to appear in court; John Ramsden, a Stocksbridge butcher, was charged with being on the premises whilst it was closed. The witness, a police officer, said that he was passing the pub at 11.30pm and heard voices, so he summoned another officer. An hour later they looked through a window and saw Moorhouse draw a pint of beer in the bar and take it into the room where they had heard voices. The chink of money was heard, which they inferred was given in payment for the beer. When they entered, the landlord denied that anyone else was there, but, armed with a candle, the police officers went and had a look. Ramsden was discovered with his face to the wall in a back kitchen, presumably hiding his face from the light of the candle. The defence was that the butcher was there on business, had stayed to have supper, and did not pay for the beer. He said he had only hidden in the kitchen because he did not want to be seen in the pub at that time of night. The men's solicitor, Mr. Muir Wilson, admitted that Ramsden had been foolish to hide himself, but that *"landlords in the country districts were so afraid of the police that they could hardly call their souls their own, and when the officers visited the house on this occasion the two men were, quite needlessly, struck with panic."* The magistrates considered there was reasonable doubt in the case, and it was dismissed.

ENOUGH SPIRITS AT STOCKBRIDGE: 1900
The pub's owner, Sheffield brewer George Lane Hooson, applied for a full licence for premises that were to be erected in Bracken Moor Lane, Stocksbridge. The pub was still a beerhouse, and according to Mr. Chambers, Hooson's solicitor, a spirit licence was needed in the area;

therefore, Hooson proposed to pull down the Miners Arms and build "*a new and superior*" pub thirty-seven yards away. Stocksbridge cricket and football grounds were within a hundred yards, and it was argued that "*it was only reasonable that the large numbers of visitors who attended should be able to obtain spirits if they wished.*" The nearest fully licensed houses were, the solicitor said, "*a very considerable distance away.*" The nearest one would be The Castle at Bolsterstone. The New Inn at the bottom of Nanny Hill was still a beerhouse at that time. Getting to any pub in the area would have involved some steep hills, certainly! The application was supported by some people but was opposed by Mr. A. Neal, on behalf of the Stocksbridge Band of Hope Temperance Society, who said that the road on which the pub stood was "*a remote country road,*" and that there was no need for a full licence in such a place. People could get spirits by going half a mile for them. After some consultation, the Bench refused the licence, principally on the ground that the proposed new public house adjoined the cricket field. Today, of course, there is a purpose-built clubhouse adjoining the cricket field.

SUPPLYING A CONSTABLE WITH DRINK
BEERHOUSE KEEPER FINED: 1907

Under the Licensing Act of 1872, any landlord who either "*harboured*" a policeman whilst he was supposed to be on duty, or who supplied him with alcohol whilst he was on duty (either as a gift, or a purchase), could be fined. In 1907, Charles Moorhouse was summoned to the West Riding Court to answer such a charge. P.C. Nicholson went to the Miners Arms on 24th October and asked for a pint of beer. Moorhouse served him and took his money. Later in the day, a sergeant found the constable drunk on duty and he left the force soon afterwards. Moorhouse admitted that he served the P.C. but argued that he did not know that he was on duty. The Magistrates regarded the offence as a serious one and imposed a fine of forty shillings, and eighteen shillings costs.[170] Superintendent Bielby said that this was the second case of this kind that had occurred in his Division within a short time, and he hoped that innkeepers would not supply officers with drink whether they were on or off duty, so long as they were wearing uniform.

When the annual licence came up for renewal the following year, Superintendent Bielby formally objected to the renewal of the Miners Arms

---

[170] The maximum fine for a first offence was £10. Moorhouse was fined forty shillings (£2).

because of Moorhouse's conviction. It was counter-argued that the conviction was the first one that had been recorded in thirty years and that Moorhouse had an excellent character and had managed the pub satisfactorily since 1899. Bielby had to concede that this offence, and a case at the Royal Hotel, Dungworth, were the only two convictions of this kind since he had been in the Division. After giving both landlords a caution as to their future conduct, the licences were renewed.

FIRST TIME AND LAST: 1908
A Stocksbridge miner called Arthur Marsh was fined fifteen shillings for refusing to leave the Miners Arms when asked to do so. In fact, he refused to leave from 6pm until 8.30pm! When he heard that he would be fined, he was heard to remark, "*It's the first time and it will be the last.*" As he does not appear in the newspaper reports again, he must have stuck to his resolution.

The 1911 census recorded Charles at the Miners Arms, his occupation being "*beer retailer, licensed beer house.*" With him was his wife Hannah, adopted daughter Lucy Moorhouse aged six, and a servant, Caroline Hardy.

Charles died on the 27th February 1914. In April, the magistrates sanctioned the transfer of the licence to his widow, Hannah. She stayed on for about two years, before transferring the licence to Thomas Dimelow in January 1916. Thomas had been born in 1863, and he worked in the steelworks as a roller. He married Ada Moorhouse in 1884 and they lived at Old Haywoods until moving to the Miners. Dimelow was fined twenty shillings in 1921 for selling beer during prohibited hours. Later that year he and his wife Ada donated the proceeds of a whist drive, £20, to the Royal Infirmary in Sheffield. Such donations were reported weekly in the newspapers. George Hooson, the brewer, had become a subscriber to the Sheffield General Infirmary in 1896.[171] This was the nearest hospital to Stocksbridge, on Infirmary Road. The site is now occupied by a supermarket.

---

[171] The Royal Infirmary opened in 1792 under the name Sheffield General Infirmary and was renamed the Royal Infirmary in 1897. It closed in 1980.

BRUTALITY AT STOCKSBRIDGE: 1922
On the 21st October George Herbert Elliott left the Miners Arms at about 10pm. As he was walking home to Bracken Moor Farm, he met two brothers, Horace and Donald Shaw. For some reason they ran at him and knocked him down; he hit his head on the kerbstone as he fell, which rendered him unconscious. His injuries confined him to bed for two weeks. In court, he said there was no reason why the two men should have attacked him. The brothers told the magistrates that they were all drunk, and as a consequence, fell on top of each other. Their version of events was dismissed, and Sir William Clegg, one of the magistrates, remarked that, *"this is a brutal and unprovoked assault, and cannot be met by the infliction of a fine. You will both be sent to prison for one month with hard labour."*

STOCKSBRIDGE RAID.
BETTING ON LICENSED PREMISES: 1923
In 1923 it was still illegal to use a public house for betting purposes; not only were the culprits in trouble but so was the landlord for allowing it. Ben Crossland was a bookmaker, formerly a miner, of Bolsterstone, and had been running bets from the Miners Arms. Police constables Driver and Kitson were in the taproom of the Miners Arms, when, in the presence of the landlord and the landlady, a man asked the landlady: *"Where's Ben?"* (referring to Crossland). She replied that he'd only just left. The man said that he wanted to back a horse called *"Juniso"* for 4 shillings, and the money was handed to the landlady. The officers visited the house each day for a week. On the second occasion, Crossland was there, and nine men and a woman were seen to make bets. The woman remarked: *"I've a quid on, Ben, but I'll have just another dollar straight win on Re-echo."* The landlord said: *"You seem to be plunging to-day,"* and she replied, *"don't forget I once won £400 on a horse."* P.C. Kitson wrote out a slip: *"Re-echo, 1s. 3d. each way. – J. Moore,"* and, walking across to Crossland, remarked, *"I think I'll back the old lady's tip."*

On the remaining days, the officers saw a similar state of affairs and laid some bets themselves. A police raid was carried out on a Saturday. There were about twenty-one people present, including Crossland, who said he wanted to keep the landlord out of it; if the constable were to say he made bets then he made them outside. Ben pleaded guilty. His solicitor said that Crossland had been making a living by bookmaking because he had suffered from nystagmus;[172] he had, however, now promised to give up betting. The landlord, Dimelow, pleaded not guilty. His solicitor said that he was deaf and had no knowledge of what was happening. The landlady, her son, and six people who were present at the time the raid took place, were bound over and ordered to pay costs. Crossland was fined £70 and Dimelow was fined £10.

Thomas Dimelow left the pub soon after, and in 1924 the new occupants were George and Mary Jane Cherry. Thomas had moved into one of the adjoining cottages known as Broomfield Cottages. When the licence came up for renewal in March 1924, the police objected because of the conviction of the former licensee. However, the licence was renewed because Dimelow was no longer there. He died on 25th August 1924.

George Cherry was married to Mary Jane Marsh. A trade directory of 1925 records George Cherry as a *"beer retailer,"* so the Miners Arms was still a beerhouse and not a fully licensed premises. The Cherrys were still in the pub when the 1939 Register was taken, and they were followed by the Marsh family.

There is a tale that miners who were coming off shift walked along the tunnel under the pub, and hit the roof with a shovel where a white cross marked the spot, which was a signal for the landlord to start pulling pints for the thirsty miners. I have no idea if this is true, but it's a great story!

And finally ... The Miners Arms had a small room to the left as you walked in which went by the nickname of *"The Kremlin."* My grandad Jack Pearson and his companions used to drink, smoke, and play cards and dominoes in there. There was always a thick fug of smoke from cigarettes and pipe tobacco, and the men who drank in there weren't exactly welcoming to strangers. He always told me that if someone intruded on their inner circle they would begin to play *"blind dominoes,"* turning all the dominoes upside down but giving secret signals with their feet as to what they'd played. Then

---

[172] Nystagmus is a vision condition in which the eyes make repetitive, uncontrolled movements. These movements often result in reduced vision and depth perception and can affect balance and coordination. These involuntary eye movements can occur from side to side, up and down, or in a circular pattern, and are painful. Also known as *"Stag,"* it was a common complaint in miners.

they would turn them all face up and they would match perfectly. I did wonder if this was one of his many tall tales, but other people have confirmed this to be true.

The Miners Arms closed its doors for the last time in 2014 and has now been converted into a private house.

SPORTSMAN'S ARMS, MANCHESTER ROAD, DEEPCAR

The Sportsman's Arms was situated on the main road at Old Haywoods, Deepcar and was known as *"Pladdey's"* after a popular couple who were the landlords for almost 40 years. The sign above the door says Tennants, which dates it to after 1916 when Tennant Brothers Brewery bought out A. H. Smith's Don Brewery, who'd had the pub previously. It closed its doors in the late 60s/early 70s and the building is now a private house.

The Sportsman's Arms was opened in about 1864 by William Helliwell. Born at Hunshelf in 1820, he married Ann Askew, the daughter of Edward Askew, blacksmith and one-time landlord of the Coach and Horses Inn at Stocksbridge. Ann's brother Elijah Askew was also the landlord of the Coach and Horses and the Friendship Hotel at Stocksbridge, and also, very briefly, the Castle Inn at Bolsterstone. Perhaps it was his wife's connection to the pub trade which prompted William to open a beerhouse. He had been living at Horner House and working as an agricultural labourer before opening the pub, which was on the corner of the main road (Manchester Road) and New Street.

FATAL ACCIDENT AT STOCKSBRIDGE: 1864
The earliest mention of the pub in the newspapers was in 1864 when the its name came up during an inquest into the death of a Bracken Moor man called Joseph Shaw, who had been found dead at the bottom of a pit shaft by coal miners working for another Mr. Helliwell, of Stocksbridge. Some of Mr. Helliwell's men found the body of Mr. Shaw, who had been employed as a coke burner, one Monday morning. He was twenty three years old and said to be "*of very intemperate habits,*" often sleeping in the cabin of a coalpit somewhere instead of going home to bed. He was apparently very drunk the previous Saturday night, and had left the Sportsman's Arms at about 10.30pm with a young woman "*to whom he had been paying his addresses.*" The couple had gone to the cabin at Mr. Helliwell's pit, the woman leaving him there sometime around midnight, and it appeared that he had fallen into the pit whilst in his drunken state. He was buried at Bolsterstone.

From 1869 all beerhouse keepers had to apply to the licensing magistrates for a licence to sell beer. At the annual Brewster Sessions held at Sheffield that year, William Helliwell duly applied for, and was granted, his licence. This new law resulted in the closure of a lot of beerhouses throughout the country because the magistrates used their new powers to close what they considered to be "*disorderly*" houses which attracted undesirable clientele or whose landlords were considered to be unsuitable.

MAD DOG AT STOCKSBRIDGE: 1870

A dog which was said to be "*mad*"[173] caused havoc when it appeared in the area. Mr. Turton was opening his shop at Deepcar when a strange dog appeared; it ran at his own dog but was driven off. A little further up the road, the mad dog bit a pup belonging to Mr. Sampson, and also the bitch which went to its rescue. It next seized a *"cur"* [mongrel] belonging to Mr. Helliwell of the Sportsman's Arms, and he went in to fetch a loaded gun before chasing the animal up the main road. The dog chased a lady in her seventies, Mrs. Pickford, who only escaped from it by turning down a lane. It ran as far as Horner House, biting several dogs and a cat on the way. Some people threw stones at it and turned it back. It then caught hold of "*a fine dog*" before being shot by Helliwell. He was probably an excellent marksman because he regularly held, and competed in, shooting competitions on land near his pub.

A HAYWOOD PUBLICAN FINED: 1876

In 1876 Helliwell was summoned for having allowed drunken men to remain on his premises. The case had been adjourned once because he had not produced his licence; in fact, he did not bring it to court this second time either, but the Bench would not allow a further adjournment. The previous week, it was alleged that Helliwell was too drunk to be brought into Court, and one of the magistrates commented that it seemed he was about the same again!

Two policemen gave evidence and told the court that they had been on patrol when they saw two drunk men in the road, arm-in-arm, rolling from one side of the footpath to the other. These men entered the Sportsman's Arms, and when the officers visited it more than half an hour later, they were still there and had beer in front of them. Helliwell's solicitor, Mr. Binney, admitted the offence, but pleaded for a mitigation of the penalty. He told the Bench that there had been a great deal of drunkenness in the neighbourhood of late, adding that it seemed to be the "*staple recreation,*" although this doesn't seem to be much of a defence because the landlord would just be adding to the problem by allowing drunkenness on his premises. When asked if Helliwell was fit to keep a public house, Mr. Binney replied that he was

---

[173] Possibly rabies. Britain was not declared free of this disease until 1922. The Sheffield papers regularly reported on cases of rabies

"*good enough for the neighbourhood*" – which doesn't seem to be very complimentary! The magistrates thought that the landlord was a "*sotted drunken man,*" and fined him forty shillings plus costs, the conviction not to be endorsed on the licence.[174]

William died in August 1876. His widow Ann then ran the beerhouse until her own death two years later in July 1878 at the age of 44. Her daughter Hannah, who had married Stephen Bradwell, was granted Administration of her effects because she did not leave a will.

A month after Ann passed away, the Don Brewery[175] advertised the pub as being available To Let, and it was taken by William Burkinshaw, a stonemason. William had been born in 1851 at Huthwaite Bank, Thurgoland, and his father, also called William, was the landlord of the Rock Inn at Green Moor from the 1860s until his death in 1877. William and his wife Esther Thompson ran the Sportsman's Arms for about thirty years, although William carried on working as a stonemason; his wife would have run the bar in his absence, with the help of a servant or two. When the 1881 census was taken, the live-in help was a 16-year-old girl called Mary Elizabeth Colley.

In 1893 William applied for a full wines and spirits licence, putting his case that, because there was no fully licensed public house nearby, there was "*a necessity*" for one. If people wanted to buy spirits, they had to travel about a mile or a mile and a half to get them. 192 people signed a "*memorial*" or petition in favour of the application. Signatories included local worthies such as Mr. Rimington Wilson (local landowner and barrister), the vicars of Bolsterstone and Deepcar, local business owners and councillors, and Mr. Herbert Ward, a doctor. There was no opposition to the application, and with the help of friends in high places, William's licence was granted.

---

[174] The Licensing Act of 1872 said that all offences were now to be recorded on the actual licence, and it could be revoked if the landlord continued to breach its conditions. For some reason, the magistrates decided that William's offence was *not* to be recorded on his licence.

[175] According to breweryhistory.com The Don Brewery (A. H. Smith & Co. Ltd) acquired the Sportsman's in April 1892, but perhaps until then they leased the actual building from whoever owned it. It was later acquired by Tennant Brothers Ltd, Exchange Brewery, when they took over the Don Brewery in 1916.

Licences had to be renewed annually, and the following year an objection had been lodged against the pub. Whoever had objected argued that a fully licensed premises in that district was *"unnecessary"* and that William's licence had not been granted by a full bench of magistrates and was thus not lawful. Burkinshaw argued that the number of houses in the neighbourhood had increased from 230 the previous year to 300 and that the nearest fully licensed house was over half a mile away. George Marsh, a grocer who lived next door, argued in favour of the full licence, saying that it would be *"of great convenience"* because at present, anyone who wanted spirits were unable to get them when they required them. The licence was renewed.

AN UNWELCOME CUSTOMER: 1896

A man named William Roebuck was summoned for having been drunk on licensed premises, and with having refused to quit the pub when asked to do so. He had gone into the Sportsman's Arms but Burkinshaw refused to serve him because he was drunk. He told him to leave, but he would not do so. Roebuck admitted the offence and was fined fifteen shillings.

In 1899, Stocksbridge Urban District Council accepted plans for a swing door to be installed in the pub.

The 1901 census records the occupants of the pub as William (licensed victualler), his wife Esther, sons Frank (a storekeeper) and William (a stonemason), and daughters Clara (22), Mary (19), Lena (12) and Florrie (9).

William retired from pub life sometime in about 1906, but he carried on living in the vicinity of the pub at Old Haywoods. In 1911 he and Esther were living with their daughter Lena, her husband Edmund Hall, and their son, 4-year-old Fred. The census recorded that William and Esther had been married for thirty-nine years, that there had been twelve children, but five of them had died.

Arthur Robertson Buttery was the next landlord. He was a silversmith by trade and moved to Deepcar from Sheffield. His wife Mabel Alice Allen was the daughter of George Allen, who was the landlord of the King and Miller at Deepcar from the turn of the century until around 1911. When the 1911 census was taken in April, Arthur was recorded at the Sportsman's Arms along with his wife Mabel Alice, their daughter Hilda Allen Buttery and a servant, Annie E. Haigh. They moved out later that year, and the Pladdeys took over.

Thomas and Elizabeth Pladdey ran the Sportsman's Arms for almost forty years. The pub became known as *"Pladdeys,"* and continued to be called this long after the couple had moved away. New Street (a steep hill at the side of the pub) was known locally as *"Pladdey's Hill."*

Thomas Pladdey had been born in Sheffield in 1875, and he was the son of Thomas Pladdey, a ship's carpenter from Sunderland, and Elizabeth Addy, from Chesterfield. Thomas senior moved south to Bradford and then to Sheffield, working as a joiner/carpenter. He died in 1888 aged 52. His widow lived at Eyre Street in Sheffield. Young Thomas was not recorded on the 1891 census – he would have been about 16 years old – but his mother had quite a houseful of visitors, including some exotic-sounding *"theatrical professionals,"* the Macarte family. Henry Macarte had been born in London, and his wife Regina in Budapest, Hungary. They had three daughters, Julia (13), Adelaide (12), and Blanche (10), who had all been born in Hamburg, Germany. The family was in town for performances at the Albert Hall, which stood in Barker's Pool, Sheffield. The Three Little Sisters Macarte were on the Holiday Bill as Gymnasts. Also appearing on the same bill was an *"extraordinary educated elephant,"* an American humourist, and Tula and Miaco, *"grotesque acrobats."* The Macarte family had been in Sheffield the previous year, performing in John Sanger's circus on Pinstone Street.

In September 1897 Thomas Pladdey married Dorothy Ann White in Derby. His occupation was a joiner, so he was following in his father's footsteps. They moved to Sheffield and had a son called Thomas Stuart Pladdey in 1898, but sadly he died the same year, and the couple had no more children. Thomas and Dorothy lived for a while at Spital Hill in Sheffield before moving to Barnsley Road where they ran a fish restaurant. In 1911 they moved to Stocksbridge to take the Sportsman's Arms.

It may well have been in the Pladdey's time that a bear was occasionally stabled behind the pub. John Holling, who was born in 1901, lived opposite the Sportsman's, where his father had a house and shop. In his memoirs he recalled the bear, which was toured around for *"entertainment"* purposes, though he doesn't mention the year:

"...as boys, we congregated together to see what sort of show was on the road, after learning the man with a bear had left the Public House at Deepcar (the "King and Miller") and was coming up the road. This entertainment, on arrival, was a dirty faced middle-aged man – long oily black hair – unshaven – dishevelled and of foreign tongue. He was accompanied by a large darkish Brown Bear. This bear had a halter around its head, similar to the ones we see today on the cattle on the Show grounds. Attached to this halter was a chain and also a pole, with which the man was able to control the various antics of the bear's performance, and also to curb its temper. After the performance the onlookers gave as they thought fit, and after satisfying the people, he proceeded to stay the night at the "Sportsmans" with his bear. In those days the rear of the Inn was a yard with stables, and the bear was put in the stables. I can remember the bear was huge, and taller than its owner, and he had on occasion to prod it to obedience with the sharpened pole."[176]

Mr. Pladdey was a keen sportsman. The pub had a football and a darts team in the 1930s, but Mr. Pladdey is perhaps best remembered for his skill as an angler, and his involvement with the Stocksbridge and District Motor Cycle & Light Car Club. The Club was formed in 1921 by a Mr. Gregory and held its first Reliability Trial[177] later that year. Mr. Pladdey was a motor enthusiast, and he sponsored the Pladdey Cup, which on this occasion was won by H. Thompson, along with the gold medal. Silver and bronze medals were also awarded. These early meetings were held at the Sportsman's Arms, and the presentations were also held there. In 1923 the second Annual dinner and prize distribution took place, presided over by Mr. Batty of the Friendship Hotel at Stocksbridge, with Mrs. Pladdey presenting the prizes. In November 1930, an Inter-Club Motor-Cycle Trial set off from The Friendship to compete for the *"Friendship"* Trophy, sponsored by Mr. Batty. The first three places went to K. Ellison, J. Armitage, and A. Hayward. The Club fell by the wayside during the Depression, but a new club containing

---

[176] The Memoires of John Holling (MSS, Stocksbridge & District History Society) written in 1959/60.
[177] An organised ride which challenges a rider to complete a course, passing through designated control points, within a pre-set time limit.

old and new members was formed after the second World War. Later meetings were held at the Rock Inn at Green Moor, and regular Scrambles were held at nearby Trunce.

Mrs. Pladdey ran a soup kitchen from the pub during the General Strike of 1926. This was a strike throughout the UK that lasted for nine days, from the 3rd to the 12th May. The strike was called by the Trades Union Council (T.U.C.) in an attempt to force the government to act to prevent wage reduction and worsening conditions for locked-out coal miners; the miners had been locked out of the mines after a dispute with the owners, who wanted them to work longer hours for less pay. In a show of solidarity, around 1.7 million workers went on strike, especially those employed in heavy industry and transport. The action was ultimately unsuccessful but was still regarded as being a *"brilliant failure,"* because it emphasised the workers' solidarity. Although the T.U.C. called off the strike, the miners maintained their resistance for a few months. They held on until December, but they were forced back to work by economic necessity. Many remained unemployed, and those that had gone back were forced to accept longer hours and lower wages, and they felt that nothing had been achieved.

The repercussions, however, lasted longer than nine days. In Stocksbridge, the miners were still on strike, which meant that there was no coal for domestic or industrial use. At the end of May, the Sheffield Independent newspaper reported that Samuel Fox's works had closed because of a lack of fuel, throwing 3,000 men and 300 women out of work. Nearly another 1,000 unemployed in the district were colliery and coke oven workers. The gas supply to Stocksbridge was cut off when the gas coke oven workers came out on strike with the miners, and they were still out. The newspapers reported on other works which had been forced to close through lack of coal, including the world's largest potteries, Sankey and Sons of Nottingham.

The Sheffield Daily Telegraph of the 29th May ran the headline: *"Stocksbridge's Plight. No Gas, No Electricity, and Little Coal."* It reported chaos at the Stocksbridge Labour Exchange when between 2,000 and 3,000 unemployed people had attended to draw their unemployment pay. Owing to the numbers, the Exchange's work had to be removed to the old Electra Picture Palace. There were some *"ugly rushes"* at times when the doors were periodically opened to let applicants in, and two men fell down, exhausted, and had to be treated by ambulance staff. Finally, the police had to be called to regulate the large queues. Many of the men stood there from 9am until 7.30pm without receiving their pay. It had been a month since any fuel had come into the district, and with the gas supply closed down and no electricity available, the position was becoming serious. The majority of people were having to exist on a ration of ½ cwt (56lbs.) of coal per week, and this was only possible because Fox's had released some of the coal from their colliery and placed it at the disposal of the local coal authority.

Not all was doom and gloom though; in May 1926, there may have been no coal or gas, but the Picture Palace was bright. The Palace and one (unnamed) public house had overcome the lighting problem. The manager of the Palace, Mr. Haines, had been making his own electricity by using a 25 horse-power gas engine. When there was no gas to power it, he borrowed a steam engine with a dynamo attached, and joined it up with his switchboard by means of a couple of cables. With the help of an engineering friend, he transformed his gas engine into a petrol engine, which, although slightly more expensive to run, worked just as effectively.

It seems the inhabitants of Garden City were the hardest hit because their fairly new houses used gas for cooking and lighting, the gas being a by-product of plant belonging to Fox's. For a few days, the Garden City residents were without gas, but their neighbours on the hillside above the village were still getting their usual supply. As the supply petered out, those living at higher altitudes were able to get it for longer than those living in the valley.

On the 9th June 1926, the directors of the Sheffield Telegraph and the Star newspapers made a gift of cheques to the Stocksbridge and Chapeltown areas. "*Stocksbridge is probably one of the hardest-hit places in the Sheffield area,*" they wrote. "*Not only has the colliery closed down, but the cessation of coal getting has thrown out of work practically all the men engaged at Samuel Fox's Steel works. A committee have got to work but they find it a difficult task to get funds since the only support they can get is from the local tradespeople. They have managed to carry on, however, and find some food for the children.*" The Vicar of Stocksbridge, the Rev. Garfield Roberts, accepted a cheque for £20 on behalf of the Relief Committee. In his thank you speech, the vicar noted that Stocksbridge had been without fuel and light for six weeks, and the conditions in the village were bad. The local Relief Committee had already collected about £90, mainly from donations from political clubs and other associations and institutes, but most of it had already been doled out to families in need. Mrs. Pladdey was doubtless one of many locals doing their best to help those who were struggling. There was a policy that "*not one child shall go hungry.*" The Sheffield Independent had a "*Feed the Children*" fund; it was still dispensing relief to Stocksbridge in late June when money and a case of milk were sent. In August, Fox's rail mill was put into operation, and work found for about 100 men. It was hoped that things were at last improving.

In December 1932 Thomas Pladdey was called to give evidence at the Sheffield Coroner's Court regarding the death of his wife's brother, a blacksmith called William Henry White. He had at one time lived with them at Spital Hill in Sheffield. The court heard how White had somehow managed to get himself onto a narrow ledge on the Furnival Road railway bridge one Friday night and "*hurled himself to death,*" falling over forty feet in "*a perfect swallow dive.*" He had been lodging at Brittain Street in Sheffield with a widow named Jessie Tattersall for about ten months. She said that he was a very reserved man and had not worked for three weeks and that he seemed very depressed because he could not get any work. He would get home and say that he was "*fed up.*"

Witnesses reported that White jumped headlong from the ledge into the road, coming through the air with his legs and arms outstretched. The police said he was not drunk, but his lips were slightly stained with iodine.[178] A policeman had tried to break White's fall and sustained a broken leg whilst doing so. Giving his evidence, Thomas Pladdey stated that his brother-in-law had a lot of friends on the London and North Eastern Railway (L.N.E.R.) and also suggested White might have got onto the ledge as a prank. "*I have known him to do silly tricks,*" he added. He said that White was used to climbing, and had been abroad, and had caught malaria, but he had never known him to have an attack.

The coroner returned a verdict that he "*committed suicide whilst in a fit of depression, due to unemployment, there not being sufficient evidence to show*

---

[178] Iodine could be used to treat malaria

the state of his mind at the time." The coroner, who said he himself had done a great deal of rock climbing and Alpine climbing, could not understand how White had got onto the ledge and worked his way along it.

The Pladdeys retired in June 1949. The Fox Magazine[179] of Autumn that year ran the following tribute to them:

"Pladdey's. We feel that many past and present employees will join us in expressing regret at the departure of Mr. and Mrs. Thomas Pladdey from "The Sportsman's Arms," Deepcar, in June, when they retired after 38 years there. As a rendezvous for local meetings of every description "Pladdeys" was known for miles. Many of these meetings were intimately connected with "the Works." Perhaps less well known were the sporting achievements of Mr. Pladdey in his early days when he was one of the keenest anglers in Yorkshire, and the generous acts of Mrs. Pladdey who, besides running a soup kitchen for children during the general strike, has helped hundreds of people in need with food and money."

There are still people around who can remember the brewery delivering barrels on a horse-drawn dray in the 1930s before steam-driven lorries were used. The pub had a small room set aside for ladies, who were not allowed in the taproom.

After the Pladdeys retired, other landlords were Mr. Lissamer, Eric Turner, and Alf Spensley. Thomas Pladdey died in 1954 aged 79, and Dorothy in 1955 aged 82.

---

[179] A magazine published for the workers of Fox's and their families, published quarterly from 1946 until 1966. Its policy was that it was "for employees, about employees, the Company and its achievements, and as far as possible, by employees." Copies are available in Stocksbridge library and can be downloaded from the website of the Stocksbridge History Society: https://www.stocksbridgehs.co.uk/archive/fox_magazines/

The sign above the door reads "*William Burkinshaw, Licensed Retailer of Ale, Beer, Porter and Tobacco*" and the one underneath it reads "*Don Brewery Celebrated Ales.*" This dates it to between about 1878 (when William Burkinshaw became the landlord) and 1893 (when the pub was granted a full licence). The pub was later extended, another door installed, and the window design changed.

THE NEW INN, STOCKSBRIDGE

Formerly a beerhouse, the New Inn was at the bottom of Nanny Hill, on the main road at Stocksbridge. It opened in about 1860 but is now a private house. I am told that there used to be a wooden plaque on the wall by the front door, which said that steelworkers who were coming off a night shift at 6am were allowed one hour in which to get a drink. Older residents recall its nickname being *"The Corner Pin."*

Photo credit: Dave Pickersgill

The New Inn at Stocksbridge began life as a beerhouse in about 1860 and continued as such for many years. When the census was taken in 1861 it was recorded as the *"New Inn, Beer House,"* its landlord being Henry Liles, whose occupation was *"Lodging House Keeper."* White's Directory of 1862 lists Henry as a beerhouse keeper and his wife Martha as a dressmaker.[180]

Henry Liles had been born at Clayton West in about 1822, and he married Martha Holmes in 1847. Unusually for the time, Martha's occupation (dressmaker) was recorded on their marriage certificate. Henry was a weaver by trade, and he and Martha lived at Ingbirchworth until around 1858 when they moved to Stocksbridge.

The couple had six children. The first four (Mary Jane, William, Jesse, and Lucy) were born at Ingbirchworth, and in the baptism records Henry's occupation was recorded as a weaver. The next two children were born at Stocksbridge (Elizabeth in 1859 and Henry in 1864).[181] Jesse married my great-great grandfather's sister Harriet Crawshaw in 1890.

ASSAULT ON THE POLICE: 1860
One Saturday night in October 1860 Henry Liles was called upon to help P.C. Samuel MacVeatty, a local policeman. MacVeatty was on duty at Stocksbridge when he heard a disturbance, and when he went to investigate, he found four men pulling a drunken man about. The men, all from Penistone, were Joseph Jubb, Allen Hoyle,[182] George Firth, and Samuel Firth. Intervening in the incident, MacVeatty told the men to be gentle with the drunk, and Jubb told him, *"Policeman, you must take the man home, or I will make you."* MacVeatty said he could not take him home, and he called upon Henry Liles to help him remove the man to his beerhouse. They started to do this, but Jubb changed his mind and told them not to take the drunken man, or he would *"have the policeman's life."* Liles retreated to his house, and the policeman let go of the man he was holding. Jubb then savagely

---

[180] During the years the Liles were at the New Inn, its location was variously listed as being in Hunshelf, Stocksbridge or Deepcar. Liles was also spelt Lisles and Lyles.
[181] Henry arrived in Stocksbridge between the birth of Lucy (at Ingbirchworth on the 7th December 1857), and Elizabeth (at Hunshelf, Stocksbridge on the 10th January 1859). The baptism register says that Elizabeth was born at Hunshelf and that her father was an inn keeper.
[182] Spelt Hoyland the second time in the newspaper report

attacked MacVeatty, knocking him down and using a great deal of violence, assisted by his companions. The case went to court, and the men were all fined. Jubb and Hoyland [sic] were fined £5 each, George Firth £2, and Samuel Firth £1.

STEALING A HAT AT HUNSHELF: 1864
Two of the men involved in the assault on P.C. MacVeatty were in trouble again four years later. George Firth and Allen Hoyle, both labourers, were charged under the Vagrancy Act with stealing a hat from the house of a Mrs. Jukes.[183] She told the court that one afternoon at around 5pm the two men called at her house asking if they could buy some bread. She refused, but she did give them some oatcake and milk. The next morning, she noticed that her son's hat (which was always hung up behind the door) was missing, and she informed the police. Her son, Joseph Charlesworth, identified the hat in court as his. Henry Liles was called to give evidence and told the court that the men had called at the New Inn that day, and that he had given them a quart of beer *"on the hat,"* which he gave to the police. P.C. Robinson said he apprehended the men three days later, and that they had both denied stealing the hat. This was apparently a first offence – there was no mention of the assault charge – and they were each sentenced to fourteen days in jail with hard labour. Mrs. Martha Jukes lived at Dyson Cote, Hunshelf, with her husband Benjamin, her son Joseph and her daughter Mary. The family also had a lodger, a policeman called Wilson.

Many public houses held auctions, although the New Inn does not seem to have been one of them. Therefore, we can probably assume that the auction held there on the 16th August 1866 involved the sale of Henry's effects prior to him leaving the business that year. When the 1871 census was taken, he was living in Stocksbridge and was working as a labourer. Items offered for sale included bedsteads, mattresses, beds, chairs, tables, a langsettle, carpets, boxes, kitchen requisites and so on.

The next landlord was Joseph Gill, who ran the place for about thirteen years until his death in 1879, after which his wife Eliza took over. Gill came from Hunshelf and he was married to Eliza Micklethwaite, the daughter of Benjamin Micklethwaite, schoolmaster at Green Moor school. After their

---

[183] The Vagrancy Act of 1824 made it an offence to sleep rough or beg.

marriage at Penistone in 1852, Joseph and Eliza lived for a while at Deepcar before taking over from Henry Liles at the New Inn. Joseph, Eliza, and their seven children were living at the New Inn when the 1871 census was taken, along with a lodger.

There were fields at the back of the pub, and Joseph held pigeon shooting matches there. Many other landlords in the area did the same. He also fielded a cricket team. In the 1920s the Stocksbridge Harriers (cross-country runners) used the New Inn as their base.

EXTRAORDINARY ACCIDENT TO CHILDREN: 1867

One Sunday afternoon in August at around 8pm a number of children were playing with one of Mr. Hinchliffe's wagons, which had been used as a platform by the Primitive Methodists during the day. Some of the bigger boys unlocked the wheels to give those mounted on the wagon a ride down the field, which was a small croft opposite the New Inn. They had not gone far when they found themselves quite unable to hold it, and they threw down the shafts and ran away. One of the children on the wagon managed to jump off, but the rest were carried with increasing speed to the bottom of the field down a very steep slope, where the wagon turned over and pitched the rest of them into the river. Fortunately, most of them were not badly hurt, but four were stunned and bruised, one of them severely.

In 1869 a law was passed which brought all beerhouses under the much stricter control of the local magistrates. All beer sellers, including beershops, now had to apply to the magistrates for a licence. The magistrates based their decisions on police reports and inspections of the premises, taking into account the suitability of the applicant, the suitability of the premises, and the needs of the locality (they may have thought that there were enough pubs in the locality already). Many magistrates used the new legislation to get rid of previously troublesome beerhouses. Joseph duly applied, and when the Brewster Sessions were held that year, his licence was granted because he was deemed to have a "*good character.*"

OBTAINING MONEY BY FALSE PRETENCES: 1876

Appearing at the West Riding Court, Fred Hurst, a 23-year-old labourer who lived at Joiner Lane, Sheffield, was charged with obtaining money by false pretences from Joseph Gill. Hurst had gone to the New Inn one Monday and asked the landlord to lend him two shillings, which he needed in order to pay the blacksmith at Deepcar, where he had left a dray to be repaired. He told Gill that he worked as a drayman for Reuben Senior of Shepley, who was a brewer, and that his master would pay the money back. Gill knew Reuben Senior well, and so he lent Hurst the money. Five days later, Gill went into The Friendship a short way up the road, and he saw Hurst borrow five shillings from the landlord Thomas Batty. Realising that they were being cheated, they summoned a police officer and P.C. Delve took Hurst into custody. In court, it was found that Hurst had ceased to be employed by the brewer the previous year. Because this was a serious crime, the case was referred to the Sessions to be tried there. He pleaded guilty to both charges and was sentenced to six months' imprisonment with hard labour.

A FRIENDLY GLASS OF BEER: 1877

In December 1877, Joseph Gill was summoned to court for opening during prohibited hours. Sergeant Wright testified that he went to the New Inn at 9.45am one Sunday morning and found a man named Joseph Illingworth in the kitchen. He was a milk seller, and *"did not live a mile away."* The distance was important because there was an exception to the law made for genuine travellers; they were allowed to obtain a drink outside of the opening hours, but they had to live at least three miles away from the pub in which they were found.[184] Illingworth had a glass of beer before him, three parts full. Gill's solicitor, Mr. Binney (solicitor for the Sheffield and Rotherham Licensed Victuallers' Association) called as witnesses the landlord and his wife, as well as Mr. Illingworth, to confirm this. The Bench said it was *"a suspicious case,"* but under the circumstances, they had no choice but to dismiss it. They also complimented the sergeant on his conduct of the case. As no other people were found in the pub, it does look as if Joseph had simply offered the milkman a drink, and because the magistrates could not prove otherwise, the case was thrown out.

Two years later, on the 24th March 1879, Joseph died at the New Inn, aged just 49. The pub stayed in the family for many years; Joseph's widow Eliza carried on as landlady until her death five years later, and she was succeeded

---

[184] An Act of 1854 had introduced the concept of a *bona fide* [genuine] traveller, in a bid to cut abuse of the existing exemption for travellers by those who just wanted a drink. An Act of 1874 further qualified this by defining a traveller as someone who was at least three miles from his previous night's lodging.

by her daughter Ruth and son-in-law Joseph Addy. After Ruth died, her son John Arthur Addy became the landlord.

According to the 1881 census, the New Inn was in the occupation of Eliza Gill, beerhouse keeper, five of her children (George, Benjamin, William, Joe, and James), and her niece Sarah Ann Gill, who was employed there as a domestic servant. There were two houses adjoining the pub, and the house next door to the pub was occupied by Eliza's daughter Ruth along with her husband Joseph Addy, their two young sons (Joseph William and John Arthur), and a 13-year-old girl called Ann Elizabeth Beachill, who was employed as their nurse.

Eliza died at the New Inn on the 3rd March 1884 aged 53. She did not leave a will, and her daughter Ruth was granted the Administration of her personal estate, which was valued at just over £643.[185]

Ruth Gill had married Joseph Addy at Thornhill Lees near Dewsbury in 1876. They lived in the house adjoining the New Inn until they took over its running, perhaps on the death of Eliza in 1884, but they were probably helping to run it earlier than that. By 1891 Ruth's brother William and his wife Amelia had moved into the house next to the pub.

The 1901 census recorded Joseph Addy as a "*beerhouse keeper*" at the New Inn. Also at the pub was a visitor called Elizabeth Ellen Moorwood. Elizabeth went on to marry Joseph's son John Arthur Addy in 1903. John Arthur was recorded on this census with his brother Joseph William at Otley Street, Walkley, both their occupations being pawn broker managers. John Arthur, having grown up in a pub, decided to take the Royal Oak at Deepcar after he married; he was there until 1913, and he later moved back to the New Inn in 1922. The two adjoining houses, the New Inn Cottages, were occupied by William and Amelia Gill, and by Ann May Drabble in 1901. The cottage which was adjacent to the pub was incorporated into it when renovations were carried out in the 1970s. The pub was given indoor toilets, the gents having been outside, and any ladies wanting the loo had previously had to queue up the stairs to use the landlady's own bathroom. At one time, the

---

[185] The equivalent of over £80,000 today, according to the Bank of England's Inflation Calculator

occupant of this adjoining cottage was one Captain Marple, who had been a Canadian Mountie. His memorabilia of those times was displayed throughout his house.

According to the 1911 census, the New Inn was still a beerhouse, and not a fully licensed premises.[186]

The pub had been holding annual Cottage Garden Society meetings since about 1877, ever since Joseph Gill was the landlord. Reports of these meetings began to appear in the Sheffield newspapers from 1901. The Sheffield Daily Telegraph of the 15th September 1913 reported that the New Inn had held the 37th annual show of plants, flowers, and vegetables, which was a *"decided success,"* and very well patronised. John Arthur Addy won a lot of the prizes on offer.

A Botanist Society met at the New Inn every Sunday, one of its members being Doctor Mossman, who at one time ran a surgery from his home at Bank House, near Ford Lane (now demolished). Frederick Vernon Mossman had been born in Devonport and had lived in various places before being appointed medical officer and public vaccination officer for Stocksbridge in 1904. He died suddenly in 1918 aged 54.

FATAL TRAIN CRASH AT CUDWORTH: 1905
There was a fatal train crash near Darfield Station, Barnsley, at around 3am on the 19th January 1905. The Scotch Express crashed into the rear of the mail train when dense fog prevented the signals from being seen. Six people were killed in the accident (four passengers, a fireman, and a guard), and one died a few days later. Both trains were wrecked, and a fire broke out. Doctors from Sheffield and Cudworth arrived, and a passenger from the Scotch Express, Driver Wright of the 105th Battery, Royal Field Artillery, was a big help in the rescue. An appeal to recognise his *"conspicuous bravery"* was organised by the Sheffield Daily Telegraph (they started it off with two guineas), and the customers of the New Inn contributed seven shillings and sixpence, worth around £50 in today's money. Mr. Hayes Fisher M.P. who had been one of the passengers, organised another appeal

---

[186] It is not known when it gained a full wines and spirits licence, but it was still a beerhouse as late as 1929, being listed as such in a trade directory of that year.

for the goods guard who had done much to help as well. The Midland Railway Company gave money and watches as gifts to various people including Driver Wright in thanks for their help and service. Two of those who were killed were brothers, Scottish boys returning to school in Berkshire after the holidays. The others were James Gray of Gateshead, Guard James Weston, engine fireman Patterson, and a commercial traveller who had not been identified. The seventh victim, who died a few days later, was a *"brilliant young Scottish artist"* called Robert Brough.

Joseph Addy died in June 1914 aged 64, and the Sheffield Daily Telegraph said that he was a well-known and respected inhabitant of the area, and one of the oldest publicans in the district. He left estate valued at just over £4,000, with net personalty of £467.[187]

The beerhouse licence was transferred to his widow Ruth, and she would no doubt have been assisted by some of her children and a few servants. Her son John Arthur Addy was the landlord of the Royal Oak at Deepcar in 1911. He left there in 1913, moving to the Old Haywoods and later to Low Lane (Victoria Road), but he moved back to the New Inn after his mother's death. He took over the licence when she died in 1922.

In 1915, Doris Micklethwaite[188] of the New Inn donated 3s. 6d. for the troops who were away fighting in the Great War. The Sheffield Independent was organising parcels for soldiers and sailors. They had struck a deal whereby they saved duty on tobacco and cigarettes, and a parcel of tobacco, cigarettes, and chocolate could be sent out for 2s. 6d. instead of 5s. 3d. They asked for donations of 2s. 6d. but many, like Doris, sent more. The parcels were sent to local regiments for distribution. Almost £2,000 had been raised when Doris contributed her money, perhaps raised from the New Inn's customers.

In 1921 the New Inn was the venue for a *"Smoking Concert"* organised for the members and friends of the Stocksbridge Church Cricket and Football Club. The cricket club had been the champions of the Norton and District League and the Sugg League the previous year, whilst the football club

---

[187] Personal estate which does not include property; it is money, possessions, furniture etc.
[188] Ruth Addy's mother had been a Micklethwaite before her marriage, so Doris was possibly a relation

carried off the Junior League honours. The chairman presented gold watches to the Treasurer Marsh Swallow, and the secretary Willie Booth; the latter would later become the landlord, in about 1924. Smoking Concerts were live performances, usually of music, and were generally for men only. As the name suggests, men would meet to smoke and speak of topics such as sport and politics, whilst listening to live music.

Ruth Addy died at the New Inn on the 19th January 1922 aged 67. Her son, John Arthur Addy, moved back into the pub after his mother's death. This seems to have been a temporary measure because by 1924 the landlord was Willie Booth. John Arthur moved out, living at Townend for a while before settling at Skelton Villas or Skelton Grove in the early 1930s. Skelton Grove is a row of houses on the corner of Hole House Lane and Pot House Lane, and it was once known by locals as Addy Row; John Arthur and his wife Elizabeth had a shop there.

SUMMONED FOR ALLOWING BETTING: 1923

John Arthur Addy was summoned to appear at the West Riding Police Court, accused of allowing his pub to be used for betting. P.C.s Kitson and Driver were in plain clothes when they visited the New Inn one day in June 1923. They alleged that they saw five men writing out betting slips and handing them to the landlord, who took the money and placed it in a tin box on a shelf. It was observed that money taken for beer was placed separately in the till. The P.C.s went back a second time and witnessed the landlord receiving a slip. They saw an old man was writing out a slip and heard the landlord say, *"You are a long while making it out – are you sorting another winner out? Bring it to the bar, when you have finished."* On a third occasion, a man handed something to the landlord and received something in return. Addy, the officers alleged, turned to the company in the room and said, *"That chap's lucky. That's the second time I have paid him out this week, and they have both been big prices."*

P.C. Kitson said that he went into the New Inn wearing overalls. He denied that on the first occasion the people in the pub knew he was a policeman, and that one man had said, *"If you had your proper clothes on you would not be here."* Sergeant Wright said he found £10 and some silver in a box, which the landlord said was spare cash for the till.

The defence was that no one would have been betting because they all knew that the men were "*police spies,*" and they argued that they were immediately recognised. One of them had said he was "*a chimney jack,*" and he was laughed at. It was said to be significant that neither officer made a bet, and no betting material was found on the landlord. Several witnesses were called to prove the house was conducted in a proper manner. The Chairman said that it was a rather complicated case, and the police had done right to bring it, but because there was some doubt, he had to dismiss it. In a place like Stocksbridge, one would have thought that all the policemen were well known to the public, which is perhaps why the element of doubt was there.

Willie Booth was the next landlord and he and his wife Emma were there from 1924 until 1932. Willie had married Emma Robinson in 1891 and had worked as a miner before moving to Common Piece in about 1916, where they ran a shop. The shop was licensed to sell beer for consumption off the premises and had previously been licensed to Edwin Bamforth. The Booths moved to the New Inn in 1924, and they ran it until John Wood took over in 1933. When Ernest Schofield set up his new company in 1920, Schofield Brothers (Stocksbridge) Ltd, Motor Transport, and Picture House Proprietors, Willie was one of the Directors. He died at Hawthorn Brook in 1935 aged 66.

John and Lily Wood were at the New Inn for two years, 1933-1935, before handing over to Harry Wilkinson Blackburn in January 1935. Harry had been born at Cleckheaton in 1883, and his family moved to the Darnall area of Sheffield. He had married Emma Elliott in 1910. According to the 1911 census, Harry was a grocer's clerk. In March 1938, Harry put himself forward as a candidate for a seat on Stocksbridge Council, but he did not get elected. Edwin Thomas Littler won one seat (1,421 votes), the other three going to Vincent Challis, Percy Schofield, and David Allan Truman. Harry Blackburn got 642 votes.

Harry died two months later on the 11th May 1938. He was 55 years old and was buried at Tinsley Park Cemetery. At his funeral, the Rev. Garfield Roberts (who had also stood, unsuccessfully, for election) attributed the virtues of "*manliness, simplicity and sympathy*" to him. Like my great-grandfather Wilfred Donkersley (who was present at the funeral as a representative of the Stocksbridge and District Tradesmen's Association),[189] Harry was a member of the R.A.O.B. or Royal Antediluvian Order of Buffaloes. *"The Buffs,"* as they are commonly known, are a fraternal organisation similar to the Freemasons, and they usually held their meetings in pubs – which also accounts for nicknames such as the *"Boozy Buffs."* They did a lot of charitable work. Wilfred Donkersley was a member of the Hand o'Friendship Lodge which met at the Friendship Hotel just up the road from the New Inn.[190] The R.A.O.B. ritual was carried out at the graveside by Mr. R. Froggatt; he would have read the Buffalo service, and any Brothers present would stand around the coffin and drop ivy leaves.

Harry's widow Emma married again the following year, to George Herbert Elliott, and they went to live at 87 Victoria Road, Stocksbridge.

We leave the New Inn history in 1939, a year after James Walter Sykes moved in after the death of Harry Blackburn. He was the son of Walt Sykes and Emma Charlesworth and was known as *"Walt junior."* Born in 1887, he married Elsie May Evans in 1911. She had been born in Stocksbridge in 1889 and was the daughter of Josiah Barber Evans. She was my great-great-grandmother Sarah Hannah Crawshaw's cousin.[191] Members of the Evans family had, like so many, come over from Samuel Fox's home village of Bradwell in Derbyshire to work in the wire-drawing business he started here in the 1840s. Young Walt had been a collier before he became the landlord of the New Inn.

And finally … One of the New Inn's customers was known as *"Mrs. Navvy Adams."* A colourful character, she lived in a house on the corner of Victoria Street and Button Row. Mrs. Adams took in lodgers, including the navvies who would have been working on the construction of the dams. She had a large family (the 1911 census listed her with eight children and recorded that she'd had 11 children but 2 had died). The long kitchen table was scrubbed until it was white as snow, and the flagstones on the floor were very smooth and clean. Apparently, she was prim and neat, always felt dressed up when

---

[189] The Tradesmen's Association's representatives were: Mr. Percy Schofield (president), Mr. G. C. Knowles (secretary), Mr. E. Jackson (treasurer) and Messrs. J. Bisby, J. Adams, Norman Knowles, W. Dimmock, Wilfred Donkersley and A. Rogers.
[190] See the chapter on the Friendship for more information on the R.A.O.B.
[191] Sarah Hannah Evans married Thomas Henry Crawshaw in 1884

she wore her white apron, but for some reason she always wore a man's flat cap. She also smoked a clay pipe, sometimes swapping it for a briar pipe [a wooden pipe made from briar wood]. She liked a glass of beer in the New Inn and joined in most pub games. She was never unkind or aggressive. Jack Branston worked for the Co-op for many years, and he remembered that she would go in every Monday and ask for a *"sixpenny knock-out bag"* for her pipe. This contained all sorts of tobacco that had fallen into the drawer bottom, and was a mix of Sweet Crop, Thundercloud, Bruno, Thick Twist, Honey Dew, and Warhorse. Which, I am told, would have tasted very odd indeed! [192]

Mrs. Navvy Adams was called Thirza (nee Radmore) and she had been born at New Brompton, Kent, in 1868. Her husband John Adams was born at Astley St. Mary, Shropshire, in 1860. In 1911 the family were living at Hayfield, Derbyshire, and in 1901 they were in Cardiff. John worked as a navvy on the reservoirs and travelled about for work. It is thought that the family moved to Stocksbridge in about 1913 when work commenced on the dams in Ewden Valley. They were here until about 1927. John died in 1934 and Thirza died in 1942; they are both buried in the churchyard at Heptonstall, West Yorkshire.[193]

---

[192] This story is taken from Jack Branston's book The History of Stocksbridge & District

[193] This paragraph is an amendment from the first printing of this book because I had confused a lady called Caroline Adams with Thirza. Caroline Adams also lived at Button Row and took in lodgers. Her husband Frederick worked for the waterboard, as did John. Thank you to Gail Adams Linaker for the correction; Gail is the great granddaughter of John and Thirza.

TRAVELLERS INN, VAUGHTON HILL, DEEPCAR

The Travellers Inn was on Vaughton Hill, Deepcar, and started out as a beerhouse run by James Vaughton in the mid-1830s. He lived at the bottom house of this row of three. This photograph was taken when Arthur Reddish was the landlord (from 1901-1908). The pub was also known as the "*Low Drop*" because it was at the bottom of the row. It was also referred to in various documents over the years as the Travellers Rest. This pub closed in 1932.

James Vaughton first ran a beerhouse from his home in the mid-1830s. The Beerhouse Act of 1830 had removed beerhouses from the control of the licensing magistrates, and any homeowner who met certain conditions could now brew and sell beer from his house once he had paid the Excise two guineas for the privilege. Beerhouses were not allowed to sell stronger drink such as wines and spirits. James was a stonemason, a trade he continued to work at after he opened the beerhouse, which his wife would have run in his absence. He was married to Elizabeth Couldwell, whose nephew Benjamin opened the Royal Oak just across the way in the 1830s, perhaps at about the same time the Travellers was opened.

In July 1836 James Vaughton gave notice to the parish officials that he intended to apply for a licence to sell wines and spirits at the upcoming Annual Licensing Meeting. He owned his own house, which was described as being on the road leading from the Turnpike Road at Deepcar (Manchester Road), to Wortley. The full licence was not granted, but no reason was given for this decision. James died the following year and his widow Elizabeth continued to run the beerhouse for over ten years with the help of her son, who was also called James. In addition, she farmed ten acres of land.

James Vaughton junior had been born in 1822, and he lived next door to his mother in the middle house of the row of three. He was a filesmith by trade and worked in the attached forge. He was first mentioned as a publican in 1858.[194] The first mention of the place being called The Travellers Inn comes at the end of June 1859 when the Sheffield newspapers printed a list of all those who were giving notice that they intended to apply for a licence at the next Brewster Sessions. This list included James Vaughton of the Travellers Inn, Deepcar, although when the licence was granted, the pub was not named; one of the newspaper reports merely said that James Vaughton lived "*near the Deepcar-road* [railway] *Station*." The pub was now fully licensed and able to sell wines and spirits. Elizabeth still lived on the premises, but it was now James's name over the door.

---

[194] When James's daughter Sarah was baptised at Bolsterstone in 1858, his occupation was "*file cutter and publican*." Despite having died in 1837, James Vaughton senior, stonemason, continues to be listed in trade directories. It was not until 1856 that his widow Elizabeth was listed alone as running a beerhouse.

James carried on working in the smithy during the day and served in the bar at night. He was married to Hannah Bramall whose father John Bramall was the first landlord of the Castle at Bolsterstone. In 1861 John was living next door to the Vaughtons, and perhaps he helped out in the bar now and again. Hannah died young, in 1865, and Elizabeth Vaughton died the following year at the age of 83.

At the West Riding Brewster Sessions in September 1860 Mr. Windle of Deepcar tried to get the licence (which had been granted to James at the previous Brewster Sessions) set aside, on the grounds that the place was "*wholly unnecessary.*" This was almost certainly Abraham Windle, who at that time lived nearby at Wortley and who owned the "*chemical works*" at Deepcar (which was later occupied by Lowood & Co.)[195] Perhaps he thought that his workforce spent far too much time in there, or in the other two public houses at Deepcar, the King and Miller and the Royal Oak. Mr. Chambers[196] appeared on behalf of Vaughton, handing in a "*respectably-signed memorial*" which said that the house was well run and a great convenience. The Bench agreed, saying that the Travellers Inn had been "*exceedingly well conducted, that it was admirably adapted for an inn, and that it would be a very great injustice if they now refused to renew the licence.*" The licence was duly renewed. Perhaps Mr. Windle was objecting to the granting of a licence to sell spirits as well as beer, but his objection referred only to the pub itself being unnecessary.

AUCTION: January 1863

Auctioneer Mr. Robert Lowe held an auction at the Travellers in January 1863. Up for sale in separate Lots was a farmhouse and quite a few acres of land. The farmhouse, barn, stable, and all the outbuildings were in the tenancy of Jonathan Swallow, and the 1861 census tells us that he lived at Lane, Deepcar (up what is now Carr Road) and that he farmed thirty acres of

---

[195] The 1861 census lists Abraham Windle's occupations as "*Farmer of 157 acres, corn miller, manufacturing chemist, timber merchant. Employing about 50 men and 10 boys.*" He had erected a new corn mill sometime between 1838 and 1849, and it stood close to the Travellers Inn on Vaughton Hill, at Mill Lane (what is now the entrance to the Don Field).

[196] Mr. Chambers is mentioned in many of the reports of the Brewster Sessions. This was perhaps John Chambers, a solicitor & attorney at law, who lived in Sheffield. In later court reports an H. W. Chambers was mentioned; probably his son, Harry Walker Chambers, solicitor & attorney - he represented the Sheffield Brewers Association.

land, which is more or less the amount that was up for sale, some of it fronting Carr Road and Manchester Road. Much of it was arable or grass, but it was also suitable for building on; some of the land was later used to build the houses at Frank Hillock Field and Netherfield Close. Lot four was rented out to Jonathan Thompson, Joseph Dronfield, and Benjamin Grayson, and consisted of three houses and a cabinet maker's shop (the latter in the occupation of Jonathan Thompson). These houses appear to have been near to the Deepcar Schools on Carr Road, and would, said the advert, be suitable for the erection of a brewery or manufactory, the land having a stream of water running through it. Some of the other Lots were The Carr and The Nook. Jonathan was married to Jane Vaughton.[197] By 1871 they had moved to Haywoods, Deepcar, and Jonathan was working as a labourer.

HIGHWAY ROBBERY AT DEEPCAR: February 1863

This rather dramatic newspaper headline does not refer to a daring robbery by a masked Dick Turpin riding a black horse, but merely to a robbery that took place on the highway. One Saturday night in February 1863, farm labourer Thomas Siddons was walking home to Town End from the Travellers Inn when he was set upon and robbed by two Wadsley men, John Bland and George Dronfield. The pair appeared in court charged with "*highway robbery*," having stolen Thomas's felt hat, a silk handkerchief, a cotton handkerchief, and two pence in money.

All the men had been drinking in the Travellers along with a Joel Bramall from Oughtibridge. Siddons was very drunk; indeed, he confessed to being rather the worse for liquor. When the pub closed, Bland and Dronfield told him they wanted to spend the night at Deepcar rather than face the long walk home. The newspapers offered different accounts of what had happened and it isn't clear whether Siddons had tried to get rid of the men, or whether he had offered them a bed and some "*real good stuff to drink*" at his house. One newspaper reported that Bramall had followed the men and Siddons, hoping that the offer of something to drink extended to him too. Siddons accused the two men Bland and Dronfield of attacking him, dragging him into the road by his neck, kicking him, and stealing his property. They, on the other hand, insisted that Siddons was so drunk that he fell over, and they could not

---

[197] Jane was born in 1827 and was the daughter of James Vaughton and his wife Elizabeth Couldwell, and the younger sister of James Vaughton junior from the Travellers Inn

get him to walk, so they left him lying in the road. Which was rather uncharitable of them, it being February.

A policeman named McVitty was summoned, and he called at the men's houses where he found the stolen property. Dronfield told him, "*I wish we had killed the old b--, and then he could not have told. I found it on the ground by the side of him when he was down.*"

As with all serious cases, this one was referred to the York Assizes the following month. Bland insisted that the whole thing was merely a drunken lark and that Siddons and the policeman had brought no one to court to prove that Dronfield had really said those words. Dronfield, defending himself, stated that Siddons was so drunk that he fell down some steps and cut his head, and so he picked up the old man's hat and coat and took them home, intending to return them the next morning (which also seems uncharitable; surely if they decided to leave him in the road it would have been kinder to have left him with his hat and coat).

The jury returned a verdict of not guilty, and the prisoners were free to go. It seems that in this case not only was the victim's version of events not believed, the policeman's word was doubted as well.

Five years later, Siddons was involved in another attack whilst drinking in the King and Miller. His son had entered the pub, arguing with James Couldwell. 60-year-old Thomas intervened in the fight by hitting Couldwell with his walking stick, but he came off worse, being severely beaten by Couldwell, who was fined £5 for the assault.[198]

James Vaughton's wife Eliza died in 1865 and his mother Elizabeth died in 1866. A month or so later he married for a second time, to Eliza Ann Gidlow,[199] but the marriage was short-lived because she died in 1867.

According to one of his descendants, James Vaughton was originally a teetotaller but later descended into alcoholism. He became unable to meet

---

[198] See the chapter on the King and Miller for full details
[199] Sister to Sarah Gidlow, who was married to James Vaughton's brother-in-law Joseph Bramall (the brother of his first wife, Hannah Bramall). The Gidlows came from Leeds.

the bills and was declared bankrupt in November 1867, resulting in him having to leave the pub. Did the deaths of two of his children (in 1861 and 1864), his mother (in 1866), and two wives in quick succession (1865 and 1867) make him seek solace in the bottle? His brother-in-law Jonathan Makin took over as the licensee of the Travellers, and James went to live in the cottage adjoining the pub, going back to his original trade of filesmith. He lived there for over twenty years. Jonathan was married to James's elder sister, Sarah Vaughton.

There was no notice in the newspapers about the pub being either sold or put up for lease, so this was could have been a private arrangement between James Vaughton and his son-in-law to satisfy his creditors. According to a descendant,[200] James was in debt to the brewery and had to give them the pub. The brewery would have been the ones to petition for a bankruptcy order against him and would have had a claim on any assets that he had; the court would order how these were to be distributed. According to the website breweryhistory.com, Thomas Rawson & Company, The Pond Street Brewery, acquired the Travellers in 1867; as James was declared bankrupt in November 1867, so there could be some truth in this. Official Assignees were chosen in December to collect proof of his debts from both himself and his creditors. When all debts had been paid and the creditors were satisfied, the Commissioners could issue a Discharge Certificate – this was granted in January 1868.

James married for a third time in 1884, to Eliza Helliwell. When she died in 1893, he moved away to live with his sons Henry and John at their farm at Stubbin, Deepcar. He was said to have had such a taste for whisky that he used to drink the bottle that was kept in the cow barn to treat sick cattle. He died in 1901 aged 78 and was buried at Bolsterstone. All three wives are commemorated on his headstone. Olwen Firth thought that James was the family's "*Black Sheep*," who inherited a great deal from his father but lost it all.

BRUTAL OUTRAGE ON A GAME WATCHER AT DEEPCAR: 1869
It was a Saturday evening in June in the Travellers Inn, and at about 11pm a dispute arose between one of Lord Wharncliffe's occasional game-watchers

---

[200] Olwen Firth, who was a teacher at Deepcar St. John's junior school.

called Edward Wragg and a 19-year-old man called Dan Moorhouse. The men were arguing because Wragg had hauled Moorhouse's younger brother George up before the magistrates for poaching, which resulted in him being fined. The argument went on for some time, and in the end, to calm things down, Wragg agreed to pay for some drink for Moorhouse. This was not enough though, because he also wanted some of his brother's fine reimbursed. Moorhouse insisted his brother had done no wrong, and that he would get his revenge on the gamekeeper. Wragg was attacked later that night at Ellen Cliffe, which was part of the Wharncliffe Estate.

Wragg was struck on the head with a large stone, which stunned him, and then he was savagely kicked and left on the ground all night until a passer-by found him at around 5am. The surgeon and a police officer were called. Wragg had severe head and eye injuries and could not be moved from his bed without danger. Moorhouse was arrested by P.C. Robertshaw and charged with unlawful assault. He confessed, "*I did it. I don't deny that,*" and he was remanded in custody.

In court, Moorhouse's solicitor insisted that what happened was the result of a quarrel brought on by Wragg, who was very drunk and who had challenged his client to a fight. His injuries, he said, were not inflicted with any malicious intent, and were partly the result of a fall; that in his "*drunken ramblings*" he must have injured himself on a stone or a tree. George Moorhouse, the prisoner's brother, gave evidence to the effect that Wragg was "*very quarrelsome,*" and thought that he was "*t'mester o'everybody at Deepcar*" [the boss of everyone]. He said he had heard the keeper ask his brother several times to go up the wood and fight him. Richard Wilson, a saddler, gave similar evidence. Moorhouse was bailed and committed for trial, charged with unlawfully and maliciously wounding Wragg. He was found guilty of common assault and sentenced to three months' imprisonment.

It was common practice for the Coroner to use public houses when inquests were held. One such inquest took place at the Travellers in November 1869. A man called Charles Wainwright had been killed at Deepcar railway station one Friday morning, and the inquest on the body was held at the pub the following day. Wainwright worked as a carter for Samuel Fox and was moving some trucks with his horse. He went to uncouple the last of the trucks whilst they were still moving, and he was caught between the buffers and killed "*almost instantaneously.*" A verdict of accidental death was returned.

In June 1870 Jonathan Makin was in trouble with the authorities for breaching the terms of his licence by allowing drinking outside of the allowed hours. Two policemen had entered the pub one Sunday morning at 11am and found eight men, six of whom were drinking. Jonathan said the men were travellers, but the Bench did not believe him, and he was fined twenty shillings plus costs. Makin was using as his defence an Act of 1854 concerning Sunday closing hours. Alcohol was only allowed be served on Sundays between 1pm and 2.30pm, and between 6pm and 10pm, but an exception was made for "*bona fide*" travellers to be served refreshment. The interpretation of this law was, of course, open to abuse, and two years after Makin was fined, in 1872, an Act was passed which clarified what constituted "*bona fide travellers.*"[201] Even after the passing of this later Act, landlords continued to use it as a handy "*get-out clause*" from the law. The prosecution had to prove that the landlord did not honestly believe that his customer was a true traveller when he chose to serve him outside of normal opening hours.

Three months later the West Riding Licensing Sessions met, and the newspapers reported on the "*blacklist,*" which contained the names of ten people who had been fined during the year. Making an appearance on this list was Jonathan Makin. What usually happened is that all of those on the blacklist would be called before the Bench and cautioned as to their behaviour in the future. In some instances, the landlord could lose their licence. If the licence was renewed, any further trouble could lead to it being revoked.

Jonathan's tenure as the landlord was not a long one, for he died in June 1871, having been the landlord for four years. His widow Sarah took over and she ran the place for over twenty years; she was still landlady in 1891 at the age of 79. When the 1881 census was taken, the row of three houses was called "*Makin Row*" after the family, and in 1891 it was "*Vaughton Row*" even though Mrs. Makin still lived at the pub.

---

[201] Bona Fide literally means "*in good faith*"; real, genuine, without intention to deceive. In this context, it refers to someone who "*goes into an inn for refreshment in the course of a journey, whether of business or pleasure.*" It did not mean one who travelled purely "*for the purpose of taking refreshment.*"

BRAWLING IRISHMEN: 1871

There was some trouble in the pub one Sunday night in December 1871, six months after Jonathan died. A policeman was called to quell a disturbance, and he walked into quite a scene. About twenty-five Irish men were fighting, tables were overturned, glasses broken, and ale spilled. It took P.C. Tomlinson and the landlord's son an hour to clear the house; the men left eventually, but threw stones at the policeman when he followed them. Six of the men, all labourers living at Stocksbridge, were summoned to appear at the West Riding Court in Sheffield where they were charged with being drunk and refusing to quit a public house. The men were James Roans, Patrick McDonald, Michael Kelly, William Robinson, John Clarke, and Richard Clarke. P.C. Tomlinson identified all the defendants except Robinson, who he said had been summoned by mistake and he was therefore discharged. The others were fined ten shillings each.

PERMITTING DRUNKENNESS: 1881

Things appeared quiet for the most part, with Sarah Makin keeping an orderly house until 1881 when she was charged with *"permitting drunkenness."* Sergeant Tingey reported that he had seen several men in front of the pub and that had he ordered them to go away, before going inside himself, where he found a large number of people. There was music and dancing in one bar, and in the taproom, he found a man called Thomas Wilkinson lying on the sofa, hopelessly drunk and fast asleep. The man was taken home by his son and by Sarah's son. In her defence, Sarah said she did not know about the drunkard in the house. The magistrates believed her, and the case was dismissed. Thomas Wilkinson was a corn miller and lived at Carr Head cottages, Deepcar.

It seems odd that pubs were places where people went to drink, and get drunk, and yet it was an offence to be seen to be drunk. It was also an offence for a landlord to permit drunkenness on licensed premises. But what constituted *"drunkenness,"* and how was it policed? The early legislation, dating back to the 17th century, made no effort to define what it meant. Over the years, police and magistrates have also struggled to interpret the law. *"Drunk"* was usually taken to mean incapable of standing up. In general, only when a person was so intoxicated would the police justify getting involved. If a man was staggering but on his way home, he would be left alone, but if he was drunk and disorderly, refused to quit the pub when asked, or was incapable, then he could be taken into custody. There was a well-known rhyme by Thomas Love Peacock that said:

> *"Not drunk is he who from the floor*
> *Can rise alone and still drink more:*
> *But drunk is he, who prostrate lies,*
> *Without the power to drink or rise."*[202]

HIGHWAY ROBBERY: 1885

A farmer named Eli Crossland from Thurgoland had been out collecting rents at Wadsley Bridge and called in at the Travellers. Despite only having £7 on him, he was heard to boast that he had between £30 and £40. He set off for his brother's farm at Low Lathe, Hunshelf, passing over Fox Bridge and past Softly [Soughly] Wood. He was followed by two men from the pub, who attacked him. One of them grabbed him by the throat and told him to *"deliver or die."* Not wanting to give up his money, Eli replied, *"why, I think I'll die then."* The bag containing the £7 was taken from him and shortly afterwards a Deepcar man named John Lindley was seen at The Sportsman's Arms at Deepcar offering to *"treat"* everyone in the room to a drink because he had won £7 on a horse race. Lindley was later apprehended by Sergeant Berry, who found a large amount of money in his house. Like all serious offences, this case was referred to the Assize Court, which was held at York a few weeks later in November. Because of some previous convictions, he was refused bail.[203] The other attacker, Charles Hazzlegrave, was jointly charged, but the prosecution could not make a case against him and the charge was withdrawn. The Grand Jury at York returned a *"No Bill,"* which means that there wasn't enough evidence to warrant a trial, and the case was dropped.[204]

---

[202] A verse from The Misfortunes of Elphin. 1929

[203] In 1882 John Lindley of Crow Edge, Thurlstone, was charged with stealing money from J. W. Dickinson. He was found guilty, several previous convictions proved, 18 months' imprisonment with hard labour. Lindley had been born at Thurlstone in 1858 and was living at Haywoods Park in 1891. He was a miner (fireman).

[204] At the start of the Assizes the Grand Jury would vet the indictments and statements and hear evidence from the prosecutors and their witnesses, but not from the defendants. If the Grand Jury believed the evidence was sufficient to warrant a trial, the case was approved as a *"true bill,"* whilst those it rejected were labelled *"ignoramus," "not found"* or *"no bill,"* and the case would be dropped.

ALLEGED CANNIBALISM AT DEEPCAR: 1885
In December 1885, the newspapers ran this rather sensational headline, though in reality it was not as gory as it sounds. It was a Monday night in December, and Deepcar man Edmund Hall, a carter, entered the Travellers rather the worse for drink. For some reason, he was carrying a rope, and he knocked a pint pot off a table with it. A lodger in the pub called Haigh told Hall that he would have to pay 3d. for the pot. Hall swore at him and said that he would not. The Landlady Sarah Makin came in and ordered Hall to leave, but he refused. He rushed across the room to where Haigh was sitting, grabbed him, and threw him on the fender. He then jumped on him and bit his ear, his teeth penetrating right through; Haigh claimed he had been unable to work since. Hall appeared in court charged with having been drunk and refused to quit and also with having assaulted Abel Makin.[205] He was fined a total of thirty shillings plus costs for the offences of refusing to quit and assault and was lucky to avoid a prison sentence.

A STRANGE GENTLEMAN FROM OLDHAM: 1887
One Friday in February 1887 it was reported that a *"strange gentleman"* called at the Travellers for refreshment and lodging - he came from Oldham, so we must assume that he was a stranger to the district as opposed to a man of odd character! He was heading for Bolsterstone to take a farm there and wanted a bed at the Travellers for the night. However, there were already two families living on the pub premises, so he was taken to Carr Head to lodge. That night, he suffered a stroke and was unable to tell anyone where his home was. The police were informed, and a spring-cart was called to take him to the workhouse. Enquiries were made, and it was discovered that the man came from Akroyd Street in Oldham, where he had a *"good business and bakery."* Sadly, he was not expected to recover.

EASTER TUESDAY AT DEEPCAR: 1890
Sarah was in trouble in 1890 for permitting drunkenness in her pub, on the 8th April. James Dalton, John Stacey, Harvey Shaw, Albert Herbert, Robert Woodhead, John Goodison and James Smith, all miners from Deepcar, were summoned for being drunk on licensed premises. Sergeant Berry had visited

---

[205] This is an error in the report; he was Abel Hague, Sarah's son-in-law. He could be the lodger referred to as Haigh, as spellings were often inconsistent at this time. Abel Hague, his wife Emma Makin and their children lived at the pub with Sarah Makin the landlady.

the inn at 2.30pm and found the men drunk, some of them unable to walk without holding onto the wall! The landlady said she had not served them with anything for an hour and had asked them to leave, especially as they were messing about, blacking each other's faces with soot. She was fined over £1 for the offence. Dalton, Stacey, and Shaw, who had been previously fined for drunkenness, were fined 21s. 6d. each, whilst the others were fined 16d. 6d.

ADULTERATED WHISKY: 1890

There was a more serious charge against the landlady the following month. P.C. Taylor had sent a man named John Palfreyman to purchase some spirits and he was sold a pint of whisky which turned out not to be "*of the nature, substance, and quality*" it should have been. The whisky was sealed in the presence of Mrs. Makin and sent off for analysis. When the case came to court, there was some disagreement as to the legality of the summons, because the whisky had been bought by a third party, but in the end, a prosecution was brought. The whisky was 36 degrees under proof, or 11 degrees more than was legal. Sarah's defence said the strength of the whisky had not been lowered beyond what was allowed by law. But the Bench disagreed, and Sarah was fined over £1.

Sarah was still the landlady when the 1891 census was taken. She was 79 years old. Her daughter Emma and son-in-law Abel Hague were living with her, along with their three young children and two servants, Elizabeth Hague and Elizabeth Jones. James Vaughton was still living next door. However, it must have been time to retire, because by January 1893 there was a new landlord in residence, George William Elliott. He had been born at the Strines Inn in 1866, his father William being the landlord there, as well as being a farmer. Sarah died in March 1894 aged 82 and was buried at Oughtibridge.

George William Elliott had married Adelaide Herbert at Bolsterstone in 1891. His occupation at that time was coke merchant. The couple lived at Haywoods where a daughter, Edith Phadorah, was born in 1892, before moving to the Travellers where a son, George Herbert, was born in 1895.

Mr. Elliott submitted a claim to the Stocksbridge Local Board in January 1893 for the loss of a horse, which had suffered a fall on some ice. He was unsuccessful. Similar claims were made over the years by people blaming the council for animals being injured because of the state of roads, walls, and footpaths.

A MINER IN TROUBLE: May 1895
John William Sanderson, a miner from High Green, was drinking in the Travellers one evening and was the "*leading spirit*" of a gang of men who were creating a disturbance in the taproom. He was summoned before the magistrates for being disorderly, refusing to quit the premises, and assaulting Mr. Elliott, who had asked him to leave, resulting in a scuffle taking place in the passage. Sanderson complained that the landlord had ill-treated him, but he was found guilty and was fined 29 shillings.

On the 4th December 1897, the London Evening Standard reported in its Estate Market section that the freehold Travellers Inn at Deepcar was sold by William Bush & Sons at Sheffield for £5,000. Mr. Elliott left to take on the Royal Oak as a tenant of its new owners, Sheffield-based brewery Whitmarsh, Watson & Co.

The next landlord was Arthur John Reddish and his wife Lydia, who were from Clowne in Derbyshire. In 1891 he and his family were living at Brightside in Sheffield, and he was working as a steel finisher. They moved to Deepcar in the early 1890s, and Arthur worked as a ganister crusher before they moved into the Travellers in 1898. Following Arthur's death in 1908 his widow Lydia took over, assisted by her daughters Blanche and Lillie. Lydia ran the Travellers until February 1926, when she transferred the licence to Frank Moxon. She died two years later at the age of 72, at Woodbine Villas, Deepcar.

Mr. Moxon and his wife Clara only stayed a couple of years before deciding to move "*down south.*" He auctioned off some of his household goods at the Travellers in 1928. John Schofield (known as Jack) was the next landlord, and also its last.

A TALE OF A LION
Marshall's fair used to come once a year to Deepcar, setting up on the Don Field, an event known fondly by locals as the "*Deepcar Feast.*" They travelled with a large menagerie which included a lion known as "*Oscar the*

Untameable." In an attempt to draw the crowds, they advertised that a well-known local publican would enter Oscar's cage. The landlord at the King & Miller, George Eyre, was the first to be asked, but he remarked, *"Not bloody likely, I had enough fighting the Jerries without taking on damned lions."* The next to be approached was Jack Schofield from the Travellers - his remarks were very much the same, only a bit stronger! However, Jack's wife, Josephine, said, *"I'll go in, I am not afraid of lions."* The following Saturday night, before a full marquee, she did indeed enter the untameable lion's cage, giving her husband a kiss beforehand, in case she didn't make it back out. The lion roared and growled but kept his place at the back of his cage with the trainer between him and Josephine. Afterwards, people thought she must have been paid to go in, but she remarked that, *"frankly, I got nowt."* The next day several of the fairground children were seen leading *"Old Oscar"* by a chain down to the River Don to be given a wash![206] Considering the number of fatal accidents involving circus animals and their trainers reported in the newspapers of the time, they were either very brave or very lucky.

NATIONAL CONSERVATIVE LEAGUE MEETING: 1931
In April 1931, the Travellers played host to the Deepcar branch of the National Conservative League. Mr. O. Mate presided over a large attendance of members, and those present included the prospective candidate, Mr. C. W. H. Glossop, Mr. F. Green, Penistone (agent), Mr. Lucock (Penistone), Mr. E. Peace, Mr. M. Gregory, and Mr. H. Clarke (hon. secretary).

But the days of the Travellers Inn were numbered, thanks in part to the Temperance Movement, which had grown in popularity during the early part of the twentieth century. Its views on the evils of drink and teetotalism permeated into society as a whole, as did their view that there were too many public houses compared with the needs of the public.

An Act had been passed in 1904 which facilitated the closing of public houses. These were to be closed via a scheme whereby the owners would be compensated for the extinguished licences out of a fund which would be levied on all the public houses in each licensing area. If the licensing

---

[206] This story is told by Jack Branston in his book The History of Stocksbridge. He gives the date as 1926, but Jack and Josephine were not the landlords of the Travellers Inn until 1928 (they were there until 1931), and George and Lucy Eyre didn't have the King and Miller until 1930 or 1931, so the probable date of this event would be 1930 or 1931

magistrates considered that a pub was a good candidate for closure, then they could submit a report to the Compensation Authority, who would decide the case. If they decided on closure, they worked out the value of the compensation; this would then be paid both to the owner of the premises and the licensee although, typically, only about 10% of the compensation went to the licensee. This provision of the 1904 Act was carried forward into the Licensing (Consolidation) Act of 1910.[207]

In 1931, notice was given (under this Act of 1910) that a meeting would be held about the renewal of fifteen licences in the West Riding area. One of these was The Travellers at Deepcar. Also on the list were the Travellers Rest at Wharncliffe Side and the Stanley Arms at Oughtibridge. In the case of The Travellers at Deepcar, the grounds for closure were that the pub was redundant, excessive [there were two other fully licensed pubs very close by, the Royal Oak and the King and Miller] and, it was alleged, had *"irreparable dampness."* Mr. J. G. Chambers, speaking for the owners, said that it was *"an ordinary old country inn,"* whereas a police witness replied, *"It is in a very shocking state of repair."* The renewal of the licence of the Travellers was turned down. In fact, all the pubs on the list except one were to close.

One of the last events to take place there was a celebration dinner, held in November after the election of Mr. Clifford W. Glossop, in what was a landslide victory for the National Government. The South Yorkshire times called it *"The most remarkable General Election in Parliamentary history,"* and it wasn't until 1997 that a party would win over 400 seats in the House of Commons.

---

[207] Pub closures: It was usually the police who were given the task of preparing a list of each public house in a given area as candidates for closure. A range of criteria were often used, which might include the quality of the accommodation offered, the level of trade, the number of times a licence had been transferred in recent years, whether the local population could justify the number of pubs in a given area, any convictions of the licensee and the structural condition of the premises. The police would also know how easy it was for them to supervise the pub and what went off in it. Many reports exist of pubs that were deemed ripe for closure, with poor sanitation, undesirable clientele, repeated reporting of nuisances and so on.

In February 1932, Jack Schofield left the Travellers and went across the road to run the Royal Oak. Joe Mills bought the pub and turned it into a butcher's shop. It is now a private house.

The landlord when this photograph was taken was Arthur Reddish, which dates it to between 1901 and 1908.

A view from Manchester Road looking down Vaughton Hill; the Travellers is the bottom house of the row of three. The toll bar once stood near here.

THE VAUGHTONS OF VAUGHTON HILL
(A poem in the local dialect)

There's a famous village called Deepcar
About eight miles from Sheffield - or more -
Where a well-known family called Vaughton lived
Rahnd abaht eighteen fifty-four

James Vaughton were t'landlord ot'
Low Drop -
T'Travellers Rest, by right
'E worked as a file-cutter in t'day-time
And served in t'pub at night.

E'd inherited t'pub from 'is father,
An' all t'row o'houses an all;
A teetotaller - 'e then started boozin' -
And that brought abaht 'is downfall.

On one side o't'ouses were t'Smithy;
Wi't'Saddlers at t'bottom o't'ill.
There were t'Toll bar for t'Langsett Turnpike,
And across t'rooad at t'bottom, t'Flour Mill

There warn't much else i'Deepcar -
A station across t'River Don,
Two more pubs, t'Oak and t'Miller,
And farms - and Stocksbridge further on.

Education were at a small school
Up in t'hive yard run by a dame;
Or, they 'ad to walk up t'pay school
All t'way up More Hall Lane.

There were nowt in t'way on amusement:
They 'ad to provide their own fun;
But t'travelling shows came every so often
When a bear danced to t'barrel organ.

Then t'Penny Gaff and t'Travelling Circus
Used to play to packed houses in t'Grove;
Yer could see three murders a night for a penny,
Wi' blood running - bright red and mauve!

In between times there were concerts
When owd James Vaughton played t'bass;
Saddler Dyson were a virtuoso on t'fiddle,
While Jim Woodcock pulled a long face.

But James Vaughton 'ad taken to t'bottle;
'E couldn't meet t'brewery bill;
So 'e 'ad to let 'em 'ave t'Travellers Rest
And move out of Vaughton Hill.

'E ended 'is days up at t'Stubbin,
Wheer 'is sons lived up on t'farm
And 'e allus sampled t'whisky
That they kept for t'sick cows in t'barn

It was said that when on 'is death bed,
A widower three times o'er,
'E said e'd like to get married ageean
If 'e could find a good number four

'E's buried up at Bolsterstooan,
Just across from t'church door,
In t'family grave wi' wives one, two and three;
Go and see t'poetic inscription set o'er

I'm one of his living descendants;
A few more are scattered about
My grandmother (Sarah Vaughton)
Married Jim Firth
But her brothers remained bachelors - so
t'name died out.

But Vaughton is still part o'Deepcar
It's still in t'middle o't'place,
Called after t'feller who built all t'row,
Not after t'one who were a disgrace.

We all have our black sheep in t'family;
James Vaughton followed this rule;
E'd 'ad but in 'is 'and
And couldn't look after it - the fool.

If there's a moral to this story,
(As there must be, when all's done and said),
It's simply - "Don't leave all yer money to t'men.
Let t'women 'ave it instead!"

Olwen Firth[208]

---

[208] Olwen was a teacher at Deepcar junior school, passionate about local history, and great-great granddaughter of James Vaughton. She inspired a love of history in a great many of her pupils, me included.

THE ROCK INN, GREEN MOOR ROAD, GREEN MOOR

The Rock Inn was in the village of Green Moor and was built for the use of workers at the nearby quarries which supplied the Green Moor stone that was widely used for building both locally and nationally. The pub was built on the site of the paymaster's office for the Green Moor Delph quarry, which stretched back from the pub and was quarried for stone roofing slates and fine-grained green stone. It has now been filled in. There were other quarries nearby; the California at Trunce, the Victoria, the Isle of Skye at the top of Hunshelf Bank and the New Biggin. The last workings closed in 1936, and the quarry face is registered as a regionally important geological site. The pub closed in about 2005/6 and houses now stand on the site. The pub had two sides and two entrances. This photograph shows one side; in recent years, the main entrance was on the other side, along with a car park. Cherry Tree Cottage once stood where the carpark was, but as quarrying encroached it was pulled down and rebuilt elsewhere.

There were several pubs or beerhouses at Hunshelf and Green Moor.

An old coaching route from Fulshaw Cross to Rotherham followed a branch of the old packhorse route, the Saltway, which passed over Hartcliff Hill along the ridge through Hunshelf. This was at one time one of the most important thoroughfares in the area, used by drovers taking cattle and pack horses carrying salt along the Cheshire to East Yorkshire Salters Way. This road became the turnpike road to Manchester in 1741. Peck Pond was a natural ancient watering hole. Walls were built through it to allow different livestock to water simultaneously.[209] The farmers at Peck Pond and Cranberry took advantage of this passing trade and turned part of their farms into alehouses. The pub at Peck Pond was called the Brown Cow and was once one of the stops for the stagecoaches. Parish officials held meetings there too. Thomas Pitt held a licence there from at least 1773, and in 1803 the licence holder was Martha Pitt, a widow. There used to be some stocks at Peck Pond, but they were re-sited opposite the Rock in 1937.

In 1654, Richard Sylvester, an alehouse keeper from Hunshelf, was fined at the Wakefield Quarter Sessions for allowing disorderly persons to be tippling, drinking and dancing on the Sabbath day [Sunday], and also allowing a piper to play in his pub, also on the Sabbath.

Before the Rock Inn opened, there was another pub at Green Moor called the Travellers Rest. It was situated a little further along the road from where the Rock later would be built, on Well Hill Road, and was popular with the local quarry workers. Its name was later changed to the Friendship Inn. It was here that Robert and Ann Rusby lived. Robert was a quarry worker and Ann ran a shop and beerhouse from her home from about 1840 until her death in 1875.[210] Her son William took it over after she died; the 1881 census recorded him at the Friendship, and a few years later he moved up the road to run the Rock Inn.

---

[209] This site was restored by Hunshelf Parish Council and the British Trust for Conservation Volunteers in 2001. Legend has it that suspected witches were dowsed in the pond.
[210] Robert died at Well Hill in 1845 aged 44 and was buried at Wortley church on the 11th December

The Brownhill family ran a shop at Hunshelf with a beerhouse attached to it, which was occasionally referred to as the Butcher's Arms, the shop being a butchers.

In 1862 William Newton was granted a licence to run a pub from his farm at Berton-under-Edge on Hunshelf Bank, which had stabling for six horses. William died in 1864, and his family went on to run The Rising Sun Inn, which was further down Hunshelf Bank towards Stocksbridge.

The earliest newspaper report to mention a public house at Green Moor was printed in 1839. The landlord's name was Francis Blackwell, but the name of his pub was never mentioned in any of the subsequent reports, census returns, parish registers etc. Francis had been born at Manchester in around 1803 and he married Ann Lingard at Bradfield church in 1828. He worked as a labourer/quarryman for a few years and became a publican in around 1834 when his third child was born.[211]

The first time The Rock Inn was mentioned by name was in a newspaper report of 1845, but I have been unable to discover exactly when it opened.

In 1839 Francis Blackwell, along with several other men, was charged with attempting to hang Isaac Walton in Blackwell's pub – a drunken escapade that could have gone very wrong.

THE HANGING OF ISAAC WALTON: 1839

Isaac Walton was of a similar age to Francis Blackwell and had been baptised at Wortley church in 1806, the son of Isaac Walton, a labourer. On the 9th January 1839 Walton was drinking in Blackwell's public house in the company of several other men. They had drunk about twelve pints each. The men got to arguing, and Blackwell threatened that if he met Walton on the road and was carrying a sword, he would cut him to pieces. In fact, he said, he would hang him before he left the pub. He then called for a rope, and when Walton got up to light his pipe at the fireplace, a noose was thrown over his head and he was drawn up to the top of the room. He became

---

[211] When Francis and Ann's son Thomas was baptised at Penistone in November 1832, Francis's occupation was stone-getter. When their daughter Mary was baptised in June 1834 his occupation had changed to publican.

insensible, and when he regained consciousness, he found himself laid on the *"lang settle"* [a long bench]. His neck was marked, and he'd had difficulty in swallowing ever since. He included all his drinking companions in his warrant for assault by hanging - Francis Blackwell, Samuel Frith, William Pate, George Clark, Thomas Downend, and John Charlesworth. Because the men were defendants, they could not be examined as witnesses unless Walton withdrew the charges, which he did for two of them. Pate and Clark were then sworn in, and they stated that no such hanging had taken place. Walton admitted that his back was turned when the noose was thrown, so he did not see who the main culprit was. The men admitted to *"some scuffling,"* but insisted that it was nothing serious.

Blackwell said that Walton was a *"nuisance to his house,"* turning up with a bundle of newspapers and sitting for five or six hours talking politics, quarrelling with the rest of the company, and all the time drinking only one glass of ale. The constable of Hunshelf said that Blackwell was a quiet man, and his pub was conducted in an orderly manner. The conclusion was that all the men were excessively drunk and didn't really know what they were doing. The case was dismissed.

Walton had told them during that evening that Lord John Russell was about to propose a bill to authorise the police putting to death all the children a woman might have beyond three, and to send all the children of paupers to Van Diemen's Land. Walton said that he had six children, and if it was law, and they chose to take three of them, he would let them. Isaac lived at Thurgoland with his wife Martha, and they did indeed have six children at that time.

INQUEST ON JAMES CROSSLAND: 1843
One Wednesday in late November, James Crossland, aged 33, was killed in the Green Moor quarry at about 8am. He was standing on a drag [wagon] and was assisting in loading it with some flagstones. As he moved one to the front end of the drag, he slipped over the side onto the ground, and the flag followed, falling onto the right side of his head and fracturing his skull; he was killed instantly. The inquest was held at Blackwell's pub at Green Moor. The jury examined several witnesses and were satisfied that no one was to blame and that it was purely an accident, and they returned a verdict of accidental death.

A STOLEN WATCH: 1845

One Monday evening in 1845, a 23-year-old navvy called Henry Slater (nicknamed *"Bilper"*) was arrested in the King and Miller at Deepcar for attempting to sell a stolen silver pocket watch belonging to Jonathan Crabtree of Thurgoland. After leaving the Rock Inn at Green Moor one night, Crabtree fell asleep in some woodland, and when he woke up, he found that his watch had gone, as well as thirty shillings. Several witnesses were called to say they had seen Slater trying to sell the watch, and when he was arrested, he handed it over to the police. Slater was charged with *"highway robbery"* and committed to be tried at the Sessions, where he was found guilty and sent to jail for three months. This is the first mention of the Rock Inn by name.

At some point Francis Blackwell formed a partnership with David Craven, and they worked as stone merchants from Green Moor. Craven was a master builder and he lived in Sheffield. Blackwell may well have carried on with the pub, no doubt aided by his wife, as well as running his other business, which lasted until the partnership was dissolved in September 1851.[212] He was entitled to vote, being the occupier of a farm and quarry at a rent of £50 per year. Francis then seems to have had a run of bad luck. In 1854 Lord Wharncliffe took action in court to recover possession of a house at Green Moor which was occupied by him. There was *"considerable argument on both sides,"* ending with the magistrates granting a warrant to recover possession. Blackwell got into debt, and the following year there was a meeting of his creditors. He was working as a quarryman. There was no further notice pertaining to bankruptcy, so perhaps he managed to satisfy his creditors.

Francis moved away from Green Moor, to the Old Punch Bowl at Crookes, Sheffield. In July 1857 he gave notice that he intended to apply for a wines and spirits licence, but when the application came before the licensing magistrates the following month, it was refused (no reason was given). The following January all his furniture and bar items were sold at auction on the premises; items included gas fittings, seating, a pump with several yards of lead piping, tables, ceiling with folding door,[213] fenders, fire irons, a weather

---

[212] The 1851 census (taken on the 30th March) recorded him as a stone merchant. A trade directory of 1852 listed him as a shop keeper.
[213] Joseph Wright's English Dialect Dictionary defines ceiling as being a wooden partition.

glass, tumbler and beer glasses, an eight-days' clock in an oak case, quart spirit pitchers, pint mugs, pewter ale measures a copper kettle and so on. He left the pub and died a few months later at Tom Cross Lane in Sheffield, aged 55. His widow died the following year at 96 Spring Street, Sheffield, in April 1859, aged 53.

The only publican listed on the 1851 for Green Moor was Ann Rusby, but she did not have The Rock Inn. Francis Blackwell was recorded as a stone merchant at Green Moor, and the next house on the census enumerator's schedule, also at Green Moor, was that of Thomas Dawson, a table blade forger. A trade directory of 1852 lists Thomas Dawson as a licensed victualler at the Rock Inn, Underbank [sic]. Electoral registers place Thomas Dawson at Green Moor from 1852 until 1859[214], but he doesn't seem to have been the landlord for that length of time.

Thomas Buckley was the landlord from at least 1856; he had previously been living at Windy Bank (on the top of Hunshelf Bank). During his tenancy he continued to work as a quarryman, and his wife and family would have assisted in running the pub. When the 1861 census was taken, Thomas and Martha were living at Green Moor with their children Henry (25 years old, quarryman and innkeeper), Emma (19), Joseph (12), and Ellen (12), who would all have had a part to play in the business.

THE DRUIDS CLUB: July 1856
The Rock Inn was the venue for the Druids Club to hold their anniversary on Monday 7th July 1856. Attended by the Clayton brass band, they walked in procession around the hills, before listening to *"an excellent sermon"* by the Rev. Daniel Brierly in the Green Moor chapel, after which a collection was made for the Sunday school. Everyone then moved on to the Rock Inn and sat down to *"an excellent dinner,"* which had been provided by Mr. Thomas Buckley, the landlord. After the cloth was withdrawn, the usual healths and toasts were given, and an enjoyable evening was had by all. The Druids Club was a fraternal organisation which later became a benefit society like the Oddfellows and the Foresters.

---

[214] He was entitled to vote by virtue of having one third of an undivided property, freehold houses, and shops, at West Street and Westfield Terrace in Sheffield. By 1861 he had moved from Green Moor to Monmouth Street, Ecclesall Bierlow, and was working as a table blade forger.

The pub was also the venue for the Wortley Rifle Club (which was founded in 1860), pigeon shooting matches, and Knur & Spell contests.

FATAL ACCIDENT: May 1859
William Illingworth of Hunshelf had been working at the quarry one Saturday afternoon and was found dead beneath a plank which crossed it. It was thought that he had overbalanced in the centre of the plank whilst wheeling some stone across and had fallen about twenty feet. An inquest was held, and a verdict of accidental death was returned. He was 33 years old.

In 1861, Buckley was charged with allowing drinking out of hours, at half-past ten on Sunday 30th June. Six men were seen in the pub by P.C. Wilson, one with a glass of gin, and another asking for some gin. It was the day of the Hunshelf Feast. Buckley's defence was that the men were relatives of his who had been invited to spend the day with him. Witnesses were called, but they only proved that three of the men were relations, and Buckley was fined ten shillings plus costs.

In September 1862, the landlord of The Rock Inn was a Mr. Ellis. When William Newton applied for a licence to open a pub at his farm, Berton-under-Edge, a solicitor objected on behalf of Mr. Ellis and Lord Wharncliffe. He must have thought that this new pub would have an impact on his trade, but William was granted a licence despite the objections.

The next landlord was William Burkinshaw, a quarry worker. He continued to work in the quarries as well as running the pub. He became the landlord between 1862 and 1868, and he was there until his death in 1877. William had been born at Hunshelf in 1812 and was the son of Richard Burkinshaw and Elizabeth Rollin. He married Martha Crossley and they lived at Thurgoland. In December 1869 he took part in a pigeon shooting match at his house, the Rock Inn, shooting against, and beating, Charles Crossland of Green Moor.

ASSAULT ON THE POLICE: 1864
A "*powerful looking man*" named Henry Rusby was charged with assaulting P.C. Robinson at Green Moor on the 4th June 1864. The constable had been ill for some time and had only resumed duty on the day he was assaulted.

The policeman saw a large group of disorderly people outside an (unnamed) public house at Green Moor, so he went over to them and asked them to disperse peacefully to their homes. They did so, but as he was walking away, Rusby called out, *"Here policeman; I want to speak to you."* The officer accordingly went up to him and was immediately knocked down by Rusby, who also pulled his hair, and screwed his thumb so violently as to dislocate it. A boy named Fieldsend, who lived at Crane Moor, stated that before the assault took place, he overheard Rusby telling another man how *"he should like to kick the policeman"* [Robinson]. Rusby was ordered to pay a fine of twenty shillings plus costs, or in default, be imprisoned for one month.

FATAL ACCIDENT AT HUNSHELF: October 1868
The Coroner held an inquest at the Rock Inn to inquire into the circumstances surrounding the death of quarry worker William Barraclough, who was killed at work in the California Quarry. His father John Barraclough of Smithy Moor saw his son fall to his death from a ledge about sixteen yards up from the quarry bottom and three yards from the top. It was 7.30am, and William had been *"baring"* a ledge[215] with another man called William Illingworth of Snowden Hill. There were another three men working above them, who were also baring, and after about half an hour one of them shouted a warning, so Barraclough and Illingworth moved to one end of the ledge they were working on, where they supposed they would be safe. They waited there a few minutes but then a large stone came over onto where they were standing and struck Barraclough on his stomach, knocking him backwards. From his position on the ground, William's father saw him fall headfirst into the bottom of the quarry. He told the coroner, *"I went to him and found he was dead. His head was smashed."* He was 27 years old. The verdict was that he was accidentally killed.

ANOTHER FATAL ACCIDENT: March 1869
The Coroner held another inquest at the Rock Inn a few months later regarding the death of John Beever, a carter employed by Messrs. Booth & Company of the Green Moor Stone Quarries. Mr. Beever was 50 years old and was killed on the 6th March when he fell under the wheels of the wagon he was driving. He had been riding on the shafts of his cart when the wheels came into contact with some large stones that had been placed on the road.

---

[215] Exposing the rock, removing overlying earth.

The impact caused him to be jerked from his seat and he fell and was run over.

The stones had been placed upon the road by a man named Taylor, under the direction of Mr. J. Haigh, one of the road surveyors. Mr. Dransfield of Penistone, solicitor, appeared for the road surveyors; he was willing to admit that the stones were there, and said that the surveyors John Haigh and George Scholey had permission to put them there and that they were not responsible for the result. The inquest was told that it was a custom that had been adopted locally for many years.

The Coroner said that it was *"preposterous, and even monstrous, to place large stones upon the highway in order to make the public travel twice the distance by twisting and twining in order to escape accident, simply to prevent the road from being worn out in the ordinary way."* He thought that the surveyors had no right to place stones or other obstructions on the highway unless it was undergoing repair. If they did so, and placed them so that they caused an obstruction, that made them a nuisance, and the surveyors should be liable to a criminal prosecution. He added that, whatever the result of the present inquiry would be, he himself would take steps to have the stones removed from the highway.

The Coroner then heard from witnesses, and the jury was told that a post-mortem had proved that Beever had died from contusion of the brain, caused by a blow or fall. After a consultation of about an hour, the jury brought in a verdict that the deceased *"came by his death by coming into contact with the stones which had been placed upon the road by the order of the surveyors, but recommended them to mercy."* The coroner said that he had nothing whatever to do with mercy; the jury must decide whether the deceased died because he did not exercise due caution, or whether his death was the result of the conduct of the surveyors in placing the stones upon the highway. The jury then consulted for another half an hour, and brought in a verdict of *"accidental death, brought about by the carelessness of the deceased."* One of the jurors remarked that they should have brought in a verdict of manslaughter, but they thought it would get the man Taylor into trouble.

The Coroner's Notebooks bring home the personal details about such cases. Mr. Beever's widow Mary Ann, of Windy Bank, Hunshelf, told the coroner's court that her husband left home about 6.15am on Saturday morning, and at around 11am his dead body was brought home. Thomas Hanson of Finkle Street, Wortley, had known Beever about twenty years and had passed him whilst driving his own cart at Wortley railway station. Beever's wagon was being pulled by two horses, one in front of the other, and they were trotting *"sharply but steadily."* He saw the accident occur and ran to assist Beever, but he died very soon afterwards.

Ann Rusby, beerhouse keeper at Green Moor, said she had known Beever for ten years. He had called at her house for a glass of beer at 9.30am on the morning of his death, before returning to his waiting horses. She said he seemed sober. About an hour and a half later she saw his dead body being brought past in a cart. Martha Burkinshaw, the wife of William, also gave evidence and told the court that Beever had been a caller at the Rock Inn for the past three years. She said that he was drunk on the Friday night before his death, and that his daughter called for him and took him home. He had called for a drink between 7am and 8am on the morning of his death and had left in a cheerful mood. There was some talk that he had fits.

When the 1871 census was taken, the landlord William Burkinshaw was working as both a stonemason and an innkeeper. Living with him were his wife Martha, son Joseph and a servant called Lois Green. William and Martha had a son William, born in 1851, and he went on to be the landlord of the Sportsman's Arms at Deepcar from about 1878 until about 1906.

TWO HAWKERS STRUCK BY LIGHTENING: June 1871
A man and woman, said to be from Barnsley, were hawking cutlery in this area when they got caught in a violent storm and were struck by lightning when on the top of Windy Bank whilst on their way to Green Moor. A witness saw them, the woman in front and the man a little way behind her, and both were seen to fall instantly to the ground. The woman wasn't injured, apart from suffering from shock, but the man was unconscious, and he was carried to a nearby house. His name was William Ellis, and he was walking around selling his cutlery despite only having one leg (the report doesn't say whether he was on crutches or had a wooden leg). He had been wearing a low-crowned hat, which had a steel wire around its brim, and it is this which seems to have attracted the lightning. The man's silver watch and its watch guard were *"shivered to atoms,"* the longest piece being not more than an

inch, while some of it could not be found. The cutlery he was carrying must also have attracted the lightning. It was reported that the wall by which he was walking was marked as if by gunshot. His left shoulder, the left side of his body, and his leg were badly burnt, and his boot was completely torn off. A surgeon and a policeman were called, and Mr. Ellis was taken to the Rock Inn, before being taken to Edward Hampshire's lodging house on Doncaster Road, Barnsley, where a surgeon was treating him.

In May 1872 William was caught serving out of hours on a Sunday afternoon. Two plain-clothes policemen went into the Rock at 3.35pm and found men drinking. In a small room, two men were found with a jug containing beer and ginger beer. In another room was a man with some beer, but he was said to be a traveller. An exemption had always existed for travellers to be able to get a drink outside of opening hours, but this was open to abuse, and in 1854 an Act introduced the concept of a *"bona fide traveller."* However, this abuse continued, and in 1874 (two years after William was caught) another Act qualified this by defining a traveller as someone who was at least three miles from his previous night's lodging. *"Travelling"* three miles for a drink then seems to have become something of a national institution. A judgement of 1893 removed the status of bona fide traveller if the main object of travel was to obtain liquor. Police Inspector Birkhill said that this was their first complaint against the landlord and that he had previously *"conducted his house in a satisfactory manner."* He was fined ten shillings plus costs, and the offence was endorsed on the back of his licence. The men who were found drinking that day also appeared in court; Jonathan Batty (who *"appeared by his father"*[216]) and Henry Brewer were charged with aiding and abetting the landlord to commit a breach of his licence. They were fined five shillings.

William was fined again in August 1876 for the same offence; this time the police found ten men with beer and ginger beer on the table in front of them at 5.20pm one Sunday.[217] There was some variation in opening hours

---

[216] He was a minor, under 21 (he was 17 in 1871) and lived at Crimbles with his parents.
[217] The usual hours when pubs had to close on Sundays were between 3pm and 5pm, but the 1872 Licensing Act (introduced in August that year) was incredibly complicated, and even the Barnsley magistrates, whose job it was to implement the Act, reported that, *"There were many clauses in the Act not quite so clear as they ought to be, but with care and attention*

throughout the country, but pubs in the Barnsley licensing district were not allowed to be open until 6pm on Sundays. The landlord did not deny the offence but said the day was very hot, and the whole of the men had been singing at a chapel anniversary in the neighbourhood, and they wanted refreshments. They had gone to wash themselves, and he had drawn them some beer and ginger beer. Once again, he was fined ten shillings plus costs, and warned to be very careful in the future. The ten men were summoned for aiding and abetting the landlord to commit a breach of his licence; they all pleaded guilty and were ordered to pay the costs. They were also warned that they had better not be thirsty again until after 6 o'clock on a Sunday evening.

AFFRAY WITH POACHERS: 1875

In August 1875 two miners, Thomas Crawshaw of Thurgoland and Solomon Crossland of Green Moor, appeared in court at Barnsley Town Hall. The men were *"noted characters"* according to the Yorkshire Post, and both had previous convictions. They were both charged with *"trespassing in pursuit of game"* on land belonging to Mr. W. Dransfield at Oxspring, and also with assaulting Mr. Dransfield the same day. Dransfield had been out on his farm with a gun when he heard voices near a wood which runs parallel with the road leading from Oxspring to Penistone. He watched for a short time and noticed two men. He asked them what they were doing there. One of them replied, *"we are doing nothing, but the dog has followed a rabbit into the wood and we are bringing her out."* When he said he wanted a word with them, the two men ran off through the wood. He chased after them and caught up with Crossland, who had two rabbits in his pocket. When Crossland refused to give up the rabbits, Dransfield threw him to the floor and knelt on him, hoping to keep hold of him until he could get help. Crawshaw went to his companion's aid, and the men ran into a turnip field and began throwing stones at their pursuer. The men then went in the direction of Green Moor. Dransfield and P.C. Windle found Crawshaw at

---

the Bench thought they could master them." They had the power to choose the opening hours for the Barnsley district, but eventually decided to adopt the hours of opening and closing which were named in the Act, with individual modifications if landlords requested it. Two years later, an Act of 1874 amended this, and shortened the hours for the sale of liquor. Pubs could open on Sundays from 1pm to 3pm, and 6pm to 11pm on Sunday evenings.

his father's house and Crossland in the Rock Inn. The two men were fined forty shillings each for the trespass, and ten shillings each for the assault. The total fines and costs amounted to £7. 8s.

REFUSING TO QUIT: 1877
John Hadcock and William Martin pleaded guilty to being drunk and refusing to quit the house of William Burkinshaw, the Rock Inn, on the 14th May 1877. They had gone into the pub and called for some beer, but they were refused service because they seemed to be drunk already. P.C. Windle proved the case and said the men were not quarrelsome, and they were fined five shillings. In September the same year Joseph Roebuck pleaded guilty to being drunk and refusing to quit the Rock Inn and was fined ten shillings.

William Burkinshaw died at Green Moor in 1877 aged 64 and was buried at Thurgoland on the 3rd November. He was succeeded at the pub by John Helliwell, who was also a stonemason. John had married Martha Burkinshaw in 1866, and they stayed at the pub until about 1882/85. Martha was William Burkinshaw's niece, her father being William's older brother James. John and his father were dry-stone wallers according to the 1861 census.

A DANGEROUS LARK AT GREEN MOOR: October 1879
Rather a dramatic headline for stealing a handkerchief and some trousers, but that is what the Barnsley Chronicle went with. A young man named William Martin was charged with stealing a pair of trousers belonging to David Barraclough, a quarryman who lived at Green Moor. Around 7pm one evening Barraclough had gone into the Rock Inn carrying a handkerchief and a pair of cotton cord trousers, which he placed on a seat by the side of him. William Martin was in the pub, and after about half an hour he got up, placed the parcel under his arm and went out. The items were worth 6s. 6d. After he had gone, Barraclough reported the theft to the police. P.C. Windle, who was stationed at Hunshelf, apprehended the young man at the house of a woman named Lydia Crabtree, and he found the stolen property in his possession. Martin replied, "*I had only taken them for a lark; I was going to take them back again.*" He swore that when he took the parcel and went out, he made the remark that he would have a walk with it and that he had intended to go back to the pub because he had left his coat there. The

magistrates thought that the case was a *"drunken spree,"* and ordered Martin to pay costs. They did not allow Barraclough any expenses.

AUCTION AT THE ROCK INN
The old Green Moor School: November 1880
Deepcar auctioneer John Bramall advertised that he had been instructed by the Hunshelf School Board to sell a stone-built dwelling house, with attached buildings, formerly known and used as the Green Moor School, which was *"substantially built and would easily convert into cottages."* He was also instructed to sell some land fronting the road from Wortley to Penistone. None of this sold and was withdrawn from sale at £162 10s., not having reached the reserve set by the Board.

The Helliwells then moved to Wortley where John continued to work as a stonemason, and the pub then passed into the hands of the Rusbys, who had it for many years. William Rusby had been born in 1839, and his parents were Robert and Ann Rusby. Ann was the daughter of John Burkinshaw. For many years, Ann (who was widowed in 1845) ran a shop and a beerhouse at Pond Cottages on Well Hill Road, which she called The Friendship.[218] In 1869 a new Licensing Act required all beerhouses to be licensed by the magistrates, and Ann duly applied to the Barnsley magistrates for a licence. Her premises were initially said to be *"insufficiently rated"* [their rateable value was too low to be a licensed premises].[219] A few weeks later there was a report from the adjourned Brewster Sessions that Ann Rusby of Hunshelf had a shop in connection with her beerhouse, and that there was an objection (not specified) to her being granted a licence. The objection in these cases was usually that the shop interfered with the closing hours of the licensed premises. Often, the applicant was required to give up either the shop or the beerhouse. However, when it was shown that Ann had kept the beerhouse since 1840 the objection was not pressed, and the licence was granted. Her son William took over at The Friendship Inn when she died in 1875, and in

---

[218] The 1869 Brewster Sessions said she had run this since 1840. She was recorded on the 1851, 1861 and 1871 census returns as running a beershop or beerhouse, although not on the 1841 census when only her husband's occupation of *"delver"* [quarry man] was recorded. She died at Green Moor in 1875 aged 68.

[219] Barnsley Chronicle 4th September 1869: Lists of persons who are not sufficiently rated included Ann Rusby, Friendship Inn, Hunshelf.

1881 he was living there with his wife Mary and their eight children.[220] He also worked as a mason. He became the landlord of the Rock Inn sometime between 1881 and 1885 and ran it until his death in 1893 when it passed to his son, also called William.

STRANGE DEATH AT HUNSHELF: 1885

One Saturday morning in June 1885 a Hunshelf labourer named George Wright was found dead in unusual circumstances. The inquest was held at the Rock Inn, of which William Rusby was now the landlord. George and his brother Arthur lodged with their sister Hannah Cole at Green Moor. George did not keep well; he had suffered with ill-health for ten years and had been having fits for the past six years. Arthur told the inquest that his brother had had a fit on Friday night, and another one on Saturday morning at 5.15am. He stayed with him until he came round and then set off for work. He saw George two hours later at Fox's works, but he told him that he felt too ill to remain and he was going home again. He was seen going towards the Rising Sun Inn, Hunshelf, but the landlord Tom Batty was not yet up, so he carried on. Around 8am George was seen by a road mender called George Firth. Firth saw him leave a basket and a can (possibly a *"mashing can"* for making a drink in) on a wall and go into a field. Half an hour later Firth was on his way home for breakfast when he noticed Wright's basket and can still sitting on the wall, so he went to look for him. He found his lifeless body kneeling by the side of a water trough face-down in the water, his cap floating on the surface. Firth went to Berton-under-Edge farm to seek assistance from the farmer there, Charles Illingworth. Mrs. Illingworth told the inquest that she laid out the body and that there were no marks of violence on it. The verdict was that he had accidentally drowned. His life was insured with the Prudential, and he was a member of the Order of Druids, so his funeral costs would have been taken care of. He was 26 years old.

William Rusby was widowed in June 1890 when Mary died at the age of 49. When the 1891 census was taken, he was still at the Rock Inn, and his six children plus a domestic servant would have helped in the running of the pub. William died two years later in September 1893. He had been suffering from

---

[220] William married Mary Burkinshaw (daughter of George Burkinshaw) at St. Mary's parish church, Bramall Lane, Sheffield, in 1863.

a complaint in his legs and often went to bed when he was having a bad day. His son found him dead in bed.[221]

One of William's sons, also called William, took over the licence of the Rock Inn following his father's death. He had been born in 1867 and married Ada Storey at Eckington in 1892.

In 1894 a man fell from a dangerous footpath one night when returning home from one of the regular pigeon-shooting competitions which were held at the pub. Harry Farrow, a miner aged 35, left the Rock Inn at 8.15pm, apparently sober. He never reached home, and the next morning his brother-in-law Richard Grayson went to look for him. When he reached the quarry at Green Moor, he called out and Farrow answered him. He was at the bottom of the quarry, holding his head. He was taken to the Sheffield Infirmary, but died there the same night. William Rusby gave evidence and said that although the footpath that Farrow had taken was a good short-cut, it was a dangerous one. It crossed the corner of the quarry, and that night had been very dark and foggy; Farrow must have missed the footpath and rolled about fifty feet down into the quarry. It was not a designated public footpath but had been used as such for a number of years. The quarry was not being worked and was rented by a Mr. Booth. The jury returned a verdict of accidental death and added a rider expressing their opinion *"that the place was dangerous, and that the quarry should be fenced off or the footpath closed."* The Coroner promised to forward the verdict to Mr. Booth. The quarry business at this time was owned by Benjamin Brodie Booth, who had inherited it after the death of his great uncle Henry Booth in 1877 (he also left effects to a value of £100,000 – well over £11 million in today's money).

More information can be found about this in the memoirs of John Holling.[222] He wrote that the quarry was to the right of Windy Bank Farm, on the brow of Hunshelf Bank, and was known as the *"Isle of Skye"* quarry. People taking short-cuts to and from Green Moor made a pathway no more than two feet

---

[221] The death was reported differently in two newspaper articles. One said that he died on Tuesday between 6pm and 6.30pm, and that his son had taken him a cup of tea at 6pm, which he said he would drink later. The other report says he was found passed away in his bed on Wednesday morning.

[222] The Memoires of John Holling (MSS, Stocksbridge & District History Society) written in 1959/60. John was born in 1901 at Deepcar.

away from the edge of the stone crater. Farrow lay at the bottom of the crater all Saturday night. When he was removed, he was taken down the hill to one of the farms. The farmer, a Mr. Illingworth, lent his milk float so that Farrow could be taken to the hospital in Sheffield. A pigeon was found in his pocket, fit and well in spite of the fall. He added that this danger spot was filled in by Fox's many years ago.

William Rusby died in 1908 at the age of 41 and his widow Ada took over the running of the pub. When the 1911 census was taken, she was recorded as the innkeeper and was living at the Rock Inn with five of her children and her brother-in-law Hector Rusby, who helped in the bar. The pub formed part of the Earl of Wharncliffe's Wortley Estate, and in January 1921 much of this Estate was put up for auction. The Rock Inn, five cottages, and Green Moor Quarry made up Lot 110. The auctioneer announced that the selling of all these properties meant *"the severance of very old associations, but in the circumstances it was unavoidable."* Despite the large attendance, bidding was far from brisk, and out of 411 lots submitted, only 24 were sold. One of the properties reported as being unsold was The Rock Inn, which was withdrawn at £950.

Ada ran the pub until 1922 or 1923 before retiring and going to live at New Houses, Green Moor, handing over the reins to her brother-in-law Joel Rusby. She died at Green Moor in December 1936.

Joel was Ada's late husband's brother. He had been born in 1881 and married Florence Micklethwaite in 1906. They lived at Thurgoland and Joel worked as a stonemason in the quarry. The couple later moved from Thurgoland to New Houses before moving into the Rock Inn when Ada left in about 1937. The Rock was a much-liked rendezvous for quarrymen and farmers, and Joel Rusby was regarded as a good publican who encouraged sportsmen of many types to use his various rooms, which of course brought in a lot of trade. The Penistone Harriers, a local hunt, also used it as one of their meeting places in the 1930s. Joel and Florence ran the pub until about 1937, before retiring to New Houses

Joel and Florence had three daughters, Eva, Gladys, and Ivy. Ivy was born in 1917 and married Joseph Bacon in 1937. She used to play the piano in the pub, and also sing.

The Rock Inn became a tied house to Truswell's Brewery in 1937. Joe and Ivy ran the pub until the 1950s, perhaps until 1955 when it was acquired by Hope and Anchor Breweries.

When the 1939 Register was taken on the eve of WWII, Joe's occupation was recorded as a labourer in the steel rolling mill – there was no mention of him being a pub landlord – and it was probably his wife who ran the bar. It was during Joe and Ivy's time that the Stocksbridge and District Motor Club held meetings at the Rock, having previously held them at The Sportsman's (Pladdy's) at Deepcar. *"Scrambles"* were regularly held at nearby Trunce.

There was a shop attached to the pub, a general store which was run by a spinster called Frances Roebuck, who rented it for many years between the 1930s and about 1950. Frances died in 1953 aged 67. After Frances left the shop, it was taken on by Sid and Peggy Wells (nee Cheetham). They lived in some rooms on one side of the inn. When they emigrated to Australia, the brewery took over both the shop and the living accommodation to enlarge and modernise the pub.

The pub's name was changed from the Rock Inn to The Rock in 1969 when Peter and Audrey Stebbing were the landlords. Previous landlords were Harold Hare, and George and Jean Hind. It closed in around 2005/6 and was demolished to make way for houses.

And finally ... a story from local author Phyllis Crossland concerning the American troops stationed in this area. One of their jobs was to transport loads of bombs to and from the bomb dumps which were sited in the remoter areas of the parish:

"For security reasons the areas in which the bomb dumps were sited were closed to the general public at that time. Local farmers, and anyone else who needed to use these small country roads near the bombsites, could obtain passes which enabled them to go through the area. Guards were posted by the Americans to ensure that no unauthorised person entered the forbidden territory. There was one incident however that caused a few laughs at their expense.

"A Hunshelf farmer by the name of George Battye, having spent an evening at Greenmoor's Rock Inn, was returning to his farm on the Stocksbridge side of the hill. He did not possess a pass, because he lived out of the area. That evening he had been unable to get a lift home so, being compelled to walk, decided to take the shortest way to his house, which happened to be through the guarded area of the bomb dumps. Whether his sojourn at the Rock had rendered him oblivious to the fact that he hadn't a pass, or whether he was consciously flouting the law for the sake of convenience, is not certain. In either event, his reaction to the challenge was commendable.

"When he found himself confronted by a big, dark-faced figure with a gun at the ready, demanding to see his pass, Gerald fumbled in his pocket. Drawing out a piece of paper, which was actually one of Goldthorpe's corn bills, he waved it at the guard nonchalantly, who, without even inspecting it, muttered quickly, "*Okay, okay,*" and hurriedly motioned him to proceed. Such was the security. If Gerald had been a master spy those guards would have been none the wiser!"[223]

---

[223] Crossland, P. Years of Grace (autobiography). Bridge Publications: 1985. p232-233

The Rock. This shows the other side of the pub to the older photograph on the title page. This was the main entrance in recent years. The car park was on this side too.

Photo credit: Glyn and Alison Stebbing.

THE BUTCHER'S ARMS, HUNSHELF

There was a beershop at Hunshelf known as the Butcher's Arms, although its precise location is not known. Its owner was, unsurprisingly, a butcher, and his name was John Brownhill.

John had been born at Langsett in around 1793, and he married Frances (Fanny) Askham. John and his family lived at Penistone (near the old Rose and Crown Inn) before moving to Hunshelf between 1857 and 1860. A trade directory of 1860 lists him as a beer retailer at Hunshelf, and the 1861 census places him at Hunshelf Bank, a *"butcher and grocer and retailer of beer."*

In 1863, John Brownhill of the Butcher's Arms, Hunshelf, applied at the Barnsley Brewster Sessions for a spirit licence[224]. Whether this was granted is not recorded, but John died the following year, in April 1864. He was trying to drive an ox into his slaughterhouse when the animal attacked him and gored him so severely that he passed away. He was 71 years old.

The Coroner held the inquest at the Butcher's Arms and various people gave evidence. His daughter Mary Ann told the inquest that her father had been strong and healthy. A man called William Horton had brought a fat bullock to the house, and her father went out to help turn it into the stable. A short while afterwards, she heard her father cry out, and she went out to find him lying on the ground, the bullock standing still a few yards away. She saw Horton coming out of the stable, and her father got up and walked into the yard. His right thigh was torn but it was not bleeding much, and he took

---

[224] There are several errors in the various newspapers, reporting a Richard Lambert as applying for a license for the Butcher's Arms at Hunshelf, when in fact it was at Hoyland

himself off to bed. She had thought he was getting better, but he started to deteriorate, and died three days later.

Benjamin Batty, a Hunshelf farmer, had been sitting with John in the taproom of the Butcher's Arms on the evening the bullock was delivered; he said that Brownhill had drunk two glasses of ale and appeared to be quite sober. Batty saw Horton leading the beast up the road and remembered that it was "*going very quietly*." Brownhill left the taproom to go and help Horton, and shortly afterwards Batty heard him cry out, so he got up and went to see what was happening. Brownhill told him, "*I'm a killed man*," and added, "*them playing children have set the beast raving mad*." There were several children looking into the yard, the top of the wall at the back being level with the ground behind. Batty thought the bullock seemed inclined to "*go at*" Brownhill again, so he took him into the privy until the animal was driven into the slaughterhouse.

William Horton, a butcher living at Hunshelf Bank, and Brownhill's "*man*," told the court that he had been to Rotherham that day and bought a fat bullock on behalf of his employer. He had driven the bullock and another beast all the way as far as the Wortley toll bar. The bullock had walked steadily on towards Brownhill's, and upon its arrival, it had been let into the yard and the gate closed behind it. Brownhill had no stick or hat, so he went into the house to fetch them. Whilst Horton was in the stable, he heard a scream and came out to see Brownhill laying on the ground and the bullock looking at him. One of its horns was bloody. It was difficult to get the beast into the stable, but it seemed to calm down afterwards. Brownhill had told him he was going to scare the children off the wall when the bullock attacked him. The verdict was that Brownhill was "*accidentally injured*."

Two of Brownhill's unmarried daughters took over the running of the shop and the beerhouse. Mary Ann was the eldest (she had been born in 1829) and Sarah a bit younger (born in 1832).

An Act of 1869 brought all beerhouses under the control of the local licensing magistrates, and Mary Ann applied for her licence at the Barnsley Brewster Sessions in September. The newspaper report from the Sessions described her as "*an elderly maiden lady living with her sister,*" and said that she had conducted the beerhouse very respectably for eight or nine years. Mary Ann was hardly elderly, at forty years old, though most women were married by that age. When the case was put to the magistrates for the licence, it was said the sisters needed the income from both their shop and the beerhouse, because neither generated enough income separately to keep them. A licence to sell off the premises was issued.

In 1870 Sarah married William Horton at Sheffield. She gave her age as 32, but she would have been 38. The 1871 census records Mary Ann Brownhill at Hunshelf Bottom, the head of the household, and a grocer. William and Sarah were living with her, William working as a butcher. Both sisters gave their ages wrong; Mary Ann said she was 36, but she was 42, and Sarah said she was 33, but she was 39.

Mary Ann appeared on the Magistrates' "*blacklist*" in 1873; she was on a list of publicans and beershop keepers against whom complaints had been made during the previous year. Mary Ann, who was still running the beer-off at Hunshelf Bank was called up with the others on the list and "*reprimanded according to their desserts.*" It was the first year of the new Act [the 1872 Licensing Act], and the magistrates had been reluctant to endorse convictions on licenses.[225] After a warning, Mary Ann's licence was renewed for another year. What she had done to breach the terms of the licence was not specified, but it could well have been selling beer outside of the permitted hours.

Mary Ann carried on running the business, which a directory of 1879 recorded as "*Brownhill & Horton,*" the shop being a grocers, drapers, butchers, and beer retailers. She was also listed in the 1881 trade directory. When the 1881 census was taken, Frederick and Sarah Horton, together with their children, Mary Ann, a domestic servant, and a boarder, were living at Low Lathe, Hunshelf. Sarah had knocked nine years off her age and Mary Ann said she was 45 (she was 49). No occupation for Mary Ann was given. By 1891 they had all moved further west along Hunshelf Bank, to between Brownhill Row and Brick Houses; William was still a butcher, and Mary Ann was living on her own means. William had retired by 1901, and they were all living at High Street, Penistone.

---

[225] The Licensing Act of 1872 codified the variety of offences which a licence holder might commit and increased the penalties. All offences were now to be recorded on the actual licence, and repeated convictions might lead to its forfeiture.

THE RISING SUN INN, HUNSHELF

Built in the 1860s to serve the growing population of Stocksbridge and situated close to the works and coal pits of Samuel Fox & Company, three generations of the Newton family ran the Rising Sun Inn, which sat on the hillside overlooking the steelworks. There was also a cottage attached to the pub known as the Rising Sun Cottage. This photo shows the pub and Prospect Cottages on the hillside (circled), behind the Office Block at Fox's. The pub is on the left, the Rising Sun Cottage cannot be seen from this angle, and the newly built Prospect Cottages are on the right.

Originally owned by the Newton family, the pub was eventually bought by Tennant Brothers Brewery, Sheffield, in 1912. It was open for a hundred years before closing in 1967. It was demolished the following year.

William Newton built the Rising Sun Inn, but he died before he got to move in. He had been born at Hunshelf in 1822 to Joshua and Mary Newton and he married Martha Grayson in 1842. They lived at Berton-under-Edge farm.[226] The farm was a large one, and a school had been opened in one of its cottages in 1811. There was also ample room to open a public house, with stabling for six horses, and so William applied to the licensing magistrates for permission to open a public house on the premises.

At the Barnsley Brewster Sessions in September 1862, a solicitor called Mr. Hamer applied on behalf of William for a licence for the farm at Berton-under-Edge. Lord Wharncliffe (the Lord of the Manor of Hunshelf) and Mr. Ellis of the Rock Inn at Green Moor opposed the application. Their solicitor, Mr. Tyas, said that there was no need for another licensed premises in the area because the population only numbered 250. It was counter-argued that the population was over a thousand. Along with several other applications, a decision was deferred until later that month, and at the adjourned Brewster Sessions the licence was granted. It was noted that there was as yet no name for the newly licensed premises (*"sign not named"*).[227]

There is a story that mysterious tapping noises were said to have been heard in the beerhouse. It had once been a weaving shed, and folk blamed the ghost of a girl called Nancy, who had drowned in a vat of dye in the early 1800s.[228]

According to Hunshelf historian Ted Spencer, in 1864 William began building a new public house further down the hill, which would become the Rising Sun, but as both the Rising Sun and its attached cottage are shown on a photograph dated 1860, either Ted has this date wrong, or William did not build the house from scratch but converted an existing building. He never got to be the landlord of the new pub, however, because he died before it was finished, in September 1864. The Rising Sun had opened by May 1865 with his widow Martha as the landlady. She was the licensee for about a year,

---

[226] Also spelt Berton, Birkin, Berthing or Burton and sometimes as *"under-the-edge"* or *"underhill."*
[227] John Tyas was a Barnsley attorney and solicitor, and Mr. Thomas Greensit Hamer was also a Barnsley solicitor. Mr Hamer died in 1869, on his way back from a holiday in Blackpool to attend the Brewster Sessions. He was only 44 years old and had an extensive Police and County Court practice.
[228] Salim, Valerie. Ghost Hunter's Guide to Sheffield. Sheffield: Sheaf Publishing 2001

then for some reason her son-in-law James Thompson took over for a few years before transferring the licence back to Martha, who then ran the pub until about 1875 or 1876 when her son Joseph became the landlord.

William Newton had been instrumental in helping the fledgling Stocksbridge Band of Hope Co-operative Society to expand. They had originally used a room in George Batty's Friendship Inn to meet and begin selling, before moving into two cottages next to the Friendship owned by Mr. Batty (using one as a shop and one as a house for the grocery manager). In the spring of 1861 a piece of freehold land was bought in Stocksbridge for just over £70 from John Ridal of Wadsley, by Samuel Fox (the owner of the steelworks), John Bower of Watson House (a farmer), and William Newton of Hunshelf, who were trustees *"for the time being"* of the Society.[229] Plans for new premises were drawn up by Joseph Hayward later that year, and the new building was completed in 1863. It was known as the New Stores (later the Central Stores).

William died in September 1864, two years after being granted the licence at Berton-under-Edge. He was just 42 years old, and had made his will the day before he died; it was read back to him by his solicitor, and he signalled that he understood what had been written, before making his mark with a cross (either because he could not write, or was too ill to sign his name). The will was proved the following February by his widow Martha, his daughter Ann's husband James Thompson junior of Well Hill, and his friend Henry Booth of Bolsterstone (who was married to Martha's sister Mary Grayson). He left all his furniture to his wife, as well as four freehold cottages at Stocksbridge, which he had recently built, from which she was to have the rental income. Two of these were being rented by John Milnes, a grocer, and the others by Thomas Marsden and Isaac Patterson. It is possible that these were what

---

[229] The land and the buildings in the course of erection upon it were mortgaged for £400 on 26th July 1862, and the mortgage was not redeemed until 1873, when Samuel Fox was the sole surviving trustee. William Newton had died in 1864 aged 42, and John Bower in 1866 aged 26 (John Bower was the landlord of the Castle Inn at Bolsterstone at the time of his death).

were known as Prospect Cottages, standing close to the Rising Sun and Rising Sun Cottage.[230]

The following month, William's executors instructed auctioneer John Haigh to sell off all his farming equipment, animals, and crops, as he had specified in his will. There were six horses, nine beasts, eight sheep, two pigs, hay, wheat and oats, various carts, and dairy utensils. All the money realised by the sale was to be divided equally between his children.

SUDDEN DEATH IN A COLLIERY: 1865

Martha was the landlady in May 1865 when the coroner held an inquest there on the body of Joseph Wilding of Hunshelf. Wilding was 42 years old and had died suddenly whilst at work in John Armitage's colliery at Henholmes. John and his family came from Lancashire; they lived at Dodworth before moving to Henholmes about eight or nine months before his death. At the inquest, Wilding's wife Jane said that he had complained about having toothache five days previously, and a chemist called Mr. Walker gave him a "*draft*" [a draught of medicine] for the pain, which had made him feel very ill. Another witness, Ann Booth, said that Wilding had told her he thought he "*would have died*" after taking the medicine, he felt so ill.

Two of Joseph's sons worked in the same pit as their father as hurriers.[231] John Wilding, who would have been about 12 years old, told the inquest that he had found his father lying dead. He had seen him only half an hour previously when his father had brought a full corve (small wagon) to his brother to hurry away, telling him to "*look sharp back*" (be quick). John's brother could have been Thomas, who would have been about eight years old.

Benjamin Hudson of Wood Royd said that he was working in the next bank to Wilding, and at about 3pm he heard Wilding's son cry out so he went to his bank and saw him lying on his side, close to a full corve. He noted that his candle was lit and in its usual place and that his own candle "*burnt right*,"

---

[230] They are not shown on a photograph from 1860, but they are on a photograph from 1868, which fits in with the timescale of William Newton having built them. A sales advert from 1920 mentions four stone-built dwelling houses known as Prospect Cottages.

[231] Hurrier is a Yorkshire word for the person who took empty coal tubs or corves to the coal face and took the loaded tubs back. Hurriers were often women or young children.

indicating there was nothing wrong with the air quality. He said the bank was 2' 4" high, which reminds us of what cramped and claustrophobic conditions the miners had to work in, and that he was working ten yards away and could hear, but not see, his colleague. Wilding was removed from the pit and Ann Booth helped to lay out his body. The Coroner's verdict was that he was found dead from natural causes.

Martha Newton's son-in-law James Thompson was a joiner by trade, and he was briefly the licensee, although there are no records at this time of any licence transfers being made (including from Berton-under-Edge). Why the licence passed from Martha to James is not known. In 1867 he was in trouble for breaching the terms of his licence; when he applied to renew it at the annual Brewster Sessions in 1868, he was told that his licence would be suspended for two weeks until his case was heard by the magistrates at the adjourned Sessions. His name was on a *"blacklist"* of landlords who had either been fined or ordered to pay costs during the previous year. What misdemeanour Thompson had committed was not recorded, but it can only have been relatively minor because he did get his licence back. His name would remain on the blacklist for the following year in case he fell foul of the law again. The Barnsley Chronicle reported that Thompson had been before the court once in the preceding twelve months, as had George Lawton of the Rose and Crown at Langsett. One of the magistrates addressed the assembled publicans and gave this speech: *"Now, the magistrates are determined to punish all breaches of the law [...]and should you be guilty of any offences against your licences between now and next Brewster Sessions this* "black list" *will appear against you, and it will be a question whether it is not the duty of the bench to suspend your licenses for three, six, nine, or twelve months, or altogether. Therefore, take our advice and be careful."*

SERIOUS ACCIDENT AT STOCKSBRIDGE: 1867
A man named Pearson fell down a flight of steps, which were said to be in a dangerous condition, in March 1867. He was knocked unconscious, and was taken to the Rising Sun, where he lay with little hope of recovery. There were no further reports of who he was, or whether he recovered, and without a full name, it is almost impossible to find out his fate.

ROBBING A FELLOW LODGER AT HUNSHELF: 1867
A case came to court in October 1867 concerning a robbery at the Rising Sun earlier that year, in February. A labourer called John Armitage was charged with stealing a pair of trousers and a shirt from John Hanwell of Hunshelf. Both men were lodgers at James Thompson's pub until Armitage suddenly left in February, following which the clothes were found to be missing. The police were informed, and a description of the thief given to them, but he was not arrested until October. Another lodger had left the pub around the same time, so the case against Armitage was not a strong one, but he pleaded guilty and was sentenced to one month's imprisonment with hard labour. The sentence would have been longer, but he had no previous convictions and was of previous good character.

James Thompson had moved out of the pub with his family by the time the 1871 census was taken, although he still lived nearby, and was working in his main trade of joiner and carpenter. Martha Newton was now officially the licensee again. Joseph's brother, Jonathan Thompson, was living at Berton-under-Edge in this year.

Martha had been born in 1822, and she was the daughter of Joseph Grayson and Sarah Helliwell. Joseph lived at Eldercliffe Farm (now Ellen Cliff), Hunshelf, and had been married before, to Elizabeth Oldham, who had died in 1814. One of Joseph and Elizabeth's sons was called John Grayson, making him Martha's half-brother. In 1829 he gained notoriety when he got into some trouble, left his new bride Sarah Crawshaw (of Langley Brook Farm), and was next heard of when he was arrested in Northampton, after being found stuck in the chimney of a banking house, having been intending to steal from it. After a trial, he was sentenced to death, but this was commuted to transportation for life to Van Diemen's Land (now Tasmania).[232] He eventually won his freedom, but he never came back to this country. He married again to Janet Forrest, herself a former convict. We know from his letters that he asked about his wife, but she seems never to have written to him. In one of his letters, he wrote, "*I am doing very well*

---

[232] John Grayson went by the alias of William Butterworth. His life has been researched in depth by W.E. Spencer (Ted), and there is a MS of his work in Stocksbridge library archives. I too have researched him, because Sarah Crawshaw was the daughter of my ancestor Thomas Crawshaw of Langley Brook Farm near Midhope. Prison and transportation records survive, as do letters written by John/William to people back home.

here, and another thing I have a small family here. I never told any of you before, but it is no use to keep it from you any longer therefore you may inform all enquiring friends I shall never return. You see I have been so long away that it is almost a man's lifetime and all people would be strangers to me, besides I am so much respected here as ever I was in England." One of his correspondents was Francis Blackwell, a one-time innkeeper at Green Moor. John/William did quite well for himself and died in 1850 at the age of 47. Several years after her husband's transportation, in 1836, Sarah had an illegitimate daughter, Mary. The vicar wrote in the baptism register that she was *"the daughter of Sarah Grayson of Middop, wife of John Grayson who was deported for life."* He seemed to be expressing his condemnation!

In 1871, the household at the Rising Sun consisted of Martha Newton (licensed victualler), her children Sam, Sarah Jane, Eliza, and Fred, together with a servant and one boarder.

FATAL ACCIDENT AT A COLLIERY AT HUNSHELF BANK: 1872

A man named Thomas Heathcote had come from Warwickshire looking for work as a bricklayer. In 1871 he was lodging at an inn at Carlecotes, before moving to take lodgings at Deepcar when he got a job at a new pit (the north pit) belonging to Fox's. On the afternoon of the 4th December he was killed at work when a rope holding the corve in which he was travelling broke, throwing him out and fracturing his skull. Heathcote's body was taken to the Rising Sun Inn to await the Coroner's inquiry, which was common practice at this time. The Coroner held the inquest at the pub, and Heathcote's cousin John Townsend accompanied Thomas's widow on the journey north for the hearing.

Heathcote had been one of a group of men who were *"arching"*[233] a new road into the pit. He met with a workmate John Marshall on the bank of the north pit where six corves were coupled together, four of them already loaded with bricks and mortar. Marshall got into the fifth corve, and Heathcote got into the last one. The line of corves was then let down the incline by a rope attached to a drum, the brake being operated by the usual man. Marshall noticed that after they had gone about twelve yards down the slope, the speed rapidly increased and the corve he was riding in left the rails and threw him

---

[233] Arching: brickwork or stonework forming the roof of an underground roadway.

out. He couldn't see much because the accident had put his lamp out, but as he made his way back up the slope, he saw Heathcote lying on the ground with some cotton from his lamp burning on the ground. His body was brought up about five minutes later. Marshall said that he had never been warned not to ride down the incline in a corve.

Joe Hoyle, a fellow bricklayer, gave evidence and said that he had gone about 180 or 190 yards down the incline when he heard some corves approaching *"at great speed."* He jumped onto a wall out of their way as they sped past. When they stopped, about 200 yards down the incline, they were all still coupled up, but some had gone off the rails.

The road the men were working on was five feet high, and the corves were about twenty inches high. They were attached by a rope made of wire, which was 7/8" in diameter, and although it had been recently checked and deemed to be in good order, the strands had snapped.

Thomas Marshall, the underviewer (supervisor), inspected the site of the accident and said that there was *"a barrowful of muck down,"* presumably a fall from the roof, some of which was on the rails, which he thought had thrown the corves off the track. The verdict was that Heathcote, who was 40 years old, had been accidentally killed.

CLUBS, SPORTS, AND SOCIETIES
The pub played host to pigeon shooting matches, knur and spell matches, and the Stocksbridge Steel and Iron Works Cricket Club. It was also the home for club meetings such as the Red, White & Blue Lodge (no. 543, Thurlstone District) of the Order of Druids (a fraternal organisation which later became a benefit society like the Oddfellows and the Foresters) and the Stocksbridge branch of the South Yorkshire Miners' Association.

William and Martha's son Thomas Newton of Hunshelf played (and lost) a game of knur and spell against A. Haigh of Oughtibridge in 1874 at the pub. In 1876, the Stocksbridge Steel and Iron Works Cricket Club held their annual closing dinner at Joseph Newton's Rising Sun Inn. Forty or so members and friends were present. During the past season, the club had played 23 matches, of which they had won 11, lost 4, and drawn 8. 1st prize for batting went to J. Williams, with 2nd prize going to W. R. Knight. Prizes for bowling were awarded to E. Smith and J. Simpson.

THE ORDER OF DRUIDS LODGE 543[234]

Several meetings of the Order of Druids Lodge were reported in the local newspapers. Each year they held their Club Feast at the Rising Sun. In 1873, about 120 members walked in procession through the streets of the village, accompanied by the Pilley brass band. A sermon was preached in Stocksbridge Church School, and a dinner was held afterwards. In 1875 members attended divine service at Deepcar school in the morning before marching through the village *"in their quaint costume,"* accompanied this year by the Stocksbridge Brass Band. A *"substantial dinner"* was provided by Mr. Newton of the Rising Sun. July 1876 saw their procession being headed by the Denby Brass Band. Members wore their *"usual insignia,"* and after a service at Bolsterstone church, a collection was made for the schools. The group then marched through Deepcar and Stocksbridge to the Rising Sun, for yet another *"substantial dinner"* – which was probably much needed after walking up and down all those hills!

THE SOUTH YORKSHIRE MINERS' ASSOCIATION – Lodge no. 80

The S.Y.M.A. was an early trade union established at Barnsley in 1858. Local *"Lodges"* were formed at individual pits or groups of pits. Stocksbridge miners must have joined in 1873 because their first annual *"demonstration"* was held in 1874. A procession started from the Rising Sun Inn at 10am, where the Lodge held their meetings, and was accompanied by the Darley Dale brass band. They marched through Deepcar, Bolsterstone, and Stocksbridge, carrying *"their splendid new banner."* The Sheffield Daily Telegraph reported that *"a substantial dinner [was] provided in Mrs. Newton's best style."* Mr. R. Braithwaite was the president, and there were about ninety members. A deputation from Barnsley was also present.

Members of the S.Y.M.A. showed their solidarity through these annual demonstrations, with miners and their families parading with music and banners. In 1873 no less than 20,000 people were reported to have congregated in the Queen's Grounds in Barnsley. The Barnsley Chronicle of 2nd August that year reported that the Association had prospered and that

---

[234] In 1885 this was referred to as the Lily of the Valley Court.

it had paid out just over £11,000 during the year to the sick, the injured, widows and orphans, for funerals and to charitable purposes. *"The proceedings on the day were of a most satisfactory nature, and each may congratulate himself on their success. The union, while strong and mighty, is eminently practical and conciliatory. The tone of the speeches breathed nought of defiance, or of strife [...]. May its conduct in the future be as marked by prudence, intelligence, and moral worth as heretofore; may it still continue to educate its workmen, to cultivate arbitration, and the powers of reason to settle differences, and to further its interest; then a bright future is in store, we shall be saved the horrors of strikes, the unpleasantness of contentions, labour and capital will go hand in hand, and all will be peace and prosperity."*

In July 1875, the procession was headed by the Sheffield Artillery Volunteers' band and a *"magnificent flag."* They made their way to Bolsterstone church via Deepcar to listen to a sermon, then returned via Hole House Lane. The weather was very showery, and the roads bad. Once more, a *"substantial dinner"* was provided by Mr. Newton at the Rising Sun. The lodge now had 107 members.

WAGON ACCIDENT AT STOCKSBRIDGE: 1873

John Oxley, a pot hawker from Thurlstone, was leaving the Rising Sun one Tuesday afternoon with his wagon loaded with pots when he had an accident. He turned a corner too sharply and his wagon caught a post, knocking one side of the shafts off their hook, causing him to slip with his feet against the horse. The animal kicked and bolted down the hill. Oxley's feet were tangled in the shafts and he was hanging upside down. He held on to the reins, but when the horse was stopped (a man caught the horse and turned him against the wall), he was unconscious and seriously injured. He was carried on a board to the Rising Sun, and a surgeon was fetched. The wagon was slightly broken, the ironwork twisted, and the pots smashed, but the horse was unhurt. John survived, and carried on in business – the 1881 census, taken eight years after his accident, records him as a 50-year-old earthenware dealer. He was still listed as an earthenware dealer/hawker on the 1911 census, aged 80. He died at the grand old age of 84 in 1912.[235]

---

[235] Ages are often contradictory in old records.

A MAN FOUND DEAD AT STOCKSBRIDGE: 1874
A 48-year-old Hunshelf man named Samuel Brooke was found dead near the Rising Sun by his son William late one Sunday night in May 1874.[236] He had been in good health, and there was no sign of violence on his body. An inquest was held at Martha Newton's Rising Sun, where his son and two others gave evidence. William Brooke told the inquest that he last saw his father at around 6pm that Sunday when he was at home with Hezekiah Mann, his son-in-law. The two men went out a little later, and when his father had not returned by midnight, he and his mother went to look for him, finding him lying face down in the road close to the Rising Sun. They took him to the house of a man called George Horner and then home. Sam Hattersley Swift of Stocksbridge, a colliery manager, told the inquest that he had seen Brooke in the Rising Sun, that he'd had a glass of beer and then left, apparently sober and healthy. Finally, Hezekiah Mann of Silkstone said that he had visited his father-in-law and slept over on Saturday night and that he seemed well. They went to the pub together that evening, Mann leaving first. It was initially thought that apoplexy or heart disease was the cause of his death, and the Coroner's verdict was that he was found dead from natural causes. Samuel left a widow and seven children.[237]

The Rising Sun was taken over by Martha's son Joseph and his wife Lydia in about 1875 or 1876. Joseph had been born in 1848 and had married Lydia Cartwright of Hepworth at Penistone church in 1869. He was a butcher by trade and had been living nearby on Hunshelf Bank. He also farmed some land. He was granted the licence, despite having been arrested for assault a few years earlier, in 1871.

ASSAULT ON A PENISTONE MAN AT STOCKSBRIDGE: 1871
Joseph Newton and Benjamin Sanderson were accused of assault by John Hirst, a farm labourer living at Kirkwood, near Penistone. On Monday 25th September, all the men were drinking in Mrs. Batty's public house at Stocksbridge, The Friendship. Hirst told the court that he did not stay long

---

[236] The report in the newspaper and the Coroner's notebook vary greatly in their versions. The newspaper reported that Thomas Newton of the Rising Sun found the body, and that Samuel had been at work in Fox's until 9.15pm. The Coroner's report stated that Brooke's son found the body and there was no mention of him having been at work that evening.
[237] In 1871 Samuel and his wife Ann were living at Hunshelf. He had been born in Doncaster. Seven children were recorded with ages ranging from 23 down to 7.

and that as soon as he left, Newton and Sanderson followed him out. Newton knocked him down, and both men kicked him, and Hirst alleged that one of them tried to strangle him, making his ears bleed. Newton and Sanderson's solicitor said that Hirst was a wrestler and that he had thrown Newton before he was attacked, a statement that Hirst denied. Andrew Hoyle, a miner living at Stocksbridge, was called as a witness and told the court that as soon as Hirst left, Newton and Sanderson began *"poising him."*[238] A Mrs. Sykes confirmed this. Newton and Sanderson argued that Haigh had gone into the pub and challenged anyone to fight or wrestle. No one responded, and when they got outside, Sanderson, a farm labourer, repeated the challenge to him. However, Haigh got the better of him, prompting Newton to interfere and try to restore order. Haigh then attacked Newton, and in the end, came off second best. The Bench were of opinion that the two defendants had committed an assault, and they were each fined forty shillings plus costs, or two months' imprisonment with hard labour.

At some point Martha moved out of the pub; by the time the census was taken in 1881, she was living at Lane Farm, Deepcar, where she was recorded as being a farmer, employing one man (John Crossley, a 73-year-old widower, who worked for her as an indoor servant). Also recorded on that night were her son Thomas (a blacksmith), son Fred (a farmer), daughter Eliza Newton, and a 4-year-old grandson, Arthur Hanwell. Martha stayed at Lane End until at least 1891 (when she was living on her own means, with her son Sam, a stone dresser) before moving to Wood Royd, Deepcar, where she lived with Sam, who was still unmarried. She died on the 30th January 1910 aged 88.

TO BREWERS, INNKEEPERS, &c. – to be sold by auction: 1879.
In June 1879, the Rising Sun and its adjoining cottage were put up for auction by order of the surviving Trustees of William Newton's will. William's son-in-law James Thompson was one of them and William's widow Martha was the other, her brother-in-law Henry Booth having died in 1870. Both properties were in the occupation of Joseph Newton, and he was under notice to quit by the 11th December. According to the advert, a *"profitable trade"* had been carried on at the pub for several years. The notice said that "*Part*

---

[238] According to Dr. George Redmonds, a Yorkshire historian and expert on local dialect, surnames, and place names, poise is local dialect for kick [see Redmonds, G. Names and History: People, Places and Things. Hambleton and London: 2004]

of the purchase money may remain on security of the property at a moderate rate of interest," meaning that the Trustees were offering a kind of private mortgage, lending the purchaser some of the money required for the purchase. A shrewd business move.

Joseph himself bought the pub from his father's estate and owned it until his death in 1911. He appears to have financed this by doing a deal with Tennant Brothers, a Sheffield Brewery, making an arrangement to lease the pub to the brewery; they would have paid him to manage it, and would have supplied the beer, turning it into a tied house. When Joseph decided to leave the pub six years later in 1885, it was left to the brewery to advertise for, and employ, a new tenant, although Joseph still owned the building.

The 1881 census recorded Joseph and his wife Lydia at the pub, together with four children, two female servants (Mary Ann Hampshire and Mary Shaw), and an ostler called Thomas Wood who would have looked after the horses.

FATAL ACCIDENT AT STOCKSBRIDGE WORKS: 1881
In September 1881, a 54-year-old quarryman named William Dysche was killed in an accident whilst engaged in getting stone near the new Bessemer Works. He had been descending a ladder to the riverbed near the fitters' shop when one of the rungs broke under his weight; he was well-built and heavy. He fell with his head against the wall and died shortly afterwards. It was thought that he had broken his neck or fractured his skull. The inquest was held at the Rising Sun, and a verdict of accidental death was recorded. Dysche was described as a very steady man who was much respected. The 1881 census, taken on the 3rd April, recorded him at 15 Florence Buildings, Deepcar, with his wife Ann, daughter Annie, stepson George Hague, and four grandchildren.

CONCEALMENT OF BIRTH AT SHARROW.
SUSPICIOUS DEATH OF A CHILD: 1883
My great-great-grandmother Elizabeth Crossley was summoned to give evidence at a Coroner's court held at Joseph Newton's Rising Sun in October 1883. Elizabeth's sister Louisa had been working as a domestic servant at the house of a solicitor in Sharrow, Sheffield, called Edmund Knowles Binns. Whilst in his employ, she had given birth to a daughter who was about a month premature. No one had known that she was pregnant, and she gave

birth in secret. The child only lived for between five minutes and an hour, and the Coroner held an inquest on the body. Various people gave evidence, and the cause of death was found to be suffocation or asphyxia. There were no signs that an abortion had been procured (which would have been a crime for which Louisa would have been tried in court), and the child's body showed no sign of violence. There was some discussion as to whether the child's death was the result of being suffocated in the bedclothes through inattention, or whether death could be brought about without there being any visible marks (it could be).

Elizabeth had gone to the Binns' house because her sister had arranged for her to take her place in the service of Mrs. Binns. Louisa became ill while she was there, and Mrs. Binns had gone in a cab to fetch a doctor; Louisa told him she had a cold, and she was hot, feverish, and shivery. The doctor saw her again at about 11.30am the following day, and Louisa told him that she felt better. She refused point-blank to let him examine her. He realised there was something wrong, and eventually she admitted to being "*6 months pregnant,*" begging him not to tell Mrs. Binns, the "*missus,*" as she was going home in a few days, so she need never know. The doctor did not know that she had already given birth, because she refused to be touched, and had covered herself up. Louisa then left the house and went home to her family. On the day of the inquest, the doctor visited Louisa at her father's house (The Coach House, Hunshelf) and she told him that she had felt ill that day and gone to the bathroom, where she "*became insensible*" for about an hour, and gave birth to the child. "*She was sure she never did anything to it.*"

Elizabeth Crossley was called to give evidence. She told the court that she had checked on her sister a few times at Mr. Binns' house, and after dinner she found Louisa on the bed, her clothes on the floor, and a body laid on top of them, its head covered by a cloth. The umbilical cord had been cut. Elizabeth then destroyed all traces of the birth and wrapped the child in a petticoat and placed it in a tin box. She said that Louisa was 29 years old and "*had never had to do with babies.*" When Elizabeth found the body of the child on the Friday, Louisa sobbed, "*oh Lizzie, I don't know what I am to do. Where shall I go? I must go home.*" The Coroner having summed up, the jury returned a verdict after half an hour's deliberation that the child was "*found dead from suffocation, the mother having been without assistance during the birth.*" No blame was attached to Louisa.

Incidentally, the Binns family was no stranger to scandal. The year before all this happened, Mr. Binns had responded to an advert in the Matrimonial News placed by a widow, Ada Caroline Milne of Tunbridge Wells, who had a fortune of £18,000 (worth over £2 million today). However, her brother, F. Liebert, took great steps to stop the marriage. When Mr. Binns met the lady at her home, her brother gave him a thrashing and turned him out of the house, repeating the beating at the railway station. He said that she was not responsible for her actions, having been confined to an asylum at some point. He made several attempts to stop the marriage, but it eventually went ahead in Sheffield, with a police presence. There may have been some truth in the brother's accusation of mental illness because Ada ended her days in an asylum in France.

PUB TO LET: 1885
"To be Let, the first-class FULL-LICENSED HOUSE, called the Rising Sun, Stocksbridge. – Apply Tennant Brothers Limited, Exchange Brewery, Sheffield."[239] Tennant Brothers' Exchange Brewery was based at Bridge Street, Sheffield. It expanded throughout the twentieth century, acquiring other breweries over the years. They leased the Rising Sun from its owner Joseph Newton, and after his death they bought the pub at auction in 1912 for £3,200.

Thomas Edward Batty answered the advert and moved from the Bridge Inn at Penistone to Hunshelf. He was no stranger to the pub trade, having been brought up in the Friendship Hotel at Stocksbridge, where his father George was the landlord. After George died, his widow (Thomas Batty's stepmother) took over, and after her death Thomas ran it for a while. The pub had actually been left to his younger half-brother Elijah, who had been born in 1857, but when his mother died he was too young to run it, being only about sixteen years of age, so Thomas, who was twenty-one, ran it on his behalf. Thomas had married Annie Hawley and they had a daughter, Lucy Gertrude, but his wife died at the Friendship only two years after their marriage. A couple of years later Thomas married Annie's sister Lucy, and he moved to become the landlord of the Bridge Hotel at Penistone; he was there when the 1881 census was taken. He took the Rising Sun in 1885 but he only stayed for about three years before leaving to go back to the

---
[239] Advertisement placed in the Sheffield Daily Telegraph 16th March 1885.

Friendship. Joseph Newton then returned, staying until about 1897 when his son Harry took over. The electoral registers record Joseph as the owner of the Rising Sun until his death in 1911.

HUNSHELF FEAST: June 1885

Thomas Batty advertised that he was taking entries for a *"Grand Three Mile Steeplechase,"* to be run on Saturday 27th June. This was to be followed on the Monday by a 120 yards juvenile handicap flat race. He also organised a Knur and Spell handicap on 20th June. It must have been successful, for the following year it was reported to be an annual event. In 1886, over a thousand people assembled at the Rising Sun to watch *"Mr. T. Batty's annual steeplechase,"* which set off from the pub and went past Underbank Hall to Dyson Cote and back, a distance of about four miles. First prize went to S. Adams of Stocksbridge (with a 3¾ minutes start), who ran the distance in 23 minutes and 10 secs. J. Walton of Deepcar (45 seconds start) was second, and W. Ibbotson of Hunshelf came third (2½ minutes start). In 1887 ten entrants ran *"a very uneven route"* of over three miles, the winner being J. Walker. An annual *"Old Man's Race"* also took place in this year, with Mr. Batty giving a timepiece to the winner. Entrants had to be over fifty years of age. There were five entrants and the winner was 65-year-old B. Oates.

DEEPCAR SPORTS: Saturday 1st August 1885

Entries for the Deepcar Sports could be bought from Mr. Thomas Batty at the Rising Sun Inn, from his half-brother Elijah Batty at the Friendship, and from Benjamin Couldwell at the Royal Oak. There was obviously a wider interest in this event because entries could be made at public houses in many locations including Thurgoland, Grenoside, Oughtibridge, Penistone, Sheffield, and Barnsley. The events included *"Trotting Matches in Harness for Horses and Ponies, Hurdle Jumping for Horses, Pony Race, Bicycle Races, and the usual events."* There were valuable prizes to be won, a gala and fireworks, and the 1st West Yorkshire Yeomanry Cavalry and the Stocksbridge Prize Bands would be in attendance.

A STOCKSBRIDGE KNUR AND SPELL ACTION AT BARNSLEY: 1888

Thomas Batty organised Knur and Spell matches, but one of these ended up before the Barnsley court. In June 1888 he sued Thomas Edon, manager at the Queen's Grounds, Barnsley, to recover the sum of £25, which was the amount of a stake deposited with him for a knur and spell match between

John Whittaker and Albert Waller on the 22nd February. Whittaker was Batty's man, and he put forward a stake of £25 for him. Thomas Edon was appointed the stakeholder. On the day, all was not well. There were accusations of unfair play, cheating even, and Batty had demanded his money back. Edon, who was also the referee, ordered play to continue the next day, but Whittaker did not turn up, because he said the play was not fair. Waller did turn up, playing the remaining rises himself, and was given the stake money of £50 as his winnings.

Edon's solicitor said that the money was subscribed as a prize for the winner and that Edon, as the referee, was perfectly within his rights to award the money to Waller, who had finished the match. Batty's barrister contended that the money was a bet, not a prize, and that Batty was also perfectly within his rights to ask for his money back.[240]

It was a long, drawn-out case, not at all straightforward, and after a lengthy hearing, the judge decided he needed some advice on this complicated matter, and so he *"reserved his decision,"* meaning he would go away and research the issue and obtain some expert advice before passing judgement.

When the court sat again, the judge gave his opinion that knur and spell was a lawful game and was not within the provisions of the Betting Act. In this case, the money was a subscription for the prize money for a lawful game, so there was no bet, and the parties could not recover their money merely because they gave notice – the game must be played out. The only way in which the money could be recovered was to show fraud or trickery in carrying out the game. Despite allegations of unfair play, the judge thought the only person who could receive the money was whoever won the match. His verdict was that it was a lawful game, there was no bet, there was *"no trace of any trickery,"* and therefore he must give a verdict in favour of Edon, not Batty.

---

[240] According to the Bank of England's Inflation Calculator, £25 in 1888 would be the equivalent of £3,274 today. The National Archives estimates it at nearer £2,000 – but that was still a substantial sum – no wonder he wanted it back! In 1890, £25 would buy you two cows, and would be what a skilled labourer would earn in 75 days.

Two months later Tom Batty left the Rising Sun to take over the Friendship from his younger half-brother Elijah, who had been fined for being *"incapably drunk on his own licensed premises"* in July 1888. When Elijah's licence came up for renewal in September, the police opposed it, and so Thomas Edward applied for it instead. The licence was granted to Tom, but Superintendent Midgley said that, although there had been no conviction against him while he had held the licence at Hunshelf, he wanted to caution him because, in his opinion, he was too fond of betting. He added that the Rising Sun was somewhat isolated, and he hoped that he would not continue the practice of betting at the Friendship, which was in a much busier place.

After Thomas Batty's departure, the Rising Sun was once more in the hands of its previous landlord, Joseph Newton. When the 1891 census was taken, the household at the Rising Sun consisted of Joseph and his wife Lydia, five of their children, a boarder, and two female servants. Joseph's occupation was recorded as *"innkeeper and farmer."* The nearby cottages known as Prospect Cottages were in the occupation of their son Harry, their daughter Ann Thompson, and Ann Grayson, who could have been a relative of Joseph's mother Martha (nee Grayson). Joseph was the landlord until at least 1896/7 when his son Harry took over the reins.

Many pubs over the years have been the venues for auctions, but not many were held at the Rising Sun. There were, however, the following two properties auctioned there by local auctioneer and valuer John Bramall of Old Haywoods:

AUCTION: WEST VIEW, HUNSHELF: 1892
A freehold stone-built dwelling house called West View, located on Hunshelf Road in the vicinity of Croft Cottages and Pea Royd Hill. West View was rented out to the family of the late Henry Clough and had three *"low rooms"* [downstairs], four bedrooms, cellars, coal places, and other conveniences, and covered about 500 square yards. According to the advertisement, it was *"very pleasantly situated, and [...] in the immediate neighbourhood of Messrs. Fox and Co.'s Works"* and was *"certain to command good tenants."* This seems to have been bought by the landlord himself, Joseph Newton – when he died in 1911, it was one of his properties that was put up for auction in 1912, fetching £290.

AUCTION: GROCER'S SHOP etc: 1893

Leasehold premises at Stocksbridge, consisting of a grocer's shop, a warehouse and storeroom, with a stone-built dwelling-house, stable, garden, and a yard. The house had four bedrooms, one living and sitting room, kitchen, and cellars, and covered about 1,327 square yards. Gas was laid on throughout, and the house and shop were warmed by a heating apparatus in the warehouse. The lease was for 780 years (from the 25th March 1880), at the yearly ground rent of £6. The premises were very close to the entrance to Fox's entrance and were *"in every way suited for carrying on an extensive Grocery Business."* These premises were for many years occupied by Mr. John Milnes, and after his death, his son.

ALLEGED SERIOUS ASSAULT: 1894

On Monday 12th November 1894 George Henry Milnes, a Stocksbridge steelworker, was assaulted by three men whilst on his way home from the Rising Sun. The three men were all colliers; John Wood of Hunshelf (aged 21), John Beever (aged 25), and Herbert Goddard[241] (aged 19). Milnes was about 30 years old. He had gone into the pub between 3pm and 4pm and stayed until closing time. He drank four or five glasses of beer and some soda water. The three men were also in the pub for some time. Milnes said that he heard Goddard and a man named Ibbotson have *"some words."* Milnes overtook Goddard and Beever on his walk home, and he remarked to Goddard, *"It's a rum do if you and Ibbotson can't agree, as you are mates."* Goddard replied, *"I have not got a --- bobby living with me if you have,"* referring to the fact that P.C. Sagar lodged with Milnes. Milnes answered that he had nothing to do with Sagar, even if he did lodge with him, but Beever accused him of telling Sagar all about him poaching, which Milnes denied. Wood, who was just in front, turned around and took a running kick at Milnes, striking him in the lower part of his body. Beever and Goddard then attacked him from behind, all three kicking him until Joseph Newton came up with a man named Crossley and drove them off. Milnes was sick from the pain. The three men then went away but Beever and Wood returned, Beever pulling off his coat, wanting to continue the fight. Newton promptly

---

[241] The newspaper report of the incident gives his name as George Goddard, but when he appeared later at the Sessions, his name was reported as Herbert. The 1891 census confirms that his name was Herbert, and that he was the son of George. They were living at 81 Haywoods Park. George Henry Milnes lived at 107 Haywoods Park and was married to Alice.

knocked Beever down and also prevented Wood from further assaulting Milnes, and the men then ran off. Milnes was examined by a surgeon, who found that he had received injuries which meant he would not be able to work for a while. The three men were committed for trial at the Sessions, which was where the more serious crimes were heard. When the case came up at the West Riding Sessions in January the following year, all three pleaded guilty. Wood and Beever were each fined forty shillings, and Goddard was bound over to keep the peace.

Joseph's son Harry Newton took over as landlord in 1896. He had been born in August 1869 and married Sarah Jane Ibbotson in 1890. On the marriage certificate, he gave his occupation as clerk. Joseph moved next door to the pub, into a newer house which was known as Hunshelf House, which he may have had built (it is not on the earlier photos of the pub). The 1901 census records him as a coal merchant and the 1911 census as a farmer. In July 1896 he placed a notice in the Sheffield Daily Telegraph that said, *"All persons allowing their pigeons, fowls, or dogs to trespass on land in the occupation of Mr. Joseph Newton, of Hunshelf Bank, Stocksbridge, after this notice, will be prosecuted."*

INQUEST AT STOCKSBRIDGE ON TOM MARSH: May 1896

The coroner Mr. Taylor held an inquest at Harry Newton's Rising Sun on the body of 26-year-old Tom Marsh, who was found shot on Sunday morning, the 17th May, in the yard of Harry Haigh on Button Row. Tom and Harry had lodged together with Mrs. Mary Ann Evans, who was the widow of James Evans (Harry and Mary Ann married sometime before the inquest). Tom had been born in 1869 and was the son of Stephen Marsh and Ann Elizabeth Bradley of Brownhill Row, Hunshelf.

Mrs. Haigh told the inquest that Tom had been suspected of stealing £8 from a box belonging to Harry Haigh that was kept in the room the two men shared. Haigh had asked Mary Ann to take a sovereign from the box to buy some items for him, and when she went to put them in the box, she noticed that everything in it was upset, and £8 was missing. She informed the police. Earlier that day, Tom had got up for work at 5.30am and returned at 8.15am for his breakfast. He then announced he was not going back to work, got changed, and said he was off to see Sanger's Circus in Sheffield. He appears to have gone to Goole and sent a letter to Haigh asking for his forgiveness for stealing the money; Haigh answered that he forgave him. A man named George Slater saw Tom drunk on Saturday night, and he helped him part of the way home. Slater said, "*I stopt to make water. I followed after him and when I was about 6 yards from him I heard him say distinctly* "I'll try the [b...] here*" and I saw a flash and heard the report of a pistol."* The next morning, Mary Ann heard some noises around 7am but took no notice. She was alerted to the fact her lodger was lying dead in the communal yard by her daughters an hour later. The wound was consistent with one a man could inflict on himself with a revolver pistol, and the verdict was that Tom had committed suicide during a fit of temporary insanity. Mary Ann and Harry moved away from Button Row to live at Horner House.

A TRAMPING MASON: January 1897

Harry Newton was faced with an unruly customer one day, and he had to summon the police. The man, Peter Naylor, was a "*tramping mason*" who had walked from Halifax to Penistone on a Friday, looking for work. He had carried on to Stocksbridge and entered the Rising Sun the next day. Harry told the Petty Sessions that the man had gone into his pub, but he had not bought a drink - rather, he drank what he could out of other people's mugs - which cannot have made him very popular! He was also wanting the men in the taproom to wrestle with him "*in the Cumberland Style.*"[242] His conduct was so bad that the police were sent for, and the policeman had "*a great job*" getting the man to the police station. Naylor was using very bad language, and when he got to the station, he was drunk, violent, and obscene. He continued to be so whilst en route to the railway station, and in the train taking him to Sheffield, behaving like a "*mad-man.*" He was locked up and

---

[242] CUMBERLAND STYLE WRESTLING: The starting backhold position involves the wrestlers standing chest to chest, grasping each other around the body with their chins on their opponent's right shoulder. The right arm of each contestant is positioned under his opponent's left arm. Once the grip is taken the umpire gives the signal to start the contest by calling "*en guard,*" then "*wrestle.*" The wrestlers attempt to unbalance their opponent, or make them lose their hold, using methods such as lifting throws known as "*hipes,*" twisting throws such as "*buttocks*" and trips like the inside click, cross click, back heel or outside stroke. This is known as a "*fall.*" If any part of a wrestler's body touches the ground aside from his feet, then he loses. If both fall down at once the last to hit the ground is deemed the winner. If it is unclear which wrestler hit the ground first the fall is disqualified and must be started again. this is known as a "*dog fall.*" A win can also be achieved if either party loses his grip on the other while his opponent still retains his hold. [Wikipedia July 2020: https://en.wikipedia.org/wiki/Cumberland_and_Westmorland_wrestling]

appeared at the Petty Sessions to answer the charge of being drunk and disorderly. The newspaper reported that he was *"an intelligent fellow,"* who pleaded hard in his own defence, but the evidence against him was overwhelming. Naylor argued that he was not a *"regular tramp,"* putting himself in a different class to those *"tramps and beggars who infested the village,"* about whom the *"respectable people of Stocksbridge"* had made frequent complaints. He was found guilty of the charge, and fined ten shillings plus costs (or, in default, he would go to prison for seven days); the fine was a lesser one than usual, to take into account that he had been in custody for a while.

A "SCHOOL" OF TOSSERS: 1898

On the 22nd March, there were eleven cases of *"tossing"* with coins brought before the Sheffield court. The cases were all tried at once, as the same information had been laid against all the defendants. The defendants were Harry Hawley, Benjamin Kay and Joseph Shaw, trammers;[243] Edward Kelly and Benjamin Crossland, colliers, of Bolsterstone; Samuel Redfern, trammer; Clement Senior and William Payne, labourers; Arthur Kay, collier, of Deepcar; and Thomas Burgin and Joseph Wragg, colliers, of Stocksbridge. The police stated in court that on the 12th March there had been a pigeon shooting match in a field adjoining the Rising Sun[244], and that about 5pm, after the match was over, the men left the field and went a short way along the road where they formed a tossing *"school."* Crossland, one of the defendants, kept watch for the police, but he did not see them until they were within about fifty yards from him. He gave the alarm, and the men hurried away. Sergeant Carter and P.C. Burrows came across Senior and Hawley, from whom they got the names of the rest of the men. Under cross-examination, the constables denied having asked for the names of the men at the pigeon shooting match or having threatened to knock Hawley against the wall if he refused to give the names of the people at the match. The men's solicitor said that they had not been tossing at all, but had been to the pigeon shooting match, and were coming away when the constables spoke to Senior and Hawley. After hearing all the evidence, Mr. Wilson Mappin, who was

---

[243] A trammer worked as an assistant to the miners, loading the broken coal onto conveyer belts, filling and hauling the corves or trams, bringing in equipment, etc.
[244] There were regular shoots on land known as the *"Rising Sun Grounds."*

hearing the cases, said that he was *"bound to believe the police,"* and he fined each defendant 7s. 6d., including costs.

"Tossing" was gambling with coins and is probably as old as coins themselves. During the reign of Elizabeth I, it was a punishable offence under the Vagrancy Act. Pitch and Toss was the most common form of coin gaming and was especially popular within mining communities. It started with a ring of players being formed called a *"school."* A quiet corner of a field was usually chosen to play in, because it was illegal, and there would be a man who was appointed as the lookout, watching for the police. Money was staked on every toss of the coins, but the rules varied according to whereabouts in the country it was played. It required just three coins to play, placed at the end of the fingers, and tossed. Because there was no equipment to set up and dismantle, it was cheap, quick, and could easily escape detection. It became a huge problem in Sheffield in the 1920s, with gangs controlling the play. Huge sums of money could be bet; a Barnsley publican called Jack White was known to regularly bet £50 on the single flip of a coin.[245]

The 1901 census records Harry Newton at the Rising Sun, together with his wife, four daughters, and two female servants.

AUCTION OF HOUSES AT HUNSHELF: 1901

In 1901, Mr. Joseph Hayward died at the age of 81, and his house was put up for auction at the Rising Sun, as were two adjoining houses. Hayward's own house was a *"substantial stone-built dwelling-house"* in Hunshelf Road, and it had three sitting rooms and four bedrooms. The two adjoining cottages were brick-built and in the occupations of Abraham Hawley and George Kay. These houses were bought by Joseph Newton. On the census returns, Hayward modestly gave his occupation as *"umbrella frame maker,"* but he was much more than that. He had been born in 1819 in Derwent Village, which is now submerged under Ladybower reservoir. He worked as a wire drawer at Hathersage, and one of his fellow apprentices was none other than Samuel Fox, founder of the steelworks in Stocksbridge. When Fox began his business in Stocksbridge in 1842, Hayward was one of his first

---

[245] For a good book about the Sheffield gangs, see Bean, J. P. *The Sheffield Gang Wars.* D&D publications: 1981

employees. Hayward had much to do with the design of the umbrella frames, and he also invented the machine for producing multiple wires, and another which would clean, straighten, and temper the ribs. His "*Paragon*" design was patented in 1852. A wonderful story is told of the men's friendship; when one of the workers found Hayward asleep on the job, he ran to tell Samuel Fox – who told him, "*Thee go and mind thy work; he is worth more to me asleep than thou art waken.*"

MR. WILL THORNE AT STOCKSBRIDGE: 1907

Will Thorne, a British trade unionist, addressed an open-air meeting of men belonging to the Gas Workers and General Labourers Union at the Rising Sun Inn in July 1907. He had helped to found the Union in 1889, becoming its general secretary, and had recently won a seat representing West Ham South in the 1906 General Election. The Sheffield Daily Telegraph reported that Thorne was "*heartily received*" by the crowd.

Councillor Padley protested against Sir James Crichton-Browne's statement that the working man had "*a good joint of meat on his table every Sunday, and that oatmeal should suffice for those who could not afford meat every day.*" Councillor Padley told the crowd that the surest means to have a joint every day was to join the Union.[246] The Union Officials said that they did not advocate strikes but preferred to settle all disputes by amicable talks with the employers. Answering a question, the Chairman said the average weekly wage of labourers in Sheffield works was about twenty shillings. There were, of course, some skilled labourers who were getting anything up to 30 shillings a week, but the wage of the ordinary labourer was from 18 to 20 shillings.

Harry's wife Sarah Jane died in 1906 aged 35, and he remarried in June 1908 to Elizabeth Brown. Sadly, the marriage lasted only one year, because Harry died on the 24th June 1909 aged only 39. He did not leave a will, his death being unexpected, and so his widow was granted Administration of his effects, which were just over £330.

---

[246] Sir James Crichton-Browne was a leading psychiatrist, neurologist, and medical psychologist, and was also known for his development of public health policies in relation to mental health.

Elizabeth then took over as the landlady. When the 1911 census was taken, she was living at the pub with three of Harry's daughters, the two eldest (Lydia Martha and Ethel Hannah) helping to run the business, whilst the youngest, Elsie, who was seven years old, was still at school. There were also two female servants. This census recorded that the Rising Sun had ten rooms. Harry's other daughter Emmie, aged 14, was away at a boarding school in York called Fulford Field House.

Joseph Newton's wife Lydia died in 1909, and Joseph died two years later on the 24th July 1911. He had first made a will in December 1909, in which he made provision for his mother Martha, then aged 88. He left her his freehold house called Hunshelf House, his furniture, and an annuity of £52 a year. Martha died in January 1910. Three days before he died, Joseph added a codicil. In the will, Joseph instructed his executors to sell all his real and personal estate, and to pay off any debts, funeral expenses, death duties, and so on, and to invest the remainder. He left money for his granddaughters Elsie and Emmie Newton (the youngest daughters of his late son Harry), and he bequeathed £1,000 each to his daughters Lois Annie Wardman (wife of George Wardman), Elizabeth Sellars (wife of George Sellars), Emily Moorhouse (wife of Ernest Moorhouse)[247] and Sarah Helson (wife of Frank Helson). Any remaining money was to remain in trust for Emmie. In the codicil, he added another granddaughter, Lydia Martha Cherry. Joseph left almost £9,000 gross, making him the equivalent of a millionaire today, according to the Bank of England's inflation calculator. Probate was granted to Gunby Howarth, butcher, and Samuel Broadhead, farmer

His executors instructed auctioneers to sell all the stock and animals at Miras [Miry] Bottom Farm[248], "*to close a trust.*" This was to take place on the 6th November 1911 and included six horses, six beasts, sixty-nine sheep, nine pigs, agricultural carriages and implements, forty fleeces of wool, and so on.

A year after Joseph Newton's death, there was an auction of his property at the Rising Sun. The pub itself was up for auction, and Lot 1 consisted of the

---

[247] Sam Ernest Moorhouse and Emily married in 1905 and ran the Royal Oak at Deepcar from 1913 until 1925.
[248] A Trade Directory of 1881 said Joseph Newton was a farmer at Miry Bottom, as well as having the Rising Sun, and the farm appears to have stayed in the family because Harry's widow was listed in Kelly's Directory of 1927 as having the Rising Sun and Miry Bottom.

pub, the adjoining cottage, a coach-house, stable, and out-offices [toilets], all of which were occupied by Harry Newton's widow Elizabeth. Joseph had also owned Hunshelf House, which was the detached house next to the pub (still standing), where he had been living.[249] There was also *"a dwelling-house and two cottages,"* which were being tenanted by Fred Rodgers, Mary Ann Laycock, and Ellis Whittaker.[250] Another house was also for sale, called *"West View"*, which was close to the other three houses, and in the occupation of a widow called Charlotte Goodram. The Rising Sun was sold to Tennant Brothers Brewery for £3,200. Hunshelf House went for £310, the dwelling-house and two cottages made £520, and West View was bought for £290.

A month after the sale of Joseph Newton's house, pub, and other properties, the trustees of his will instructed auctioneers to sell his household effects, and the sale took place at his former home, Hunshelf House. There was lots of mahogany furniture on offer, as well as carpets, crockery, cutlery, rugs, etc. Also for sale was a *"handsome Cheffonier"* in *walnut*[251], with a mirror and a marble top, a piano in walnut, a grandfather clock by Sykes of Huddersfield, a barometer, a *"massive walnut sideboard with plate-glass centre back and two side mirrors,"* a large copying press,[252] and four-poster beds with hangings.

After purchasing the pub, Tennant Brothers kept Harry's widow Elizabeth Newton on as the landlady. One of the first things they did was apply to make structural alterations to the pub; a report from the Brewster Sessions in February 1914 reported that these had been sanctioned.

---

[249] The 1911 records another house called Hunshelf House, near Croft Cottages / Brick Lump, in the occupation of James Bulloss Nichols, ex-landlord of the Castle Inn at Bolsterstone.

[250] These were not Prospect Cottages as I had first thought. Looking at the census enumerator's schedule and the map, these three properties seem to have been in the vicinity of Brownhill Row, at Croft, near Pea Royd Hill; they adjoined the road from *"Underbank to Stocksbridge and Penistone"* [Hunshelf Road]. These had been sold at auction in 1901 when their owner Joseph Hayward died. West View was *"near or opposite"* the three houses, and also adjoined the same road. The previous year's census of 1911 recorded Fred Rodgers at *"Johnson Cottages"* on Hunshelf Bank. Prospect Cottages were occupied by Alfred Job Wright and Fred William Thompson. One was empty.

[251] A chiffonier or Chiffonier is similar to a sideboard, differing in that the whole of the front is enclosed by doors.

[252] A metal device for copying letters

War broke out on the 28th July that year.

STOCKSBRIDGE D.C.M. ENTERTAINED: 1915

Frank Thickett, one of our *"local heroes,"* was in the 1st/4th Battalion of the York and Lancaster Regiment (the Hallamshire Rifles) and was the son of Charles Thickett. He had been nominated for the Distinguished Conduct Medal for his conspicuous bravery whilst serving in Flanders in July and August 1915. He was expected to come home in order to be presented with his medal but was delayed when he was wounded in his back and shoulders, necessitating some time in hospital. He finally made it home and set off to Sheffield to receive his medal from the Lady Mayoress at an awards ceremony on the 30th October.

The ceremony had to be delayed because a serious accident had happened on the Bitholmes whilst Frank was on his way to town to collect his medal. It was a very foggy day, and the bus he was travelling in was in collision with a lorry and a motorcycle & sidecar. He was sitting at the front on the top deck when the accident occurred, and he jumped down into the road to assist the injured. The Indian motorbike was being ridden by a young man called Harry Sanderson of Wharncliffe Side, a well-known local man who was a footballer and a member of the Stocksbridge church team. He was returning from Sheffield where he had taken some birds to a show and had a 7-year-old boy named Thomas Wordsworth in the sidecar. Sanderson had overtaken the motor car, and run straight into the bus, and was then hit from behind by the car he had just passed. He was killed instantly. The boy was trapped under a wheel, and Thickett helped get him out, but his injuries were so severe he later died in the Infirmary.

The newspapers reported that 10,000 people gathered in Sheffield town centre for the event. About a hundred men from the Hallamshire Rifles, who were stationed at Endcliffe Hall, marched into town, headed by their band. As Thickett mounted the platform to receive his medal there were huge cheers from the crowd, and the band played *"Have you got another little girl at home like Mary?"* He was joined on the platform by his parents and friends, Colonel Branson (ex-commander of the Hallamshires), Major Wortley and Captain Hay, and a group of wounded soldiers from the Sheffield Base hospital.

The D.C.M. was conferred upon him for conspicuous gallantry on the Yser Canal on 13th - 14th July. During a heavy artillery bombardment, when all telephone communication was cut, he carried an urgent message from the firing line to headquarters. In order to do so, he had to wade across the canal. On the night of 8th - 9th August he performed a similar feat, crossing the canal by a single plank. An officer in the crowd said that if not for Thickett's heroic deed, he might not be alive now, and there were men in the Base Hospital from Thickett's regiment who also praised his heroism which, as they put it, saved them from being wiped out.

A few days later, Frank was honoured at an event in the Rising Sun where he was entertained by his fellow workers from Fox's. The works manager Dr. Percy Longmuir presided, and presented him with a gold watch, suitably inscribed, which had been paid for by his workmates. I am told that he survived the War.

The Penistone, Stocksbridge and Hoyland Express published a letter which Thickett had written to a friend:

"It was on the 13th July that the enemy bombarded our trenches for half-an-hour before our guns replied, and the message came down that they were attacking. Our shells were falling short, and the shrapnel flying in our trenches. All communications were cut off, and the nearest signal station was about 800 yards off, just behind the firing line but in the same direction. Our officers wondered what to do to stop it, and asked if anyone would go. I volunteered, and one of the officers went with me. We had to cross the canal and the bridge had half of it blown away. I went as far as possible, then jumped in, being up to my waist in mud. I struggled out and assisted the officer, and we landed under terrible shell-fire without being injured. All our men congratulated me when things had settled down. It was my duty, so in any case, better luck next time. I shall never forget looking over the parapet, with the guns in action; it was like a picture to see one continuous line of fire. You will have heard about some of the Stocksbridge boys being wounded, also F. Eastwood,[253] we were all very sorry, but he died a hero; and if the

---

[253] Private Frank Eastwood. Like Frank Thickett, he was also in the 1st/4th Battalion of the York and Lancaster Regiment. He was killed in action on the 13th July 1915 (the day

young men in England saw how the poor fellows suffer they should be glad to do their little bit."

After the war, Elizabeth Newton married again to John William Bisby. They married at Bradfield Church on the 14th May 1919 and held an "*at home*" at the Rising Sun the following week. Bisby was previously the licensee of the Blue Ball at Wharncliffe Side. A temporary transfer from Elizabeth was granted in June, with it being finalised on the 1st July. Bisby had only been landlord of the Blue Ball for about a year, having previously had the Cock Inn at Oughtibridge. He too had been widowed; his first wife was Mary Agnes Helliwell, and she had died in 1918 aged 46.

MINERS' FRACAS: September 1919

Five men had been playing cards for money in the Rising Sun, and a fight broke out afterwards outside the pub. The men were all miners, and their names were Frank Revitt[254], George Cheetham, Isaac Cheetham, Joseph Ashton, and Harry Marsden. They were summoned to court accused of assaulting Herbert Smith, of Chapel Road (probably Chapel Row) Stocksbridge. Smith and Marsden had been arguing over the winnings in a card game, and once outside the pub, Smith was knocked to the ground, and all the men had "*set about him*," one of them kicking him in the head. The defence argued that Revitt was the only one who had hit Smith, and only after Smith had struck him first. All the men were fined ten shillings each; on top of this, they were all fined another ten shillings for using obscene language whilst walking home along Hawke Green.

This case had repercussions for the landlord of the Rising Sun, who was in trouble for allowing gambling on his licensed premises. In October that year John William Bisby appeared in court to answer this charge. Herbert Smith, the man who was assaulted, appeared as a witness for the prosecution, along with one of his attackers, Harry Marsden, and two other men, James Oates and a man named Thorpe. They admitted playing a card game called "*Don*" for money but said that it was impossible for anyone else in the public house to know that they were gambling. Bisby's defence was that he was not even

---

Thickett writes about in his letter). Eastwood was the son of George and Frances Eastwood of "*Woodville*," Rundle Road, Stocksbridge. He was 19 years old and was buried at Talana Farm Cemetery, West-Vlaanderen, Belgium.

[254] Also spelt Revill in the same newspaper report.

in the pub that night, because he was away in Scotland with his wife. The Bench decided not to convict him.

Bisby had been before the courts before. In 1906 he was fined for selling watered whisky at the Wharncliffe Arms, and in 1916 he was fined for selling liquor during prohibited hours at the Cock Inn, Oughtibridge.

AUCTION: 1924
A sale of horses, cattle, harness, carts, etc., removed to the Rising Sun for convenience, as instructed by Mr. F. Bowers.

AUCTION: 1927
A *"Capital Small Farm with Milk Round, Avice Royd Farm, Stocksbridge, with Vacant Possession."* Avice Royd Farm, Stocksbridge, covered just over 31 acres, of which 26 acres were grass, the remainder being arable. The house was stone-built with a stone slate roof, and had six rooms, a dairy, and an outside washhouse. The farm buildings included a barn to house up to fourteen cows, a stirk[255] place for five, two loose boxes, a stable for two horses, a large barn, turnip house, granary, cart shed, two pigsties, and a large timber-built cart shed. Also for sale as a separate lot was over four acres of land at Hunshelf Hall Lane.

In 1932 John Bisby transferred the licence to George Hobson and moved to Oughtibridge, where he and his wife took over the White Hart from John W. Fisher. Elizabeth's son Thomas Walton Bower had lived and worked at the Rising Sun as a barman, and he moved to the White Hart with the Bisbys, along with his wife Mary Jane (nee Sams), where he continued to work in the pub. Elizabeth Bisby died in 1940, Thomas Walton Bisby died in 1945 aged 47, and John William died in 1856 aged 78.

George Hobson was married to Lucy Robinson and had previously worked as a coal carter, and they ran the pub until at least the 1940s. One of their sons, also called George, was killed in an accident in November 1934. He had been riding his bicycle along Haywood Lane in Deepcar when he collided with a lorry which was coming in the opposite direction. James Marratt of the Steel houses, Deepcar, had been standing on the back of the

---

[255] A young bull or cow.

lorry when he saw Hobson, who had just come down Quarry Hill, on the wrong side of the road going very fast, the front wheel of his bike wobbling. Errors of judgement meant that he hit the lorry, with fatal consequences. He was 26 years old and had been living at the Rising Sun with his parents and his wife, Edith Annie.

When the 1939 Register was taken on the eve of World War II, George and Lucy were at the Rising Sun along with their son Cyril Hobson, a lorry driver and a relative of Lucy's, Gladys Sturr. George's occupation was not given as publican but as a worker in the Siemen's department in the steelworks. No doubt he did both.

The Rising Sun closed its doors in 1967. It was bought by the British Steel Corporation and demolished in 1968 after being open a hundred years. Prefab offices were put on the site, which are no longer there; the site has been derelict for years and new eco-houses are planned. Hunshelf House still stands, and at the time the Rising Sun was demolished was being used by the Marketing Department of the steel works. It reverted back to a private dwelling in the 1980s. The last landlords of the Rising Sun before it closed were Allen and Carole Hill.

And finally ... The name The Rising Sun was often given to pubs which faced east, towards where the sun rose every morning. The Rising Sun pub on Hunshelf Bank faces the setting sun. This apparent contradiction can be explained in that William Newton's original pub at Berton-under-Edge did indeed face the rising sun. The name and the licence would have been transferred down the hill to the new location. Other pubs with this name took their name from heraldry; the sun's rays featured on one of the badges of Edward III, for example.

THE FRIENDSHIP HOTEL, MANCHESTER ROAD, STOCKSBRIDGE

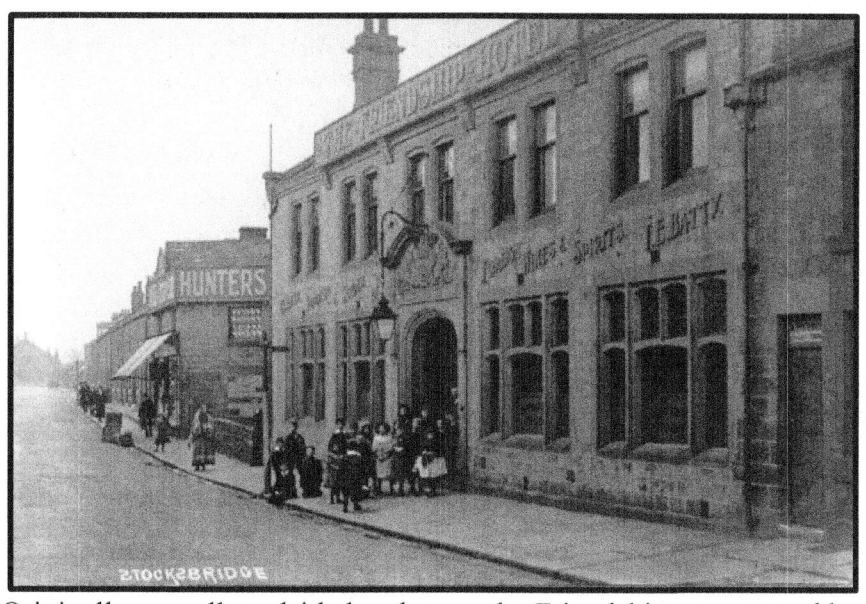

Originally a small roadside beerhouse, the Friendship was opened by George Batty in the 1850s, becoming fully licensed in 1860. The building was much enlarged over the years, and in 1903 it was re-built, and a new ornate facia added. Two of George's sons went on to run the pub, Elijah and Thomas Edward (Tom). Tom Batty ran the pub twice, the second time for almost fifty years; he was much respected, and he played a huge part in local life. He enlarged the premises, turning The Friendship into a successful hotel and a home for many clubs and organisations. It is still open today. This photo dates to about 1903.

George Batty owned a row of houses which were situated on the main road through Stocksbridge, and in the 1850s he turned part of his home into a small beerhouse. The Friendship's humble origins would have been a barrel of beer on a counter in George's front room, with additional barrels being kept in the cellar or an outhouse. Unfortunately, there are no known photographs of the pub before it was altered in 1903. After a few years, George applied for a wines and spirits licence. His application was initially refused, but he applied again, and a full licence was granted at the September Brewster Sessions in 1860. The following year he was in trouble for the offence of permitting drunkenness and his name was entered on the magistrates' blacklist. He did not appear before the Bench, and his licence was suspended for a month, during which time he would not have been allowed to open and would have had to remove his pub sign. George remained the landlord until his death in 1865 at the age of forty.

George had been born in 1825 and was the son of Thomas Batty, a shoemaker, and his wife Amelia, who lived at Thurlstone. He had been apprenticed as a wheelwright to Charles Ramsden of Horner House, and like many landlords at the time, he carried on working at his trade alongside running the pub. His wife Hannah was the daughter of a publican, Edward Askew of the Coach and Horses, a little further along Manchester Road. Edward had worked as a blacksmith at the smithy next to the Coach and Horses before becoming its landlord. Hannah's younger sister Ann ran the Sportsman's Arms at Old Haywoods with her husband William Helliwell from about 1864.

George and Hannah Batty had seven children including Thomas Edward, who later became the Friendship's long-serving landlord. After Hannah died in 1856, George married again to Harriet Bradbury, and they had a son Elijah in 1858. Elijah was bequeathed the Friendship in his father's will, although he was too young to run it at the time.[256]

CLEVER CAPTURE OF COINERS: 1859
In May 1859 George was a witness in the trial of three men who were accused of *"uttering"* counterfeit coins (passing counterfeit money whilst knowing it

---

[256] George left his property to his widow, until his youngest child reached the age of 21 years. Elijah was to have the Friendship after his mother's death.

to be so). Albert Smith of Manchester, Joseph Byram of Marsden near Huddersfield, and John Wood of Sheffield appeared in court, and were described by the newspaper as being "*somewhat respectably dressed.*" They were charged with possessing counterfeit coins, and with several specific instances of trying to spend these coins, knowing them to be fake. The men had visited many public houses, using the coins to buy drinks as a way to obtain genuine money in their change. One of these cases involved George Batty of the Friendship beerhouse and his daughter, described in the newspaper report as "*a little girl.*"[257] Albert Smith had gone into the Friendship one Monday afternoon and handed over a five-shilling piece (a crown, worth a quarter of a pound) in payment for a glass of beer. He had been served by Batty's daughter, and when she gave her father the coin, he soon realised it was fake. He took it to his workbench and cut a piece out of it, finding it to be soft. He returned the coin to Smith, who said he had no idea it was fake, adding that he wished he had a thousand like it. He took it back without hesitation, and obtaining change for a good sovereign from Batty, paid for his beer out of the change. He threw the coin onto the fire, where it melted like lead.

The three men spent the day visiting various public houses, including Mrs. Green's Wagon and Horses at Langsett and Mrs. Downing's Wharncliffe Arms. A filesmith called Henry Robinson was present in the Wharncliffe Arms when Byram was trying to spend his counterfeit coin. He suspected him to be a swindler, and followed him when he left the pub. He saw Byram meet up with his two partners in crime, and he followed them to Oughtibridge, where the three men separated. John Wood went into Mrs. Turner's White Hart and paid for a glass of gin and a cigar with a counterfeit crown piece. He took a seat in the bar, but unfortunately for him, two policemen were present. Wood was arrested, and Henry Robinson went after the others, meeting a policeman called French along the way. The two men saw that they were being followed and threw something into the woods at the Forge Bank plantation. They were arrested, but it was too dark to see what they had thrown away. The next day a bag was found which contained forty-seven counterfeit half-crowns, and four counterfeit crowns, all wrapped carefully in separate pieces of paper and tied together. Nearby was another parcel containing eighteen florins (a florin was worth two shillings). The

---

[257] It could have been Ann (age 13), Amelia (11), Elizabeth (10) or Emma (8)

three prisoners were remanded in custody until communication had been made with the Royal Mint.

Two weeks later, the men were back in court. Byram and Wood admitted trying to spend the money, their defence being that they did not know the coins were bad. Batty's daughter was one of those who gave evidence. A Sheffield silversmith called Thomas Robinson examined the coins, declaring them all to be fakes. The jury did not believe the men's stories about how they had come into possession of the coins and found them all guilty. They were sentenced to two years' imprisonment in the House of Correction. Smith was 30 years old and a warehouseman, Byram was 37 and a cloth-dresser, and Wood, 23, was a blacksmith.

EMBEZZLEMENT: 1861
A man named Eli Andrews was charged with embezzlement by John Vernon, a cordial manufacturer of Oborne Street, Bridgehouses, in Sheffield. Andrews had been employed by Vernon for seven or eight years, and for the last two years had taken orders and collected money. However, after his boss had spoken to him about some irregularities in his money transactions, he absconded. It was discovered that he had received several sums of money which he had not accounted for. Amongst these were ten shillings which he had collected from George Batty at the Friendship. Eli was arrested, and at his trial, he was found guilty and was sentenced to four months in prison.

When the 1861 census was taken George Batty was recorded at the Friendship Inn as a *"wheelwright and victualler,"* living with his wife Harriet, his children by his first wife Hannah, and his son with Harriet, young Elijah.

AUCTIONS
The Friendship regularly held auctions on its premises. Some of the early auctions which took place there included:
- 1861: freehold property at Horner House. This included two stone-built cottages fronting the main road, occupied by tenants James Rusby, William Helliwell and Ann Grayson; six stone-built cottages, three fronting the main road, with gardens front and back, occupied by Benjamin Brearley, William Whittaker, Joseph Moorhouse, Thomas Shaw, William Webster and Edward Wragg; two stone-built

cottages and a shop, fronting the main road, with gardens front and back, occupied by Joseph Hoyle and Thomas Firth. All these were recently built, and there was land available for further building, houses being in great demand because of the continued growth of the steelworks.
- 1873: four freehold, recently erected houses and shops, with the outbuildings, yards, etc., occupied by Thomas Woodhead, John Ives, George Walker Vernon Ibbotson, and one other.
- 1881: eight stone-built houses and outbuildings at Stocksbridge fronting the main road, in the occupations of Thomas Holland, Aaron Sanderson, William Liles, Joseph Barrett, W. Broadbent, and others. This was Farmer's Terrace, just a few yards along the road from the Friendship.

A PLACE FOR MEETINGS

Pubs were much used as meeting places, and the Friendship played host to a great many clubs and organisations over the years. The pub boasted a large "*club room*" where such meetings could be held.

One of the groups that met in the pub was the Ancient Order of Druids, a fraternal benevolent society. The Lodge which met at the Friendship was known as the Lily of the Valley Lodge no. 594. In June 1862 they held their annual feast when, after a parade through the village and a service in the Independent chapel led by the Rev. Robertshaw, they retired to the Friendship for dinner. A meeting in December that year was called to see what could be done for assisting the "*distressed operatives in Lancashire,*" and it was unanimously resolved that they would send £3 to their "*distressed Druid brethren*" in that county.[258] The Lodge continued to hold anniversary meetings at the pub throughout the 1870s. In 1871, about seventy members held a parade before dinner.

The Stocksbridge Brass Band also met at the pub. At their annual meeting in 1876, around 35 people sat down to supper, business being attended to

---

[258] There was a depression in the textile industry which became known as The Lancashire Cotton Famine, or the Cotton Panic (1861–65). There was prolonged unemployment, reduced earnings, and poorer work conditions. The mill operatives faced a long period of poverty and uncertainty.

after the cloth had been removed. Mr. Wright (one of the trustees) was elected to the chair, and the secretary Mr. John Eastwood read the accounts. The band was reported to be in a *"very fair state of proficiency,"* having lately secured the services of Mr. John Berry, of the well-known Meltham Mills band, as their teacher. The usual loyal toasts were made, and the band played several *"difficult pieces."*

The Stocksbridge Horticultural Society also met there.

CO-OPERATIVE SOCIETY COMES TO STOCKSBRIDGE: 1860
The founders of The Stocksbridge Band of Hope Industrial Co-operative Society Limited held their early meetings in the Friendship, George Batty being one of their number. The origins of the Society were written about by Joseph Kenworthy in a book commemorating the Society's jubilee in 1910.[259] A few men who had heard of the success of a new movement in Rochdale met in the steelworks and in their homes to discuss starting their own movement. They decided to form themselves into a Society, and they held their first meetings at George Batty's *"little wayside inn"* to discuss the matter. His enthusiasm to the cause *"excited the admiration and gratitude of his comrades."* The symbol of the Society was clasped hands, and this symbol, carved in stone, can still be seen today over the door of the pub. Early in 1860, a public meeting was convened in the Friendship's club room, at which between twenty and thirty men were present, with George Batty being one of those appointed to inaugurate the movement. Their aim was to raise money, using members' voluntary subscriptions, to purchase stock to re-sell. They used the club room as a salesroom as well as an office in these early days. The Society called themselves the Band of Hope, but they had no connection with the Temperance Movement which went by the same name.

George Batty had just built two houses at the top of Gibson Lane (previously called Water Lane), and he gave the Society a good start by letting them have these rent-free for three months. One was used as a provision shop and the other as a dwelling house for the grocery manager. They also had a butchery

---

[259] Kenworthy, Joseph. Stocksbridge Band of Hope Jubilee History 1860-1910. Co-operative Printing Society Ltd, Manchester: 1910

department further down Gibson Lane in a little shed on George's land, which served both as a slaughterhouse and a shop.

A piece of freehold land was bought in the spring of 1861 and plans for new premises were drawn up by Joseph Hayward later that year. The land was bought for just over £70 from John Ridal of Wadsley by Samuel Fox (owner of the steelworks), John Bower of Watson House, a farmer, and William Newton of Hunshelf, the landlord of the pub at Berton-under-Edge, *"trustees for the time being of the Society."*[260] This new building became known as the New Stores (later the Central Stores) and was completed in 1863. It was not far from the Friendship, on the opposite side of the road.

FATAL ACCIDENT AT STOCKSBRIDGE: 1862

A family called Howe had recently moved to Stocksbridge from Bradwell, Derbyshire. The head of the family, Elijah, worked as a labourer, and he and his wife Martha lived with their seven children at Hunshelf Bottom. The two youngest children were Henry and Walter. One Sunday afternoon, Henry was killed when some flagstones fell on him whilst he was playing a few yards from his home, where a new building was being erected. His younger brother ran into the house to fetch their mother, who hurried out with their lodger, Harvey Elliott. Elliott pulled the flags off the boy, and Martha carried her son inside; he gave a few sobs and then expired. He was only eight years old. The inquest was held at the Friendship, and the jury returned a verdict of accidental death.

THE DEATH OF GEORGE BATTY: 1865

George Batty died on the 25th March 1865 at the relatively young age of forty. His will, made just a month before he died, was proved by his widow Harriet and his brother-in-law George Littlewood of Penistone, a grocer and provision dealer. The effects were under £300. He left all his property to his wife Harriet, which she was to have the benefit of until their youngest child reached twenty-one years of age; this included the rental income from various properties that he owned. After his wife's death, the Friendship was to go to his youngest son Elijah Batty. He was only about eight years old

---

[260] The land and the buildings in the course of erection upon it were mortgaged for £400 on 26th July 1862, and the mortgage was not redeemed until 1873, when Samuel Fox was the sole surviving trustee. William Newton had died in 1864 aged 42, and John Bower in 1866 aged 26. John Bower was landlord of the Castle Inn when he died.

when his father died, and Harriet took over the licence, running the pub for almost nine years until she passed away on 28th January 1877. George requested that his two sons, Thomas Edward and Elijah, should be put into *"respectable trades."* Thomas was apprenticed to a joiner (which was also George's trade) and Elijah went away to a boarding school at Brampton Bierlow.

Eldest daughter Ann was bequeathed nineteen guineas. The next three daughters were each left a house. The house adjoining the Friendship (then being rented to John Booth) was left to second daughter Amelia. The next house (rented to Ralph Crossley) was left to his third daughter Elizabeth, and the next adjoining house (rented to Thomas Brown) went to his fourth daughter Emma Eliza. If any of them wished to sell their house, their brother Elijah was to have the first refusal. George's eldest son, Thomas Edward, was left two houses at Thurlstone, which were at a place known as Batty Lane Top, along with a barn, mistal (cow shed), stable, pigsty, and a garden. Youngest daughter Edna was bequeathed £80.

CELEBRATION OF THE LIBERAL VICTORY: 1868
The Liberals of Stocksbridge and district held a public meeting at the Friendship in December 1868 to celebrate the return of Lord Milton and Mr. Beaumont. About 200 people sat down to *"an excellent knife-and-fork tea"* provided by Mrs. Batty. The usual loyal toasts were given, including to *"The County Members,"* *"Mr. Gladstone and the Liberal Party,"* *"The Hostess,"* and *"The Ladies."* The Stocksbridge brass band was in attendance and played at intervals.

FATAL ACCIDENT IN A BRICKFIELD: January 1871
William Brooke, a 20-year-old man, was killed while at work in a claypit at Stocksbridge. He was in the pit when some clay fell onto him, inflicting injuries from which he died soon afterwards. The inquest was held at the Friendship, where a verdict of *"Accidentally killed by a fall of clay"* was returned.

The 1871 census was taken on the 2nd April, and the residents of the Friendship that night were Harriet (innkeeper), her husband's daughter Edna, and three lodgers (Herbert and Emma Hollins and their son Solomon).

1871: Wanted, a General Servant, of good character, for a public-house in the country; age from 20 to 25 - Apply at the Friendship Inn, Stocksbridge.

Harriet died at the Friendship on the 28th January 1874 aged 51. Elijah had inherited the pub by his father's will, but he was still too young to run it, being about sixteen years of age, and so Harriet's stepson Thomas Edward Batty took over the reins. He was only three years old when his mother died, and Harriet had helped George to bring up his children and run the pub. Having grown up in the pub, it was perhaps only natural that Thomas Edward would take over following the death of his stepmother. Tom had previously moved away to be apprenticed to a joiner, and when the 1871 census was taken, he was living at Spring Vale in Penistone with his father's sister Annis Batty and her husband George Littlewood. He turned twenty-one in 1874. Tom held the licence for the Friendship twice; once after Harriet's death for a few years, and then again in 1888; the second time he was the licensee until he retired in 1935.

Thomas organised pigeon shooting ledgers and knur and spell matches. In April 1876, about 500 spectators turned up to watch Charles Walton of Deepcar play John Whittaker of Stocksbridge in a game of knur and spell.

On the 3rd November 1874 Tom married Annie Hawley at Ecclesfield church; he was 21-years old and a publican. Annie was 19. A daughter, Annie Gertrude, was born the following year and baptised at Penistone church on the 19th November 1875.

Sadly, Tom's young wife Annie died in August 1876 aged just 21 years. He went on to marry Annie's sister Lucy Hawley at St. Pancras church, London in December 1878. Tom was 25 years old, a widower, and he gave his address as St. Pancras, his occupation as carpenter, and his father's name as George, a carpenter. Lucy was 21, a spinster, living at St. Pancras, the daughter of Joseph Hawley, a builder. Why they married in London is not known, unless Lucy was in service down there.

Tom and Lucy then returned north and took the Bridge Hotel in Penistone – a newspaper report puts them there in April 1879. When the census was taken in April 1881, Tom was recorded as the landlord. Then in 1885 he answered an advert placed by Tennant Brothers Brewery, Sheffield, who were looking for someone to run the Rising Sun Inn at Hunshelf Bank, Stocksbridge. He spent three years there, before returning once more to the Friendship, taking over the licence from his half-brother Elijah Batty.

In 1878 Tom's maternal uncle, Elijah Askew, advertised for a tenant for his own pub, the nearby Coach and Horses, so that he could run the Friendship when Tom left. Elijah Askew had been born in 1837 and had married Mary Coldwell in 1858, the daughter of Benjamin Couldwell junior of the Royal Oak at Deepcar. After Mary died in 1866, Elijah had married again to Ann Bower, the widow of John Bower of the Castle Inn, and the daughter of Samuel Knutton and Mary Bramall (previous landlords of the Castle).

Elijah and Ann were at the Friendship in April 1881 when the census was taken, along with their children. Harry Bower, Ann's son, was also recorded there (he was working as a waiter) and there was also a domestic servant called Lily Wade.

In November 1880 Elijah Askew chaired a meeting of the creditors of a surgeon called Beaumont Rowley Connolly. Elijah's occupation was recorded as a grocer. Whilst he was still at the Coach and Horses, Elijah had been in partnership with a butcher called John Ramsden, but this partnership was dissolved when Ramsden died in 1876, making Elijah the sole owner of the business, which he carried on for some years. Connolly had debts of over £500, of which he could pay around £130, and the creditors (one of whom was another grocer, James Lunn) agreed that the doctor's assets could be liquidated, and the debtor discharged.

The doctor was a well-travelled man. Born in Woolwich in 1843, he was the son of an army man who ended his career as Captain of the Royal Engineers. Connolly had a commission in the 72nd Highlanders. He did his medical training in Yorkshire and married a Huddersfield girl, Emily Mary Thomas, in 1877. They moved to Stocksbridge and he was in partnership with another doctor, James Edgar Davison. This partnership was dissolved in March 1880. Connolly's wife died in childbirth in April, and after discharging his debts he moved back down south, marrying again in 1881. He went back and forwards to Madeira several times in the ensuing years with the British & African Steam Navigation company, and he died at Funchal, on the south side of the island, in 1912 aged 69.

Ann Askew died in 1882 and Elijah married for a third time to Lydia Grayson (nee Bramall), who was the widow of John Grayson of Spink Hall. Lydia and John had only been married for seven months when John was killed in a carriage accident, leaving his widow a wealthy woman. She married Elijah Askew in 1884 and he went to live with her at Spink Hall. By the time the 1891 census was taken, Elijah's occupation was given as *"living on his own means."* He died at Spink Hall in 1892. He left property from which rental incomes were derived, although there were mortgages and insurance payments to meet. He left an allowance for his son Tom, who had been adopted by the Staniforths of Bolsterstone and who had been *"feeble-minded from birth"* according to the 1901 census, and bequests to his surviving children. His wife Lydia was wealthy in her own right, and he wrote in his will, *"I acknowledge that such of the furniture and effects at Spink Hall aforesaid as belonged to my wife before her marriage and also the live and dead farming stock and effects are the separate property of my said wife and no provision is made for her by this my Will at her wish owing to the fact that she is already sufficiently provided for."*

Elijah Batty then returned to the Friendship. He was Thomas Edward's half-brother and had been born in 1858 to George Batty and his second wife Harriet Bradbury. The 1871 census records him as a scholar at a boarding school at Brampton Bierlow, which is between Elsecar and Wath. In 1881 he was living at Johnson Street, Stocksbridge, and his occupation was recorded as a gardener. He would probably have taken over the Friendship when Elijah Askew married Lydia Grayson in 1882 and went to live at Spink Hall.[261]

Elijah Batty had married Elijah Askew's daughter Harriet Elizabeth in July 1877 (she was the daughter of Elijah and his first wife Mary Couldwell).[262] They had four children: George Askew Batty (1878), Harriet Ann (1880),

---

[261] In various records, Elijah's Batty's occupation is given as publican, labourer, and gardener. He gave his occupation as publican during the time that Elijah Askew had the Friendship. As I can find no record of him having a license anywhere else, I think he must have worked in the pub on and off until he was granted the license himself.

[262] Mary Couldwell's family had the Royal Oak at Deepcar. Harriet was baptised at Bolsterstone 29th June 1860, daughter of Elijah and Mary Askew of the Coach and Horses Inn. Elijah's occupation was blacksmith and innkeeper.

Marian (1883), and Elizabeth (1885-1886). Elijah's wife died in 1888 aged 27.

Elijah Batty had been in trouble with the law a couple of times, but this did not stop him from being granted a licence. In May 1877 he had been fined twenty shillings for having been drunk at Deepcar railway station, *"contrary to the by-laws of the company."* The following year he, along with a group of men, were summoned for *"game trespass."* The other men were Edward Ryan, Walter Wood, John Buckley, and William Rodgers, and they were accused by Mr. Rimington Wilson of Broomhead Hall of trespassing on land over which he had the shooting rights. The land in question was occupied by a farmer called Mr. Bird. P.C. Bell was on the road between Lee House and Allen Croft, and gave evidence in court that he saw one of the men, Edward Ryan, in Mr. Bird's field, and that he had two dogs with him, a snap dog [whippet] and a white terrier. The other four men were also there, on the other side of the wall, in a field belonging to Mr. Stewart, a farmer who lived at Allen Croft, Bolsterstone.[263] The men were said to have been urging the dogs on to work, and Elijah Batty was pointing a gun. P.C. Bell crouched down behind a wall, observing the men, but a passer-by called out to the men that there was *"a bobby"* under the wall, and all five men ran away. The men were said to have been well-known to the police, and P.C. Bell recognised them all. Mr. Stewart was called to give evidence for the defence and told the court that he had given the men permission to shoot crows in his field. A rabbit ran into the wall whilst they were there, and in order to get at it they went into Mr. Bird's field. That was, apparently, the reason they were on Mr. Rimington Wilson's land. The Bench thought the case was too weak to stand and discharged the defendants.

Elijah was only at the Friendship for about six years, and there are not many references to him in the newspapers. In September 1887, his solicitor opposed an application by William Broadhead, a butcher and grocer of Horner House, for an *"off"* beerhouse licence. Samuel Fox and Co. also opposed the application, as did a Mr. Hawley, who also held an *"off"* licence.

---

[263] From 1892 Allen Croft became an isolation hospital, or the *"Fever Hospital"* as it was known. In 1891 it was a small cottage with 3 rooms in the occupation of John Barton, a boiler stoker. The cottage stood in ¾ acre of land and a hospital was erected on the land. Initially there were 7 beds and there was separate accommodation for smallpox patients. Many who were admitted were children, with scarlet fever.

Broadhead's solicitor produced a memorial in support of the application, which had been signed by 107 residents. His shop was said to be no more than 150 yards away from the Friendship and Mr. Hawley's (which meant it was not *"necessary"*), and of the 150 houses close to Broadhead's, 60 were owned by Samuel Fox and Co., who were opposing the licence. The application was refused.

A THEFT OUTSIDE THE FRIENDSHIP: February 1888
Stocksbridge man Edmund Taylor Race, a steelworker, appeared at the West Riding Court at Sheffield Town Hall charged with stealing four rabbits and several haddocks belonging to Henry Hooson, a hawker, of Langsett Road. Henry had a beerhouse and grocery shop, and one Saturday he had been hawking his wares around Stocksbridge. He called in at the Friendship, leaving his cart in charge of a boy for about half an hour. When he got home, he discovered that four rabbits and some haddocks had been taken from his cart. The boy who had been minding it, Fred Ashton, said that Edmund had come out of the Friendship and asked him to fetch him a penny smoke, and he would look after the cart whilst he was gone. The boy told the court that when he came back from his errand, he saw Edmund putting fish into his pocket. The man then sent the boy to fetch him some tripe, and when he returned from this second errand, he noticed that the rabbit hamper had been tampered with. A labourer called John Bower was called to give evidence and said that Edmund had given him a rabbit and some fish that Saturday night. Walter Woods, forge-man, said that Edmund had left some rabbits at his house the same night, saying he would call for them on Sunday. Sergeant Berry arrested Edmund on Sunday. In court, he confessed to being drunk at the time and received a fine of fifty shillings, including costs.

A LANDLORD FINED FOR DRUNKENNESS: July 1888
Elijah Batty was summoned to court for being incapably drunk on his own licensed premises in July 1888. At around 8pm one Saturday night, P.C.s Morley and Gunson had found him drunk, and later that night, at 10pm, Sergeant Berry found him rolling about in the passage leading from the bar. There were six stools in the passage, and Batty fell over them. Batty denied that he was drunk. His solicitor said his client was *"only excited,"* having been served with a writ earlier in the day. Batty was fined over £1, and this offence counted as a black mark against him; at the Licensing Sessions in September, his licence was not renewed. The case was adjourned until later

in the month, and it was noted that Superintendent Midgley had given notice that he would oppose the renewal. At the end of September, the case came up at the adjourned sessions, and an application was made by Elijah's older half-brother Thomas Edward Batty for the Friendship licence to be transferred to himself. Superintendent Midgely did not oppose this transfer to Tom, who was at the time the licensee of the Rising Sun at Hunshelf Bank, and against whom there were no black marks. He did, however, warn Tom that he thought he was too fond of betting, and he hoped he would not continue the practice at the Friendship. The transfer of the licence was granted. Perhaps this was his reason for leaving the Rising Sun and returning to the Friendship – to keep it in the family.

MAN SHOT AT A RABBIT COURSING LEDGER

The writ referred to could have been concerning the shooting of a man at a rabbit coursing ledger the previous year, in 1887. William Gill sued Elijah Batty for £50 for having shot him in the foot, and the case came up at Sheffield County Court in May 1889.

William Gill lived at Old Haywoods and worked as a furnaceman. He told the court that on the 26th November 1887 he attended a rabbit coursing match at Stocksbridge, which was being promoted by Elijah Batty. Batty was the starter, and his job was to fire the gun to start the dogs. Instead of firing the gun into the air, he fired it on the ground, shooting Gill in the foot. As soon as Batty saw what he had done, he ordered Gill to be taken to a doctor, who found that his toes were injured, necessitating the removal of a piece of bone from one of them. A few days later, Batty visited Gill and promised to make him *"all right."* Gill was not able to walk for nine weeks and was off work for 27 weeks. His wages before the accident were £1 4s. a week, which brought the amount for actual loss of work to over £28. The doctor's bill amounted to over £8, and the balance of the amount claimed for was suffering and for the permanent injury he had sustained. On the 29th March the following year, Batty visited Gill and said he would pay him nothing because he had no money.

In his defence, Batty claimed that Gill was a trespasser in his field on the day of the accident. He had been asked by the gatekeeper to pay, but he refused, and he and another man entered the field by climbing over a fence. As soon as the dogs were on their respective marks, Batty said he ordered the crowd to stand back, which they all did except for Gill, who was so eager to see the sport that he took up a position close behind Batty, who carried a gun loaded with blank cartridge. He fired, and Gill shouted, *"Oh, Batty, you've shot me!"* Batty gave instructions for him to be taken to Mr. Firth's house, contributed £1 towards a subscription made for him, and supplied him with brandy during his illness. Batty said it was common to fire on the ground when starting the dogs. His Honour Judge Ellison *"reserved his judgement,"* meaning he delayed passing judgement until he could review the evidence and perhaps take expert advice. Upon reconvening, the judge found in Elijah Batty's favour, and that if there was any negligence at all, it was all on Gill's part, who had not obeyed the order to stand back, and must have been stood very near to Batty when he fired the gun because the wadding had struck his food. However, he did not ask Gill to pay Batty's costs, because Batty had broken his promise to help him out financially.

EXPLOSION AT STOCKSBRIDGE: February 1889

Elijah moved out of the Friendship after losing the licence and went to live at Temperance Terrace (Button Row, now demolished). One Sunday afternoon, three of his children were playing when George, the eldest, was injured by an explosion of gunpowder which he had been playing with. George would have been about 11, Harriet 9, and Marian 6. As a keen shooter, Elijah would have kept a supply of gunpowder available for his guns.

Elijah died on the 8th July 1889, two months after the court case. He made his will on the day he died, and he made his brother Tom Batty of the Friendship his sole executor and trustee as well as the guardian of his three children, George Askew, Harriet Ann and Marian. Elijah left all his property to his brother to invest on their behalf, with the power to postpone the sale of any real estate or property as he saw fit. The gross value of his estate was just over £188 (equivalent to over £24,000 today).

The eldest, George Askew Batty, was recorded with his uncle Tom Batty at the Friendship when the 1891 census was taken. He was 13 years old. He married Ethel Bradwell in 1902 and they lived at Victoria Street. The 1911 census records him as a waiter in a hotel, which must have been the Friendship. George's two younger sisters Harriet and Marian lived with their aunt Edna [nee Batty] and her husband George Nield at Worsbrough.

Tom Batty was once more behind the bar at the Friendship, and he continued to run the pub from 1888 until his retirement in 1935, a period of 47 years. He had been a licensee for sixty-one years in total, from the age of 21 when he was the landlord of the Friendship for the first time, until he retired at the age of eighty-two. He was a member of the Sheffield, Rotherham, and District Licensed Victuallers' Association all that time, with the exception of the five years when he held a licence for the Bridge Hotel at Penistone (which was out of the Sheffield area). He had perhaps been a member of the Barnsley Licensed Victuallers, for, along with his wife, he was listed among the attendees at their annual ball in 1891. The L.V.A. held some of its meetings at the Friendship, as well as social events.

Lucy Batty died in 1892 aged 34. She and Tom did not have any children. In 1893 Tom married for a third time to Mary Meakin, a widow.[264] Tom and Mary were at the Friendship when the 1901 census was taken, but by 1911 the couple were no longer living together. Tom was at the Friendship with a housekeeper, Mrs. Kate Trees, and a domestic servant, Miss Nellie Smith, whilst his wife was living with her widowed mother in Derby. She remained in Derby until at least 1925[265] before moving to Bognor Regis on the south coast. I am told by Tom's great-granddaughter Jeanne that Mary was an alcoholic and that Tom paid her an allowance after they ceased to live together. He did not mention her in his will, and she contested it; Tom's daughter was then obliged to pay for her upkeep. In 1939 Mary was living with another widowed lady in Bognor Regis and she died there in 1949 aged 89.

1893: Wanted, respectable man, single, as groom-waiter; one who will make himself generally useful; to live in. Apply personally to T. E. Batty, Friendship Inn, Stocksbridge.

---

[264] Mary was born in 1861 at Saltney, Cheshire, the daughter of Charles and Mary Pope. Saltney is a town adjoining Chester. She married George Meakin, a railway engine stoker, in 1883, and they lived in Derby. He died in 1891 aged 32, and his widow married Tom Batty in 1893.

[265] The electoral registers record her living at London Road, Derby until 1925 (this is the latest year available online). In 1920 her younger brother Arthur Pope was also at that address with her.

1893: Wanted, General Servant, about 30, able to do plain cooking. – Apply Friendship Inn, Stocksbridge, near Sheffield.

DRUNK AND REFUSING TO QUIT: 1894
Thomas Firth, a Stocksbridge labourer, was summoned for being drunk at the Friendship and refusing to quit when asked. On the night of the 17th February, he entered the concert room and asked for a glass of beer, but the landlord, seeing his condition, refused to serve him. Firth became abusive and would not leave when asked to do so by the landlord. Tom Batty and the waiter eventually managed to eject him, but later that evening one of the windows of the pub was broken, and Batty was told that Firth had caused the damage. Firth did not appear in court and was fined £1, or in default 14 days in prison.

ACCIDENT TO A POLICEMAN: November 1894
Tom Batty was a keen sportsman, and one of his shooting companions one afternoon was a local policeman, Sergeant Frederick Tom Gunson. He was stationed at Stocksbridge, and once a month he had a day off duty. On Thursday 8th November 1894, he chose to spend his day off with a party of men who were going out shooting rabbits, though he did not take a gun himself. Tom Batty was one of the men, along with another policeman Constable Baldwin, and Joseph Cutts of Parkwood Springs. The men drove to Brookhouse near Langsett, where Tom Batty rented some shooting rights, leaving Stocksbridge at about two o'clock in the afternoon. While the ferrets were being used Mr. Cutts got too near the hole, and Mr. Batty asked him to go a little further away. He stepped backwards and caught his foot on some rock and fell to the ground. He was holding a double-barrelled breech-loading gun, and the shock of the fall caused the gun to go off. The barrels happened to be pointing towards Gunstone, and the charge struck him full in the right leg below the knee, shattering his leg. The others did all they could to stop the bleeding before driving Gunson to the Sheffield Infirmary about fifteen miles away. A surgeon was called in, but he had to amputate the leg just below the knee. Gunson had to stay in the hospital for five weeks.

Sergeant Gunson had been in the service for nearly nine years and was much respected by both his colleagues and the general public. During his time at Stocksbridge, he had been awarded a merit badge for saving the lives of two children who were drowning.[266] He was thirty years old and had only been married for a year.

In February 1895, there was a presentation evening in Sheffield for Sergeant Gunson at the King's Head Hotel, Change Alley. He was presented with a cheque and an illuminated address. An illuminated address looks like a certificate, often very ornate and colourful, and includes elements of the person's history in a series of images. Because Gunson's accident had not occurred whilst he was on duty, he was not eligible for a police pension, and it was felt by many people that some recognition should be made for his valuable service. Superintendent Bielby set up a subscription list to raise money for him. Circulars were issued to all the influential residents in the district, and a committee consisting of 24 men was formed to look after the money and to form a scheme which would benefit the Sergeant; £300 was collected from about 1,200 people, who gave sums ranging from half-a-crown to £10. In addition to this, the Sergeant was granted the sum of £56. 18s. out of the Pension Fund, and a collection was made for him among the county police force, which raised over £70. In total, over £427 was raised.[267] He had already received some of this money, and the remainder, £300, was handed over to him by cheque at the presentation evening. He also received the illuminated address which had been drawn up by a Mr. E. Siddall, of Page Hall Road. Tom Batty was amongst those in attendance, and there were many toasts made, and musical entertainment was also provided.

The Sheffield Independent reported that, since the accident, the sergeant's wife, Mary Ann, had been appointed matron at the headquarters of the

---

[266] According to the Independent newspaper he rescued two children, but it appears Gunson rescued just the one child, in May 1889. Frank Haigh, aged 4½, lived at Florence Buildings, Deepcar with his widowed mother Martha. The boy had been playing by the side of the river Don near his home when he fell in. P.C. Gunson was in plain clothes, and he jumped into the river, following the current, wading and swimming for about a quarter of a mile, trying to find him. A Deepcar man named Eli Fielding ran along the bank acting as lookout, and finally spotted the boy's body floating on the water near Bitholme's wood. He jumped in and pulled the boy out just as Gunson arrived. They wrapped him in a blanket and managed to revive him. He boy had been in the water for fifteen minutes, but luckily, he had not sunk because of the fast current and the buoyancy of his clothes. A few days later the Independent reported that Gunson had been promoted to the merit class of constables, *"a distinction much prized and difficult to obtain."*
[267] The Bank of England's inflation calculator estimates this as equivalent to £56,567 today.

Sheffield branch of the Society for the Prevention of Cruelty to Children, at the Jeffie Bainbridge Shelter in Surrey Street, and that this is where the couple would live. However, they must only have been there for a year, because in June 1896 they had their first child, George Frederick, baptised at St. Silas Church in Broomhall, and the parish register recorded that they were living at 79 Broomhall Street and that Fred was a tobacconist. Their second child Bernard was born there, but by 1899 they had taken a pub, the Sportsman's Inn at Stock's Hill, Ecclesfield. Four more children were born to them in Ecclesfield. By 1911 they had moved to 182 Northfield Road, Crookes, and Fred was running a fish and chip shop.

ELECTED TO STOCKSBRIDGE COUNCIL: December 1894

Tom Batty stood for election to the Stocksbridge Council in 1894, and was amongst those voted in, with the second-highest number of votes (434). There was a lot of rivalry between the various candidates, and many leaflets were distributed. Tom Batty published a leaflet, in which he said:

"I have been invited by a number of Electors of this Parish to allow myself to be nominated as a Candidate for election for the Urban District Council. After due consideration I have decided to do so.

"I may say I am no stranger to you, having lived in the parish or near to the whole of my life. Consequently, I have a thorough knowledge of the requirements of the district.

"I have likewise time at my disposal to attend to the duties necessary for a member of the Council.

"I am neither a teetotaller nor prominent in politics – two qualifications I consider unnecessary for a Candidate for this election. I do not approve of this election being fought on party or political lines. If I am returned, I shall study your interests strictly independently. I consider myself more temperate in my views, though a publican, than many who profess to advocate teetotalism.

"I advocate providing suitable Recreation Grounds for the numerous working-class children in the district.

"I am strongly opposed to the introduction of a School Board and Burial Board into the district, as I consider that as we are situated at the present time there is no immediate requirement for either, and, further than this, their introduction would involve an unnecessarily large increase in the rates to be levied on the working class.

"I may say that I feel justified in opposing the teetotal party by my candidature on account of the insults and insinuations of bribery on my part in respect to the sad accident which happened to Sergeant Gunsone in my presence.[268]

"I have confidence that you will show by your support on the day of the poll that I still hold the respect of the majority.

"In the event of being returned, I promise that nothing shall be wanting on my part to merit your respect and confidence."

Tom Batty was a Conservative candidate, and the Conservatives had the majority that day.

TROUT POISONING AT EWDEN: 1895

Tom Batty was called to give evidence in court against two men who were accused of poisoning trout in the Ewden stream, where the landowner Mr. Rimington Wilson of Broomhead Hall held the fishing rights. Tom had bought some fish from one of the men, Fred Lee. The two accused men, both from Stocksbridge, were Oswald Wragg, a 42-year-old collier, and Fred Lee alias Brownhill, a 44-year-old labourer.

Mr. Rimington Wilson's gamekeeper James Dyson also gave evidence. He was near Broomhead Mill at 4.30am when he saw two men going into the stream. When he was about twenty yards away, the men saw him and ran away. Wragg threw down a home-made spear, a long shaft with a dinner fork attached to the end of it. Dyson gave chase and caught Lee. Finding nothing on him he went after Wragg but was unable to catch him. On returning to where he had left Lee, he found that he had gone. A few hours later he examined the stream with Mr. Charles Ward, the head gamekeeper, and they found some dead trout, which appeared to have been recently poisoned, the water discoloured with lime. They found a hidden bag, which smelt of chloride of lime and fish. The police visited Wragg, who was found to have some chloride of lime in one of his pockets; later it was discovered that his son had purchased a pound of this at Mr. Marsden's chemists shop, Wragg waiting outside the shop whilst his son made the purchase. He was taken to the police station at Hillsborough. Tom Batty said that he had bought 5¾ lbs. of trout from Lee. When the police examined them, they

---

[268] On the 8th November

found evidence that the fish had been poisoned, and that they had spear marks on them. Wragg insisted he was after rabbits that morning, whereas Lee confessed, and said that Wragg had *"led him into it."* Both men were remanded in custody to await trial at the Sessions, where the more serious crimes were tried. The case came up the following month, and Wragg, who was no stranger to the courts, having a long record for game trespass, stealing, and drunkenness, was committed to prison for six months. Lee, who had no previous convictions, was sentenced to one month.

THROWN OUT THRICE: October 1896
Albert Barden, a striker by trade, pleaded guilty to having been drunk at the Friendship Inn and having refused to quit. Tom Batty said that the man had gone into the taproom on Saturday night, 26th September, but because he was already drunk, he had refused to serve him and had asked him to leave. He refused to go, so Batty ejected him. He was soon back a second time, and once again Batty put him out. He made a third appearance at half-past ten, and this time Batty called in the assistance of P.C. Dalby, who, finding that Barden *"turned to deaf ear to friendly counsels,"* ejected him a third time. He was summoned to court and was fined fifteen shillings.

HE POCKETED THE PEWTER: October 1896
Steelworker Herbert Chandley of Cubley was charged with having stolen two electro-plated half-pint drinking cups from the Friendship valued at just over £1. Chandley had come to Stocksbridge that day with a football team. He had gone into the Friendship on Saturday afternoon, but Tom Batty had refused to serve him because he appeared to have had enough already. Chandley said he only wanted to look for a friend, and so he was allowed to go into the smoke room. A miner called Frank Marsh gave evidence and told the court that he had been in the same room as Chandley, who was sitting on the edge of a table, on which were the two cups. Chandley had asked him what time it was, and as he looked at the clock, he saw Chandley put something in his pocket and leave the room at once. Marsh noticed the cups were missing and told the landlord, who followed him to a barber's shop. He asked for the cups to be returned to him; Chandley denied having them, but Batty felt in his pockets and found them. Superintendent Bielby said that when Chandley was locked up, which was about three hours after the theft, he was drunk. Because he had previously been of good character with no previous convictions and was the only support of his widowed mother, Tom

Batty did not press the case, and he was let off with a fine of £1, including costs (or 14 days' imprisonment).

A PUBLIC HOUSE MOB: 1898

In his diary, Alfred Moxon (who was on the committee of the Stocksbridge Band of Hope Co-operative Society, and a teetotaller) wrote about some events involving Benjamin Jackson Manknell, a local joiner and undertaker. These were not reported in the Sheffield or Barnsley newspapers. On the 18th April 1898, Mr. Manknell was tied to a lamp post opposite the Friendship by a *"public house mob."* Moxon does not give any explanation as to what prompted this. On the 24th April, Mr. Moxon went to visit Mr. Manknell to persuade him to give up drinking and sign the Pledge – to agree to abstain from *"all liquors of an intoxicating quality, whether ale, porter, wine, or ardent spirits, except as medicines."* He wrote in his diary that Mr. Manknell was *"deeply impressed with what I say and promises to amend his ways. He sheds tears when I tell him of the grief he is causing his parents."* Benjamin's parents lived in Sheffield, and his father (also Benjamin) had been tee-total for a long time.[269] On 27th April, Moxon noted that Manknell went to work and promised to reform his behaviour, and Moxon's son Leonard took the Pledge Book for him to sign, which he did the following day. Moxon wrote, *"Manknell signs the Pledge and goes to work again and his home is bright once more. – Age 36 years."* Mr. Moxon was fond of passing comments on the evils of drink in his diary; on the 20th April 1898, he noted the death of John Thickett of Midhope at the age of 65 years. He wrote, *"Another victim of drink – Doctors say 'Pneumonia'"*

Benjamin Jackson Manknell had married Edith Walton, the daughter of James Walton of Stocksbridge, in November 1886. She died the following year aged just 22. In 1889 he married again to Louisa Hattersley of Half Hall, the daughter of James Hattersley, a mason. In 1891 they were living at Skelton Villa on Pot House Lane, and Benjamin's occupation was joiner and undertaker. They had a four-month-old daughter, Edith.

---

[269] His obituary in the Sheffield Daily Telegraph 5th November 1901 said that he had been connected to the United Methodist Free Chapel for 30 years, and had been for a long time a very active worker in connection with the Band of Hope Union, and was a *"very old abstainer."*

In 1896, he put some property up for auction at the Friendship; four dwelling houses, two of which were in Victoria Street and occupied by himself and Joseph Briggs, known as West View, and the remaining two occupied by Jesse Liles and William Hance. Also, the joiner's and builder's workshops in the rear, in his own occupation. The house occupied by Mr. Manknell contained seven rooms including a bathroom and had hot and cold water laid on. There was also a greenhouse. At the auction, these were bought by Friendship landlord Tom Batty for £850 – about £114,000 in today's money. Manknell continued to live there, paying rent to Tom.

It was two years after the sale of this property that Manknell was attacked outside the Friendship. He signed the Pledge in April 1898. Then on 2nd February 1899, Moxon wrote that the *"Bums"* had taken possession of Mr. Manknell's house and workshop.[270] A few days later he added that the furniture and stock-in-trade had been sold *"by virtue of Her Majesty's Sheriff."* There is no evidence of Manknell being declared bankrupt, and according to the Sheffield Independent of 4th February 1899, it was Mr. Manknell himself, of West View, Victoria Street, who ordered the local auctioneer John Bramall to sell the whole of his household furniture as well as the joiner's shop tools and materials, his horse, some pigeons, and a dray. He and his family then moved to Half Hall.

Benjamin died in 1905 aged 43 after being knocked down by a governess car (a two-wheeled horse-drawn cart) as he was crossing the road near the Filesmith's Arms at Oughtibridge. The driver of the cart was Mr. Downes, landlord of the Earl Gray pub on Ecclesall Road, Sheffield. He took Manknell to a doctor, who thought he was drunk, and asked Downes to take him to the police station, which he did. The police took him home, but he died on the way there. The cause of death was a fracture of the skull; the doctor had missed the wound when he examined him.

THE SHEFFIELD EQUALISED INDEPENDENT DRUIDS

In May 1897, a meeting was held in a large room at the Friendship to present Brother Leonard Crapper of the Stocksbridge Pride Lodge with a compensation grant of £100 after he accidentally lost his sight. Brothers Rodman (president) and Shaw (treasurer) were present and spoke about the

---

[270] Bum was slang for bailiff, after bum-bailey or bum-bailiff, a term coined by Shakespeare

advantages of the Order. Dr. W. M. Robertshaw was initiated as an honorary member. The Sheffield Equalised Druids were an offshoot of the Order of Druids, formed in about 1890 when they had split from the Ancient Order of Druids. The A.O.D., which was a fraternal organisation, suffered a number of splits in its history, mainly due to some of the members wishing to form true friendly societies like the Oddfellows or the Ancient Order of Foresters. The two major splits were Lodges which went on to form the United Ancient Order of Druids in 1833 and the Order of Druids in around 1850. The Sheffield Order went their own way. "*Equalised*" refers to the fact that equal benefits for sick and funeral pay were paid to members across the whole district rather than being down to individual Lodges.

SHEFFIELD LICENSED VICTUALLERS' ASSOCIATION

In June 1901 one of the monthly committee meetings of the L.V.A., of which Tom Batty was a member, was held at The Friendship. The cash accounts were passed as satisfactory, and the chairman complimented the members upon the continued progress of the association. He urged upon them the importance of conducting their houses according to the law in order to avoid prosecution. A report was given about a conference which some of the committee had attended the previous month at Bristol. Topics discussed were The Child Messenger Bill, Habitual Drunkards[271], Teetotal Bias on the Bench, and Sunday Closing Bills.

The Child Messenger Bill was passed in 1901 and came into operation in the New Year of 1902. It forbade the practice of parents sending children under the age of fourteen to buy alcohol for home consumption unless it was to be of a pint measure and supplied in a corked and sealed vessel. The reasoning behind this was to prevent children from being on licensed premises unnecessarily, which, it was said, would have a good and moralising effect. The Temperance Movement was having a big influence on society and was seeking to amend the laws on drinking by petitioning the licensing

---

[271] The Child Messenger Bill and the Habitual Drunkards formed part of the 1902 Licensing Act. With regard to Habitual Drunkards, the police were given the power to arrest anyone found drunk in the street or in a public place (including licensed premises) whilst in charge of a child under seven years of age. The husband or wife of a habitual drunkard was enabled to obtain a maintenance or separation order, and under certain circumstances the drunk could be committed to a retreat for inebriates. The sale of intoxicants to habitual drunkards was prohibited.

authorities, getting people to sign the Pledge against the evils of drink, and managing to get teetotal magistrates onto the licensing boards. The breweries were increasingly worried about this because the magistrates had the power to prevent the renewal of public house licences; this was a time of massive brewery expansion and tied houses, and they were worried for the future of their investments, being dependent on the whims of the licensing boards, many of which contained temperance campaigners. It was also seen as an injustice because brewers who were also Justices of the Peace were prohibited from being on the licensing board.

When the Child Messenger Bill was discussed by Licensed Victuallers' Associations all over the country, some landlords said that they would not only follow the law but take it further, refusing to serve children under fourteen in any circumstances. However, plenty of people were fined for breaking this new law. Landlords were fined for serving children beer in vessels that were not properly corked and sealed, and parents were fined for sending their child to obtain the beer. There was also confusion about what vessels were permitted; in one case, a parent thought that sending their child with a bottle instead of a jug was OK but both he and the landlord were fined. In Lancaster, one case involved a parent knowingly breaking the law when a child had been taught to say that she was carrying milk.

The first case in Sheffield came before the courts in February 1902 when George Allen, of 15 Court, 5 house, Scotland Street, was fined ten shillings for sending an 8-year-old boy called Stuart Turner to The Fortune of War public house in Scotland Street on the 2nd February with an open jug. Allen was also in trouble for encouraging the boy to commit perjury by lying about being sent for the beer. There was no record of the landlord's name and no mention of whether he was fined, as he should have been.[272]

---

[272] The landlord at this time was John Carlton. He appeared in court on 4th February charged with criminally assaulting his 12-year-old daughter Evelyn one night whilst his wife was absent. His defence was that the girl was guilty of misconduct, and frequented music halls and other places unsuitable for girls of her age, and that she often told lies. He alleged that some of her relatives had urged her to accuse him, and that *"certain people"* had been trying to get up a case of this kind against him for ten years. The jury took ten minutes to reach a verdict of not guilty and he was discharged. There was applause in the court. John had moved out of the pub by 1902 and handed over to George Green. The magistrates tried to

The first case in the Child Messenger Bill to come before the Barnsley magistrates was also in February. George Hall, a beer seller living at Milton Street, Wombwell, was charged with allowing his daughter Bertha to sell beer to a child under the age of 14 years.[273] Sidney Parker was nine years old, and the pint bottle of beer he was seen carrying by a policeman was not properly corked and sealed and did not have a label. The boy said the label had fallen off, which it had. Bertha told the policeman that she had sealed the bottle with the seals which had been provided by the brewery and had affixed a gummed label over the cork and the bottle neck. It was thought that she must have dislodged the label when she wiped the bottle. The fine was a small one, because it was the first case that had been brought, and the child's father does not appear to have been fined, his defence being that he did not know that the Act was in force.

The Sheffield Daily Telegraph reported that the first prosecution in the West Riding Court occurred when George Medley, a Stannington butcher, was summoned for sending a child under 14 to the Queen's Hotel, Stannington, for half a pint of whisky on the 1st February. The landlady refused to serve the child. Medley could also have been charged with sending the child for less than a pint, but the magistrates thought that Medley might not have fully understood the law because the Act had been in force for such a short time. The summonses were withdrawn on payment of the costs.

In April 1904, at another meeting at the Friendship, a report was presented about a deputation from the L.V.A. who had been to London to meet local M.P.s about a proposed Licensing Bill, and it was mentioned that large petitions had been presented to Prime Minister Arthur Balfour, urging him to bring the Bill in as soon as possible.[274]

---

rescind the pub's licence in 1903, on the grounds of it being a disorderly house, but it remained open. John tried to take another pub, but his character was deemed to be "*so bad as to render him an unsuitable tenant.*" He moved to Darnall Road, where he lived with his wife and children, including Evelyn.

[273] Bertha Hall was only about 13 years of age herself. It was not until 1823 that the sale of, and purchase of, alcohol was restricted to those aged 18 and above (with the exception that a 16-year-old could have beer, port, perry or cider with a meal).

[274] After a landmark case in 1891, magistrates could refuse to renew a license on the grounds that it was surplus to requirements or unnecessary; previously refusals were dependent on misconduct charges being proven against the licensee. Trade delegations protested against

In 1908 the government proposed yet another Licensing Bill when the Chancellor of the Exchequer, Herbert Asquith, argued for an acceleration in the suppression of licences, with the aim of closing a third of all public houses in England and Wales. He also wanted a reduction in Sunday opening hours and a ban on the employment of women in pubs. Not surprisingly the brewing trade was horrified by these proposals, especially those pertaining to the removal of licences with reduced compensation, and they immediately began a series of actions designed to defeat the Bill. On the 19th March meetings were held locally at the Friendship and the King and Miller to protest against this proposed new Bill. And on the same day, a public meeting was held in favour of the Bill at the British School, presided over by Dr. W. M. Robertshaw. This meeting would have been attended by members of the Temperance Society and those who wanted to see the Bill passed by parliament. The Bill was defeated in November.

---

the over-zealous actions of some of the licensing magistrates, and although the P.M. was sympathetic to their case, he was slow to act. Political pressure was applied by supporting opposition parties in by-elections, and the government took the hint and passed the 1904 Licensing Bill, known as the Balfour Act, which introduced a compensation scheme (which was funded by a levy on all licensed properties). If a pub was closed for reasons other than misconduct, then a compensation payment could be claimed.

By 1903 the Friendship Hotel had been open for over forty years, and Tom Batty undertook some rebuilding work, adding a new façade as well. A postcard from this time (shown below) advertises it as being, *"re-built, re-furnished and up-to-date."*

Stonework above the door shows the date 1903 and the initials T.E.B. for Thomas Edward Batty. Above his initials a handshake is depicted, symbolising the Stocksbridge Band of Hope Co-operative Society, whose early meetings were held in the pub when Thomas's father George Batty was the landlord. This stonework is still there today, but other aspects of the new façade have now gone – on one side of the stonework were the words *"T. E. Batty, Importer and Bonder"* and on the other side *"Foreign Wines and Spirits, T. E. Batty."*

The interior of the pub was almost certainly remodelled at the same time. More and more pubs were coming under the control of the major breweries, who undertook large-scale refurbishment projects. They added prominent advertising boards, ornate sculptures, huge lamps, ironwork, carvings, elaborate window surrounds on the exterior, and an abundance of mirrors, tiles, and lights inside. Tom Batty ran a free house, something that he must have been proud of, for it was mentioned in a lot of his advertising material. He had not sold out to the big breweries, and he was letting everyone know! He probably borrowed some of the improvement ideas from the breweries, with prominent advertising on the outside (his own name displayed, not a brewery's), the ornate carving above the door, and the use of floor to ceiling tiles in various shades of green in the entrance lobby. A lot of this still exists today, and the bar itself – the counter, top section, and the fittings behind the bar - are also original. The room to the left of the bar was originally the Tap Room, and it retains its original bench seating which wraps around the room.

There are still some bell pushes encased in a wooden panel above the seating, which would have been used to summon the waiter.

Tom Batty would have had to have his plans approved by the licensing magistrates, because the Licensing Act of 1902 gave the magistrates power over structural alterations. It allowed them to keep control over such matters as multiple and side entrances to pubs, and compartments and snugs within them. All these things made police supervision more difficult, and they were seen as encouraging excessive or secretive drinking, particularly by women. Consent was now required if alterations created additional facilities for drinking or concealed any part of the premises from effective police observation.

```
The Friendship Hotel
T. E. BATTY         STOCKSBRIDGE              Telephone
Proprietor          (Free, Full Licensed)     No. 9 Stocksbridge

BOTTLER OF BASS' AND
WORTHINGTON'S PALE ALES

SHEFFIELD AND BURTON ALES ON DRAUGHT AND
IN BOTTLE FROM THE LEADING BREWERIES ONLY
```

This old advertising postcard (above) tells us that The Friendship was a free house (not under brewery control) and that Tom Batty was also a bottler of Bass and Worthington's Pale Ales. Ales from both Sheffield and Burton were available both on draught and in bottles. The pub also had a telephone (No. 9 Stocksbridge). There was a public call office at Deepcar, which was open at any hour for calls, but the Friendship, the Royal Oak (Deepcar), and the Coach and Horses (Stocksbridge) also functioned as additional call offices; these telephones could be used on payment of 1d. for local calls, and 2d. for Sheffield district (the costs in 1908).

From about 1905 Tom Batty advertised regularly in the Sheffield papers, aiming his publicity at tourists. An early advert, placed on the 3rd June 1905, said: *"All Tourists and Cyclists call at Friendship Hotel, Stocksbridge, Deepcar, (Free, fully Licensed). Billiards, etc. Centre for Langsett Reservoirs and Famous Moorland Walks. Catering Terms Moderate. Prop., T. E. Batty."* Another from November that year said: *"At Stocksbridge,*

Deepcar, Centre of Langsett Reservoirs and Moorland Walks. Commercials Catered for. Every Accommodation. Billiards. Friendship Hotel, Prop., T. E. Batty. Telephone, 9, Stocksbridge. Conveyances meet most trains." The 1911 census recorded that the Friendship had a total of fourteen rooms.

In 2020 the Friendship was given planning permission to reinstate hotel rooms, and once again the Stocksbridge area is being marketed as a tourist destination, with the emphasis on walking and cycling. Stocksbridge hosted the finish of the Tour de Yorkshire cycle race in 2017 and was voted second in the Ramblers *"Britain's Best Walking Neighbourhood"* in 2018.

The postcard below (left) advertises the fact that the fare from Sheffield to Deepcar Station, G. C. (Great Central) was 1/- return, and that conveyances to and from the hotel met all trains, for a fee. There was also First-Class Accommodation for Commercials (commercial travellers, or reps.) The Friendship was the *"Only Free Fully Licensed Road-Side Hotel in the District."* There were stables at the back for the horses. The postcard on the right advises that *"Motor Buses pass the door every Twenty Minutes."*

1904: Youth, sharp, Wanted; billiard mark, wait on, etc. - Friendship Hotel, Stocksbridge, Sheffield.

MINERAL WATER MAKER'S APPLICATION: 1903
In February 1903, Ernest Schofield, mineral water manufacturer of Victoria Street, applied for a wine and spirit off-licence. Solicitor Mr. Muir Wilson opposed this on behalf of the Friendship Inn and a Mr. Howe opposed for the *"residents of the district."* Schofield's solicitor argued that *"it would be greatly to the advantage of the residents if he could sell wines and spirits by retail."* Both opposing solicitors said that there was not the slightest

necessity for the licence, and the justices refused it. An advert of 1908 boasted that Schofield's were *"Manufacturers of high-class mineral waters and cordials. Bottles of Bass and Worthington's Pale Ales, and Guinness's Extra Stout. Pint beers of the Finest Quality. Beer and Stout supplied in Cask at reasonable prices. Cider and Tobacco Merchants."*

CONSERVATISM AT STOCKSBRIDGE: 1904

In February 1904, the Hallamshire Conservative and Unionist Association held a *"smoking concert"* at the Friendship. Smoking Concerts were live performances of music and were usually for men only. As the name suggests, men would meet to smoke and speak of topics such as sport and politics, whilst listening to live music. The Conservatives held regular meetings at the Friendship, and Tom Batty was their local treasurer. He was later the President of the Stocksbridge and Deepcar Conservative and Unionist Association, which was founded in 1925. The latter also held a Debating Society at the pub. There were branches of the Association for men, for women, and for juveniles. The men's section held their political meetings and entertainment evenings at the Friendship, but in 1925 it was decided that there was a need for more suitable headquarters, particularly for the ladies and juvenile branches; presumably, they thought that a pub was not a suitable venue for them. Arrangements were then made to lease a building in Hoyle [Hole] House Lane, which was known as the Stocksbridge Dancing Academy. Extensive renovations were then carried out there, *"thanks to the kindness of Mr. T. E. Batty, the owner."* The first general meeting took place there in November 1925, however the men continued to hold meetings and social events at the Friendship.

Knur and Spell matches continued to be played at the Friendship Grounds. In 1907 about a hundred spectators attended a match for £10 played between two local men, S. Revitt and H. Hoyle. Revitt won this match.

ARRESTED ON LEAVING PRISON.
CHRISTMAS & NEW YEAR'S DAYS IN PRISON: 1907

Joseph Waller, a nineteen-year-old bricklayer of no fixed abode, left Hull prison early on the morning of Boxing Day 1907 and was immediately arrested on a warrant charging him with stealing a gentleman's silver English lever watch, valued at fifty shillings. He appeared before the Sheffield West Riding magistrates a few hours later. The court heard that the watch, belonging to Charles Clark of Stocksbridge, was missed from the shop of Joseph Shaw, also at Stocksbridge, where it was being kept for the purpose of timing, in September. On the 21st September, Waller had sold the watch in the Friendship for ten shillings. He had only just served two months' imprisonment for theft. When he was arrested, he confessed, saying, "*I stole it. I sold it to a man in the Friendship Inn for 10s.*" He was remanded into custody to await trial at the Quarter Sessions. The Sessions took place in the New Year, and, as well as being charged with stealing the watch at Stocksbridge on the 21st September (to which he pleaded guilty), Waller was also charged with having stolen a coat, a pair of brown boots, and a metal watch belonging to Arthur Day of Mexborough on the 17th September. He had gone to obtain lodgings at Day's house dressed in a soldier's uniform, saying he was on furlough, but he subsequently made off with the items mentioned. Because he already had several previous convictions, he was sentenced to two years' imprisonment, with a recommendation to the Commissioners that he should be treated under the Borstal system.

MORE MEETINGS...

PRESENTATION FOR MR. F. W. HILL: May 1908

The Friendship was the venue for a large gathering of foremen and workpeople from Fox's Works, who were making a presentation to Mr. F. W. Hill, late manager of the rail mill and Bessemer department, who had recently taken up an appointment at Cammell Laird & Company's Penistone works. Mr. Edward Thickett, who officiated as chairman, presented Mr. Hill with a gold watch and chain, together with an oak-framed list of the many people who had subscribed to this gift (the lettering of which had been neatly done by the subscription secretary, Mr. S. Atkinson). There was also a gold-mounted silk umbrella for his wife. Mr. Thickett said he had known Mr. Hill nearly all his (Mr. Hill's) life and had always found him a "*good fellow,*" and the gifts showed that the feeling of good fellowship - which was essential between foremen and workmen - had always existed between Mr. Hill and his men. During the evening, there were songs and music.

PRESENTATION FOR MR. V. B. OAKLEY: November 1924

A large gathering of departmental managers and staff at Fox's took place at the Friendship, the occasion being a presentation to Mr. V. B. Oakley, who had been an engineer at the works for fourteen years. He was leaving to take up a new job in London. The gift, a gold hunter watch, was presented by Mr. W. Walker, foundry manager, who had been with the firm for almost sixty years. Mrs. Oakley was presented with a cake stand. Mr. J. Hattersley, the manager of the joinery department, who had 53 years' service, occupied the chair. This was possible Vincent Bertram Oakley (1883-1866).

PRESENTATION FOR MR. D. BREWSTER: March 1926
Another presentation at the Friendship took place, this time to present a cheque for £125 as a disablement grant to Mr. D. Brewster, who lost the sight of an eye whilst at work. Mr. H. Lake made the presentation on behalf of the Iron and Steel Trades Confederation.

PRESENTATION FOR MR. J. N. KILBY: April 1932
Mr. J. N. Kilby, who had been the assistant works manager at Fox's, was presented with a walnut secretaire, suitably inscribed, by Mr. Walter Dodgson on behalf of the Siemens' melting shop staff and workmen, upon his leaving to take up an important post with the Cargo Fleet Iron and Steel Company Ltd. of Middlesbrough.

BOLSTERSTONE AND DISTRICT RIFLE CLUB: 1909
On the 7th December 1909, the Bolsterstone and District Rifle Club held their annual dinner at the Friendship. More than fifty club members and local gentlemen sat down to a meal, followed by entertainment and prize giving. Mr. Muscroft and Mr. Mounsey of the Sheffield Male Glee and Madrigal Society sang several songs.[275]

FARMERS' UNION: 1909
The Friendship hosted a meeting of the Farmers' Union, which was well attended.

STOCKSBRIDGE FLORAL, HORTICULTURAL, AND COTTAGE GARDENERS' SOCIETY: 1909
The 34th annual exhibition and athletic sports of this Society was held one Saturday in August in a field near the Friendship and was attended by a large

---

[275] A Glee was a *"part song;"* Glee Club dates to the 18th century and the term referred to a small group of men singing parlour songs, folk songs and amusing ditties in close harmony, normally without accompaniment – what we would probably now call Barber Shop.

number of people. The Stocksbridge Old Brass Band played, and there was a gala after the show. The categories in the show were vegetables, flowers, farm produce, bread, industrial and fine art, photography, poultry, pigeons, and dogs.

THE ROYAL ANTEDILUVIAN ORDER OF BUFFALOES

The R.A.O.B.[276] is a fraternal society which is still in existence today. It is often called the Working Man's – or Poor Man's – Masonry because it is run along similar lines, but Masons are quick to point out that it is not a Masonic organisation. It is however classed as a Secret Society due to the signs and passwords used in the workings of each Lodge (local) and Province (larger area). The R.A.O.B. was very popular between the Wars but has gone into considerable decline since, and many Lodges have now been lost. The Lodge that met at the Friendship – since at least 1901 – was known as the *"Hand o' Friendship"* Lodge (no. 649), and they held their meetings every Wednesday at 8pm. Tom Batty was its treasurer.

The R.A.O.B. had been founded in London in 1822. Other Lodges came into existence in London, all working independently, and so to introduce some regularity, the Metropolitan Lodges joined together to form the Grand [Primo] Lodge of England in 1866 and formulated successful plans for both central and provincial organisation and administration. The meetings were essentially convivial gatherings, and the original initiation ceremony was intended as a burlesque on Freemasonry. In the 1860s the Order organised a Widows and Dependents Fund, and the dispensing of charitable relief became its main object. At its peak, the order had three convalescent homes and two children's homes.

The R.A.O.B. is administered along Masonic lines, with a Grand Lodge headed by a Grand Primo [Grand Master]. Below this are Provincial Lodges, and Subordinate Lodges and Chapters. Each has its own Officers. Membership of a Lodge is open to all adult males without distinction as to social position, religious faith, or political belief. The prospective member has to convince the Lodge members that he is a loyal citizen and that he

---

[276] *"Royal"* was originally *"Loyal"* and *"Antediluvian"* (literally meaning *"before the flood"*) was used as a pretence to the antiquity of the Order. *"Buffaloes"* comes from a ballad sung in meetings, *"will chase a buffalo."*

genuinely wishes to take part in their work on the basis of giving *"to the extent of his power"* – in cash or services – whatever is required to meet the needs of a less fortunate Brother or the dependent widow and children of a deceased Brother. They should also be known personally to a member who acts as a sponsor. Should a Brother or his dependents need help from the R.A.O.B., the Grant is not related to what the brother had given, but to what is needed. Members take a secret oath and wear regalia consisting of aprons, a sash, and jewels (medals) according to their rank. The apron, sash, and certificate are usually decorated with symbols, some of which are common to Freemasonry. The main symbol is, of course, the Buffalo. The original burlesque ritual was dropped back in 1866, and in the 1930s the rituals were revised.

Members of a Lodge can be awarded four Degrees (ranks), for which jewels (medals) are given. These can only be acquired on the vote or approval of the Lodge members. The initiatory membership is the Kangaroo and lasts at least one year. This is followed by Certified Primo (C.P.), obtained when a member had passed an examination on how to chair and keep a Lodge in proper running order. The next level, the Knight Order of Merit (K.O.M.) can be obtained after at least three years spent as a C.P. Finally, the 4th degree is the Roll of Honour (R.O.H.), which can be obtained after five years as a K.O.M.

The Sheffield newspapers regularly reported on Lodge meetings, usually on the evenings when members were raised to the next level. On these occasions, men would attend from other Lodges. Just a few of the local men named in these reports from the 1920s were Brothers F. H. Bainbridge, F. Barden, E. Conduit, J. P. Davey, Albert Elson, C. F. Fletcher, Harry France, G. Herbert, J. W. Holloway, W. H. Lockwood, F. Nutt, H. Oates, F. H. Stockton, David A. Truman, B. Wood, and my great-grandfather Wilfred Donkersley.

Wilfred, *"Brother Donkersley,"* was awarded his first Degree in 1915 and made Certified Primo a year later. He attained the Knight Order of Merit in 1919. His medals bear the inscription, *"nemo mortalium omnibus horis sapit"* [no man is at all times wise], and also *"Justice, Truth, Philanthropy,"* which is their general motto. The K.O.M. medal reads: *"This order of Merit and Honor* [sic] *of Knighthood was conferred on W. Donkersley C.P. by the members of the Hand o' Friendship Lodge no. 649 in recognition of his services in the cause of Buffaloism and their esteem & regard for him as a man. 9 July 1919."* In 1919 he was a delegate at the R.A.O.B. Convention in Harrogate, which is where their headquarters, the Grand Lodge of England, is situated. The Hand o' Friendship lodge closed in the 1960s.

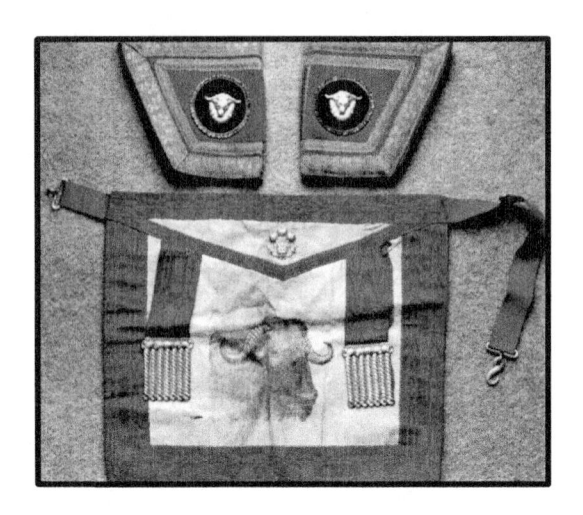

R.A.O.B. Regalia – apron and cuffs

Most Lodge meetings were usually held in rooms rented in clubs or public houses, where alcohol and tobacco could easily be obtained. These two items often played a big part in the social side of a Lodge. Like all Lodges, the Hand o' Friendship was involved in doing good works. In November 1918, for example, during World War One, they held their annual concert to raise money to provide Christmas presents for local sailors and soldiers. They were later reported to have raised £100 for St. Dunstan's Hostel for sailors and soldiers blinded in the War. In July 1919 they organised a carnival and procession (which took place in beautiful weather) to raise money for the building of a War Memorial Hall.

Mr. Albert Elson of Haywoods Park was the secretary of the Hand o'Friendship Lodge for thirty years, from about 1901 until his death on the 21st January 1931 at the age of 70. A great many people attended his funeral, including members of the R.A.O.B., the Oddfellows, church representatives, and representatives from Fox's, where he had worked for 52 years. After the committal, the Buffalo service was read at the graveside by the Provincial

Grand Primo of the Sheffield Province. Any Brothers present would stand around the coffin and drop ivy leaves.

PROPERTY AUCTIONS continued

- 1909: to be sold by order of the County Court of Yorkshire, held at Barnsley; a freehold cottage at Ford Lane known as Hawthorn Cottage, together with three fields belonging to it called House Field, Long Field and Top Piece, which was, or had been, in the occupation of William Hoyle.
- 1909: Re. Mr. David Button, deceased. A block of freehold property consisting of 12 houses and conveniences fronting Manchester Road and Victoria Street. This is what was known as Button Row, and it was also known as Temperance Terrace. The houses were being rented to Messrs. Adams, Hague, Hawley and others at a gross annual rent of £118. These sold for £1,400.
- 1912: Properties owned by the late Amos Ridal. Lot 1: Stocksbridge Hall, with grounds called *"The Park,"* covering just over eight acres, occupied by Samuel Fox & Co., or their under-tenant.[277] Also two cottages (formerly The Lodge, at the bottom of Park Drive), occupied by Cyril Dibb and Ernest Broomhead. Lot 2: Horner House Farm with barn, stables, cow houses, garden, cart shed, corn chamber, and outbuildings covering just over fourteen acres, occupied by Samuel Broadhead. Also, six cottages adjoining the farmhouse. There were many more lots of building land for sale, which afforded *"an excellent opportunity for builders and others to acquire plots of valuable freehold land admirably adapted for building purposes in a populous and growing district, and within a convenient distance of the extensive works of Messrs. S. Fox and Co., Ltd."* Stocksbridge Hall sold for £975, Horner House farm and cottages fetched £1,100, and the various building lots were bought by Mr. B. Schofield, John Cutts Kenworthy, J. B. Marsden, and Mr. Lindley.
- 1913: Four stone houses with gardens and vacant land known as Ling Bank, on Hoyle House Lane [Hole House Lane], Common Piece. These properties were said to command good tenants, and the present tenants were Ernest Bacon, Mark Firth, Mrs. Longford, and Robert Moore.

---

[277] In 1911, this was Isaiah Bagnall, the manager of the steel rolling mills

- 1913: Lot 1: Three stone-built freehold houses on Manchester Road at Deepcar known as Grove Row, in the occupations of Messrs. Firth, Allabone, and Beale. Each house had four rooms and a pantry, and there was a right of way from Henholmes Lane to the rear of these houses over the adjoining property. Lot 2: Four modern houses in Coronation Road, on the Hoyle House Estate, currently tenanted by Messrs. Couldwell, Fieldsend, Hulse and Littlewood.
- 1915: Twelve houses in Johnson Street. Seven of these houses (numbers 9, 11, 13, 15, 17, 19, and 20) faced Johnson Street and the other five were in the yard at the rear of the seven (numbers 10, 12, 14, 16, and 19). Four of the tenants were Hague, Longden, Tune and Westwood.
- 1919: Eight stone-built houses and a sales shop, outbuildings, and vacant land, adjoining the Friendship. Tenants were Knowles, Pickering, Swallow, Webster, Whittaker and others.
- 1920: Four stone-built houses called *"Prospect Cottages,"* close to the Rising Sun Inn, in the occupations of Messrs. Chandley, Kenworthy, Whittaker, and one other.

1915: Handyman wanted, to live in, respectable, reliable; personal application preferred. – T. E. Batty, Friendship Hotel, Stocksbridge.

BOWLING AT THE FRIENDSHIP
In January 1919, the Green 'Un newspaper reported that Tom Batty had taken over the Viola Bank bowling green and merged two bowling clubs, the Viola Bank and the Arundel Bowling Clubs, naming the new club the Friendship Hotel Bowling Club. They held their first meeting, which was well attended, at the Friendship. Mr. Batty, the *"genial host of the Friendship Hotel"* was said to be *"a bowler of no mean ability."* It was believed that, with the green under Tom's control, there was not the slightest doubt that the club would be successful.

Later that year Tom Batty decided to lay a bowling green on land behind the pub and he placed a notice in the Sheffield Daily Telegraph in November, putting this work out to tender. This green is still there today; it is currently used by Stocksbridge Friendship Bowling Club on a long-term lease.

Tom Batty was a particularly good bowler himself, and he loved sport. He also fielded a football team on land that he owned opposite the pub, on the other side of Manchester Road (this land was the site of the open market, then the college, and now the Co-operative Stores). Reports of the bowling matches appear regularly in the newspapers.

The Sheffield Daily Telegraph of 17th December 1920 reported on the annual dinner and prizegiving of the Friendship Club, and noted that *"with a new green, which will be one of the finest in South Yorkshire, great things are expected from the players next season."* The new green was opened one Tuesday evening in April 1921 by the club's president Mr. W. H. Robinson. He and Tom Batty played the first game, Batty winning by 21 to 18. *"The green – 40 yards square – was in splendid condition, and the members are looking forward to a very successful year,"* reported the Sheffield Daily Telegraph.[278] Mr. P. Schofield promised to present a cup, and Mr. W. H. Robinson would present another, to be called the *"Friendship Challenge Cup,"* the winner of which would also receive a set of bowls. After the opening, tea was served and there was a concert.

Later that year, in November, the club held its annual dinner and prize distribution at the Friendship, and around a hundred people attended. The club's main achievement was winning the Sheffield Association League Cup, for which the club received a silver trophy, and the fifteen players each received a gold medal. The Friendship Challenge Cup was won by F. Fieldsend, who also received a pair of bowls, and the runner-up, F. Stockton, was handed a gold medal. Other prizes were awarded, and the evening also had musical entertainment.

The bowling green was re-laid in 1924, the cost of which was defrayed by Tom Batty himself. The re-laying hampered practice, but the club still reached the final of the Sheffield and Hallamshire League (they were beaten by Dinnington Colliery). The Sheffield Daily Telegraph, reporting on the club's annual dinner in November 1926, called it *"one of the most important annual social functions in Stocksbridge and district."* Mr. G. E. Stembridge, J.P. proposed a toast to the club, congratulating it upon its healthy and vigorous state, and eulogising the great financial assistance rendered to the

---

[278] 21st April 1921

Sheffield Association by Tom Batty, who, it was said, was "*beloved by the members of the club.*" Congratulations went to Mr. J. Aspinall for his "*green wizardry*" and on his obtaining fourth prize in the Sheffield and Hallamshire Greenkeepers' Competition. The following year the club came second in the Greenkeeper's competition, and it was said that, had the owners and members not kindly loaned it out for an outside competition, it would have won. The Sheffield Association used it on several occasions.

In September 1927 one of the club's vice-presidents died. He was Albert Deakin Barge of Abbey Lane, Sheffield, and he was well known in business circles. He had been a director of the Sheffield Free Brewery Company (which supplied the Friendship), and for many years he had been an inspector of the United Yeast Company.

In 1930 another member of the club died, Charles Hampshire of Bracken Moor. He was 57 years old and was one of the most proficient bowlers in the Sheffield district, winning many trophies as a member of the Stocksbridge Friendship and the Stocksbridge and District Bowling Clubs. Representatives of both clubs attended his funeral.

The annual meeting and prize giving of 1930 was delayed because Tom Batty was ill. It took place the following April when he was by then "*happily restored to health.*" Mr. T. Dungworth proposed the toast of "*The Friendship Hotel Bowling Club,*" and, in doing so, said the name "*Friendship*" was synonymous with the name of Mr. Batty, one of the greatest sportsmen in the district. The secretary, Councillor Joseph Vardy, was too ill to attend, and he died in June that year. Vardy had been the secretary for two years, and for the previous four years, he had been the president of the local carnival held annually on behalf of local charities. In addition, he had been a member of the Stocksbridge and District Conservative Association, and for twenty-six years had been in the West Riding Police Force, eighteen of which were spent at Deepcar. For six years he was a member of the Stocksbridge Urban Council and was also a member of the Wortley Board of Guardians and the Old-Age Pensions Committee. He was Market Inspector at Stocksbridge for the last six years. He lived at Haywoods Lane, Deepcar, and was 56 years old.

1925: Barmaid, good, all-round, Wanted, respectable; age about 30; good wages and usual outings; no family; references. - Friendship Hotel, Stocksbridge.

STOCKSBRIDGE AND DISTRICT MOTOR-CYCLE CLUB
Involving himself in a different kind of sport, Tom Batty also provided a trophy for the Stocksbridge and District Motorcycle Club. In November 1930 six teams competed for the *"Friendship Trophy"* in an inter-club Reliability Trial, starting from the Friendship.[279] The club held a lot of their early meetings at Thomas Pladdey's Sportsman's Arms at Deepcar, and these were sometimes presided over by Tom Batty. Later meetings were held at the Rock Inn, Green Moor.

Tom Batty played a big part in Stocksbridge life, with the pub at its centre. He organised sporting events (football, bowls, knur and spell, races), shooting matches (birds and rabbits), he invested in property, hosted meetings of all kinds, and was active in organisations such as the R.A.O.B., the Licensed Victuallers' Association and the Conservatives. He also stood for, and was elected to, the Local Board (Council). As well as all this, he was one of the first directors on the board of the Schofield Brothers' Picture Palace venture in 1920.

Schofield Brothers (Stocksbridge) Ltd was registered as a company on the 13th February 1920. They were to take over, from 1st March, the motor transport business carried on by A. E. Schofield and P. Schofield on Manchester Road. They had capital of £25,000 in £1 shares, and Tom Batty was a director of this new company. They held their first meeting at the Friendship in March, and Percy Schofield was appointed chairman and managing director. It was decided that they should immediately embark on the business of picture house proprietors (as well as running the motor transport business). Articles in the newspapers talked of their plans to build a new, up-to-date picture palace in the centre of Stocksbridge.

Early films had been shown since 1911 in the former public hall, renamed the Electric Theatre. The Schofield Brothers had bought this from the West

---

[279] An organised ride which challenges a rider to complete a course, passing through designated control points, within a pre-set time limit.

Riding Electric Theatres, and closed it soon afterwards, in February 1922, a year after they opened the new Picture Palace (in May 1921). The new cinema cost £30,000 and had accommodation for 1,000 people including 300 in the circle, and an orchestra. It also had a café, and it was opened by Mr. R. H. Rimington of Broomhead Hall.

Two years later, towards the end of 1923, they felt that they should go into voluntary liquidation in order to set up a new company to run the cinema, separate from the motor business.[280] The cinema,[281] the public hall (the former Electric Theatre), and the motor garages and buildings were all offered for sale separately. These would not necessarily be sold to the highest bidder, so in the case of the cinema, presumably the purchaser would have had to agree to let the Schofield Brothers carry on running it as before. Whoever bought the Public Hall (where the Electric Theatre had been) had to agree not to run it as a cinema or theatre for at last ten years. They registered the new company in February 1924 as the Palace (Stocksbridge) Ltd. Percy Schofield was once again made chairman. The cinema closed on the 23rd July 1966 and became a bingo hall. The building still stands today and houses various businesses.

STOCKSBRIDGE TRADESMAN DEAD: October 1926

Mr. Alfred Marshall died on the 26th October 1926 at the age of 44. He had been the head of the firm of Marshall Brothers, coal factors, and had built up a successful business after starting his working life work as a joiner's apprentice at Stocksbridge. Mr. Marshall was an active member of the Friendship Bowling Club and the local R.A.O.B. Lodge, and he left a widow and one child.

WOMEN'S BRANCH, STOCKSBRIDGE BRITISH LEGION: 1928

The British Legion was founded in 1921 to help ex-servicemen. One of its founders was Earl Haig. It is said that, after forming the organisation, he thought something was missing, and he later told Lady Haig that what was missing was *"the wife of the British Legion."* Women's sections were formed

---

[280] The coaches etc. were auctioned off in March 1923, and included 28- and 18-seater charabancs, a Daimler limousine, a Ford touring car, a 14-seater saloon car, and others.

[281] Described as *"built in 1920, and one of the finest cinemas in the West Riding. Handsomely decorated and equipped throughout."*

all over the country, and the Stockbridge branch was formed in February 1928, the year Haig died.

They held their first annual dinner at the Friendship in February 1929, and the Sheffield Daily Telegraph reported on it, with the headline *"Women's Dinner. Novelty for Stocksbridge British Legion."* They added that the guests, artistes and attendees were all women, and that *"the members of the fair sex present were not reluctant to indulge in speech-making."* The evening was a great success, and the branch was thriving, with a growing bank balance and increasing membership. The secretary was Mrs. E. Gill, with Mrs. H. Brown as treasurer, and Mrs. G. Stanley was chair. Mrs. Gill was presented with a silver and china two-tiered fruit stand, and Mrs. Brown received a silver fruit dish, as a thank you for their hard work over the past year. Members of the Deepcar branch, an offshoot, were also present, and after dinner, there were toasts and music. The Telegraph said that the women's section *"should never forget that it was a great privilege to belong to the British Legion."*

The male members of the British Legion held their dinner later that month, also at the Friendship, with Captain H. E. Rimington Wilson of Broomhead Hall presiding. Tom Batty was presented with a silver cigar case on behalf of the branch.

THE VOLUNTEER FIRE BRIGADE: 1931
In April 1931 members of the Stocksbridge Urban Council were the guests of the Stocksbridge Volunteer Fire Brigade at a dinner held at the Friendship. First Officer Len Charlesworth presided over a large attendance, which included ex-Captains Ernest Jackson and J. Adams, previous members of the brigade. Tribute was paid to the work of the brigade by Councillor B. Butcher, chairman of the Fire Brigade Committee, and other members of the Council.[282]

OLD MOTHER WORKMAN
In his book The History of Stocksbridge, Jack Branston tells the tale of one of the characters that frequented the Friendship, a widow called Mrs. Emma

---

[282] I have written a history of the Stocksbridge Fire Brigade, which can be found here: https://www.stocksbridgetimespast.co.uk/stocksbridge-fire-brigade

Workman, who lived at Bramall House, which was on Bramall Lane, behind the steelworks. Her husband Edward was originally from London and came to Stockbridge to work as a navvy on the construction of the reservoir at Midhope, later finding work in Fox's. He died in 1926 aged 76 and Emma stayed in the little house on Bramall Lane. Old Mother Workman, as she was known, had always been neat and tidy, wearing her white aprons from the days when she worked in service. However, when her husband died, he lay in the house for three days before she told anyone of his passing. She took in a lodger to help pay the bills and break the loneliness, and he was called Thomas Cattell. The 1939 Register shows her living at Bramall Cottage along with Thomas, a retired steelworker. Tom was apparently a teetotaller, but not Mrs. Workman, who Jack says took to the bottle after losing her husband. Jack Branston, who worked for the Co-op, said that:

"Every Friday evening she would come into the village to do her shopping. She would come into the Co-op shop at precisely 7.45 p.m. and ask for her "lucky bag" which contained all the pairings which fell off our bacon machine blade, fat, bone, rind, string etc. for this she paid sixpence, we saved all this from one visit to the next. Once she had got this "lucky bag," that signalled her shopping was over. Next port of call was Tom Batty's at the Friendship Hotel. Once in the hotel she would stay until five minutes to ten, ten o'clock was turning out time in those days, this just gave her time to catch the Sheffield bus at Victoria Street for Half Hall. Nine times out of ten she got "tipsy" and had to be helped on the bus. When the bus arrived at the Half Hall terminus, she was assisted off the bus by the bus crew and handed over to old Tom who was there with his wheelbarrow. On one occasion Tom got the barrow and her ladyship too near the deep gutter which runs down the roadside in the Underbank, with the result that she lay there for quite some time underneath the barrow, old Tom shouting for help for he could not get her free. Help did eventually come when a workman who had knocked-off the ten o'clock shift, removed the barrow off Mrs. Workman, then lifting her back into it, left the rest to old Tom to get her safely home." Emma died in 1943 at the age of 79 at Netherfield Buildings in Thurlstone, Penistone; sadly, she ended her days in the Workhouse.

Tom Batty retired in July 1935 after being a licensee for sixty-one years. At 82 years of age, he was the oldest licensee in the Sheffield district, and had started in the pub trade when he was 21 years old. Members of the Sheffield,

Rotherham and District Licensed Victuallers' Association organised a presentation in his honour, giving him a chair to commemorate his 82nd birthday and to celebrate the fact that he had been a member of the Association for 61 years. Three other veteran licensees paid tribute to his work for the Association; Mr. E. Watts (aged 78), Mr. C. Matthews (73), and Mr. C. I. Needham (66). The event was held at the Magnet Hotel, Southey. The assembled company heard that Tom Batty had been a licensee since the age of 21 when he first became the landlord of the Friendship. In that same year (1874) he joined the Sheffield, Rotherham and District Licensed Victuallers' Association and, with the exception of five years, when he held a licence in Penistone, which is out of the Sheffield area, he had been a member of the Association ever since.

The presentation was made by Mr. Harry Watts, the president of the Association. Mr. G. H. Greenfield (secretary) described Mr. Batty as an *"old stalwart"* of the Association, who was looked up to by all the members. He had been a senior trustee of the L.V.A.'s Benevolent Fund for thirty years.

Tom continued to live at the Friendship after he retired. The 1936 electoral register recorded a Doris May Rodgers listed as living there as well. The 1937 electoral register recorded Annie and Edwin Bamforth as being in residence. At one time this couple ran the corner shop at the top of Smithy Hill which had previously been run by Edwin's parents Edwin and Bethia. Just before moving back to Stocksbridge Edwin and Annie had been living at Brightside in Sheffield.

Thomas Edward Batty died two years after retiring, on the 15th May 1937, aged 83. He passed away at the Claremont nursing home in Sheffield. Obituaries praised him as a generous benefactor to the village and said that Stocksbridge mourned a good friend. The Sheffield Independent printed a large list of mourners at the funeral and commented that it was one of the biggest funerals that Stocksbridge had known for many years. Members of the Hand o' Friendship R.A.O.B. Lodge headed the cortege, followed by members of the British Legion, and the Brass Band in uniform.

The service was held at Stocksbridge Church, and the Rev. J. Garfield Roberts payed tribute to Mr. Batty's qualities and generosity to good causes.[283] The burial took place at Bolsterstone, where an R.A.O.B. service was conducted. There were representatives from a great many places, including the Licensed Victuallers' Association, the Sheffield Free Brewery, the Old Albion Brewery, Stocksbridge Urban District Council, the licensing trade, The Hand o' Friendship R.A.O.B. Lodge, the Stocksbridge Branch of the British Legion, Stocksbridge Old Brass Band, Stocksbridge Bowling Club, Stocksbridge Fire Brigade, the Yorkshire Bowling Association, Sheffield and Hallamshire Bowls Association, and many others.

His will was proved by his daughter Lucy Gertrude, the wife of Arthur Hoyland.[284] He left just over £21,626 (net £6,877).[285] Gertrude inherited some property including the Friendship, houses, shops, the market (which was held on land opposite the pub) and several fields. The pub was sold at auction, and she derived a rental income from the other property. Her son Frank (known as Dick) was the usual rent collector.

The death of Tom Batty saw the end of an era for the Friendship pub, which had been opened by his father George in about 1859 as a wayside beerhouse and been expanded to become a successful hotel and pub. The Friendship was put up for sale in October 1937 and was bought by Truswell's Brewery for £25,250. The bidding had started at £10,000 and rose rapidly by increases of £500 to £25,000 when it was raised to £25,250 by the brewery's representative, who had been a keen bidder throughout.

Having bought the pub, the brewery installed someone to run it, and that was George Henry Rogerson. In January 1938, Lucy Hoyland transferred the licence to Rogerson *"under an agreement with Messrs. Truswell's Brewery;"* this included an off-licence and also a music licence. George was married to

---

[283] When the Rev. Roberts died in 1939, there was an R.A.O.B. service held at his funeral. He lay in state at St. Matthias church, five women parishioners keeping an all-night vigil by the side of his coffin. He had been the vicar there for over fifteen years. A large number of people attended his funeral, and he was laid to rest in Midhope churchyard. As with Tom Batty's funeral two years earlier, there were representatives present from the many organisations he had been involved with.

[284] Lucy Gertrude married Arthur Hoyland at Penistone church in 1897. She gave her father's occupation as "wine and spirit merchant" on the marriage certificate. The couple and their family lived at Ecklands Hamlet, Thurlstone. Arthur owned an engineering firm and a garage at the Flouch.

[285] The Bank of England's Inflation Calculator estimates this as £1,424.190 (£452,888)

Florence (nee Hadfield), and had previously been a cutlery manufacturer. His father, also George, had been a grocer and beer retailer in Sheffield. Previous to their move to Stocksbridge, the Rogersons had been living in Rotherham. Their son Joe was a fairly well-known golfer, who played at the Sitwell Park Golf Club in Rotherham. He helped his father in the running of the pub, including keeping the books, and during the War, he also worked as an ambulance driver.

The Friendship is still open as a pub today, but, as with all the pubs in this book, we end in 1939, when Britain was at the very beginning of World War II. Great Britain declared war on Germany on the 3rd September 1939.

And finally ... A downed German plane, a Messerschmitt 109, once made an appearance on land behind the Friendship. It was also put on view at Barker's Pool in Sheffield. It was shot down over the south of England (apparently it did not have the range to fly as far north as Sheffield), and it was then put on tour around the country to raise funds. Money was collected from people who wanted to see it or sit in it.

In this photograph, taken in about 1905, a group of boys are standing outside the Friendship. Some of them have blackened faces so they have probably just come from the pit. There are three balls hanging above the shop next to the pub, the sign of the pawnbroker. On the right, W. Hoyle's shop can be seen at the bottom of Johnson Street; this row has been demolished, as have the houses on the far right.

A MISCELLANY

THE OFFICIAL ALE-TESTER
Writing in 1909, F. W. Hackwood said that a couple of hundred years ago, ale was tested for no impurity other than sugar. If beer had been watered down, this could be disguised by the addition of sugar. Believe it or not, there was a way of testing this out….

The official ale tester wore leather breeches. "He would enter an inn unexpectedly, draw a glass of ale, pour it on a wooden bench, and then sit down in the little puddle he had made. There he would sit for thirty minutes by the clock. He would converse, he would smoke, he would drink with all who asked him to, but he would be very careful not to change his position in any way. At the end of the half-hour he would make as if to rise, and this was the test of the ale; for, if the ale was impure, if it had sugar in it, the tester's leather breeches would stick fast to the bench, but if there was no sugar in the liquor no impression would be present – in other words, the tester would not stick to the bench."[286]

TIPPLING ON SUNDAY
Tippling on Sunday during the hours of divine service was punished by the offender being placed in the stocks. In 1790 nine men were locked in the stocks at Sheffield all at one time for this offence. In some places,

---
[286] Hackwood, F. W. Inns, Ales and Drinking Customer of Old England. London. T. Fisher Unwin: 1909

churchwardens would go around the parish looking into the public houses to see if anyone was drinking during the time the church service was being held. This was going on until at least the 1850s. The last case of an offender being placed in the stocks for drunkenness occurred at Newbury, Berkshire, in 1872.

1603: AN ACT TO RESTRAIN THE INORDINATE HAUNTING AND TIPLING IN INNS, ALEHOUSES AND OTHER VICTUALLING HOUSES:
Steps have always been taken to prevent the establishment of places for people to congregate and misspend their time and money by idleness and excessive drinking. This extract is from an Act passed in the first year of the reign of James I, 1603: "*The ancient, true, and principal use of inns, taverns, alehouses, victualling houses, and other houses for common entertainment, is for [the] receipt, relief and lodging of travellers and strangers, and the refreshment of persons upon lawful business [...] and are not intended for entertainment and harbouring lewd or idle people to spend and consume their money or time there.*" The objects of the law were "*to prevent intemperance and nurseries of vice and debauchery.*"

AND FINALLY – WHY NOT
Writing on men in the East End of London, Sir Walter Besant said, "*There is the public house for a club, and perhaps the workman spends, night after night, more than he should upon beer. Let us remember, if he needs excuse, that his employers have found him no better place and no better amusement than to sit in a tavern, drink beer (generally in moderation), and talk and smoke tobacco. Why not? A respectable tavern is a very harmless place; the circle which meets there is the society of the workman: it is his life: without it he might as well have been a factory hand of the good old time – such as hands were forty years ago; and then he would have made but two journeys a day – one from bed to mill, and the other from mill to bed.*"
Sir Walter Besant (1836-1901), As We Are And As We May Be
Novelist, historian, philanthropist, and social reformer

A (VERY) BRIEF HISTORY OF LICENSING LAW

I do not pretend vast and expert knowledge of the complexities surrounding the licensing laws, but a bit of knowledge is needed to put things into context. But if you don't really understand them, take comfort from the fact that many others did not understand them either, including the magistrates whose job it was to interpret them. A 19th century Lord Chief Justice described it as "*a labyrinth of chaotic legislation.*"

The 1872 Licensing Act was incredibly complicated, and the Barnsley magistrates, whose job it was to implement the Act, were on record as saying that "*there were many clauses in the Act not quite so clear as they ought to be, but with care and attention the Bench thought they could master them.*"

"*Most aspects of the law relating to offences on licensed premises have at one time or another – and in many cases a number of times – been the subject of careful consideration in the courts; but in spite of all the time and skill that have been expended upon them many points are still far from being beyond argument.*" – meaning that they are open to interpretation and discussion.[287]

Ever since beer was first sold, attempts were made to control the brewing and sale of it, and over the years more and more legislation has been passed which encompasses everything from religious and class issues to a desire to exert authority and to raise revenue through taxes. As time went on, the Temperance Movement waged war on public houses and the evils of drink, influencing the magistrates who had the power to close public houses. A

---

[287] The Journal of Criminal Law, Volume 11, July 1947

piece in the Gentleman's Magazine in September 1736 claimed that public houses were corrupting and debauching the nation, ruining honest labourers, and fostering crime.

BREWSTER SESSIONS
Authority over the sale of alcohol was in the hands of the Justices of the Peace (J.P.s), who held annual licensing sessions, known as Brewster Sessions. This is where the granting of new licences, the renewal of existing licences, and the transfer of licences was dealt with. There were often two sittings, with the second Sessions being used to hear appeals and make decisions which had been deferred from the first Sessions. Publicans had to attend in person, and it was here that the "**BLACKLIST**" was considered; any landlord who had broken the law had to face the magistrates to learn whether they would be fined or have their licence suspended or revoked.

LICENCES
A licence was granted for one year and came with certain conditions – no adulteration of drink, no drunkenness or disorder allowed on the premises, no unlawful games, no short measures, no allowing criminals or prostitutes to gather, no gambling, and so on. Pubs were not allowed to open during church services on Sundays, Christmas Day, and Good Friday.

1830 – THE BEERHOUSE ACT
There had been a huge increase in the number of people drinking spirits, especially gin, and the government took steps to curb this by passing an Act in 1830 to promote the sale of beer. The evils of society were increasingly blamed on gin, whereas beer was seen as being both nutritious and often safer to drink than water (in fact, the early Temperance Movement promoted moderate beer drinking rather than total abstinence). William Hogarth's famous engraving entitled *"Beer Street"* pictured the merits of beer drinking whilst his *"Gin Lane"* depicted the horrors of gin consumption, with a half-naked mother letting her baby fall to the ground. Beer had always been a common drink, usually home-brewed, and even children drank it, though they would have had *"small beer"* which was much weaker. Andrew Boorde, a 16th physician, decreed that water was *"not wholesome solely by itself for an Englishman."* In many towns and villages, it was not healthy to drink the water, which was often contaminated.

This Act brought in a major change. From 1830 until 1869, the pub trade was split into either fully licensed premises (selling beer, wine, and spirits) or beerhouses (selling just beer). The former were licensed by the magistrates and the latter obtained a certificate to sell beer direct from the Excise. In an attempt to increase the consumption of beer rather than spirits, the Act abolished the duty on beer. From 1830, any householder of good character whose house was assessed to a certain rateable value could now sell beer from their premises without obtaining a licence from the justices; they paid the small sum of two guineas direct to the Excise. This beer could be brewed at home or bought from a brewery. A great many householders then began to sell beer from the front rooms of their homes; in Liverpool 20,000 beerhouses were opened, almost overnight! It was common for a woman to run the beerhouse whilst her husband was at work, for there was little profit to be made by selling beer alone. Farmers' wives would also brew and sell beer to local workers or passers-by. Beerhouses had more restrictive opening hours than fully licensed premises.

Local pubs that opened as beerhouses in the 1830s include the Castle Inn, Coach and Horses, Royal Oak, Sportsman's Arms at Wigtwizzle, and the Travellers Inn at Deepcar.

Following this 1830 Act, tens of thousands of new beerhouses opened up, but (not surprisingly) this did nothing to reduce public drunkenness, as had been hoped, and many of the new places were unhygienic and unsuitable. In London, the number of beerhouses had grown so vast that the licensing authorities invited applications for full wine and spirit licenses so that they might gain some control over the sale of alcohol. In 1834 "*off*" licences were granted for the sale of beer "*not to be consumed on the premises,*" and in villages and towns all over the country, many shopkeepers opened their own beershop, and sold beer alongside their usual goods. Beerhouses often became the haunt of criminals and prostitutes and many of them were hard to police, being in out-of-the-way locations. In 1869, almost forty years after the Act was passed, all beerhouses were once again brought under the stricter control of the licensing magistrates.

1860 REFRESHMENT HOUSES AND WINE LICENCES ACT
This Act was introduced to free up the sale of wine, a temperance measure which aimed to promote the sale of light wine and decrease the consumption

of strong spirits. Duty on wine was reduced and shopkeepers could now sell wine for consumption off the premises (it was decanted from barrels into bottles). Places that offered entertainment and food could also now sell wine to their customers. In 1861 this measure was explicitly extended to beerhouses, although the take-up was relatively low. It seems contradictory that, while these measures were being taken to decrease the consumption of spirits, from 1861 grocers could apply for a licence to sell spirits. The idea was to allow *"respectable people"* to buy spirits without needing to enter a public house. It was argued that this increased secret drinking among women, especially the middle and upper classes, and a woman who would never have dreamt of entering a public house would now be able to buy spirits alongside her groceries.

1869 WINE AND BEERHOUSE ACT

The huge growth in the number of beerhouses had led to this new legislation, and magistrates were then able to close disorderly beerhouses and make it much harder for someone to obtain a new beerhouse licence. A licence could be refused if the house had been *"disorderly"* and frequented by thieves, prostitutes and persons of bad character. A licence could be refused if the applicant himself was not of good character or if he had previously lost a licence because of misconduct. An Act of 1872 decreed that a licence would not be issued if the house in question was of too low a rateable value. Over the subsequent decades many beerhouses closed, but some were purchased by breweries or became fully licensed public houses. The J.P.s based their decisions to grant licences on police reports and inspections of the premises; the applicant had to be suitable, his premises had to be suitable, and the needs of the locality were taken into account - if there were already several licensed premises nearby, the new premises would be deemed *"unnecessary"* and the application would be refused.

BEING DRUNK ON LICENSED PREMISES

It was, believe it or not, an offence to be drunk in a pub. The Licensing Act of 1872 stated that: *"Every person found drunk in any highway or other public place whether a building or not or on any licensed premises shall be liable to a penalty..."* A landlord could be fined for permitting drunkenness on his licensed premises, and he could lose his licence for being drunk on his own licensed premises. Passed during the Victorian era, this law was probably concerned with keeping the workforce sober enough to be productive. In fact, it remains an offence for a landlord to sell or attempt to sell alcohol to a customer who is drunk. It was not easy for the police to prove in court that someone was drunk – after all, what defines *"drunk?"* Cumberland magistrate Sir Wilfred Lawson recalled a day when he was sitting on the Bench, and there was a long discussion about whether a man in a certain case was actually drunk. A witness, a retired barmaid, said that in her opinion a man was really drunk *"When he falls down and cannot get up again."*[288] In 1864 the landlady of a pub in Beverley, who had been summoned for permitting drunkenness on her licensed premises, defined drunkenness as the inability to stand up, referring to a customer who had been drinking for nine hours Christmas Eve and was *"merry, and quite jolly, but not lushy."*[289] There was a well-known rhyme by Thomas Love Peacock that said:

> *"Not drunk is he who from the floor*
> *Can rise alone and still drink more:*
> *But drunk is he, who prostrate lies,*
> *Without the power to drink or rise."*

This difficulty also extended to proving that a landlord had been responsible for serving a customer so much alcohol that they got drunk. How could he tell if a customer was already drunk when he came into his pub? Again, what defines *"drunk?"* Who would the magistrates believe? The police, the landlord, or the allegedly drunk person and his drinking companions? The landlord of the Friendship, Elijah Askew, was summoned to court for being *"incapably drunk on his own licensed premises"* in 1888, but in court his solicitor argued that he was not drunk, merely *"excited."*

LICENCE TRANSFER DATES

Certain days were set aside every year for the transfer of licences. The Brewster Sessions were held annually, but other dates were set aside throughout the year because licences would need to be transferred when the pub changed hands or the licensee died (the executors of the deceased's will would apply for a transfer to themselves and would then, after probate had

---

[288] Cited in Russell, G. W. E. (ed.) Sir Wilfred Lawson: A Memoir. London: Smith, Elder: 1909. p.124

[289] Cited in Crowther, J. Beverly in Mid-Victorian Times. Beverley: Hutton Press 1990. p.119

been granted, transfer the licence on – in many cases, to the widow of the late landlord).

PROTECTION ORDERS
Protection Orders were granted when the Bench gave permission for a new landlord to take over the house before an official transfer day. The official transfer would then be granted on the appointed day. Without the protection order, the landlord or landlady could be prosecuted for selling intoxicating liquor without a licence.

WWI and WWII
During WWI, there were four big changes in the way public houses were run. The Defence of the Realm Act was passed in 1914 immediately after the outbreak of war and was designed to support the Allies. It now became illegal to "*treat*" someone to a drink, that is, to buy another person a drink. There was no credit given, and it was made illegal to serve a "*long-pull*" (serving more than the correct measure to attract custom). Opening hours were also drastically reduced, with pubs only being allowed to open for a few hours at noon and a few hours in the evening. Off-sales hours were also reduced; off-sales of beer ceased at 8pm, and off-sales of spirits was limited to the hours of 12 noon until 2.30pm on weekdays only, an exception being made for medical emergencies. The price of drink rose, and its strength fell. Dilution of whisky, brandy and rum was made compulsory.

In 1915 measures were introduced to control the supply of liquor to those employed in supplying and transporting war materials. These measures especially applied to London, the seaports and the large industrial centres.

Another change was that more women were seen in pubs, usually those who had been enlisted in the factories to help with the war effort. The drinking of women in public offended a great many people. Drinking was also seen to interfere with workers' productivity.

The shortage of munitions that jeopardised the war effort during the early weeks of 1915 was attributed to drink. David Lloyd George, the minister for munitions, made a speech in 1915 in which he claimed that "*Drink is doing us more damage in the War than all the German submarines put together."*[290] To a deputation from the Shipbuilding Employers' Federation a month later he declared, *"We are fighting Germany, Austria and Drink; and, as far as I can see, the greatest of these three deadly foes is Drink.*" He was not a teetotaller, but he did initiate a campaign for complete abstinence for the duration of the war, even managing to persuade King George V to support this. A statement was issued that *"no wines spirits or beer will be consumed in any of His Majesty's houses after today, Tuesday April 6th, 1915."* The letter columns of The Times were filled with debate about prohibition.

The maximum penalty for defying Government orders was six months' imprisonment. Most of these measures were repealed after the end of the War, with the exception of the afternoon gap in opening hours, which was not repealed until as late as 1988.

A completely different stance was taken in WWII, when pubs became the friend of the nation, not its enemy. The supply of beer was deemed to be vital to morale, but it was not just the beer; pubs became an escape from the bombs and the bad news and the blackout, and even people who would never have normally gone into a pub found themselves seeking them out. Pubs were now social hubs, and even women were more tolerated. Early on in the war, A. P. Herbert, a politician and novelist, commented that *"the British pub, the people's club, has justified its existence as perhaps it never did before. For it has been the one human corner, a centre not of beer but bonhomie; the one place where after dark the collective heart of the nation could be seen and felt, beating resolute and strong."*[291] The pub cellars provided a refuge from the bombing raids and gave a sense of camaraderie to those who found themselves hunkered down there. A condition of the licence was that the pub had to be open when it was supposed to be, and even pubs with bomb damage would try their best to open for business, instilling a sense of normality and routine among the chaos. And it wasn't just civilians that relied on the pub; so too did the armed forces, including the Americans stationed over here. There was a booklet published which gave

---

[290] A speech made by Lloyd George at Bangor 28th February 1918.
[291] Sir Alan Patrick Herbert C. H. (1890-1971), an English humourist, novelist, playwright and law reform activist who served as an Independent M.P. for Oxford University from the 1935 general election to the 1950 general election, when university constituencies were abolished.

humorous guidance about how they should behave. Of pubs it said: *"The British are beer drinkers and can "hold it." Beer is now below peace-time strength but can still make a man's tongue wag at both ends. You will be welcome in British taverns as long as you remember one thing – the inn or tavern is the poor man's club or gathering place where men have come to see their friends not strangers."*[292]

---

[292] A Short Guide to Great Britain. War & Navy Departments. Washington: 1942

GLOSSARY

ALEHOUSE: where householders sold their home-brewed ale.

ASSIZES: The Courts of Assize, or the Assizes, were periodic courts held around the country and heard mainly criminal cases, although they did hear the occasional civil case. These courts were where the most serious cases were heard, which were committed to the Assizes by the Quarter Sessions. They were heard by visiting judges from the higher courts based in London. The judges conducted trials dealing with the most serious offenders such as forgers, highwaymen, burglars, murderers, rapists, and, historically, could pass the death sentence or commit someone to be transported overseas to one of the Colonies such as Australia or Van Diemen's Land (Tasmania). These courts also had juries consisting of twelve men. Civil cases heard here would be those concerning entitlement to land or money.

BEERHOUSE: Allowed to sell beer, often home-brewed, but not stronger drinks.

BEERSHOP: Allowed to sell beer for consumption off the premises.

BREWSTER SESSIONS: When the licensing magistrates sat to deal with licensed premises; they considered new applications for pub licences, renewals of existing licences, and the transfer of licences.

CENSUS: The Census is an official survey of the population, noting details such as age, marital status, occupation, place of birth, and so on. As far as family historians are concerned, the first useful census was taken in 1841; it noted name, age (rounded up or down to the nearest five years for adults), address (often just the name of the village or hamlet), whether male or female, occupation and whether or not someone was born in the county in which they were living. There was also space to write whether someone was born in Scotland, Ireland, or foreign parts. Successive census returns were taken in every ten years. The 1921 census will not become available until the hundred-year closure rule ends. Each census included progressively more information; relationships to the head of household were recorded, and a more precise place of birth. Ages were more accurate, although only as accurate as someone knew or was prepared to say. Addresses also became more specific although house numbers might not be included (and if they were, they could have changed over time). The number of rooms was also sometimes recorded. The 1911 census was the first one that a householder filled out themselves, and it asked how long a couple had been married, how many children they'd had, and whether any had died. The census is a snapshot of the entire country on one particular night of the year it was taken.

CENSUS ENUMERATOR: The Census Enumerator was employed to collect and record the census details from householders. Each Enumerator had a specific area to cover.

CLUB ROOM: A large room separate from the rest of the pub – often upstairs – which was used by clubs and societies for meetings. Members often had to pay a *"wet rent"* to the landlord – in other words, they were expected to buy a drink whilst there.

COMMERCIAL ROOM: A better-quality room where commercial travellers and better-off tradesmen could gather. The Rising Sun on Hunshelf Bank advertised that it had a commercial room.

FREE HOUSE: A pub not tied to a brewery, whose landlord can source his supplies from wherever he likes

INN: similar to a tavern but also somewhere a traveller could find lodging. Inns usually only sold beer and ale.

MONEY, WEIGHTS AND MEASURES: Money, weights and measures in this book are those that were in use at the time. Before 1971 our currency was pounds, shillings, and pence (£sd or Lsd). There were 4 farthings in a penny, 12 pennies in a shilling and 20 shillings in £1. A guinea was worth

21 shillings (just over a pound) and a florin was worth two shillings. Other coins included a ha'penny (half a penny), thruppenny bit (worth three pennies) and a sixpence (worth six pennies), a half-crown (two shillings and sixpence) and a crown (five shillings). Weights and measures include inches, feet, yards, rod/perch/pole, chains, furlongs, mile, acres; ounces, pounds, stones, hundredweight, and ton; gills, pints, quarts, and gallons. There are plenty of good conversion charts online.

PETTY SESSIONS: These were local courts presided over by magistrates and usually heard cases without a jury. They were the lowest tier in the court system and heard cases of a less serious nature such as petty theft, poaching, assault, neighbourhood disputes, drunkenness, evasion of turnpike tolls, bastardy examinations, absconding apprentices, and so on. If a case was serious, it would be referred on from here to be tried at the Quarter Sessions. The Sessions met frequently, every few weeks on average, and so local matters were dealt with quickly.

POLICE: Our concept of a police force is a relatively recent one. Each parish in England had a parish constable, and, along with the other parish posts such as Overseer of the Poor and Church Warden, the Constable was usually unpaid, although he could claim expenses.

Constables were originally chosen by the manor court and sworn in by a magistrate, and they were almost wholly responsible for the maintenance of law and order in the parishes for many centuries. In 1842 the power to choose a constable was transferred to the church vestry.[293] The various parish posts were often rotated amongst householders, and a man could refuse to serve, but he would have to pay a fine.

Inns and alehouses came under the Constable's watchful eye, and he would report drunkenness, unlawful gaming, keepers of *"bawdy houses"* [brothels], drinking during church services, serving out of hours, and other wrongdoings.

---

[293] The vestry was a decision-making body which took its name from the room in which it sat. By the Act of 1842, the requirement to hold the office of constable was that a man had to occupy lands or tenements assessed to the rates (poor rate or county rate) of £4 or more.

The parish constable had a huge range of duties to perform. There was so much to do that some constables could not manage, and some just did what they could and what they deemed most important. W. E. Tate suggests that many constables contented themselves with levying a modest poor rate, whipping an occasional vagrant, leaving rogues alone so long as they made no attempt to interfere with him, and attending the Sessions.[294] In 1745 Thomas Crawshaw, Bradfield constable for that year, submitted expenses of £12 16s. 2d. These included journeys to Sheffield, Rotherham and Doncaster, meetings with the chief constable, delivering the names of Catholics to Doncaster, as well as land tax and window tax warrants, attending the Coroner's Courts, and providing coal and taking it to the [night] Watch at Bolsterstone and Stannington.[295]

QUARTER SESSIONS: Quarter Sessions were courts that sat in the seat of the county or county borough. They were held four times a year (hence "*quarter*" sessions) and trials were held before justices of the peace. These Sessions dealt with a range of crimes that were deemed to be too serious to be dealt with at the Petty Sessions but were usually less serious crimes than those tried at the Assize Courts. They also had civil jurisdiction to deal with matters such as licensing, supervision of the highways, and offences against the poor laws. They were abolished in 1971.

SALOON BAR: Also known as the "*best room*," the saloon would have a carpet and upholstered seats. Any women that went in the pub (usually accompanied by a man) would sit in this bar.

SMOKE ROOM: Another better-quality room where men could relax and smoke (although there was no restriction on smoking in the other rooms).

SNUG: A smaller room set apart from the taproom and the saloon, but still with access to the bar. It was more private, and the window glass might be frosted. There are very few snugs left, as they were incorporated into the rest of the pub when modernisations took place. The police didn't like them because they encouraged secret drinking (they were harder to supervise),

---

[294] Tate, W. E. The Parish Chest. Cambridge University Press: 1969
[295] From the Bradfield Guard Book, parish chest records held by Sheffield Archives, Shoreham Street

although the police themselves were known to sneak in for a quick drink now and again.

TAPROOM: Also known as the public bar. The taproom was more basic than the "*best room*," and would have either a tiled floor or bare floorboards. These were usually covered with sawdust to absorb the spitting and spillages. There would be bare wooden benches and stools, and maybe pub games too. Traditionally, drinks were slightly cheaper in the taproom, and it was also where the men congregated.

TAVERN: A place to drink and eat, and also to do business in. A tavern usually sold wine; its earliest meaning was "*wine shop.*"

TIED HOUSES A great many publicans had always brewed their own beer and run their pubs whilst pursuing another occupation; in this area, there were landlords who also worked as blacksmiths, wheelwrights, farmers, and stonemasons. Wives and children would run the pub in the landlord's absence, and many women carried on running the pub after they were widowed. In the early 18th century, about two-thirds of publicans brewed their own beer, and records for public houses in this area record that there were brew-houses attached to certain pubs including the Castle Inn, the Royal Oak and the King and Miller. It wasn't really until the early 20th century that this changed. The Sheffield Daily Telegraph of 1927 reported that "*The question of holders of on-licences engaged in other employment or occupation had been further considered, and the [Sheffield licensing justices'] committee, whilst still holding to the opinion that a licensee should give his whole time to the conduct of his house, had decided to continue to consider each case on its merits when applications for licences or transfers were received.*"

The big change to this way of doing things happened when breweries began to take control of pubs. They often offered loans, credit, or investment, and landlords gradually became "*tied*" to the breweries, buying their supplies from one particular brewery only. Breweries also began to buy up public houses when they came up for auction. Sheffield lagged behind the national trend for a while, retaining a higher proportion of publicans who brewed their own beer, but this eventually changed. Tom Batty of the Friendship ran a free house for a lot longer than did any of the others locally. When he died, the pub was bought at auction by a Sheffield brewery. Publicans gradually lost their independence as more and more pubs became tied to the breweries, and pubs tended to change hands more frequently as the breweries installed tenants, who they could soon get rid of if things did not work out. Breweries added new facias, advertising boards, ornate windows, and so on, and often enlarged the pubs they bought.

1939 REGISTER With WWII looming, the government announced that a National Register would be compiled (similar to the previous census returns) should war break out. Germany invaded Poland on 1st September 1939, and Britain declared war on the 3rd. Consequently, the plans for the Register were activated, and a National Registration Day took place on 29th September. The purpose of this was to co-ordinate the war effort at home, and the register would also be used to issue identity cards, organise rationing, etc. It was later used when the N.H.S. was being formed. Because the 1931 Census was destroyed in an air-raid, and the 1941 census was never taken, the 1939 Register is an important resource for historians. It lists address, name, marital status, actual date of birth, and occupation. For women, this was usually *"unpaid domestic duties."*

The Prime Minister Winston L. S. Churchill was recorded at Admiralty, Whitehall, SW1; born 30th November 1874, occupation 1st Lord of the Admiralty. Another hand has written above this, "Prime Minister." It was a working document, and when a woman married her new surname would be added. If a person was also employed in war work – A.R.P. Warden, ambulance driver, First Aid worker, or auxiliary fireman, this was also recorded.

"One Autumn night, in Sudbury town,
Across the meadows bare and brown,
The windows of the wayside inn
Gleamed red with fire-light through the leaves
Of woodbine, hanging from the eaves
Their crimson curtains rent and thin."
As ancient is this hostelry
As any in the land may be,
Built in the old Colonial day,
When men lived in a grander way,
With ampler hospitality;
A kind of old Hobgoblin Hall,
Now somewhat fallen to decay,
With weather-stains upon the wall,
And stairways worn, and crazy doors,
And creaking and uneven floors,
And chimneys huge, and tiled and tall.
A region of repose it seems,
A place of slumber and of dreams,
Remote among the wooded hills!
For there no noisy railway speeds,
Its torch-race scattering smoke and gleeds;
But noon and night, the panting teams
Stop under the great oaks, that throw
Tangles of light and shade below,
On roofs and doors and window-sills.
Across the road the barns display
Their lines of stalls, their mows of hay,
Through the wide doors the breezes blow,
The wattled cocks strut to and fro,
And, half effaced by rain and shine,
The Red Horse prances on the sign.

An extract from Tales of a Wayside Inn by Henry Longfellow, 1863
This was a collection of poems by Henry Wadsworth Longfellow, an American, and depicts a group of people at the Wayside Inn. It is very evocative of how we imagine an *olde worlde* English inn to be, but in fact the Wayside Inn was in Sudbury Massachusetts.

BIBLIOGRAPHY

BOOKS
Branston, J. History of Stocksbridge & District
Hackwood, F. W. Inns, Ales, and Drinking Customs of Old England. London: T. Fisher Unwin 1909
Hunter, Joseph: The History and Topography of the Parish of Sheffield. London: 1819
Jennings, Paul. The Local: A History of the English Pub. Stroud: Tempus 2007
Kenworthy J. The Broken Earthenware of Midhope Potteries. Wharncliffe Press 1928
Kenworthy, J. The Early History of Stocksbridge & District: Handbook 14: Bolsterstone 1915
Kenworthy, J. The Early History of Stocksbridge and District: Handbook 15: Bolsterstone 1915
Roebuck, Neville. It 'appened at t'pub. Privately printed 2002
Ward, G.H.B. Across the Derbyshire Moors. Sheffield Telegraph & Star 1946
Wright, J. The English Dialect Dictionary. Oxford: Henry Frowde 1905
The Stocksbridge Almanacs 1908-1910. My family has a copy of this, which is three issues bound together.
The Penistone Almanacs 1894-1958. Available in Stocksbridge Library. Some of these are available to download from penistonearchive.co.uk

WEBSITES
National Library of Scotland: maps.nls.uk
Victorian Crime and Punishment: http://vcp.e2bn.org
https://convictrecords.com.au/ships/hive

www.breweryhistory.com
http://www.pubhistorysociety.co.uk/
For equivalent values of money today I mainly used:
https://www.bankofengland.co.uk/monetary-policy/inflation/inflation-calculator
But there is also this site [values tend to differ from the Bank of England, but it is interesting to see what your money would have bought at that time]:
https://www.nationalarchives.gov.uk/currency-converter

The following websites for the census, 1939 Register, parish records, trade directories, electoral registers, Coroner's notebooks, probate records, newspapers, military records, public house licences, immigration and travel, historical parish documents, etc.

www.ancestry.co.uk
www.findmypast.co.uk
www.familysearch.org
http://specialcollections.le.ac.uk/
www.britishnewspaperarchive.co.uk
www.bradfieldarchives.co.uk
https://probatesearch.service.gov.uk/#calendar [wills 1858-1996]

FURTHER READING
Sheffield Archives hold many records relating to licensing as well as two boxes of archives from the Duncan Gilmore & Co Ltd. brewery which include property deeds and papers. Also records from Tennant Brothers Ltd. ref. MD7518 and A. H. Smith ref. X816.
Brown, P. Man Walks into a Pub, A Sociable History of Beer. Macmillan. 2003
Burke, T. The English Inn. London: Longmans, Green. 1930
Harper, Charles G. The Old Inns of England vols. 1 & 2, A Picturesque Account of the Ancient and Stories Hostelries of Our Own Country. London: Chapman & Hall Ltd. 1906
Lamb, D. A Pub on Every Corner. Sheffield: The Hallamshire Press. 1996
Lamb, D. Last Orders. Sheffield: Pickard Publishing. 2000
Parry, D., Parry, D. & Walker, A. Bygone Breweries of Sheffield. Neil Richardson. 1982

Pickersgill, D. (ed.) Sheffield's Real Heritage Pubs 3rd edition. Sheffield: CAMRA and 221 Creative. 2019. This is also available as a free download at https://sheffield.camra.org.uk/SheffieldsRealHeritagePubs.pdf

Richardson, A. E. The Old Inns of England. London: B. T. Batsford. 1934

Wrigley, J. R. T'Owd Locals. Sheffield: Youbooks. 2008